25

CBSE

Class 12

CHEMISTRY

Chapter-wise, Topic-wise & Skill-wise

Previous Year Solved Papers (2013 - 2023) Powered with Concept Notes

DISHA™
Publication Inc

DISHA Publication Inc.

A - 23, FIEE Comples,
Okhla Industrial Area Phase-II, New Delhi-110020
Tel: 49842349/ 49842350

Edited by : Kalpana Bhargav

Kavita Agarwal

Typeset By
DISHA DTP Team

Buying books from DISHA

Just Got A Lot More Rewarding!!!

We at DISHA Publication, value your feedback immensely and to show our apperciation of our reviewers, we have launched a review contest.

To participate in this reward scheme, just follow these quick and simple steps:
- Write a review of the product you purchase on Amazon/Flipkart.
- Take a screenshot/photo of your review.
- Mail it to *disha-rewards@aiets.co.in*, along with all your details.

Each month, selected reviewers will win exciting gifts from DISHA Publication. Note that the rewards for each month will be declared in the first week of next month on our website.

https://bit.ly/review-reward-disha.

Write To Us At

feedback_disha@aiets.co.in

CONTENTS

Trend Analysis (Year 2023-2019)
CBSE All India & Delhi

CH. No.	Chapter Name	Year of Examination				2021				
		2023		2022			2020		2019	
		All India	Delhi	Term-I	Term-II		All India	Delhi	All India	Delhi
1.	Solutions	4	2	9	–		4	3	2	2
2.	Electrochemistry	4	6	–	2		3	4	3	1
3.	Chemical Kinetics	4	4	–	1		3	2	1	2
4.	The *d* and *f*- Block Elements	3	3	–	2		2	1	1	2
5.	Coordination Compounds	4	4	–	1		2	3	2	3
6.	Haloalkanes and Haloarenes	4	2	10	–		3	2	2	1
7.	Alcohols,Phenols and Ethers	2	3	6	–		3	2	2	2
8.	Aldehydes,Ketones and Carboxylic Acids	5	3	3	–		3	2	1	2
9.	Amines	2	4	–	2		2	2	2	2
10.	Biomolecules	3	4	7	–		3	2	1	2
	Total	35	35	35	8		26	23	17	19

The 2021 column reads: Exam not held in 2021 due to Covid-19 pandemic

Note: In this book all 25 papers (Years 2023-2013) including CBSE sample papers 2021-22, 2022-23 & 2023-24 are divided as per latest CBSE chapter-wise, topicwise & skill-wise – K (= Knowledge based), U (= Understanding), Ap (= Application based) & A (= Analysis) marked below the question.

Chapter 1: Solutions

1   *Multiple Choice Questions*

1. Which of the following is an example of a solid solution?
   [CBSE Sample 2021-22, K]
   - (a) sea water
   - (b) sugar solution
   - (c) smoke
   - (d) 22 carat gold

2   *Assertion Reason/Two Statement Type Questions*

Given below are two statements labelled as Assertion (A) and Reason (R). Select the most appropriate answer from the options given below:

- (a) Both (A) and (R) are true and (R) is the correct explanation of (A).
- (b) Both (A) and (R) are true, but (R) is not the correct explanation of (A).
- (c) (A) is true, but (R) is false.
- (d) (A) is false, but (R) is true.

2. **Assertion (A):** Molarity of a solution changes with temperature.

   Reason (R): Molarity is a colligative property.
   [All India 2021-22, Term-I, K]

1   *Multiple Choice Questions*

1. Solubility of gas in liquid decreases with increase in
   [All India 2023, Set-I, K]
   - (a) Pressure
   - (b) Temperature
   - (c) Volume
   - (d) Number of solute molecules

2. An unknown gas 'X' is dissolved in water at 2.5 bar pressure and has mole fraction 0.04 in solution. The mole fraction of 'X' gas when the pressure of gas is doubled at the same temperature is
   [All India 2022, Term-I, Ap]
   - (a) 0.08
   - (b) 0.04
   - (c) 0.02
   - (d) 0.92

3. Solubility of gases in liquids decreases with rise in temperature because dissolution is an:
   [CBSE 2021-22, Term-I, K]
   - (a) endothermic and reversible process
   - (b) exothermic and reversible process
   - (c) endothermic and irreversible process
   - (d) exothermic and irreversible process

2   *Assertion Reason/Two Statement Type Questions*

Given below are two statements labelled as Assertion (A) and Reason (R). Select the most appropriate answer from the options given below:

- (a) Both (A) and (R) are true and (R) is the correct explanation of (A).
- (b) Both (A) and (R) are true, but (R) is not the correct explanation of (A).
- (c) (A) is true, but (R) is false.
- (d) (A) is false, but (R) is true.

4. **Assertion (A) :** Aquatic species are more comfortable in cold waters rather than in warm waters.

   Reason (R) : Different gases have different K_H values at the same temperature   **[CBSE Sample 2020-21, U]**

 **Short Answer Questions (2 or 3 Marks)**

5. Answer the following questions:

[CBSE Sample 2022-23, U]

(a) State Henry's law and explain why are the tanks used by scuba divers filled with air diluted with helium (11.7% helium, 56.2% nitrogen and 32.1% oxygen)?

(b) Assume that argon exerts a partial pressure of 6 bar. Calculate the solubility of argon gas in water. (Given Henry's law constant for argon dissolved in water, $K_H = 40$ kbar)

Topic-3: Vapour Pressure of Liquid Solutions, Ideal and Non-ideal Solutions

 **Multiple Choice Questions**

1. An azeotropic mixture of two liquids will have a boiling point lower than either of the two liquids when it

[All India 2023 Set-II, U]

(a) shows a negative deviation from Raoult's law

(b) forms an ideal solution

(c) shows a positive deviation from Raoult's law

(d) is saturated

2. 1 mole of liquid A and 2 moles of liquid B make a solution having a total vapour pressure 40 torr. The vapour pressure of pure A and pure B are 45 torr and 30 torr respectively. The above solution.

[Delhi 2023 Set-I, Ap]

(a) is an ideal solution

(b) shows positive deviation

(c) shows negative deviation

(d) is a maximum boiling azeotrope.

3. Which one of the following pairs will form an ideal solution? **[All India 2022, Term-I, K]**

(a) Chloroform and acetone

(b) Ethanol and acetone

(c) n-hexane and n-heptane

(d) Phenol and aniline

4. Which of the following formula represents Raoult's law for a solution containing non-volatile solute ?

[All India 2022, Term-I, K]

(a) $p_{solute} = p^\circ_{solute} \cdot x_{solute}$

(b) $p = K_H.X$

(c) $p_{total} = p_{solvent}$

(d) $p_{solvent} = p^\circ_{solvent} \cdot x_{solvent}$

5. An azeotropic solution of two liquids has a boiling point lower than either of the two when it

[All India 2022, Term-I, K]

(a) shows a positive deviation from Raoult's law.

(b) shows a negative deviation from Raoult's law.

(c) shows no deviation from Raoult's law.

(d) is saturated.

6. On mixing 20 mL of acetone with 30 mL of chloroform, the total volume of the solution is

[All India 2022, Term-I, U]

(a) < 50 mL   (b) $= 50$ mL

(c) > 50 mL   (d) $= 10$ mL

7. Identify the law which is stated as:

"For any solution, the partial vapour pressure of each volatile component in the solution is directly proportional to its mole fraction."

[All India 2021-22, Term-I, K]

(a) Henry's law

(b) Raoult's law

(c) Dalton's law

(d) Gay-Lussac's Law

8. When 1 mole of benzene is mixed with 1 mole of toluene The vapour will contain: (Given : vapour of benzene $= 12.8$ kPa and vapour pressure of toluene $= 3.85$ kPa).

[CBSE Sample 2020-21, U]

(a) equal amount of benzene and toluene as it forms an ideal solution

(b) unequal amount of benzene and toluene as it forms a non ideal solution

(c) higher percentage of benzene

(d) higher percentage of toluene

 **Assertion Reason/Two Statement Type Questions**

Given below are two statements labelled as Assertion (A) and Reason (R). Select the most appropriate answer from the options given below:
(a) Both (A) and (R) are true and (R) is the correct explanation of (A).
(b) Both (A) and (R) are true, but (R) is not the correct explanation of (A).
(c) (A) is true, but (R) is false.
(d) (A) is false, but (R) is true.

9. **Assertion (A) :** The enthalpy of mixing $\Delta_{mix}H$ is equal to zero for an ideal solution.

   Reason (R) : For an ideal solution the interaction between solute and solvent molecules is stronger than the interactions between solute-solute or solvent-solvent molecules. **[All India 2023, Set-I, K]**

10. **Assertion (A) :** Nitric acid and water form maximum boiling azeotrope. **[CBSE Sample 2020-21, U]**

    Reason (R) : Azeotropes are binary mixtures having the same composition in liquid and vapour phase.

 **Very Short Answer Questions (1 Mark)**

11. The vapour pressure of pure liquid X and pure liquid Y at 25 °C are 120 mm Hg and 160 mm Hg respectively. If equal moles of X and Y are mixed to form an ideal solution, calculate the vapour pressure of the solution.

    [All India 2023, Set-I, Ap]

 **Short Answer Questions (2 or 3 Marks)**

12. State Raoult's law for a solution containing volatile components. What is the similarity between Raoult's law and Henry's law? **[Delhi 2020, K]**

13. Give reasons for the following: **[All India 2019, U]**
    (a) Aquatic species are more comfortable in cold water than warm water. **[All India 2019, U]**
    (b) At higher altitudes, people suffer from anoxia resulting in inability to think.

    [All India 2019, U]

14. What type of azeotropic mixture will be formed by a solution of acetone and chloroform? Justify on the basis of strength of intermolecular interactions that develop in the solution. **[All India 2019, U]**

15. State Raoult's law for a solution containing volatile components. Write two characteristics of the solution which obeys Raoult's law at all concentrations.

    [Delhi 2019, K]

16. Write two differences between an ideal solution and a non-ideal solution. **[All India 2019, Set-II]**

17. (i) Gas (A) is more soluble in water than gas (B) at the same temperature. Which one of the two gases will have the higher value of K_H (Henry's constant) and why ? **All India 2016, K**

    (ii) In non-ideal solution, what type of deviation shows the formation of maximum boiling azeotropes ?

    [All India 2016, K]

18. What is meant by positive deviations from Raoult's law ? Give an example. What is the sign of $\Delta_{mix}H$ for positive deviation ? **[Delhi 2015, K]**

19. Define azeotropes. What type of azeotrope is formed by positive deviation from Raoult's law ? Give an example.

    [??????]

20. Define an ideal solution and write one of its characteristics. **[Delhi 2014, K]**

 **Topic-4:** ***Colligative Properties and Determination of Molar Mass, Abnormal Molar Masses***

 **Multiple Choice Questions**

1. Which of the following aqueous solution will have highest boiling point? **[Delhi 2023, Set-I, U]**
   (a) 1.0 M KCl
   (b) 1.0 M K_2SO_4
   (c) 2.0 M KCl
   (d) 2.0 M K_2SO_4

2. If molality of a dilute solution is doubled, the value of the molal elevation constant (K_b) will be

   [Delhi 2023 Set-I, U]
   (a) halved
   (b) doubled
   (c) tripled
   (d) unchanged

3. Out of the following 1.0 M aqueous solutions, which one will show largest freezing point depression?

[Delhi 2023 Set-III, U]

(a) NaCl 　　　　　(b) Na_2SO_4

(c) $C_6H_{12}O_6$　　　(d) $Al_2(SO_4)_3$

4. Elevation of boiling point is inversely proportional to

[All India 2022, Term-I, K]

(a) molal elevation constant (K_b)

(b) molality (m)

(c) molar mass of solute (M)

(d) weight of solute (W)

5. The boiling point of a 0.2 m solution of a non-electrolyte in water is (K_b for water = 0.52 K kg mol^{-1})

[All India 2022, Term-I, Ap]

(a) 100 °C　　　　　(b) 100.52 °C

(c) 100.104 °C　　　(d) 100.26 °C

6. In the following diagram point, 'X' represents

[All India 2022, Term-I, U]

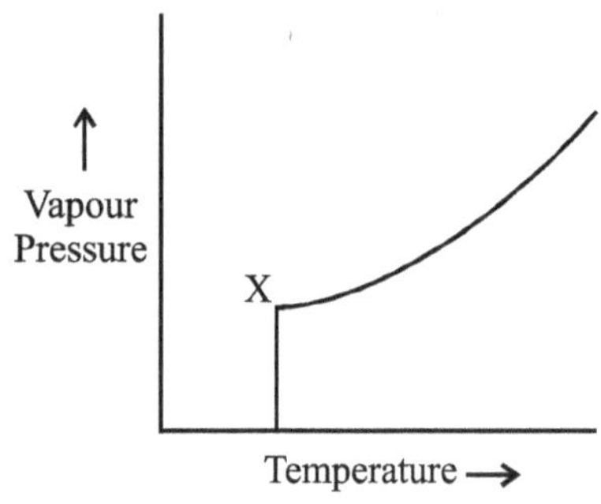

(a) Boiling point of solution

(b) Freezing point of solvent

(c) Boiling point of solvent

(d) Freezing point of solution

7. In which of the following cases blood cells will shrink:

[CBSE Sample 2021-22, U]

(a) when placed in water containing more than 0.9% (mass/volume) NaCl solution.

(b) when placed in water containing less than 0.9% (mass /volume) NaCl solution.

(c) when placed in water containing 0.9% (mass/ volume) NaCl solution.

(d) when placed in distilled water.

8. How much ethyl alcohol must be added to 1 litre of water so that the solution will freeze at –14°C?

(K_f for water = 1.86°C/mol)

[CBSE Sample 2021-22, Ap]

(a) 7.5 mol　　　　　(b) 8.5 mol

(c) 9.5 mol　　　　　(d) 10.5 mol

9. Water retention or puffiness due to high salt intake occurs due to: **[CBSE Sample 2021-22, K]**

(a) diffusion

(b) vapour pressure difference

(c) osmosis

(d) reverse osmosis

2 *Assertion Reason/Two Statement Type Questions*

Given below are two statements labelled as Assertion (A) and Reason (R). Select the most appropriate answer from the options given below:

(a) Both (A) and (R) are true and (R) is the correct explanation of (A).

(b) Both (A) and (R) are true, but (R) is not the correct explanation of (A).

(c) (A) is true, but (R) is false.

(d) (A) is false, but (R) is true.

10. **Assertion (A):** Elevation in boiling point is a colligative property. **[All India 2023 Set-II, U]**

Reason (R): The lowering of vapour pressure of solution causes elevation in boiling point.

11. **Assertion (A):** A raw mango placed in a saline solution loses water and shrivel into pickle.

Reason (R): Through the process of reverse osmosis, raw mango shrivel into pickle.

[All India 2022, Term-I, K]

12. **Assertion (A):** Cryoscopic constant depends on nature of solvent. **[CBSE Sample 2021-22, U]**

Reason (R): Cryoscopic constant is a universal constant.

13. **Assertion (A):** Elevation in boiling point is a colligative property. **[Delhi 2020, Set-I]**

Reason (R): Elevation in boiling point is directly proportional to molarity.

14. **Assertion (A):** 0.1 M solution of KCl has greater osmotic pressure than 0.1 M solution of glucose at same temperature.

Reason (R): In solution, KCl dissociates to produce more number of particles. **[Delhi 2020, U]**

4 *Very Short Answer Questions (1 Mark)*

15. Identify which liquid will have a higher vapour pressure at 90°C if the boiling points of two liquids A and B are 140°C and 180°, respectively. **[All India 2020, U]**

16. What are isotonic solutions ? **[Delhi 2014, K]**

 **Short Answer Questions (2 or 3 Marks)**

17. A 5% solution of $Na_2SO_4.10H_2O$ (MW = 322) is isotonic with 2% solution of non– electrolytic, non volatile substance X. Find out the molecular weight of X. **[CBSE Sample 2023-24, U]**

18. When 19.5 g of $F – CH_2 – COOH$ (Molar mass = 78g mol^{-1}). is dissolved in 500 g of water, the depression in freezing point is observed to be FC. Calculate the degree of dissociation of $F – CH_2 – COOH$.
   [Given : K_f for water = 1.86 K kg mol^{-1}]
   [All India 2023, Set-I, Ap]

19. For a 5% solution of urea (Molar mass = 60 g/mol), calculate the osmotic pressure at 300 K. [R = 0.0821 L atm K^{-1} mol^{-1}] **[All India 2020, U]**

20. Visha took two aqueous solutions – one containing 7.5 g of urea (Molar mass = 60 g/mol) and the other containing 42.75 g of substance Z in 100 g water, respectively. It was observed that both the solutions froze at the same temperature. Calculate the molar mass of Z.
   [All India 2020, U]

21. Calculate the mass of ascorbic acid (Molar mass = 176 g mol^{-1}) to be dissolved in 75 g of acetic acid, to lower its freezing point by 1.5°C. (k_f = 3.9 K kg mol^{-1})
   [All India 2020, Ap]

22. A 0.01 m aqueous solution of $AlCl_3$ freezes at –0.068 °C. Calculate the percentage of dissociation.
   [Given: K_f for water = 1.86 K kg mol^{-1}]
   [Delhi 2020, Ap]

23. At 300 K, 30 g of glucose present in a litre of its solution has an osmotic pressure of 4·98 bar. If the osmotic pressure of a glucose solution is 1·52 bar, at the same temperature what would be its concentration?
   [All India 2019, Ap]

24. A 4% solution(w/w) of sucrose (M = 342 g mol^{-1}) in water has a freezing point of 271.15 K. Calculate the freezing point of 5% glucose (M = 180 g mol^{-1}) in water. (Given: Freezing point of pure water = 273.15 K)
   [Delhi 2019, Ap]

25. Calculate the freezing point of a solution containing 60 g glucose (Molar mass = 180 g mol^{-1}) in 250 g of water.
   (k_f of water = 1.86 K kg mol^{-1}) **[All India 2018, Ap]**

26. Given reasons for the following : **[All India 2018, U]**
   (a) Measurement of osmotic pressure method is preferred for the determination of molar masses of macromolecules such as proteins and polymers. **[All India 2018, U]**
   (b) Aquatic animals are more comfortable in cold water than in warm water. **[All India 2018, U]**
   (c) Elevation of boiling point of 1 M KCl solution is nearly double than of 1 M sugar solution. **[All India 2018, U]**

27. Define the following terms : **[Delhi 2017, K]**
   (i) Colligative properties
   (ii) Molality (m)

28. A 10% solution (by mass) of sucrose in water has freezing point of 269.15 K. Calculate the freezing point of 10% glucose in water, if freezing point of pure water is 273.15 K. **[Delhi 2017, Ap]**
   Given : (Molar mass of sucrose = 342 g mol^{-1}) (Molar mass of glucose = 180 g mol^{-1})

29. Calculate the boiling point of solution when 4g of $MgSO_4$ (M = 120 g mol^{-1}) was dissolved in 100 g of water, assuming $MgSO_4$ undergoes complete ionization.
   (K_b for water = 0.52 K kg mol^{-1}) **[All India 2016, Ap]**

30. Why does a solution containing non-volatile solute have higher boiling point than the pure solvent?
   Why is elevation of boiling point a colligative property?
   [All India 2015, K]

31. Calculate the freezing point of the solution when 31 g of ethylene glycol ($C_2H_6O_2$) is dissolved in 500 g of water (K_f for water = 1.86 K kg mol^{-1})
   [All India 2015, Ap]

32. 3.9 g of benzoic acid dissolved in 49 g of benzene shows a depression in freezing point of 1.62 K. Calculate the van't Hoff factor and predict the nature of solute (associated or dissociated).
   (Given : Molar mass of benzoic acid = 122 g mol^{-1}, K_f for benzene = 4.9 K kg mol^{-1}) **[Delhi 2015, Ap]**

33. Calculate the mass of compound (molar mass = 256 g mol^{-1}) to be dissolved in 75 g of benzene to lower its freezing point by 0.48 K (K_f = 5.12 K kg mol^{-1}).
   [Delhi 2014, Ap]

34. 18 g of glucose, $C_6H_{12}O_6$ (Molar Mass = 180 g mol^{-1}) is dissolved in 1 kg of water in a sauce pan. At what temperature will this solution boil?

(K_b for water = 0.52 K kg mol^{-1}, boiling point of pure water = 373.15 K)   **[Delhi 2013, Ap]**

35. Determine the osmotic pressure of solution prepared by dissolving 2.5×10^{-2} g of K_2SO_4 in 2 L of water at 25°C, assuming that it is completely dissociated.

(R = 0.0821 L atm K^{-1} mol^{-1}, Molar mass of K_2SO_4 = 174 g mol^{-1}).   **[Delhi 2013, Ap]**

> **6**   *Long Answer Questions*

36. (a) What is the effect of temperature on the solubility of glucose in water?   **[CBSE Sample 2023-24, K]**

    (b) Ibrahim collected a 10mL each of fresh water and ocean water. He observed that one sample labeled "P" froze at 0°C while the other "Q" at –1.3°C. Ibrahim forgot which of the two, "P" or "Q" was ocean water. Help him identify which container contains ocean water, giving rationalization for your answer.

        [CBSE Sample 2023-24, Ap]

    (c) Calculate Van't Hoff factor for an aqueous solution of $K_3[Fe(CN)_6]$ if the degree of dissociation (α) is 0.852. What will be boiling point of this solution if its concentration is 1 molal? (Kb = 0.52 K kg/mol)

        [CBSE Sample 2023-24, Ap]

37. (a) What type of deviation from Rault's Law is expected when phenol and aniline are mixed with each other? What change in the net volume of the mixture is expected? Graphically represent the deviation.

        [CBSE Sample 2023-24, K]

    (b) The vapour pressure of pure water at a certain temperature is 23.80 mm Hg. If 1 mole of a non–volatile non–electrolytic solute is dissolved in 100g water, Calculate the resultant vapour pressure of the solution.   **[CBSE Sample 2023-24, Ap]**

38. (i) Why is boiling point of 1M NaCl solution more than that of 1M glucose solution?

        [Delhi 2023, Set-I, Ap]

    (ii) A non-volatile solute 'X' (molar mass = 50 g mol^{-1}) when dissolved in 78g of benzene reduced its vapour pressure to 90%. Calculate the mass of X dissolved in the solution.   **[Delhi 2023, Set-I, Ap]**

    (iii) Calculate the boiling point elevation for a solution prepared by adding 10g of $MgCl_2$ to 200g of water assuming $MgCl_2$ is completely dissociated.

(K_b for Water = 0.512 K kg mol^{-1}. Molar mass $MgCl_2$ = 95g mol^{-1})   **[Delhi 2023, Set-I, Ap]**

39. (i) Why is the value of Van't Hoff factor for ethanoic acid in benzene close to 0.5?

        [Delhi 2023, Set-I, Ap]

    (ii) Determine the osmotic pressure of a solution prepared by dissolving 2.32×10^{-2}g of K_2SO_4 in 2L of solution at 25 °C, assuming that K_2SO_4 is completely dissociated.

(R = 0.082 L atm K^{-1} mol^{-1}, Molar mass K_2SO_4 = 174g mol^{-1})   **[Delhi 2023, Set-I, Ap]**

    (iii) When 25.6g of Sulphur was dissolved in 1000g of benzene, the freezing point lowered by 0.512 K. Calculate the formula of Sulphur (S_x).

(K_f for benzene = 5.12 K kg mol^{-1}. Atomic mass of Sulphur = 32g mol^{-1})   **[Delhi 2023, Set-I, Ap]**

40. (a) A 10% solution (by mass) of sucrose in water has a freezing point of 269.15K. Calculate the freezing point of 10% glucose in water if the freezing point of pure water is 273.15K   **[All India 2017, Ap]**

    Given:

    (Molar mass of sucrose = 342 g mol^{-1})

    (Molar mass of glucose =180 g mol^{-1})

    (b) Define the following terms: **[All India 2017, K]**

    (i) Molality (m)

    (ii) Abnormal molar mass

41. (a) 30 g of urea (M = 60 g mol^{-1}) is dissolved in 846 g of water. Calculate the vapour pressure of water for this solutions if vapour pressure of pure water at 298 K is 23.8 mm Hg.

        [All India 2017, Ap]

    (b) Write two difference between ideal solutions and non-ideal solutions.   **[All India 2017, K]**

42. (a) Calculate the freezing point of solution when 1.9 g of $MgCl_2$ (M = 95 g mol^{-1}) was dissolved in 50 g of water, assuming $MgCl_2$ undergoes complete ionization. (K_f for water = 1.86 K kg mol^{-1})

        [Delhi 2016, Ap]

    (b) (i) Out of 1 M glucose and 2 M glucose, which one has a higher boiling point and why ?

        [Delhi 2016, U]

    (ii) What happens when the external pressure applied becomes more than the osmotic pressure of solution ?   **[Delhi 2016, U]**

43. (a) When 2.56 g of sulphur was dissolved in 100 g of CS_2, the freezing point lowered by 0.383 K. Calculate the formula of sulphur (S_x).

(K_f for CS_2 = 3.83 K kg mol^{-1}, Atomic mass of Sulphur = 32 g mol^{-1}] **[Delhi 2016, Ap]**

(b) Blood cells are isotonic with 0.9% sodium chloride solution. What happens if we place blood cells in a solution containing **[Delhi 2016, U]**

(i) 1.2% sodium chloride solution ?

(ii) 0.4% sodium chloride solution ?

44. (a) Define the following terms : **[All India 2014, K]**

(i) Molarity

(ii) Molal elevation constant (K_b)

(b) A solution containing 15 g urea (molar mass = 60 g mol^{-1}) per litre of solution in water has the same osmotic pressure (isotonic) as a solution of glucose (molar mass = 180 g mol^{-1}) in water. Calculate the mass of glucose present in one litre of its solution. **[All India 2014, Ap]**

45. (a) What type of deviation is shown by a mixture of ethanol and acetone? Give reason.

[All India 2014, K]

(b) A solution of glucose (molar mass = 180 g mol^{-1}) in water is labelled as 10% (by mass). What would be the molality and molarity of the solution?

(Density of solution = 1.2 g mL^{-1})

[All India 2014, Ap]

46. (a) State Raoult's law for a solution containing volatile components. How does Raoult's law become a special case of Henry's law? **[All India 2013, Ap]**

(b) 1.00 g of a non-electrolyte solute dissolved in 50 g of benzene lowered the freezing point of benzene by 0.40 K. Find the molar mass of the solute. (K_f for benzene = 5.12 K kg mol^{-1}) **[All India 2013, Ap]**

47. (a) Define the following terms : **[All India 2013, Ap]**

(i) Ideal solution

(ii) Azeotrope

(iii) Osmotic pressure

(b) A solution of glucose ($C_6H_{12}O_6$) in water is labelled as 10% by weight. What would be the molality of the solution? **[All India 2013, Ap]**

(Molar mass of glucose = 180 g mol^{-1})

 *Case Based Questions*

48. Henna is investigating the melting point of different salt solutions. She makes a salt solution using 10 mL of water with a known mass of NaCl salt. She puts the salt solution into a freezer and leaves it to freeze. She takes the frozen salt solution out of the freezer and measures the temperature when the frozen salt solution melts. She repeats each experiment. **[CBSE Sample 2022-23, A]**

S.No.	Mass of the salt Used in g	Melting point in °C	
		Readings Set 1	Reading Set 2
1	0.3	–1.9	–1.9
2	0.4	–2.5	–2.6
3	0.5	–3.0	–5.5
4	0.6	–3.8	–3.8
5	0.8	–5.1	–5.0
6	1.0	–6.4	–6.3

Assuming the melting point of pure water as 0°C, answer the following questions:

(a) One temperature in the second set of results does not fit the pattern. Which temperature is that? Justify your answer.

(b) Why did Henna collect two sets of results?

(c) In place of NaCl, if Henna had used glucose, what would have been the melting point of the solution with 0.6 g glucose in it?

What is the predicted melting point if 1.2 g of salt is added to 10 mL of water? Justify your answer.

Solutions

Topic-1: *Types of solutions, Expressing Concentration of Solutions*

1. **(d)** 22 carat gold (it is an alloy so solid in solid solution) **(1 Mark)**

2. **(c)** Molarity of a solution changes with temperature. Molarity is not a colligative property. **(1 Mark)**

Topic-2: *Solubility*

1. **(b)** Temperature;

   The solubility of gas in the decreases with increase in temperature as the kinetic energy of the gas increases. Which is increases the escaping tendency from liquid. **(1 Mark)**

2. **(a)** We know that;

   $$\frac{P_1}{P_2} = \frac{\chi_1}{\chi_2}$$

   Here;

   P_1 = initial pressure; P_2 = final pressure; χ = mole fraction

   $$\frac{2.5}{5} = \frac{0.04}{\chi_2}$$

   $\chi_2 = 0.08$ **(1 Mark)**

3. **(b)** Exothermic and reversible process (according to Le -Chatlier principle solubility of gases in liquids decreases with rise in temperature) **(1 Mark)**

4. **(b)** Aquatic species are more comfortable in cold water because solubility of oxygen in water is more in cold water than in warm water. **(1 Mark)**

5. **(a)** Henry's law: the partial pressure of the gas in vapour phase (p) is proportional to the mole fraction of the gas (x) in the solution. **(1 Mark)**

   The pressure underwater is high, so the solubility of gases in blood increases. When the diver comes to surface the pressure decreases so does the solubility causing bubbles of nitrogen in blood, to avoid this situation and maintain the same partial pressure of nitrogen underwater too, the dilution is done.

   (1 Mark)

(b) $p = K_H x$

   mole fraction of argon in water $x = p/k = 6/40 \times 10^3$

   $= 1.5 \times 10^{-4}$ **(1 Mark)**

Topic-3: *Vapour Pressure of Liquid Solutions, Ideal and Non-ideal Solutions*

1. **(c)** When a solution shows positive deviation from Raoult's law, the intermolecular attractive forces between the solute-solvent molecules are weaker than those between the solute-solute and solvent-solvent molecules. This will increase the vapour pressure and results in positive deviation. Hence, the azeotropic mixture of the two liquids will have a boiling point lower than either of the two liquids.

   (1 Mark)

2. **(b)** Total vapour pressure, $P_{Total} = P_A + P_B$

   $$P_{Total} = X_A P_A^\circ + X_B P_B^\circ$$

   $$= \left(\frac{1}{3} \times 45\right) + \left(\frac{2}{3} \times 30\right)$$

   $= 15 + 20$

   $= 35$ torr

   Since, the actual vapour pressure of solution is 40 torr which is greater than the calculated value. It means the solution shows positive deviation from the ideal solution. **(1 Mark)**

3. **(c)** n-heptane and n-hexane obeys Raoult's law at all temperature and concentration. Hence; they will form an ideal solution. **(1 Mark)**

4. **(d)** Formula of Raoult's law for a non-volatile solute is:

   $$P_{solvent} = P_{solvent}^\circ \cdot \chi_{solvent}$$ **(1 Mark)**

5. **(a)** Azeotropes are of two types:

   (i) The solution which shows large positive deviation from Raoult's law form minimum boiling azeotrope at a specific composition.

   (ii) The solution which shows large negative deviation from Raoult's law form maximum boiling azeotrope at a specific composition. **(1 Mark)**

6. **(a)** The mixture of acetone and chloroform show negative deviation due to which the total volume of the solution will be less than 50. **(1 Mark)**

7. **(b)** Raoult's law. **(1 Mark)**

8. **(c)** The vapour will contain higher percentage of benzene. **(1 Mark)**

9. **(c)** For ideal solution, $\Delta_{mix} H = 0$
   Solute – Solvent interaction = Solute – solute or
   Solvent – solvent interaction **(1 Mark)**

10. **(b)** Nitric acid and water solution show large negative deviation from Raoult's law. **(1 Mark)**

11. $p_x^0 = 120$ mm Hg, $p_y^0 = 166$ mm Hg at 25°C
    Equal moles of X and Y.

$\therefore \quad \chi_x$ = mole fraction of X = $\dfrac{1}{2}$

χ_y = mole fraction of Y = $\dfrac{1}{2}$ **(½ Mark)**

$p_{Total} = p_x + p_y$ **(½ Mark)**

$\quad = \chi_x p_x^0 + \chi_y p_y^0$

$\quad = \left(\dfrac{1}{2} \times 120 + \dfrac{1}{2} \times 160\right)$ mm Hg **(½ Mark)**

$\quad = 140$ mm Hg **(½ Mark)**

The vapour pressure of the solution = 140 mm Hg.

12.

Topper's Answer

Ans2: Raoult's law state that in a solution of volatile components, the partial pressure of each volatile component is directly proportional to their partial pressures mole fraction in the solution.

Let 2 volatile components be A and B
then, $p_A \propto x_A$ and $p_B \propto x_B$
$\Rightarrow p_A = p_A^0 x_A$ $\Rightarrow p_B = p_B^0 x_B$
p_A^0, p_B^0 : proportionality constants.

On the other hand, Henry law states that partial pressure of a (volatile) gas in a liquid is directly proportional to its mole fraction.
$p \propto x \Rightarrow p = K_H x$
K_H = Henry's constant

By comparing the two equations, we see they are very similar and it seems as the Raolts Law is special case of Henry's law in which $K_H = p^0$

Raoult's law: For a solution of volatile liquids, the partial vapour pressure of each component of the solution is directly proportional to its mole fraction in solution, $P \propto x$; $P = x P°$.

by Henry's law,

$P = x.K_H$

Here, P is the partial pressure of gas, x is mole fraction of it in the solution and K_H is the Henry's law constant.

In both Henry's law and Raoult's law, partial pressure of volatile component is directly proportional to mole fraction of it in the solution. **(1 + 1 = 2 Marks)**

13. (a) Solubility of gases in liquid is inversly proportional to temperature. As temperature increases, solubility of dissolved gases in water decreases. Hence, aquatic species find difficult to breath in warm water due to decreased availability of oxygen.

(1 Mark)

(b) Henry's Law states that the solubility of a gas in a liquid at a given temperature is directly proportional to the partial pressure of the gas.

At higher altitude, partial pressure of oxygen is less than that at ground level, so low O_2 in blood causes climbers to become weak and makes them unable to think clearly. **(1 Mark)**

14. Maximum boiling azeotropes mixture will be formed by mixing of acetone and chloroform. In these solutions, the A—B interactions are stronger than the A—A and B—B molecular interactions present in the two liquids forming the solution. Hydrogen bonding will decrease the escaping tendency of the molecules.

(1 + 1 = 2 Marks)

15. According to Raoult's law for a solution containing volatile components.

"The partial vapour pressure of each component of the solution is directly proportional to it's mole fraction present in solution"

The characteristics of the solution which obeys Raoult's law at all concentrations are as follows:

(i) In a binary solution of components, A and B, the enthalpy of mixing $\Delta H_{mix} = 0$, i.e., in prepration of an ideal solution no thermal change is observed.

(ii) In an ideal solution, the volume of mixing $\Delta V_{mix} = 0$, i.e., the final volume of the solution is equal to the sum of volumes of components being mixed.

(1 + 1 = 2 Marks)

16.

Topper's Answer

8.

Ideal Solution	Non–Ideal Solution
(a) The solution obeys Raoult's law over the entire range of concentration. The vapour pressure of solution is nearly equal to that predicted by Raoult's law.	(a) The solution does not obeys Raoult's law. The vapour pressure of the solution is either higher or lower than that predicted by Raoult's law.
(b) The intermolecular interactions between solute–solvent particles are of similar order to that of solute–solute particles and solvent–solvent particles. i.e. $\Delta_{mix} H = 0$ & $\Delta_{mix} V = 0$	(b) The intermolecular interactions between solute–solvent particles is either stronger or weaker than that existing between solute–solute particles & solvent–solvent particles. i.e. $\Delta_{mix} H > 0$, $\Delta_{mix} V > 0$ (+ve deviation) OR $\Delta_{mix} H < 0$, $\Delta_{mix} V < 0$ (–ve deviation)
e.g. Solution of n-hexane & n-heptane	e.g. Solution of …

17. (i) According to Henry's law, the solubility of a gas is inversely related to the Henry's constant (K_H) for that gas. Hence, gas (B), being less soluble, would have a higher K_H value than gas(A). **(1 Mark)**

Henry's law only works if the molecules are at equilibrium. It does not work for gases at high pressure and if there is a chemical reaction between the solute and solvent.

(ii) The non-ideal solution which shows large negative deviation from Raoult's law form maximum boiling azeotrop at a specific composition. Example, nitric acid and water. **(1 Mark)**

18. Positive Deviation: When the experimenty determined vapour pressures of a binary liquid-liquid solution having different compositions are greater than calculated values of vapour pressure using Raoult's law, this is known as positive deviation.

In positive deviation the interaction between A-B is weaker than A-A and B-B. Where A and B are the two constituents liquid of binary solution. **(2 Marks)**

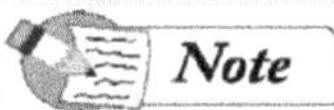

In positive deviation the interaction between A – B is weaker than A – A and B – B while in negative deviation the interaction between A – A and B – B is weaker than A – B. Where A and B are the two constituents liquids of binary solution.

19. Azeotropes are the binary mixtures of solution that have the same composition in liquid and vapour phases and that have constant boiling points.

A minimum boiling azeotrope is formed by solutions showing a large positive deviation from Raoult's law at a specific composition.

Example: An ethanol – water mixture containing approximately 95% ethanol by volume. **(2 Marks)**

20. The solutions which obey Raoult's law over the entire range of concentration are known as ideal solutions. For an ideal solution, the A-B interactions are nearly same as the A-A and B-B interactions. Where A and B are the two components of the solution. **(2 Marks)**

Topic-4: Colligative Properties and Determination of Molar Mass, Abnormal Molar Masses

1. **(d)** All the given species are strong electrolytes so they dissociate completely in the aqueous solution.

The species that gives the highest number of particles upon dissociation will have the highest boiling point.

1.0 M KCl = 1 mole K^+ ions + 1 mole Cl^- ions.

2.0 M KCl = 2 moles K^+ ions + 2 mole Cl^- ions.

1.0 M K_2SO_4 = 1 × 2 = 2 moles K^+ ions + 1 mole SO_4^{2-} ions.

2.0 M K_2SO_4 = 2 × 2 = 4 moles K^+ ions + 2 moles SO_4^{2-} ions.

Therefore, 2.0 M K_2SO_4 will give the highest number of particles and therefore its boiling point will be highest.

Therefore, option **(d)** is correct. **(1 Mark)**

2. **(d)** Since, the value of molal elevation constant (K_b) is constant for a particular solvent. Hence, it will remain unchanged when molality of the solution is doubled. **(1 Mark)**

3. **(d)** Freezing point depression is given by,

$\Delta T_f = i \times K_f \times m$

$\Rightarrow \Delta T_f \, \alpha \, i$ (Van't Hoff factor)

NaCl dissociates to give 2 ions. Na_2SO_4 dissociates to give 3 ions. $C_6H_{12}O_6$ dissociates to give no ions. $Al_2(SO_4)_3$ dissociates to give 5 ions.

Hence, $Al_2(SO_4)_3$ will exhibit largest freezing point depression due to highest value of Van't Hoff factor ($i = 5$). **(1 Mark)**

4. **(c)** The formula of elevation in boiling point is:

$\Delta T_b = K_b \times m$

$$\Delta T_b = \frac{K_b \times W_A}{M_B \times W_B (Kg)}$$

$\therefore$ Elevation in boiling point is inversely proportional to molar mass of solute (M_B). **(1 Mark)**

5. **(c)** $\Delta T_b = K_b \times m$
$= 0.52 \times 0.2$
$\Delta T_b = 0.104$
$T_b = T_b^\circ + \Delta T_b$
$= 100 + 0.104$
$= 100.104°C$ **(1 Mark)**

6. **(b)** The point 'X' represents the freezing point of solvent. The freezing point of a substance may be defined as the temperature at which the vapour pressure of the substance in its liquid phase is equal to the vapour pressure in the solid phase. **(1 Mark)**

7. **(a)** When placed in water containing more than 0.9% (mass/volume) NaCl solution because fluid inside blood cells is isotonic with 0.9% NaCl solution. **(1 Mark)**

8. **(a)** 7.5 mol

$$\Delta T_f = K_f\, m$$

$$\Delta T_f = K_f\, \frac{n_2 \times 1000}{w_1}$$

$$14 = 1.86 \times \frac{n_2 \times 1000}{1000}$$

$n_2 = 7.5$ mol **(1 Mark)**

9. **(c)** Osmosis **(1 Mark)**

10. **(a)** Elevation in boiling point depends on the number of solute molecules rather than their nature. So, it is a colligative property.

$\Delta T_b = K_b$, molality

When a non–volatile solute is added to a solvent, the vapour pressure of the resulting solution is lower than that of pure solvent. Thus, a greater amount of heat must be supplied to the solution for it to boil. This increase in the boiling point of the solution is the elevation of boiling point. **(1 Mark)**

11. **(c)** A is true but R is false. When raw mango is placed in a saline solution to prepare pickle the mango looses water due to osmosis and get shrivel. This event does not occur due to reverse osmosis.

(1 Mark)

Note

In reverse osmosis the direction of osmosis is reversed by making pressure larger than the osmotic pressure and is applied to the solution side. In this, pure solvent flows outside of the conc. solution through a semipermeable membrane.

12. **(c)** Cryoscopic constant depends on nature of solvent. Cryoscopic constant is not a universal constant. Cryoscopic constant varies with type of solvent.

13. **Topper's Answer**

(c) Elevation in boiling point is directly proportional to molality. **(1 Mark)**

14. **(a)** KCl is an electrolyte, thus in solution it produces more number of particles than glucose. Hence, solution of KCl has greater osmotic pressure than glucose. **(1 Mark)**

15. Liquid A has higher vapour pressure. **(1 Mark)**

16. Two solutions having same osmotic pressure at a given temperature are called isotonic solutions. **(1 Mark)**

17. $\pi_1 = \pi_2$ **(1/2 Mark)**

$iC_1RT = C_2RT$ **(1/2 Mark)**

$$\frac{3 \times 5}{322} = \frac{2}{M}$$ **(1/2 Mark)**

$$M = \frac{2 \times 322}{3 \times 5}$$ **(1/2 Mark)**

$M = 42.9$ g

18. 19.5 g of $F - CH_2 - COOH$: $n_1 = \dfrac{19.5}{78} = 0.25$ mol **(½ Mark)**

Molality of solution (m) $= \dfrac{0.25}{0.5} = 0.5$ (m)

Depression of freezing point due to dissociation $= 1°$

$\therefore$ $\Delta T_f = i\, m K_f$

$\therefore$ $i = \dfrac{1}{0.5 \times 1.86} = 1.075$ **(½ Mark)**

$$F - CH_2 - COOH \longrightarrow F\, CH_2\, COO^- + H^+$$

0.25 mol

$0.25(1-x)$ mol $\qquad$ 0.25x mol $\qquad$ 0.25x mol

[Suppose x is the degree of dissociation]

$\therefore$ Total no. of particles

$= 0.25(1-x) + 0.25x + 0.25x$ **(½ Mark)**

$= 0.25 + 0.25x$

$i = \dfrac{\text{Total no. of moles of particles after dissociation}}{\text{Total no. of moles of particles before dissociation}}$ **(½ Mark)**

$\therefore$ $i = \dfrac{0.25(1+x)}{0.25} = 1.075$ **(½ Mark)**

or $\quad 1 + x = 1.075$

or $\quad x = 1.075 - 1 = 0.075$

$\therefore$ Degree of dissociation of $F - CH_2 - COOH = 0.075$.

(½ Mark)

19. 5% urea solution means. 5g urea is present in 100 mL of solution.

Molarity of solution

$$C = \frac{5g}{60 \text{ g/mol}} \times \frac{1000}{100 \text{ L}}$$

$$C = \frac{10}{12} \text{mol/L} \qquad \textbf{(1 Mark)}$$

Osmotic pressure, $\pi = CRT$

$$\pi = \frac{10}{12} \times 0.0821 \times 300$$

$$= 20.525 \text{ atm} \qquad \textbf{(1 Mark)}$$

20. It is given that the depression in freezing points of the two given aqueous solution are same.

$$(\Delta T_f)_{\text{urea}} = (\Delta T_f)_z \qquad \textbf{(½ Mark)}$$

$$m_{\text{urea}} \times (k_f)_{\text{water}} = m_z \times (k_f)_{\text{water}}$$

$$\Rightarrow \quad \frac{\dfrac{7.5}{60}}{\dfrac{100}{1000}} = \frac{\dfrac{42.75}{M_z}}{\dfrac{100}{1000}} \qquad \textbf{(½ Mark)}$$

$$\Rightarrow \quad M_z = 342 \text{ g/mol} \qquad \textbf{(1 Mark)}$$

21. Let 'w' be the required mass of ascorbic acid.

Molality of ascorbic and

$$m = \frac{(w/176)}{(75/1000)} \quad \Rightarrow \quad m = \frac{w}{176} \times \frac{1000}{75} \qquad \textbf{(½ Mark)}$$

$$(k_f)_{\text{acetic}} = 3.9 \text{ K kg mol}^{-1} \qquad \textbf{(1 Mark)}$$

$$\Delta T_f = 1.5 \,°C \quad \Rightarrow \quad \Delta T_f = 1.5 \text{ K}$$

$$\Delta T_f = m.k_f \qquad \textbf{(½ Mark)}$$

$$\Rightarrow \quad 1.5 = \frac{w}{176} \times \frac{1000}{75} \times 3.9$$

$$\Rightarrow \quad w = 5.08 \text{ g} \approx 5g \qquad \textbf{(1 Mark)}$$

22.

Topper's Answer

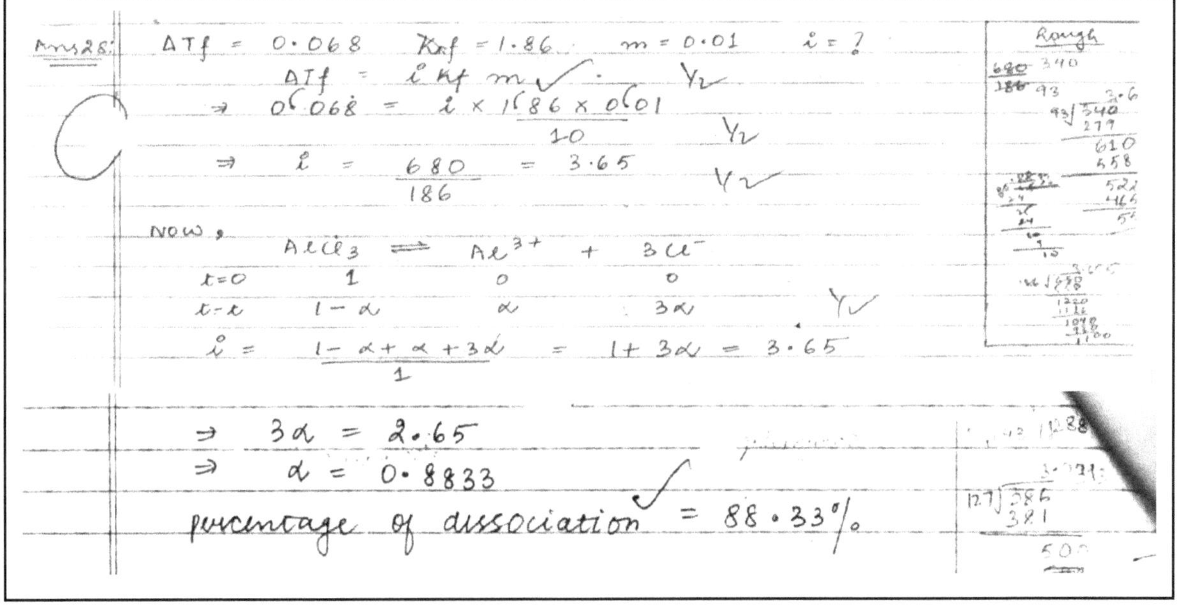

$m = 0.01$; $\Delta T_f = 0.068\,°C$; $k_f = 1.86$ K kg mol^{-1}

If i is the van't Hoff factor for the aqueous solution of AlCl$_3$, then

$$\Delta T_f = i.K_f.m \qquad \textbf{(½ Mark)}$$

$$\Rightarrow \quad i = \frac{\Delta T_f}{K_f.m}$$

$$= \frac{0.068}{1.86 \times 0.01} \qquad \textbf{(½ Mark)}$$

$$= 3.66 \qquad \textbf{(½ Mark)}$$

$$AlCl_3 \longrightarrow Al^{3+} + 3Cl^- \qquad \textbf{(½Mark)}$$

initial	1	0	0
at equilibrium	$1-x$	x	$3x$

$$i = \frac{(1-x) + x + 3x}{1} \qquad \textbf{(½ Mark)}$$

$$\Rightarrow \quad 3.66 = 1 + 3x \quad \Rightarrow \quad x = 0.89$$

x is degree of dissociation.

∴ Percentage of dissociation = 89%. **(½ Mark)**

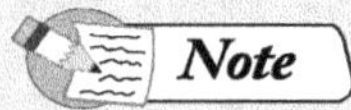

$$i = \frac{\text{Total number of moles after dissociation/association}}{\text{Total number of moles before dissociation/association}}$$

23. Osmotic pressure,

$$\pi = CRT$$

$$\pi_1 = C_1RT \qquad \textbf{(1 Mark)}$$

$$4.98 = \frac{30/180}{1}RT \qquad \text{... (i)}$$

$$1.52 = C_2RT \qquad \text{... (ii)}$$

24.

Divide equation (i) by (ii)

$$\frac{4.98}{1.52} = \frac{1}{6 \times C_2} \Rightarrow C_2 = 0.0508 \text{ mol L}^{-1} \quad \textbf{(1 Mark)}$$

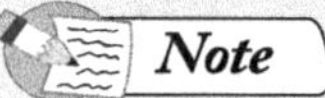

The measurement of osmotic pressure can be used to determine molecular weight of compounds and is also used in the desalination and purification of sea water, which involves the process of reverse osmosis.

Topper's Answer

14 Concentration of solution = 4% (w/w) (sucrose)

Considering 100 g of solutions

Mass of Sucrose = 4 g (m_s)

Mass of water = 100 − 4 = 96 g (m_w)

Molar mass of Sucrose, M_s = 342 g mol⁻¹

Moles of Sucrose molecules

$$n_s = \frac{m_s}{M_s} = \frac{4}{342} \text{ mol} = \frac{2}{171} \text{ mol}$$

$$\text{Molality of Solution} = \frac{n_s}{m_w \text{(in kg)}}$$

$$m = \frac{2(1000)}{171(96)} \text{ mol kg}^{-1}$$

$$m = \frac{2000}{171 \times 96} \text{ mol kg}^{-1}$$

Freezing point of solution = 271.15 K

Depression in freezing point = (273.15 − 271.15) K

$$= 2K = \Delta T_f$$

Now, $\Delta T_f = K_f \, m$

where K_f = molal depression constant of water.

Substituting values,

$$2 = \frac{K_f \times 2000}{171 \times 96}$$

OR $K_f = \frac{2 \times 171 \times 96}{2000} = \frac{171 \times 96}{1000} \; K \, kg \, mol^{-1}$ ——①

Now, given 5% glucose solution.
Considering 100 g of solution.
Mass of glucose = 5g = m_g [Mass of water = 95g]
Molar mass of glucose = 180 g mol^{-1} = M_g
moles of glucose, $n_g = \frac{m_g}{M_g} = \frac{5}{180} \, mol = \frac{1}{36} \, mol$

Molality of solution = $\dfrac{n_g}{\text{mass of water (in kg)}}$

$m = \dfrac{1}{36(95)} \, 1000 \; mol \, kg^{-1} = \dfrac{1000}{36 \cdot 95} \, mol \, kg^{-1}$

Using, $\Delta T_f = K_f \, m$

$\Delta T_f = \dfrac{171 \times 96}{1000} \times \dfrac{1000}{36 \times 95}$ (from ①)

$\Delta T_f = \dfrac{171 \times 96}{36 \times 95} \; K = 4.8 \, K$

So, actual freezing point = 273.15 K − 4.8 K
= 273.15
  4.80
  ────────
  268.35

= 268.35 K

Hence, the freezing point of 5% glucose solution in water is 268.35 K.

We know, $\Delta T_f = k_f m$

or $\quad \Delta T_f = \dfrac{k_f \times w_{sucrose} \times 1000}{E_{sucrose} w_{water}}$ ...(i)

(1 Mark)

$\Delta T_f = 273.15 - 271.15 = 2 \text{ K}$

put the value in (i) for 4% solution of sucrose in water

$2 = \dfrac{k_f \times 4 \times 1000}{342 \times 100} \Rightarrow k_f = 17.1 \text{ K kg mol}^{-1}$

For 5% solution of glucose

$\Delta T_f = \dfrac{k_f \times w_{glucose} \times 1000}{M_{glucose} \times w_{water}}$

(1 Mark)

$= \dfrac{17.1 \times 5 \times 1000}{180 \times 100} = 4.75 \text{ K}$

$T_f = 273.15 - 4.75 = 268.4 \text{ K}$ **(1 Mark)**

25. Given : Mass of glucose $(C_6H_{12}O_6)$, $w_2 = 60$ g

Mass of water, $w_1 = 250$ g

Molecular mass of (glucose) $(M_2) = 180 \text{ g mol}^{-1}$

$k_f = 1.86 \text{ K kg mol}^{-1}$

Freezing point of solution, $T_f = ?$

We know,

$\Delta T_f = i k_f m$

for glucose, $i = 1$

$\therefore \quad \Delta T_f = k_f m$

$= k_f \times \dfrac{w_2}{M_2} \times \dfrac{1000}{w_1}$ **(1 Mark)**

$\Delta T_f = 1.86 \times \dfrac{60}{180} \times \dfrac{1000}{250} = 2.48 \text{ K}$

Now,

$\Delta T_f = T_f^0 - T_f$

$2.48 = 0\,^\circ C - T_f$

$\therefore \quad T_f = -2.48\,^\circ C$

$= 270.67 \text{ K}$ **(1 Mark)**

26. (a) Osmotic pressure method is preferred for the determination of molar masses of macromolecules. This is because it is done around room temperature and molarity of solution is used instead of molality. as compared to other colligative properties, its magnitude is large even for very dilute solutions. this method is preferred for biomolecules as they are not stable at higher temperatures and polymers have poor solubility. **(1 Mark)**

(b) Aquatic animals are more comfortable in cold water than in warm water. This is because as temperature increase, solubility of gases in water decreases (from Le-chatelier's principle). Thus, in warm water the amount of oxygen available decreases. As a result, aquatic animals are more comfortable in cold water. **(1 Mark)**

(c) Elevation of boiling point for 1M KCl solution is nearly double than that of 1 M sugar solution. This is because elevation of boiling point depends on the value of 'i'. KCl being a strong electrolyte completely dissociates in water to give K^+ and Cl^- ions. Thus, $i = 2$ for KCl. On the other hand, sugar does not dissociate/associate in water so $i = 1$ for sugar solution. Hence $\Delta T_b\,(kCl) = 2\Delta T_b\,(sugar)$ **(1 Mark)**

27. (i) Properties which depend on the number of solute particles irrespective of their nature relative to the total number of particles present in the solution are called colligative properties. **(1 Mark)**

(ii) Molality (m): The number of gram molecule or moles of solute dissolved in 1 kg of solvent represents the molality of solution.

$\text{Molality} = \dfrac{\text{Number of gram molecule of solute (mol)}}{\text{Mass of solvent (in kg)}}$

(1 Mark)

28. Freezing point of surcose $(T_f) = 269.15 \text{ K}$

Freezing point of water $(T^\circ_f) = 273.15 \text{ K}$

Molar mass of surcose $= 342 \text{ g mol}^{-1}$

$\Delta T_f = 273.15 - 269.15 = 4 \text{ K}$

Molar mass of glucose $= 180 \text{ g mol}^{-1}$

Freezing point of glucose $= ?$

For sucrose $m = \dfrac{\text{moles of solute}}{W\,(in\text{ kg})}$ **(1 Mark)**

$= \dfrac{w \times 1000}{M_{sucose} \times W} = \dfrac{10 \times 1000}{90 \times 342}$

$\Delta T_f = K_f \times m$

$4 = K_f \times \dfrac{10 \times 1000}{90 \times 342}$

$K_f = 12.30 \text{ K kg mol}^{-1}$

For glucose $\Delta T_f = K_f \times m$ **(1 Mark)**

$\Delta T_f = 12.30 \times \dfrac{10 \times 1000}{90 \times 180}$

$\Delta T_f = 7.7 \text{ K}$

Freezing point of glucose $= T_f = 273.15 - 7.7 = 265.45\,K$

(1 Mark)

29. $K_b = 0.52$ K kg mol^{-1}

Mass of solute, $MgSO_4 = 4$g

Mass of solvent, water $= 100$ g

So, Molality of the solution, $m = \dfrac{4}{120} \times \dfrac{1000}{100}$

$$m = 0.33 \text{ mol/kg} \qquad \textbf{(1 Mark)}$$

Also, $MgSO_4$ undergoes complete ionisation, thereby yielding 2 moles of consituent ions for every mole of $MgSO_4$.

$\therefore \quad i = 2$ **(½ Mark)**

Now, elevation in boiling point is given as

$\Delta T_b = iK_b m$ **(½ Mark)**

$\qquad = 2 \times 0.52 \times 0.33$

$\qquad = 0.34$ K

$\because \Delta T_b = T_b - T_b^{\circ}$

$0.34 = T_b - 373.15$K

$T_b \quad = 373.15 + 0.34$

$\qquad = 373.49$ K **(1 Mark)**

Therefore, the new boiling point of the solution is 373.49 K.

30. Boiling point is the temperature at which vapour pressure of the substance becomes equal to atmospheric pressure. As the vapour pressure of the solution containing non-volatile solute is lower than that of the pure solvent and vapour pressure increases with increase in temperature. Hence, the solution has to be heated more to make its vapour pressure equal to the atmospheric pressure so that it starts boiling.

Elevation of boiling point is a colligative property because, it depends upon the number of particles of solute dissolved in solution. **(1 + 1 = 2 Marks)**

31. $W_2 = 31$g, $W_1 = 500$ g, $K_f = 1.86$ K kg mol^{-1}

$M_2 (C_2H_6O_2) = 24 + 6 + 32 = 62$ g mol^{-1}

$$\Delta T_f = \dfrac{1000 K_f \times W_2}{W_1 \times M_2} \qquad \textbf{(1 Mark)}$$

$$= \dfrac{1000 \times 1.86 \times 31}{500 \times 62} = 1.86 \text{ K} \qquad \textbf{(1 Mark)}$$

Freezing point of pure water $= 273.15$ K

$\therefore$ Freezing point of solution $= T_f^{\circ} - \Delta T_f$

$\qquad\qquad = 273.15 - 1.86$ K

$\qquad\qquad = 271.29$ K **(1 Mark)**

32. $\Delta T_f = K_f \times$ molality

Molality $= \dfrac{3.9 \times 1000}{122 \times 49} = 0.612$ m **(½ Mark)**

Now, $\Delta T_f = 4.9 \times 0.612 = 2.99$ K **(1 Mark)**

$$i = \dfrac{\text{observed } \Delta T_f}{\text{calculated } \Delta T_f} \qquad \textbf{(½ Mark)}$$

ΔT_f observed $= 1.62$ K (given)

$\therefore \quad i = \dfrac{1.62}{2.99} = 0.54$

As i < 1, benzoic acid is an associated solute. **(1 Mark)**

33. **Given :** $\Delta T_f = 0.48$ K

$M_2 = 256$ g mol^{-1}

$w_1 = 75$ g

$K_f = 5.12$ K kg mol^{-1}

To find : $w_2 = $?

Solution $\Delta T_f = K_f m$ **(½ Mark)**

$$\Delta T_f = K_f \times \dfrac{w_2}{M_2} \times \dfrac{1000}{w_1}$$

$$\Rightarrow \quad w_2 = \dfrac{\Delta T_f \times M_2 \times w_1}{K_f \times 1000} \qquad \textbf{(½ Mark)}$$

$$= \dfrac{0.48 \times 256 \times 75}{5.12 \times 1000}$$

$\Rightarrow \quad w_2 = 1.8$ g **(1 Mark)**

34. $W_2 \quad = 18$ g

$M_2 \quad = 180$ g mol^{-1}

$W_1 \quad = 1$ kg $= 1000$ g

$K_b \quad = 0.52$ K kg mol^{-1}

$$\Delta T_b = K_b \times \dfrac{W_2}{M_2} \times \dfrac{1000}{W_1} \qquad \textbf{(½ Mark)}$$

$$= 0.52 \times \dfrac{18}{180} \times \dfrac{1000}{1000} = \dfrac{0.52}{10} \qquad \textbf{(½ Mark)}$$

$$= 0.052 \text{ K}$$

Now, $\Delta T_b = T_s - T^{\circ}$ **(½ Mark)**

$0.052 = T_s - 373.15$

$\therefore \quad T_s = 373.15 + 0.052 = 373.202$ K

$\therefore$ Boiling point of solution $= 373.202$ K. **(½ Mark)**

35. $\pi = iCRT = i\dfrac{W}{M} \times \dfrac{R \times T}{V}$ **(½ Mark)**

For $K_2SO_4 \rightleftharpoons 2K^+ + SO_4^{2-}$ **(½ Mark)**

$i = 3$

$$\dfrac{3 \times 2.5 \times 10^{-2} (\text{gram}) \times 0.0821 \text{ L atm K}^{-1}\text{mol}^{-1} \times 298\text{K}}{174(\text{g mol}^{-1}) \times 2 \text{ L}}$$

(1 Mark)

$= 5.27 \times 10^{-3}$ atm **(1 Mark)**

36. (a) Addition of glucose to water is an endothermic reaction. According to Le Chat elier's principle, on increase in temperature, solubility will increase.

(1 Mark)

(b) Q is ocean water, due to the presence of salts it freezes at lower temperature (depression in freezing point) **(1 Mark)**

(c) $K_3[Fe(CN)_6]$ gives 4 ions in aqueous solution

(½ Mark)

$i = 1 + (n - 1)\,\alpha$ **(½ Mark)**

$i = 1 + (4 - 1) \times 0.0.852$

$i = 3.556$ **(½ Mark)**

$\Delta Tb = iKb\,m = 3.556 \times 0.52 \times 1 = 1.85$ **(1 Mark)**

$Tb = 101.85°C$ **(½ Mark)**

37. (a) Negative Deviation is expected when phenol and aniline are mixed with each other. The net volume of the mixture will decrease, $\Delta V < 0$ due to stronger intermolecular interactions.   **(1 Mark)**

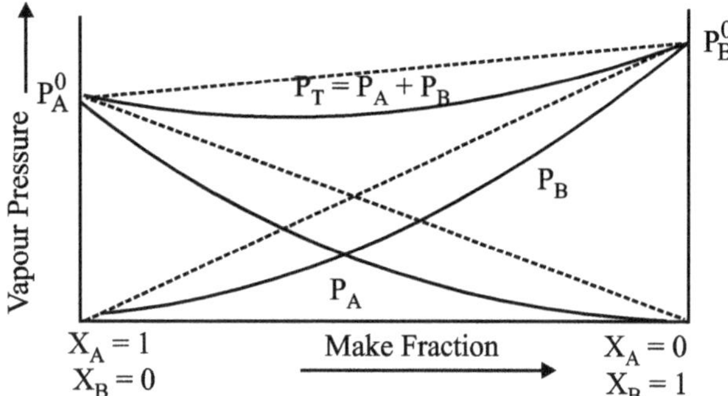

P-X Diagram for Solutions Showing Negative Deviation from Raoult-Law

(1 Mark)

(b) Relative lowering of vapour pressure $= (P° - P)/P°$
$= x_2$ **(½ Mark)**

$x_2 = n_2/n_1$

$n_2 = 0.1$

$n_1 = 100/18$

$x_2 = 0.1/5.55 + 0.1 = 0.1/5.65 = 0.018$ **(½ Mark)**

$P° = 23.8$ mm Hg

Relative lowering of vapour pressure $= (23.80 - P)/23.80$
$= 0.018$ **(½ Mark)**

$23.80 - P = 0.428$ **(½ Mark)**

$P = 23.80 - 0.428 = 23.37$ mm Hg   **(1 Mark)**

38. (i) The boiling point of 1 M NaCl solution more than that of 1 M glucose solution because NaCl is an ionic compound that dissociates into ions Na^+ and Cl^- in aqueous solutions while glucose does not.

Boiling point is a colligative property that increases with an increase in the number of particles. **(1 Mark)**

(ii) The vapour pressure is reduced to 90% when certain mass of 'X' is dissolved in 78 g of benzene.

If $P°_{benzene} = 1$ atm,

$P°_{Benzene} - P_{Benzene} = 0.1$ atm   **(½ Mark)**

$M_{Benzene} = 78.11$ g/mol ≈ 78 g/mol

$M_X = 50$ g/mol, $W_{Benzene} = 78$ g

$$\Rightarrow x_X = \frac{\dfrac{W_X}{M_X}}{\dfrac{W_X}{M_X} + \dfrac{W_{Benzene}}{M_{Benzene}}} = 0.2 \quad \textbf{(½ Mark)}$$

$$= \frac{\dfrac{W_X}{50}}{\dfrac{W_X}{50} + 1} = 0.2$$

$$= \frac{W_X}{W_X + 50} = 0.2 \quad \textbf{(½ Mark)}$$

$\Rightarrow \quad 0.2W_X + 10 = W_X$

$\Rightarrow \quad W_X - 0.2W_X = 10$

$\Rightarrow \quad 0.8W_X = 10$

$\Rightarrow \quad W_X = \dfrac{10}{0.8} = \textbf{12.5 g}$ **(½ Mark)**

(iii) $\Delta T_b = iK_b m$

$$= iK_b \left[\frac{1000 \times W_2}{M_2 \times W_1}\right] \quad \textbf{(1 Mark)}$$

i for $MgCl_2 = 3 \times 0.512 \times \left[\dfrac{1000 \times 10}{95 \times 200}\right]$

$= 0.808$ K   **(1 Mark)**

39. (i) The value of Van't Hoff factor for ethanoic acid in benzene is determined by its association in benzene. It forms a dimer in benzene so:

$$i = \frac{\text{no. of particles present}}{\text{Theoretical no. of particles}} = \frac{1}{2} = \textbf{0.5}$$

(1 Mark)

(ii) Osmotic pressure $(\pi) = \dfrac{i \times n_2 \times R \times T}{V}$ **(½ Mark)**

i for $K_2SO_4 = 3$ **(½ Mark)**

$$n_2 = \frac{m_2}{M_2} = \frac{2.32 \times 10^{-2}\ g}{174\ g/mol} = 1.33 \times 10^{-4}\ \text{moles}$$

$$\Rightarrow \pi = \frac{3 \times (1.33 \times 10^{-4}) \times (0.082) \times (298)}{2}$$

(½ Mark)

$= 0.00487$ atm or 4.87×10^{-3} atm.   **(½ Mark)**

(iii) $\Delta T_f = K_f \cdot m = K_f \left[\dfrac{1000 \times W_2}{M_2 \times W_1} \right]$ **(½ Mark)**

$\Rightarrow M_2 = \dfrac{K_f \times W_2 \times 1000}{\Delta T_f \times W_1}$

$= \dfrac{(5.12)\,(25.6)\,(1000)}{0.512 \times 1000} = \mathbf{256\ g}$ **(½ Mark)**

$\Rightarrow$ Molecular formula of Sulphur

$= \dfrac{M_{sulphur}}{At.\ mass} = \dfrac{256\ g}{32\ g/mol} = 8$ **(½ Mark)**

$\Rightarrow$ Molecular formula $= S_8$. **(½ Mark)**

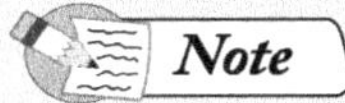 *Note*

Relative lowering of vapour pressure, osmotic pressure, elevation in boiling point and depression in freezing point are all colligative properties that are determined by the number of particles of the solute only. Further association or dissociation is determined by the Vant Hoff Factor (i) that gives the actual value of the property.

40. (a) Here $\Delta T_f = (273.15 - 269.15)\ K = 4\ K$

Molar mass of sugar $(C_{12}H_{22}O_{11})$

$= 12 \times 12 + 22 \times 1 + 11 \times 16 = 342\ g\ mol^{-1}$

10% solution (by mass) of sucrose (cane sugar) in water means 10 g of cane sugar is present in $(100 - 10)g = 90\ g$ of water.

Now, number of moles of cane sugar

$= \dfrac{10}{342} = 0.0292\ mol$ **(1 Mark)**

Therefore, molality (m) of the solution,

$= \dfrac{0.0292 \times 1000}{90} = 0.3244\ mol\ kg^{-1}$

Applying the relation, $\Delta T_f = K_f \times m$

$\Rightarrow K_f = \dfrac{\Delta T_f}{m} = \dfrac{4}{0.3244}$

$= 12.33\ K\ kg\ mol^{-1}$ **(1 Mark)**

Molar mass of glucose $(C_6H_{12}O_6)$

$= 6 \times 12 + 12 \times 1 + 6 \times 16$

$= 180\ g\ mol^{-1}$

10% glucose in water means 10 g of glucose is present in $(100 - 10)\ g = 90\ g$ of water.

$\therefore$ Number of mole of glucose

$= \dfrac{10}{180}\ mol = 0.0555\ mol$

Therefore, molality (m) of the solution

$= \dfrac{0.0555 \times 1000}{90} = 0.6166\ mol\ kg^{-1}$

Applying the relation, $\Delta T_f = K_f \times m$

$= 12.33\ K\ kg\ mol^{-1} \times 0.6166\ mol\ kg^{-1}$

$= 7.60\ K$ (approximately)

Hence, the freezing point of 10% glucose solution is $(273.15 - 7.60)\ K = 265.55\ K$ **(1 Mark)**

(b) **(i) Molality :** It is defined as the number of moles of a solute present in 1000 g (1kg) of a solvent.

$$\text{Molality } (m) = \frac{\text{Number of moles of solute}}{\text{Weight of solvent in kg}}$$

(1 Mark)

 *Note*

The relation between molarity and molality is

$$Molality\ (m) = \frac{Molarity(M)}{(Density\ of\ the\ solution(\rho) - molarity)} \times molecular\ wt.\ of\ solute$$

It can be used to determine the molarity if molality is given or vice versa.

(ii) Abnormal molar mass : Due to association or dissociation of molecules, the expected molar mass is either lower or higher than calculated molar mass. Such molar mass is called abnormal molar mass. **(1 Mark)**

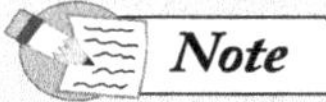 *Note*

Abnormal molar mass is the experimentally determined molar mass and is used to find the value of van't Hoff factor (i). To account for the extent of dissociation or association following relation can be used.

$$i = \frac{Normal\ molar\ mass}{Abnormal\ molar\ mass}.$$

41. (a) It is given that vapour pressure of water, $P_1^\circ = 23.8$ mm of Hg

Weight of water taken, $w_1 = 846\ g$

Weight of urea taken, $w_2 = 30g$

Molecular weight of water, $M_1 = 18\ g\ mol^{-1}$

Molecular weight of urea, $M_2 = 60\ g\ mol^{-1}$

Now, we have to calculate vapour pressure of water in the solution we take vapour pressure as P_1.

Relative lowering of vapour pressure equation can be written as :

$$\frac{P_1^0 - P_1}{P_1^0} = \frac{n_2}{n_1 + n_2}$$

For dilute solution $(n_2 \ll n_1)$

$$\frac{P_1^0 - P_1}{P_1^0} = \frac{n_2}{n_1} \qquad \textbf{(1 Mark)}$$

$$\Rightarrow \quad \frac{23.8 - P_1}{23.8} = \frac{(30/60)}{(846/18)} \qquad \textbf{(1 Mark)}$$

$$\Rightarrow \quad \frac{23.8 - P_1}{23.8} = \frac{1}{94}$$

$$\Rightarrow \quad P_1 = 23.5501 \text{ mm of Hg}$$

Hence, the vapour pressure of water in the given solution is 23.5501 mm of Hg and its relative lowering is 0.0105. **(1 Mark)**

(b) Ideal solutions and non-ideal solutions

	Ideal Solutions	**Non-Ideal Solutions**
1.	Solutions which obey Rault's law over the entire range of concentration are known as ideal solutions.	Solutions which do not obey Raoult's law over the entire range of concentration are known as non-ideal solutions.
2.	Intermolecular force of attraction between the molecules of solute (A – A) and those between the molecules of solvent (B – B) are nearly equal to those between solute and solvent molecules (A – B).	Intermolecular force of attraction between the molecules of solute (A – A) and those between the molecules of solvent (B – B) are not equal to those between solute and solvent molecules (A – B).

(1 + 1 = 2 Marks)

42. (a) Given

$$K_f = 1.86 \text{ K kg mol}^{-1}$$

mass of solute = 1.9 g

mass of solvent = 50 g

Therefore,

Molality of the solution, $m = \dfrac{\text{no. of mole of solute}}{\text{wt. of solvent in kg}}$

$$= \frac{1.9 \times 1000}{95 \times 50} = 0.4 \text{ m} \qquad \textbf{(1 Mark)}$$

$$MgCl_2 \longrightarrow Mg^+ + 2Cl^-$$

No. of ion = 3

$$i = 3$$

$$\Delta T_f = i\, K_f\, m$$
$$= 3 \times 1.86 \times 0.4$$
$$= 2.232 \text{ K} \qquad \textbf{(1 Mark)}$$

$$T_f(MgCl_2) = T_f(water) - \Delta T_f$$
$$= 273 - 2.232$$
$$= 270.77 \text{ K} \qquad \textbf{(1 Mark)}$$

(b) (i) The elevation in the boiling point of a solution is a colligative property, therefore it is affected by the number of particles of the solute. Since the amount of solute is higher in 2M glucose solution as compared to 1M glucose solution, the elevation in the boiling point is higher. Hence, 2M glucose solution has a higher boiling point than 1 M glucose solution.

(1 Mark)

(ii) When the external pressure applied become more than the osmotic pressure, pure solvent starts flowing out of the solution through the semipermeable membrane. This process is known as reverse osmosis. **(1 Mark)**

43. (a) Weight of sulphur $(w_2) = 2.56$ g, $M_2 = 32$ g/mol

Weight of solvent = 100 g

$$K_f = 3.83 \text{ K kg/mol}$$

$$\Delta T_f = K_f \times \frac{W_2}{M \times w_1} \times 1000 \qquad \textbf{(1 Mark)}$$

$$0.383 = \frac{3.83 \times 2.56 \times 1000}{M \times 100}$$

$$M = 256 \text{ g/mol} \qquad \textbf{(1 Mark)}$$

Formula of sulphur

One atom of S = 32 g/mol^{-1}

so atoms of S in molecule $= \dfrac{256}{32} = 8$

Formula = S_8 **(1 Mark)**

(b) (i) 1.2% Sodium chloride is hypertonic with respect to 0.9% sodium chloride, hence cells will shrink and water flows out of the cells. Plasmolysis will take place. **(1 Mark)**

(ii) 0.41% Sodium chloride solution is hypotonic with respsect to 0.9% sodium chloride. Hence water flows into the cell and cells will swell. Endo osmosis will take place. **(1 Mark)**

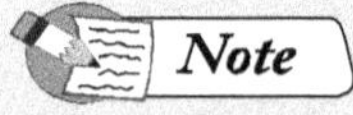

Isotonic solution : Concentration of solute inside the cell is same as in the solution outside.
Hypotonic solution : Outside solution has lower concentration of solute than inside the cell.
Hypertonic solution : Outside solution has greater solute concentration than inside the cell.

44. **(a)** **(i)** **Molarity:** It is defined as number of moles of solute per litre of the solution. Its units are mol L^{-1}.

$$\text{Molarity (M)} = \frac{\text{No. of moles of solute}}{\text{Volume of solution}}$$

(1 Mark)

(ii) **Molal elevation constant (Kb):** It is defined as the elevation in boiling point when the molality of the solution is unity, i.e., 1 mole of the solute is dissolved in 1 kg of the solvent.

(1 Mark)

(b) **Given:**

Urea	Glucose
$w_1 = 15$ g	$M_2 = 180$ g
$M_1 = 60$ g	

To find: $w_2 = ?$

As the solutions are isotonic, we have

$$\pi_1 = \pi_2 \qquad \text{(½ Mark)}$$
$$C_1RT = C_2RT$$
$$C_1 = C_2 \qquad \text{(½ Mark)}$$
$$\frac{n_1}{V_1} = \frac{n_2}{V_2}$$

$$\Rightarrow \quad n_2 = \frac{n_1}{V_1} \times V_2$$

$V_1 = V_2$ as vol. is 1 litre

$$\therefore \quad \frac{n_2}{M_2} = \frac{n_1}{M_1} \frac{w_1}{M_1}$$

(1 Mark)

$$w_2 = \frac{w_1}{M_1} \times M_2$$

$$= \frac{15}{60} \times 180 = 45$$

$\therefore$ mass of glucose $= 45$ g **(½ + ½ = 1 Mark)**

45. **(a)** A mixture of ethanol and acetone shows positive deviation from Raoult's law. This is because acetone molecules enter between alcohol molecules thus breaking the H-bonds between ethanol molecules and hence showing +ve deviation.

(1 + 1 = 2 Marks)

(b) **Given:** 10% solution of glucose $\Rightarrow$ 10 g of glucose in 100 g of solution

molar mass of glucose, $M_2 = 180$ g mol^{-1}

density of solution, $d = 1.2$ g mL^{-1}

To find: (i) molality, m

(ii) molarity, M

(i) Molality,

$$m = \frac{\text{Moles of solute}}{\text{Mass of solvent (in g)}} \times 1000 \quad \text{(½ Mark)}$$

$$m = \frac{(10/180)}{(100-10)} \times 1000$$

$$m = \frac{10}{180 \times 90} \times 1000 = \frac{100}{18 \times 9}$$

$$m = 0.617 \text{ mol kg}^{-1} \qquad \text{(1 Mark)}$$

(ii) Molarity,

$$m = \frac{\text{Moles of solute}}{\text{Volume of solution (in mL)}} \times 1000 \quad \text{(½ Mark)}$$

$$M = \frac{(10/180)}{V_{sol}} \times 1000$$

$$V_{sol} = \frac{m_{sol}}{d} = \frac{100}{1.2}$$

$$M = \frac{10/180}{100/1.2} \times 1000 = \frac{2}{3}$$

$$\therefore \quad M = 0.66 \text{ mol L}^{-1} \qquad \text{(1 Mark)}$$

46. **(a)** **Raoult's law :** For a solution of volatile liquids, the partial vapour pressure of each component of the solution is directly proportional to its mole fraction present in solution.

For two components A and B

$$p_B = p_B^{\circ} \times x_B \qquad p_A = p_A^{\circ} \times x_A \qquad \text{(1 Mark)}$$

Raoult's law as a special case of Henry's law :

According to Raoult's law, for any volatile component of the solution.

$$p_A = p_A^{\circ} \times x_A$$

Now, for a solution in which a gas is the solute and liquid is the solvent, then according to Henry's law

$$p_A = k_H \times x_A$$

i.e., partial pressure of the volatile component (gas) is directly proportional to the mole fraction of that component (gas) in the solution.

Thus, Raoult's law and Henry's law become identical except that their proportionality constants are different. **(2 Marks)**

(b) $W_2 = 1.00$ g

$W_1 = 50$ g

$\Delta T_f = 0.40$ K

$K_f = 5.12$ K kg mol^{-1}

$$M_2 = \frac{1000 \times K_f \times W_2}{W_1 \times \Delta T_f}$$ **(1 Mark)**

$$= \frac{1000 \times 5.12 \times 1.00}{50 \times 0.40}$$

$$= 256 \text{ g mol}^{-1}$$ **(1 Mark)**

47. (a) (i) Ideal solution : (I) The solution which obey Raoult's law at all temperatures and concentrations (II) $\Delta H_{mix} = 0$ i.e. no heat is evolved or absorbed when components are mixed to form the solution (III) $\Delta V_{mix} = 0$ i.e. no change in volume. **(1 Mark)**

(ii) Azeotrope : A liquid mixture, having a definite composition, and boiling point like a pure liquid, is called a constant boiling mixture or an azeotrope. **(1 Mark)**

(iii) Osmotic pressure : The minimum excess pressure that has to be applied to the solution to prevent the entry of the solvent into the solution through the semipermeable membrane due to osmosis is called the osmotic pressure. **(1 Mark)**

(b) 10% glucose solution by weight means

Mass of solute $(W_2) = 10$ g

Mol. mass of solute $(M_2) = 180$ g mol^{-1}

Mass of solvent $(W_1) = 100 - 10 = 90$ g

Molality (m) $= \dfrac{W_2}{M_2} \times \dfrac{1000}{W_1}$ **(1 Mark)**

$$= \frac{10}{180} \times \frac{1000}{90}$$

$$= 0.617 \text{ m}$$ **(1 Mark)**

48. The melting point of ice is the freezing point of water. We can use the depression in freezing point property in this case.

(a) 3rd reading for 0.5 g there has to be an increase in depression of freezing point and therefore decrease in freezing point so also decrease in melting point when amount of salt is increased but the trend is not followed on this case. **(1 Mark)**

(b) two sets of reading help to avoid error in data collection and give more objective data. **(1 Mark)**

(c) ΔT_f (glucose) $= 1 \times K_f \times \dfrac{0.6 \times 1000}{180 \times 10}$ ....(1)

  (1/2 Mark)

ΔT_f (NaCl) $= 2 \times K_f \times \dfrac{0.6 \times 1000}{58.5 \times 10}$ **(1/2 Mark)**

$3.8 = 2 \times K_f \times \dfrac{0.6 \times 1000}{58.5 \times 10}$ ....(2)

Divide equation 1 by 2

$\dfrac{\Delta T_f \text{ (glucose)}}{3.8} = \dfrac{58.5}{2 \times 180}$ **(1/2 Mark)**

ΔT_f (glucose = 0.62 Freezing point or Melting point $= -0.62 \,^{\circ}C$ **(1/2 Mark)**

OR

depression in freezing point is directly proportional to molality (mass of solute when the amount of solvent remains same) **(1 Mark)**

0.3 g depression is 1.9 °C

0.6 g depression is 3.8 °C

1.2 g depression will be $3.8 \times 2 = 7.6\,^{\circ}C$ **(1 Mark)**

2 Chapter — Electrochemistry

1   *Multiple Choice Questions*

1. Consider the following standard electrode potential values: **[Delhi 2023, Set-I, Ap]**

   $Fe^{3+}(aq) + e^- \rightarrow Fe^{2+}(aq)$ $E° = +0.77$ V

   $MnO_4^-(aq) + 8H^+ + 5e^- \rightarrow$

   $\qquad Mn^{2+}(aq) + 4H_2O(l)$ $E° = +1.51$ V

   What is the cell potential for the redox reaction?

   (a) -2.28 V

   (b) -0.74 V

   (c) $+0.74$ V

   (d) $+2.28$ V

2. A voltaic cell is made by connecting two half cells represented by half equations below:

   [Delhi 2023, Set-I, U]

   $Sn^{2+}{}_{(aq)} + 2e^- \rightarrow Sn_{(a)}$ $E° = -0.14$ V

   $Fe^{3+}{}_{(aq)} + e^- \rightarrow Fe^{2+}{}_{(aq)}$ $E° = +0.77$ V

   Which statement is correct about this voltaic cell?

   (a) Fe^{2+} is oxidised and the voltage of the cell is -0.91 V

   (b) Sn is oxidised and the voltage of the cell is 0.91 V

   (c) Fe^{2+} is oxidised and the voltage of the cell is 0.91 V

   (d) Sn is oxidised and the voltage of the cell is 0.63 V.

3. In an electrochemical process, a salt bridge is used

   [Delhi 2020, K]

   (a) as a reducing agent

   (b) as an oxidizing agent

   (c) to complete the circuit so that current can flow

   (d) none of these

1   *Multiple Choice Questions*

1. Consider the following standard electrode potential values: **[Delhi 2023 Set-III, U]**

   $Sn^{2+}{}_{(aq)} + 2e^- \rightarrow Sn_{(s)}$ $E° = -0.14$ V

   $Fe^{3+}{}_{(aq)} + e^- \rightarrow Fe^{2+}{}_{(aq)}$ $E° = +0.77$ V

   What is the cell reaction and potential for the spontaneous reaction that occurs?

   (a) $2\,Fe^{2+}{}_{(aq)} + Sn^{2+}{}_{(aq)} \rightarrow 2Fe^{3+}{}_{(aq)} + Sn_{(s)}$

       $E° = -0.91$ V

   (b) $2\,Fe^{3+}{}_{(aq)} + Sn_{(s)} \rightarrow 2\,Fe^{2+}{}_{(aq)} + Sn^{2+}$

       $E° = +0.91$ V

   (c) $2\,Fe^{2+}{}_{(aq)} + Sn^{2+}{}_{(aq)} \rightarrow 2\,Fe^{3+}{}_{(aq)} + Sn_{(s)}$

       $E° = +0.91$ V

   (d) $2\,Fe^{3+}{}_{(aq)} + Sn_{(s)} \rightarrow 2\,Fe^{2+}{}_{(aq)} + Sn^{2+}{}_{(aq)}$

       $E° = +1.68$ V

5   *Short Answer Questions (2 or 3 Marks)*

2. (a) Calculate $\Delta_r G°$ and $\log K_c$ for the following cell :

   $Ni(s) + 2\,Ag^+(aq) \rightarrow Ni^{2+}(aq) + 2Ag(s)$

   Given that $E°_{cell} = 1.05$V, $F = 96{,}500$ Cmol^{-1}.

   [All India 2022, Term-II, Ap]

3. (b) Calculate the e.m.f. of the following cell at 298K :

   $Fe(s)|Fe^{2+}(0.001\,M)||H^+(0.01M)|H_2(g)(1\,bar)|Pt(s)$

   Given that $E°_{cell} = +0.44$ V

   $[\log 2 = 0.3010 \quad \log 3 = 0.4771 \quad \log 10 = 1]$

   [All India 2022, Term-II, Ap] 

4. Represent the cell in which the following reaction takes place. The value of E° for the cell is 1.260 V. What is the value of E_{cell} ? **[CBSE Sample 2021-22, Term-II, Ap]**

$$2Al(s) + 3Cd^{2+} (0.1M) \rightarrow 3Cd\ (s) + 2Al^{3+} (0.01M)$$

5. (a) The cell in which the following reaction occurs:

[All India 2017, Ap]

$$2Fe^{3+}\ (aq) + 2I^-\ (aq) \longrightarrow 2Fe^{2+}\ (aq) + I_2(s)$$

has $E_{cell}^{\circ} = 0.236$ V at 298 K. Calculate the standard Gibbs energy of the cell reaction

(Given: 1 F = 96,500 C mol^{-1})

(b) How many electrons flow through a metallic wire if a current of 0.5 A is passed for 2 hours ?

(Given: 1F = 96,500 C mol^{-1})

6. Calculate emf of the following cell at 25 °C :

[Delhi 2015, Ap]

$$Fe\ |\ Fe^{2+}\ (0.001\ M)\ \|\ H^+(0.01\ M)\ |\ H_2(g)\ (1\ bar)\ |\ Pt(s)$$

$$E°(Fe^{2+}\ |\ Fe) = -0.44\ V,\ E°(H^+\ |\ H_2) = 0.00\ V$$

7. Write two differences between 'order of reaction' and 'molecularity of reaction'. **[Delhi 2014, K]**

8. The standard electrode potential (E°) for Daniel cell is + 1.1 V. Calculate the $\Delta G°$ for the reaction $Zn(s) + Cu^{2+}$ (aq) $\longrightarrow Zn^{2+}$ (aq) + Cu(s)

(1F = 96500 C mol^{-1}). **[All India 2013, Ap]**

9. Calculate the emf of the following cell at 25°C :

[All India 2013, Ap]

$$Ag\ (s)\ |Ag^+\ (10^{-3}\ M)\ \|\ Cu^{2+}\ (10^{-1}\ M)\ |\ Cu\ (s)$$

Given $E_{cell}^{\circ} = + 0.46$ V and log $10^n = n$.

10. Calculate the emf of the following cell at 298 K :

$$Fe(s)\ |\ Fe^{2+}\ (0.001\ M)\ \|\ H^+\ (1\ M)\ |\ H_2\ (g)\ (1\ bar),\ Pt\ (s)$$

(Given $E_{cell}^{\circ} = +0.44V$) **[Delhi 2013, Ap]**

6   *Long Answer Questions*

11. Calculate e.m.f of the following cell at 298 K :

[Delhi 2016, Ap]

$$2Cr(s) + 3Fe^{2+}(0.1M) \rightarrow 2Cr^{3+}\ (0.01M) + 3\ Fe(s)$$

Given : $E°(Cr^{3+}\ |Cr) = -0.74V$, $E°(Fe^{2+}\ |\ Fe) = -0.44$ V

12. Calculate e.m.f and ΔG for the following cell :

$$Mg(s)\ |\ Mg^{2+}\ (0.001\ M)\ \|\ Cu^{2+}\ (0.0001\ M)\ |\ Cu\ (s)$$

Given : $E_{(Mg^{2+}/Mg)}^{\circ} = -2.37V$,   **[All India 2015, Ap]**

$$E_{(Cu^{2+}/Cu)}^{\circ} = + 0.34V.$$

 **Topic-3:**   *Conductance of Electrolytic Solutions*

1   *Multiple Choice Questions*

1. Which of the following solutions will have the highest conductivity at 298 K? **[CBSE Sample 2023-24, K]**

(a) 0.01 M HCl solution

(b) 0.1 M HCl solution

(c) 0.01 M CH$_3$COOH solution

(d) 0.1 M CH$_3$COOH solution

2. Which of the following relations is incorrect?

[All India 2023, Set-I, K]

(a) $R = \dfrac{1}{k}\left(\dfrac{l}{a}\right)$ (b) $G = k\left(\dfrac{a}{l}\right)$

(c) $G = k\left(\dfrac{l}{a}\right)$ (d) $\wedge_m = \dfrac{k}{c}$

3. Which of the following solutions KCl will have the highest value of molar conductivity?

[All India 2023 Set-II, U]

(a) 0.01 M   (b) 1 M

(c) 0.5 M   (d) 0.1 M

4. The unit of molar conductivity is

[Delhi 2023 Set-III, K]

(a) S cm^{-2} mol^{-1} (b) S cm^2 mol^{-1}

(c) S^{-1} cm^2 mol^{-1} (d) S cm^2 mol

5. The molar conductivity of CH$_3$COOH at infinite dilution is 390 Scm^2/mol. Using the graph and given information, the molar conductivity of CH$_3$COOK will be:

[CBSE Sample 2022-23, Ap]

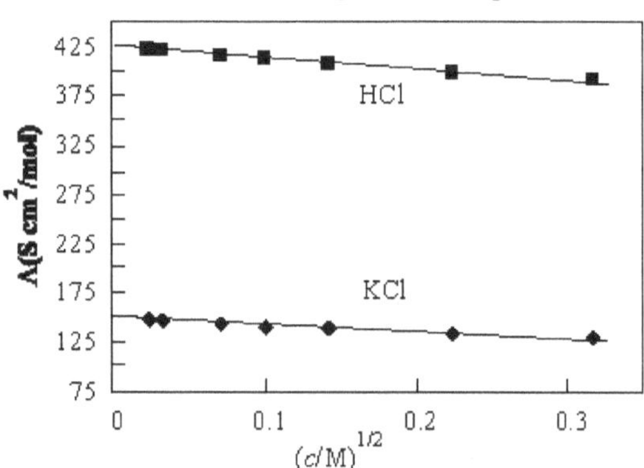

(a) 100 Scm^2/mol   (b) 115 Scm^2/mol

(c) 150 Scm^2/mol   (d) 125 Scm^2/mol

6. What is the molar conductance at infinite dilution for sodium chloride if the molar conductance at infinite dilution of Na^+ and Cl^- ions are 51.12×10^{-4} Scm^2/mol and 73.54×10^{-4} Scm^2/mol respectively?

[CBSE Sample 2022-23, Ap]

   (a) 124.66 Scm^2/mol (b) 22.42 Scm^2/mol

   (c) 198.20 Scm^2/mol (d) 175.78 Scm^2/mol

7. Which of the following option will be the limiting molar conductivity of CH_3COOH if the limiting molar conductivity of CH_3COONa is 91 Scm^2mol-1? Limiting molar conductivity for individual ions are given in the following table. **CBSE Sample 2020-21, Ap]**

S.No.	Ions	Limiting molar conductivity/Scm^2 $mole^{-1}$
1	H^+	349.6
2	Na^+	50.1
3	K^+	73.5
4	OH^-	199.1

   (a) 350 Scm^2mol^{-1} (b) 375.3 Scm^2mol^{-1}

   (c) 390.5 Scm^2mol^{-1} (d) 340.4 Scm^2mol^{-1}

8. Kohlrausch gave the following relation for strong electrolytes:

$$\wedge = \wedge_0 - A\sqrt{C}$$

Which of the following equality holds? **[Delhi 2020, U]**

   (a) $\wedge = \wedge_0$ as $C \to \sqrt{A}$ (b) $\wedge = \wedge_0$ as $C \to \infty$

   (c) $\wedge = \wedge_0$ as $C \to 0$ (d) $\wedge = \wedge_0$ as $C \to 1$

2   *Assertion Reason/Two Statement Type Questions*

Given below are two statements labelled as Assertion (A) and Reason (R). Select the most appropriate answer from the options given below:

(a) Both (A) and (R) are true and (R) is the correct explanation of (A).

(b) Both (A) and (R) are true, but (R) is not the correct explanation of (A).

(c) (A) is true, but (R) is false.

(d) (A) is false, but (R) is true.

9. **Assertion (A) :** Molar conductivity decreases with increase in concentration. **[All India 2023, Set-I, K]**

Reason (R) : When concentration approaches zero, the molar conductivity is known as limiting molar conductivity.

10. **Assertion (A):** Conductivity decreases with decreases in concentration of electrolyte. **[All India 2023 Set-II, U]**

Reason (R): Number of ions per unit volume that carry the current in a solution decreases on dilution.

11. **Assertion (A) :** Conductivity of an electrolyte increases with decrease in concentration.

Reason (R) : Number of ions per unit volume decreases on dilution. **[Delhi 2020, U]**

4   *Very Short Answer Questions (1 Mark)*

12. The conductivity of 0.001M acetic acid is 7.8×10^{-5} S cm^{-1}. Calculate its degree of dissociation if Λ°_m for acetic acid is 390 S cm^2 mol^{-1}. **[All India 2022, Term-II, Ap]**

5   *Short Answer Questions (2 or 3 Marks)*

13. (a) Can we construct an electrochemical cell with two half-cells composed of $ZnSO_4$ solution and zinc electrodes? Explain your answer.

[CBSE Sample 2023-24, Ap]

   (b) Calculate the λ^0_m for Cl^- ion from the data given below: $\Lambda^0_m MgCl_2 = 258.6$ Scm^2mol^{-1} and $\lambda^0_m Mg^{2+} = 106$ Scm^2mol^{-1} **[CBSE Sample 2023-24, Ap]**

   (c) The cell constant of a conductivity cell is 0.146 cm^{-1}. What is the conductivity of 0.01 M solution of an electrolyte at 298 K, if the resistance of the cell is 1000 ohm? **[CBSE Sample 2023-24, Ap]**

14. Solutions of two electrolytes 'A' and 'B' are diluted. The Λ_m of 'B' increases 1.5 times while that of A increases 25 times. Which of the two is a strong electrolyte? Justify your answer. Graphically show the behavior of 'A' and 'B'. **[CBSE Sample 2021-22, Term-II, U]**

15. Calculate the degree of dissociation (α) of acetic acid if its molar conductivity (Λ_m) is 39.05 S cm^2mol^{-1}. Given $\lambda^0(H^+) = 349.6$ S cm^2 mol^{-1} and $\lambda^0(CH_3COO^-) = 40.9$ S cm^2 mol^{-1} **[Delhi 2017, Ap]**

16. (a) Following reactions occur at cathode during the electrolysis of aqueous silver chloride solution : **[Delhi 2015, K]**

$$Ag^+(aq) + e^- \longrightarrow Ag(s) \quad E^\circ = +0.80 \text{ V}$$

$$H^+(aq) + e^- \longrightarrow \frac{1}{2}H_2(g) \quad E^\circ = 0.00 \text{ V}$$

On the basis of their standard reduction electrode potential (E°) values, which reaction is feasible at the cathode and why ?

   (b) Define limiting molar conductivity. Why conductivity of an electrolyte solution decreases with the decrease in concentration ? **[Delhi 2015, K]**

17. State Kohlrausch's law of independent migration of ions. Why does the conductivity of a solution decrease with dilution? **[All India 2014, K]**

18. The conductivity of 0.20 M solution of KCl at 298 K is 0.025 S cm^{-1}. Calculate its molar conductivity. **[Delhi 2013, Ap]**

6   *Long Answer Questions*

19. (a) Conductivity of 2×10^{-3} methanoic acid is 8×10^{-5} cm^{-1}. **[All India 2023, Set-I, Ap]** Calculate its molar conductivity and degree of dissociation of $\wedge_m^o$ for methanoic acid is 404 S cm^2 mol^{-1}.

(b) Calculate the $\Delta_r G^o$ and log K_c for the given reaction at 298 K:

$$Ni(s) + 2Ag^+(aq) \rightleftharpoons Ni^{2+}(aq) + 2Ag(s)$$

Given: $E^o_{Ni^{2+}/Ni_1} = -0.25V, E^o_{Ag^+/Ag} = +0.80V$

1 F = 96500 C mol^{-1}. **[All India 2023, Set-I, Ap]**

20. (a) Write the cell reaction and calculate the e.m.f. of the following cell at 298 K : **[All India 2018, Ap]**

$$Sn(s)\,|\,Sn^{2+}(0.004\,M)\,\|\,H^+(0.020\,M)\,|\,H_2(g)\,(1\,bar)\,|\,Pt(s)$$

$$\left(Given : E^o_{Sn^{2+}/Sn} = -0.14V\right)$$

(b) Give reasons : **[All India 2018, U]**

   (i) On the basis of E° values, O_2 gas should be liberated at anode but it is Cl_2 gas which is liberated in the electrolysis of aqueous NaCl.

   (ii) Conductivity of CH_3COOH decreases on dilution.

21. (a) Calculate E°$_{cell}$ for the following reaction at 298 K:

$$2Al(s) + 3Cu^{2+}(0.01M) \longrightarrow 2Al^{3+}(0.01\,M) + 3Cu(s)$$

Given : E_{cell} = 1.98 V **[All India 2016, Ap]**

(b) Using the E° values of A and B, predict which is better for coating the surface of iron $[E^o_{(Fe^{2+}/Fe)} = -0.44V]$ to prevent corrosion and why ?

Given : $E^o_{(A^{2+}/A)} = -2.37V$

$$E^o_{(B^{2+}/B)} = -0.14\ V \quad \textbf{[All India 2016, Ap]}$$

22. (a) The conductivity of 0.001 mol L^{-1} solution of CH_3COOH is 3.905×10^{-5} S cm^{-1}. Calculate its molar conductivity and degree of dissociation (α). Given $\lambda^0(H^+) = 349.6$ S cm^2 mol^{-1} and $\lambda^0(CH_3COO^-) = 40.9$ S cm^2 mol^{-1} **[All India 2016, Ap]**

(b) Define electrochemical cell. What happens if external potential applied becomes greater than E°$_{cell}$ of electrochemical cell ? **[All India 2016, U]**

7   *Case Based Questions*

The following questions are case based questions. Read the passage carefully and answer the questions that follow:

23. Rahul set-up an experiment to find resistance of aqueous KCl solution for different concentration at 298 K using a conductivity cell connected to a Wheatstone bridge. He fed the Wheatstone bridge with a.c. power in the audio frequency range 550 to 5000 cycles per second. Once the resistance was calculated from null point he also calculated the conductivity K and molar conductivity Λ_m and recorded his readings in tabular form.

[Delhi 2023, Set-I, A]

S. No	Conc. (M)	 S cm^{-1}	Λ_m S cm^2 mol^{-1}
1.	1.00	111.3×10^{-3}	111.3
2.	0.10	12.9×10^{-3}	129.0
3.	0.01	1.41×10^{-3}	141.0

Answer the following questions :

(a) Why does conductivity decrease with dilution ?

(b) If Λ_m^0 of KCl is 150.0 S cm^2 mol^{-1}, calculate the degree of dissociation of 0.01 M KCl.

(c) If Rahul had used HCl instead to KCl then would you expect the Λ_m values to be more or less than those per KCl for a given concentration. Justify.

OR

(c) Amit a classmate of Rahul repeated the same experiment with CH_3COOH solution instead of KCl solution. Give one point that would be similar and one that would be different in his observations as compared to Rahul.

Topic-4: *Electrolytic Cells and Electrolysis*

---

1   *Multiple Choice Questions*

1. Four half reactions I to IV are shown below:

I. $2Cl^- \rightarrow Cl_2 + 2e^-$ **[Delhi 2023, Set-I, U]**

II. $4OH^- \rightarrow O_2 + 2H_2O + 2e^-$

III. $Na^+ + e^- \rightarrow Na$

IV. $2H^+ + 2e^- \rightarrow H_2$

Which two of these reactions are most likely to occur when concentrated brine is electrolysed?

(a)   I and III

(b)   I and IV

(c)   II and III

(d)   II and IV

---

2   *Assertion Reason/Two Statement Type Questions*

Given below are two statements labelled as Assertion (A) and Reason (R). Select the most appropriate answer from the options given below:

(a)   Both (A) and (R) are true and (R) is the correct explanation of (A).

(b)   Both (A) and (R) are true, but (R) is not the correct explanation of (A).

(c)   (A) is true, but (R) is false.

(d)   (A) is false, but (R) is true.

2. **Assertion (A):** During electrolysis of aqueous copper sulphate solution using copper electrodes hydrogen gas is released at the cathode.

[CBSE Sample 2023-24, U]

Reason (R): The electrode potential of Cu^{2+}/Cu is greater than that of H^+/H_2

---

4   *Very Short Answer Questions (1 Mark)*

3. How much charge in terms of Faraday is required to reduce one mol of MnO_4^- to Mn^{2+} ?

[Delhi 2020, Set-I]

4. How much charge is required for the reduction of 1 mol of Zn^{2+} to Zn ?   **[All India 2015, K]**

---

5   *Short Answer Questions (2 or 3 Marks)*

5. (i)   What should be the signs (positive/negative) for E°_{Cell} and ΔG° for a spontaneous redox reaction occurring under standard conditions?

[Delhi 2023, Set-I, U]

(ii)   State Faraday's first law of electrolysis.

[Delhi 2023, Set-I, K]

6. Calculate the emf of the following cell at 298 K:

[Delhi 2023, Set-I, U]

$Fe_{(s)}|\ Fe^{2+}\ (0.01M)\|H^+_{(1M)}|H_{2(g)}\ (1\ bar),\ Pt_{(s)}$

Given $E^{\circ}_{Cell} = 0.44$ V.

7. Calculate $\Delta_r G^{\circ}$ and log K_c for the following reaction:

[All India 2019, Ap]

$Cd^{2+}(aq) + Zn(s) \longrightarrow Zn^{2+}(aq) + Cd(s)$

Given: $E^{\circ}_{Cd^{2+}/Cd} = -0.403$ V

$E^{\circ}_{Zn^{2+}/Zn} = -0.763$ V

8. When a steady current of 2A was passed through two electrolytic cells A and B containing electrolytes $ZnSO_4$ and $CuSO_4$ connected in series, 2 g of Cu were deposited at the cathode of cell B. How long did the current flow?

What mass of Zn was deposited at cathode of cell A? [Atomic mass: Cu = 63.5 g mol^{-1}, Zn = 65 g mol^{-1}; 1F = 96500 C mol^{-1}]   **[Delhi 2020, Ap.]**

9. E°_{cell} for the given redox reaction is 2.71 V

[Delhi 2019, Ap]

$Mg(s) + Cu^{2+}(0.01\ M) \longrightarrow Mg^{2+}(0.001\ M) + Cu(s)$

Calculate E_{cell} for the reaction. Write the direction of flow of current when an external opposite potential applied is

(i)   less than 2.71 V and

(ii)   greater than 2.71 V

10. Chromium metal is electroplated using an acidic solution containing CrO_3 according to the following equation: **[All India 2019, Ap]**

$CrO_3(aq) + 6H^+ + 6e^- \longrightarrow Cr(s) + 3H_2O$

Calculate how many grams of chromium will be electroplated by 24,000 coulombs. How long will it take to electroplate 1.5 g chromium using 12.5 A current?

[Atomic mass of Cr = 52 g mol^{-1}, 1 F = 96500 C mol^{-1}]

6   *Long Answer Questions*

11. (a) Why does the cell voltage of a mercury cell remain constant during its lifetime?

[CBSE Sample 2022-23, K]

(b) Write the reaction occurring at anode and cathode and the products of electrolysis of aq KCl.

[CBSE Sample 2022-23, U]

(c) What is the pH of HCl solution when the hydrogen gas electrode shows a potential of –0.59 V at standard temperature and pressure?

[CBSE Sample 2022-23, Ap]

12. (a) Molar conductivity of substance "A" is 5.9×10^3 S/m and "B" is 1×10^{-16} S/m. Which of the two is most likely to be copper metal and why?

[CBSE Sample 2022-23, Ap]

(b) What is the quantity of electricity in Coulombs required to produce 4.8 g of Mg from molten $MgCl_2$? How much Ca will be produced if the same amount of electricity was passed through molten $CaCl_2$? (Atomic mass of Mg = 24 u, atomic mass of Ca = 40 u). **[CBSE Sample 2022-23, Ap]**

(c) What is the standard free energy change for the following reaction at room temperature? Is the reaction spontaneous?

$Sn(s) + 2Cu^{2+}(aq) → Sn^{2+}(aq) + 2Cu^{+}(s)$

[CBSE Sample 2022-23, Ap]

13. (a) Out of the following pairs, predict with reason which pair will allow greater conduction of electricity:

[All India 2020, Ap]

(i) Silver wire at 30°C or silver wire at 60°C.

(ii) 0.1 M CH_3COOH solution or 1 M CH_3COOH solution.

(iii) KCl solution at 20°C or KCl solution at 50°C.

(b) Give two points of differences between electro chemical and electrolytic cells.

[All India 2020, K]

14. (a) A steady current of 2 amperes was passed through two electrolytic cells X and Y connected in series containing electrolytes $FeSO_4$ and $ZnSO_4$ until 2.8 g of Fe deposited at the cathode of cell X. How long did the current flow? Calculate the mass of Zn deposited at the cathode of cell Y.

(Molar mass: Fe = 56 g mol^{-1} Zn = 65.3 g mol^{-1}, 1F = 96500 C mol^{-1}) **[Delhi 2019, Ap]**

(b) In the plot of molar conductivity (Λ_m) vs square root of concentration ($c^{1/2}$), following curves are obtained for two electrolytes A and B:

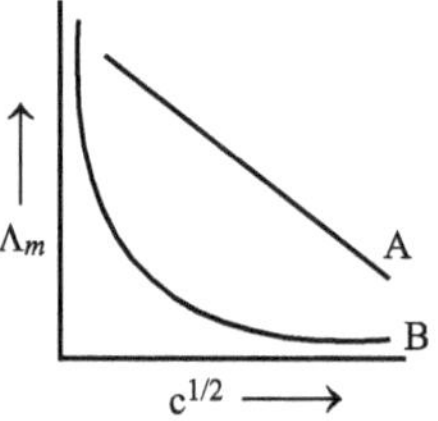

Answer the following: **[Delhi 2019, U]**

(i) Predict the nature of electrolytes A and B.

(ii) What happens on extrapolation of Λ_m to concentration approaching zero for electrolytes A and B?

15. (a) State Faraday's first law of electrolysis. How much charge in terms of Faraday is required for the reduction of 1 mol of Cu^{2+} to Cu.

[Delhi 2014, U]

(b) Calculate *emf* of the following cell at 298 K :

Mg (s) | Mg^{2+} (0.1 M) || Cu^{2+} (0.01) | Cu(s)

[Given E°_{cell} = +2.71 V, 1F = 96500 C mol^{-1}).

[Delhi 2014, Ap]

 **Topic-5:** *Batteries, Fuel Cells, Corrosion*

1   *Multiple Choice Questions*

1. Which of the following cell was used in Apollo space programme? **[Delhi 2023, K]**

(a) Mercury cell   (b) Daniel cell

(c) $H_2 - O_2$ Fuel cell   (d) Dry cell

4   *Very Short Answer Questions (1 Mark)*

2. Out of zinc and tin, whose coating is better to protect iron objects? **[All India 2020, K]**

5   *Short Answer Questions (2 or 3 Marks)*

3. Define fuel cell with an example. What advantages do the fuel cells have over primary and secondary batteries?
    [All India 2023, Set-I, K]

4. Give reasons: **[All India 2023, Set-I, U]**
   (i) Mercury cell delivers a constant potential during its life time
   (ii) In the experimental determination of electrolytic conductance Direct Current (DC) is not used.

5. Corrosion is an electrochemical phenomenon. The oxygen in moist air reacts as follows:
    [CBSE Sample 2022-23, U]
$$O_2(g) + 2H_2O(l) + 4e^- \rightarrow 4OH^- (aq).$$
   Write down the possible reactions for corrosion of zinc occurring at anode, cathode, and overall reaction to form a white layer of zinc hydroxide.

6. Name the cell used in hearing aids and watches.
    [Delhi 2020, Set-I]

7. Using the E^0 values of X and Y, predict which is better for coating the surface of iron to prevent rust and why?

   Given: $[E^°_{(Fe^{2+}/Fe)} = -0.44$ V   **[All India 2019, Ap]**

   $E^°_{(X^{2+}/X)} = -2.36$ V

   $E^°_{(Y^{2+}/Y)} = -0.14$ V]

8. Write the name of the cell which is generally used in transistors. Write the reactions taking place at the anode and the cathode of this cell.   **[All India 2017, K]**

9. (a) Calculate the mass of Ag deposited at cathode when a current of 2 amperes was passed through a solution of $AgNO_3$ for 15 minutes. **[Delhi 2017, Ap]** (Given : Molar mass of Ag = 108 g mol^{-1} 1F = 96500 C mol^{-1})
   (b) Define fuel cell.   **[Delhi 2017, K]**

10. From the given cells :   **[Delhi 2016, K]**
    Lead storage cell, Mercury cell, Fuel cell and Dry cell
    Answer the following :
    (i) Which cell is used in hearing aids ?
    (ii) Which cell was used in Apollo Space Programme ?
    (iii) Which cell is used in automobiles and inverters ?
    (iv) Which cell does not have long life ?

11. (a) Calculate $\Delta_r G°$ for the reaction
    $$Mg\,(s) + Cu^{2+}\,(aq) \rightarrow Mg^{2+}\,(aq) + Cu\,(s)$$
    Given : $E°_{cell} = +2.71$ V, 1 F = 96500 C mol^{-1}
    (b) Name the type of cell which was used in Apollo space programme for providing electrical power.
        [All India 2014, K]

6   *Long Answer Questions*

12. (a) Calculate $\Delta G°$ for the reaction
        [All India 2020, Ap]
    $$Zn(s) + Cu^{2+}(aq) \longrightarrow Zn^{2+}(aq) + Cu(s)$$
    Given: E° for $Zn^{2+}/Zn = -0.76$ V and
    E° for $Cu^{2+}/Cu = +0.34$ V
    R = 8.314 JK^{-1} mol^{-1}
    F = 96500 C mol^{-1}
    (b) Give two advantages of fuel cells.
        [All India 2020, K]

13. (a) For the reaction   **[All India 2018, Ap]**
    $$2AgCl\,(s) + H_2\,(g)\,(1\text{ atm}) \longrightarrow$$
    $$2Ag\,(s) + 2H^+\,(0.1\text{ M}) + 2Cl^-\,(0.1\text{ M}),$$
    $\Delta G° = -43600$ J at 25°C
    Calculate the e.m.f of the cell.
    $[\log 10^{-n} = -n]$
    (b) Define fuel cell and write its two advantages.
        [All India 2018, K]

14. (a) The conductivity of 0.20 mol L^{-1} solution of KCl is 2.48×10^{-2} S cm^{-1}. Calculate its molar conductivity and degree of dissociation (α). Given $\lambda^°\,(K^+) = 73.5$ S cm^2 mol^{-1} and $\lambda^°\,(Cl^-) = 76.5$ S cm^2 mol^{-1}.
        [All India 2015, Ap]
    (b) What type of battery is mercury cell? Why is it more advantageous than dry cell?   **[All India 2015, K]**

15. (a) Define the following terms :   **[Delhi 2014, Ap]**
    (i) Limiting molar conductivity
    (ii) Fuel cell
    (b) Resistance of a conductivity cell filled with 0.1 mol L^{-1} KCl solution is 100Ω. If the resistance of the same cell when filled with 0.02 mol L^{-1} KCl solution is 520Ω, calculate the conductivity and molar conductivity of 0.02 mol L^{-1} KCl solution. The conductivity of 0.1 mol L^{-1} KCl solution is 1.29×10^{-2} Ω^{-1} cm^{-1}.   **[All India 2015, Ap]**

16. The lead–acid battery represents the oldest rechargeable battery technology. Lead acid batteries can be found in a wide variety of applications including small–scale power storage such as UPS systems, ignition power sources for automobiles, along with large, grid–scale power systems. The spongy lead act as the anode and lead dioxide as the cathode. Aqueous sulphuric acid is used as an electrolyte. The half–reactions during discharging of lead storage cells are: **[CBSE Sample 2023-24, A]**

Anode: $Pb(s) + SO_4^{2-}(aq) \rightarrow PbSO_4(s) + 2e^-$

Cathode: $PbO(s) + 4H^+(aq) + SO_4^{2-}(aq) + 2e^- \rightarrow$
$$PbSO(s) + 2H_2O$$

There is no safe way of disposal and these batteries end – up in landfills. Lead and sulphuric acid are extremely hazardous and pollute soil, water as well as air. Irrespective of the environmental challenges it poses, lead–acid batteries have remained an important source of energy.

Designing green and sustainable battery systems as alternatives to conventional means remains relevant. Fuel cells are seen as the future source of energy. Hydrogen is considered a green fuel. Problem with fuel cells at present is the storage of hydrogen. Currently, ammonia and methanol are being used as a source of hydrogen for fuel cell. These are obtained industrially, so add to the environmental issues.

If the problem of storage of hydrogen is overcome, is it still a "green fuel?" Despite being the most abundant element in the Universe, hydrogen does not exist on its own so needs to be extracted from the water using electrolysis or separated from carbon fossil fuels. Both of these processes require a significant amount of energy which is currently more than that gained from the hydrogen itself. In addition, this extraction typically requires the use of fossil fuels. More research is being conducted in this field to solve these problems. Despite the problem of no good means to extract Hydrogen, it is a uniquely abundant and renewable source of energy, perfect for our future zero–carbon needs.

Answer the following questions:

(a) How many coulombs have been transferred from anode to cathode in order to consume one mole of sulphuric acid during the discharging of lead storage cell?

(b) How much work can be extracted by using lead storage cell if each cell delivers about 2.0 V of voltage? (1 F = 96500 C)

(c) Do you agree with the statement – "Hydrogen is a green fuel." Give your comments for and against this statement and justify your views.

OR

Imagine you are a member of an agency funding scientific research. Which of the following projects will you fund and why?

(i) safe recycling of lead batteries

(ii) extraction of hydrogen

Solutions

Topic-1: *Electrochemical Cells, Galvanic Cells*

1. (c) Cell potential (standard) of a cell reaction:

$$E^0_{cell} = E^0_{cathode} - E^0_{anode} = E^0_{Right} - E^0_{Left}$$

Now, among the two reactions, the one with the higher value of the standard electrode potential will act as the cathode and vice-versa.

Thus, the second reaction (reduction of manganate ion) will be the reduction half-cell reaction and therefore the E^0_{cell} will be:

$$E^0_{cell} = E^0_{MnO_4^-/Mn^{2+}} - E^0_{Fe^{3+}/Fe^{2+}}$$

$$= (+1.51\ V) - (+0.77\ V)$$

$$= +0.74$$

Therefore, option (c) is correct. **(1 Mark)**

2. (b) Among the two half-cell reactions, the half-cell reaction having a higher value of the standard electrode potential will be the reduction half-cell reaction and vice-versa.

Thus, cathode half-cell reaction is $Fe^{3+} + e^- \longrightarrow Fe^{2+}$ and the anode half-cell reaction is $Sn^{2+} + 2e^- \longrightarrow Sn$ which takes place is $Sn \longrightarrow Sn^{2+} + 2e^-$.

So, Sn is oxidized and Fe^{3+} is reduced.

$$E^0_{cell} = E^0_{cathode} - E^0_{anode} = E^0_{Fe^{3+}/Fe^{2+}} - E^0_{Sn^{2+}/Sn}$$

$$= (+0.77\ V) - (-0.14\ V)$$

$$= +0.91\ V$$

Therefore, option **(b)** is correct. **(1 Mark)**

3. (c) Salt bridge is used to complete the circuit so that current can flow. **(1 Mark)**

Topic-2: *Nernst Equation*

1. (b) The cell reaction is

$$Sn(s) + 2\ Fe^{3+}(aq) \to 2\ Fe^{2+}(aq) + Sn^{2+}(aq)$$

$$E^{\circ}_{cell} = E^{\circ}_{oxd.} + E^{\circ}_{red.}$$

$$E^{\circ}_{Sn/Sn_{2+}} + E^{\circ}_{Fe^{3+}/Fe^{2+}}$$

Given:

$$E^{\circ}_{Sn^{2+}/Sn} = -0.14V \Rightarrow E^{0}_{Sn/Sn^{2+}} = -(-0.14V)$$

$$= +0.14V$$

$$E^{\circ}_{Fe^{3+}/Fe^{2+}} = +0.77V$$

Thus, $E^{\circ}_{cell} = +0.14 + 0.77\ V = +0.91V$ **(1 Mark)**

2. (a) $Ni(s) + 2Ag^+(aq) \longrightarrow Ni^{2+}(aq) + 2Ag(s)$

$$\Delta G^{\circ} = -n\ FE^{\circ}_{cell}$$

$$= -2 \times 96500 \times 1.05$$

$$= -202{,}650\ J\ mol^{-1} \quad \textbf{(1 Mark)}$$

$$\Delta G^{\circ} = -RT\ \ln K_c = -2.303\ RT\ \log K_c$$

$$-202.650 = -8.314 \times 298 \times 2.303\ \log K_c \quad \textbf{(1 Mark)}$$

$$\log K_c = 35.52 \quad \textbf{(1 Mark)}$$

3. (b) $Fe(s)|Fe^{2+}(0.001M)||H^+(0.01M)|H_2(g)(1\,bar)|Pt(s)$

$$E_{cell} = E^{\circ}_{cell} - \frac{2.303\ RT}{nF} \log \frac{[P]}{[R]}$$

$$= 0.44 - \frac{2.303 \times 8.314 \times 298}{2 \times 96500} \log \frac{[0.001]}{[0.01]} \quad \textbf{(1 Mark)}$$

$$= 0.44 + \frac{5705.85}{193000} \log [10] \quad \textbf{(1 Mark)}$$

$$= 0.44 + 0.0296$$

$$E_{cell} = 0.469\ V \quad \textbf{(1 Mark)}$$

4. $Al(s)\,|\,Cd^{2+}(0.1M)\,||\,Al^{3+}(0.01M)\,|\,Cd(s)$ **(½ Mark)**

$$2Al(s) + 3Cd^{2+}(0.1M) \to 3Cd(s) + 2Al^{3+}(0.01M)$$
(½ Mark)

$$E_{cell} = E^{\circ}_{cell} - \frac{0.059}{n} \log \frac{\left[Al^{3+}\right]^2}{\left[Cd^{2+}\right]^3}$$

$$E_{cell} = 1.26 - \frac{0.059}{6} \log \frac{(0.01)^2}{(0.1)^3} \quad \textbf{(½ Mark)}$$

$$= 1.26 - \frac{0.059}{6}(-1) \quad \textbf{(1 Mark)}$$

$$= 1.26 + 0.009 \quad \textbf{(½ Mark)}$$

$$= 1.269\ V$$

5. (a) Here $n = 2$, $E^0_{cell} = 0.236$ V, T = 298 K

We know that

$$\Delta G^0 = -nFE^0_{cell} = -2 \times 96500 \times 0.236$$
$$= -45548 \text{ J mol}^{-1}$$
$$= -45.548 \text{ kJ mol}^{-1} \qquad \textbf{(1 Mark)}$$

(b) $i = 0.5$ A

$t = 2$ hours $= 2 \times 60 \times 60$ s $= 7200$ s

Thus $Q = i \times t = 0.5$ A $\times 7200$ s $= 3600$ C

$$\textbf{(1 Mark)}$$

We know that 96500 C

$= 6.023 \times 10^{23}$ number of electrons

Then, no. of electrons in 3600 C

$$= \frac{6.023 \times 10^{23} \times 3600}{96500} = 2.25 \times 10^{22}$$

Hence, 2.25×10^{22} number of electrons will flow

through the wire. **(1 Mark)**

6. For the given cell representation, the cell reaction will be

$$Fe(s) + 2H^+(aq) \longrightarrow Fe^{2+}(aq) + H_2(g)$$

The standard emf of the cell will be

$$E^\circ_{cell} = E^\circ_{(H^+/H_2)} - E^\circ_{(Fe^{2+}/Fe)}$$

$\Rightarrow \quad E^\circ_{cell} = 0 - (-0.44) = 0.44$ V **(½ Mark)**

The Nernst equation for the cell

$$E_{cell} = E^\circ_{cell} - \left[\frac{0.0591}{2}\log\frac{[Fe^{2+}]}{[H^+]^2}\right] \qquad \textbf{(1 Mark)}$$

$$= 0.44 - \left[\frac{0.0591}{2}\log\frac{0.001}{(0.01)^2}\right]$$

$$= 0.44 - [0.02955\ (\log 10)] \qquad \textbf{(½ Mark)}$$

$$= 0.44 - 0.02955$$

$$E_{cell} = 0.41 \text{ V} \qquad \textbf{(1 Mark)}$$

7.

	Order of reaction	Molecularity of reaction
(i)	The sum of powers of the concentration of the reactant in the rate law expression is the order of reactant.	The number of reacting species taking part in an elementary reaction is called molecularity of a reaction.
(i)	It is an experimental entity. It can be zero and even a fraction.	It cannot be zero or a non-integer.

(2 Marks)

8. $\Delta G^\circ = -n FE^\circ_{cell}$ **(½ Mark)**

$$= -2 \times 96500 \text{ C mol}^{-1} \times 1.1 \text{ V} \qquad \textbf{(½ Mark)}$$

$$= -212300 \text{ J mol}^{-1} \text{ (J = C.V)}$$

$$= -212.3 \text{ kJ mol}^{-1} \qquad \textbf{(1 Mark)}$$

9. For the given cell, the redox reaction is

$$2Ag(s) + Cu^{2+}(aq) \longrightarrow 2Ag^+(aq) + Cu(s)$$

$\therefore \quad n = 2$

$$Ecell = E^\circ_{cell} - \left[\frac{0.0591}{n}\log\frac{[Ag^+]^2}{[Cu^{2+}]}\right] \qquad \textbf{(½ Mark)}$$

$$= 0.46 - \left[\frac{0.0591}{2}\log\frac{(10^{-3})^2}{10^{-1}}\right] \qquad \textbf{(½ Mark)}$$

$$= 0.46 - [0.02955\log 10^{-5}]$$

$$= 0.46 - [0.02955 \times (-5)] \qquad \textbf{(1 Mark)}$$

$$= 0.46 + 0.14775$$

$$= 0.60775 \text{ V.} \qquad \textbf{(1 Mark)}$$

10. $Fe + 2H^+ \rightarrow Fe^{2+} + H_2$, $n = 2$ **(½ Mark)**

$$E_{cell} = E^\circ_{cell} - \left[\frac{0.0591}{2}\log\frac{[Fe^{2+}]}{[H^+]^2}\right]$$

$$\textbf{(½ Mark)}$$

$$= (0.44) - \left[\frac{0.0591}{2}\log\frac{10^{-3}}{(1)^2}\right] \qquad \textbf{(1 Mark)}$$

$$= 0.44 + 0.0886 = 0.5286 \text{ V} \qquad \textbf{(1 Mark)}$$

11. The half cell reaction for the cell

$$[Cr \longrightarrow Cr^{3+} + 3e^-] \times 2,$$
$$[2e^- + Fe^{2+} \longrightarrow Fe] \times 3$$

$$E^\circ_{cell} = E^\circ_R - E^\circ_L = -0.44 - (-0.74)$$

$$E^\circ_{cell} = +0.30 \text{ V} \qquad \textbf{(1 Mark)}$$

Hence $= n = 6$, $T = 298$ K, $R = 8.314$ J K^{-1} mol^{-1}

Nearest equation for the cell

$$E_{cell} = E^\circ_{cell} - \frac{2.303RT}{nF}\log\frac{[Cr^{3+}]^2}{[Fe^{2+}]^3} \qquad \textbf{(1 Mark)}$$

$$= 0.30 - \frac{2.303 \times 8.314 \times 298}{6 \times 96500}\log\frac{[0.01]^2}{[0.1]^3}$$

$$= 0.30 - \frac{0.059}{6}\log 10^{-1}$$

$$= 0.30 + \frac{0.059}{6}$$

$$E_{cell} = 0.3098 \text{ V} \qquad \textbf{(1 Mark)}$$

e.m.f. of the cell is 0.3098

12. $Mg + Cu^{2+} \longrightarrow Mg^{2+} + Cu$

$$E_{cell} = E^{\circ}_{cell} - \left[\frac{0.0591}{2} \log \frac{[Mg^{2+}]}{[Cu^{2+}]} \right]$$ **(1Mark)**

$$= \left[0.34 - (-2.37) \right] - \left[\frac{0.0591}{2} \log \frac{10^{-3}}{10^{-4}} \right]$$ **(1Mark)**

$$= 2.71 - 0.02955(\log 10)$$

$$= 2.68 \text{ V}$$ **(1Mark)**

$$\Delta G = -nFE_{cell}$$ **(1Mark)**

$$= -2 \times 96500 \times 2.68 \text{ J}$$

$$= -517240 \text{ J mol}^{-1} = -517.24 \text{ kJ mol}^{-1}$$

(1 Mark)

Topic-3: *Conductance of Electrolytic Solutions*

1. (b) 0.1 M HCl solution, conductivity is higher for strong electrolyte, conductivity decreases with dilution
(1 Mark)

2. (c) $G = K\left(\dfrac{l}{a}\right)$

Conductance (G) is directly proportional to area (a) of the conductor, conductivity of the medium and inversely proportional to the length of the conductor. **(1 Mark)**

3. (a) Molar conductivity $(\Lambda_m) = \dfrac{K}{C}$

Since, molar conductivity $\alpha \dfrac{1}{\text{concentration}}$

Lower the concentration, higher will be its molar conductivity under similar conditions.

Thus, 0.01 M K will have highest value of molar conductivity. **(1 Mark)**

4. (b) The unit of molar conductivity is S cm^2 mol^{-1}.

Molar conductivity $(\Lambda_m) = \dfrac{K}{C}$ **(1 Mark)**

5. (b) 115 Scm^2/mol
$\Lambda^{\circ}CH_3COOK = \Lambda^{\circ}CH_3COOH + \Lambda^{\circ}KCl - \Lambda^{\circ}HCl =$
$390 + 150 - 425 = 115$ Scm^2/mol **(1 Mark)**

6 (a) 124.66×10^{-4} Sm^{2}mol^{-1}
Molar conductance of $NaCl = \lambda^+_{Na} + \lambda^+_{Cl}$
$= 51.12 \times 10^{-4} + 73.54 \times 10^{-4}$
$= 124.66 \times 10^{-4}$ Sm^{2}mol^{-1} **(1 Mark)**

7. (c) **(1 Mark)**

8. (c) $\wedge = \wedge_0$ as $C \to 0$

$\wedge = \wedge_0 - A\sqrt{C}$

when $C = 0$, $\wedge = \wedge_0$ **(1 Mark)**

9. (b) Molar conductivity (Λ_m) decreases with increase in concentration can be explained by Debye – Huckel – Onsager equation.

$\Lambda_C = \Lambda_0 - A\sqrt{C}$

↑ Limiting molar conductivity ↑ Concentration

As the concentration of the electrolyte increases the ion-cloud surrounding the a' particular ion increases as the ion-cloud is created by oppositely charged ions. Therefore, the movement of desired ion towards the electrode gets hindered. As the dilution increases the counter ion-cloud is simultaneously decreases and conductivity increases. **(1 Mark)**

10. (a) Conductivity always decreases with decrease in concentration for both weak and strong electrolytes because the number of ions per unit volume that carry the current in a solution decreases on dilution. **(1 Mark)**

11. (d) Conductivity of an electrolyte decreases with decrease in concentration because number of ions per unit volume decreases on dilution. **(1 Mark)**

12. $\lambda_m = \dfrac{K}{c} = \dfrac{7.8 \times 10^{-5} \text{Scm}^{-1}}{0.001 \text{mol L}^{-1}} \times \dfrac{1000 \text{cm}^3}{L}$

$= 78.05$ cm^2 mol^{-1}

$\alpha = \dfrac{\lambda_m}{\lambda^{\circ}_m} = \dfrac{78.0 \text{ Scm}^2\text{mol}^{-1}}{390 \text{ Scm}^2\text{mol}^{-1}} = 0.2$ **(1 Mark)**

13. (a) Yes, if the concentration of $ZnSO_4$ in the two half cell is different, the electrode potential will be different making the cell possible. **(1 Mark)**

(b) $\Lambda^0_m (MgCl_2) = \lambda^0_m (Mg^{2+}) + 2\lambda^0_m (Cl^-)$
$258.6 = 106 + 2\lambda^0_m (Cl^-)$
$\lambda^0_m(Cl^-) = 76.3$ Scm^{2}mol^{-1} **(1 Mark)**

(c) cell constant $G^* = k \times R$
$k = G^*/R = 0.146/1000 = 1.46 \times 10^{-4}$ Scm^{-1}.
(1 Mark)

14. B is a strong electrolyte. The molar conductivity increases slowly with dilution as there is no increase in number of ions on dilution as strong electrolytes are completely dissociated. **(½ + ½ = 1 Mark)**

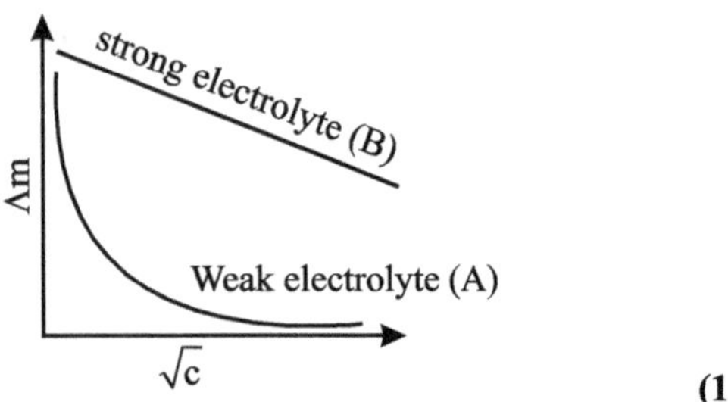

 (1 Mark)

15. $CH_3COOH \longrightarrow CH_3COO^- + H^+$

$$\Lambda^{\circ}_{(CH_3COOH)} = \lambda^{\circ}_{(CH_3COO^+)} + \lambda^{\circ}_{(H^+)}$$
$$= 40.9 + 349.6$$
$$= 390.5 \quad \textbf{(1 Mark)}$$

Now degree of dissociation (α)

$$\alpha = \frac{\Lambda_m}{\Lambda^{\circ}} = \frac{39.05}{390.5} = 0.1 \quad \textbf{(1 Mark)}$$

The degree of dissociation of acitic acid is 0.1.

16. (a) We have given

$$Ag^+(aq) + e^- \longrightarrow Ag(s) \qquad E^{\circ} = +0.80\ V$$
$$H^+(aq) + e^- \longrightarrow \frac{1}{2} H_2(g) \qquad E^{\circ} = 0.00\ V$$

The relationship between the standard free energy change and emf of a cell reaction is given by

$$\Delta G^{\circ} = -nFE^{\circ}_{(cell)}$$

Thus, the more positive the standard reduction potential of a reaction, the more negative is the standard free energy change associated with the process, and consequently, the higher is the feasibelity of the reaction.

Since $E^{\circ}_{Ag^+/Ag}$ has a greater positive value than $E^{\circ}_{H^+/H,}$ the reaction which is feasible at the cathode is given by

$$Ag^+(aq) + e^- \longrightarrow Ag(s) \qquad \textbf{(1 Mark)}$$

(b) Limiting Molar Conductivity: At infinite dilution or at approximately zero concentration $(V \to \infty,\ C \to 0)$ the molar conductivity attain limiting value and become constant. At infinite dilution, this limiting value of electrolyte is expressed by limiting molar conductivity (Λ°_m).

Conductivity of an electrolyte solution decreases with the decrease in concentration because with decrease in concentration number of ions per unit volume decreases. **(1 Mark)**

17. According to Kohlrausch law of independent migration of ions, the limiting molar conductivity of an electrolyte is the sum of the limiting ionic conductivities of the cation and the anion each multiplied with the number of ions present in one formula unit of the electrolyte.

i.e., Λ°_m for $A_xB_y = x\lambda^{\circ}_+ + y\lambda^{\circ}_-$ **(1 Mark)**

The conductivity of a solution decreases with dilution because the number of current carrying particles, i.e., ions per cm^3 of the solution become less and further decreases on dilution. **(1 Mark)**

18. Conductivity (κ) = 0.025 S cm^{-1}

Molarity = 0.20 M

$$\Lambda_m = \frac{\kappa \times 1000}{\text{Molarity}} = \frac{0.025 \times 1000}{0.20} \quad \textbf{(1 Mark)}$$

$$= 125\,S\,cm^2\,mol^{-1}. \quad \textbf{(1 Mark)}$$

19. (a) $HCOOH \rightleftharpoons HCOO^- + H^+$

$K = 8 \times 10^{-5}$ S cm^{-1} for concentration = 2×10^{-3} M

$$\therefore \text{Molar conductivity } (\Lambda_m) = \frac{K}{} \quad \frac{8 \times 10^{-5}}{2 \times 10^{-3}}$$
 (1 Mark)

$$= 4 \times 10^{-2}\ S\ M^{-1}\ cm^{-1}$$
$$= 4 \times 10^{-2}\ S\ mol^{-1}\ L\ cm^{-1}$$
$$= 4 \times 10^{-2} \times 10^3\ S\ mol^{-1}\ cm^2$$
$$= 40\ S\ cm^2\ mol^{-1} \quad \textbf{(½ Mark)}$$

$$\therefore \quad \alpha = \frac{\Lambda_m}{\Lambda^0_m} = \frac{40}{404} \approx 0.099 \quad \textbf{(1 Mark)}$$

Degree of dissociation = 0.099 **(½ Mark)**

(b) $Ni\,(s) + 2Ag^+\,(aq) \rightleftharpoons Ni^{2+}\,(aq) + 2Ag\,(s)$

Anodic reaction: $Ni \longrightarrow Ni^{2+} + 2e$

Cathodic reaction: $2Ag^+ + 2e \longrightarrow 2Ag$ **(½ Mark)**

$$\Delta_r G^0 = -nFE^0_{cell}$$
$$= -2 \times 96500 \times 1.05\ J\ mol^{-1}$$
$$= -202{,}650\ J\ mol^{-1}$$
$$= -202.65\ kJ\ mol^{-1} \quad \textbf{(½ Mark)}$$

$$E^0_{cell} = E^0_{Ni/Ni^{2+}} + E^0_{Ag^+/Ag}$$
$$= (0.25 + 0.80)\ V$$
$$= 1.05\ V \quad \textbf{(½ Mark)}$$

$$\therefore \quad \Delta_r G^0 = -RT \ln K_C = -202.65$$

$$\text{or,} \quad \log K_C = \frac{202.65 \times 10^3}{2.303 \times 8.314 \times 298} = 35.52$$

$$\Delta_r G^0 = -202.65\ kJ\ mol^{-1}$$
$$\log K_C = 35.52 \quad \textbf{(½ Mark)}$$

20. **(a)** Given : $E^\circ_{Sn^{2+}|Sn} = -0.14$ V

To find : cell emf. $E_{cell} = ?$

Solution :

The cell reaction is:
$$2Sn(s) + 2H^+(aq) \rightarrow Sn^{2+}(aq) + H_2(g)$$

Number of electrons n = 2

$$E^\circ_{cell} = E^\circ_{cathode} - E^\circ_{Anode} = 0 - (-0.14) = 0.14 \text{ V}$$

From Nernst equation,

$$E_{cell} = E^\circ_{cell} - \frac{RT}{nF}\ln\frac{\left[Sn^{2+}\right]}{[H^+]^2} \qquad \textbf{(1 Mark)}$$

$$E_{cell} = E^\circ_{cell} - \frac{0.059}{2}\log\frac{[Sn^{2+}]}{[H^+]^2}$$

$$= 0.14 - \frac{0.059}{n}\log\frac{[Sn^{2+}]}{[H^+]^2}$$

$$= 0.14 - \frac{0.059}{2}\log\frac{0.004}{(0.02)^2} \qquad \textbf{(1 Mark)}$$

$$= 0.14 - \frac{0.059}{2}\log\frac{0.004}{0.02 \times 0.02}$$

$$E_{cell} = 0.1105 \text{ V} \quad \textbf{(1 Mark)}$$

Thus the emf of the cell is 0.1105 V.

(b) **(i)** On the basis of E° values, O_2 gas should be liberated at anode but Cl_2 gas is liberated. This is because of over-potential required for O_2 which makes the process difficult to occur. **(1 Mark)**

(ii) Conductivity depends on the number of ions per unit volume. On dilution, the number of ions per unit volume decreases and hence conductivity of CH_3COOH decreases with dilution. **(1 Mark)**

21. **(a)** Given: $2Al(s) + 3Cu^{2+}(0.01 \text{ m}) \longrightarrow$
$$2Al^{3+}(0.01 \text{ m}) + 3Cu(s)$$

$$E_{cell} = E^\circ_{cell} - \left[\frac{2.303\,RT}{nF}\log Q\right] \qquad \textbf{(1 Mark)}$$

$$E^\circ_{cell} = E_{cell} + \left[\frac{2.303\,RT}{nF}\log Q\frac{[Al^{3+}]^2}{[Cu^{2+}]^3}\right]$$

$$E^\circ_{cell} = 1.98 + \left[\frac{0.0591}{6}\log\frac{(0.01)^2}{(0.01)^3}\right]$$

$$E^\circ_{cell} = 1.98 + \left[\frac{0.0591}{6} \times \log 10^2\right] \qquad \textbf{(1 Mark)}$$

$$E^\circ_{cell} = 1.98 + \left[\frac{0.0591}{6} \times 2\right] = 1.99 \text{ V} \qquad \textbf{(1 Mark)}$$

(b) Corrosion is basically a process of oxidation, so oxidation potential is considered here.

Oxidation potential of Fe = 0.44 V

Oxidation potential of A = 2.37 V

Oxidation potential of B = 0.14 V

Since A has a higher oxidation potential than that of iron, so it will oxidise faster than Fe. Therefore A is better for coating. **(2 Marks)**

22. **(a)** $\Lambda_m = \dfrac{\kappa}{C} \times 1000 = \dfrac{3.905 \times 10^{-5} \times 1000}{0.001}$
$$= 39.05 \text{ S cm}^2\text{mol}^{-1} \quad \textbf{(1 Mark)}$$

$$\Lambda^\circ_m = \lambda^\circ_{H^+} + \lambda^\circ_{CH_3COO^-}$$

$$\Lambda^\circ_m = 349.6 + 40.9$$

$$\Lambda^\circ_m = 390.5 \text{ S cm}^2 \text{ mol}^{-1} \qquad \textbf{(1 Mark)}$$

$$\alpha = \frac{\Lambda_m}{\Lambda^\circ_m} = 39.05/390.5 = 0.1 \qquad \textbf{(1 Mark)}$$

(b) An electrochemical cell is a device capable of generating electrical energy from chemical reaction. If external potential is higher than E°_{cell} potential value of the cell, the flow of current and cell reactions are reversed. The cell now functions as electrolytic cell, a device for using electrical energy to carry non-spontaneous chemical reactions. **(2 Marks)**

23. **(a)** Conductivity (k) of an electrolytic solution decreases with dilution because the number of ions per unit volume of the solution decreases upon dilution. **(1 Mark)**

(b) Since, $\dfrac{\Lambda_m}{\Lambda^0_m} = \alpha$

We need to calculate and determine the value of Λ_m.

Now, $\Lambda_m = 141.0$ S cm^2 mol^{-1} (from table)

$$\Rightarrow \quad \alpha = \frac{141.0}{150.0} = 0.94 \qquad \textbf{(1 Mark)}$$

(c) The value of molar conductivity Λ_m of HCl would be **higher** than that of KCl for the same concentration. This is due to the higher value of conductivity of the H^+ ions. **(1 Mark)**

OR

(c) Amit is using a weak electrolyte CH_3COOH instead of a strong electrolyte KCl.

Similarity: Conductivity would decrease upon dilution. **(½ Mark)**

Difference: Molar conductivity would increase steeply on dilution instead of a slow increase. **(½ Mark)**

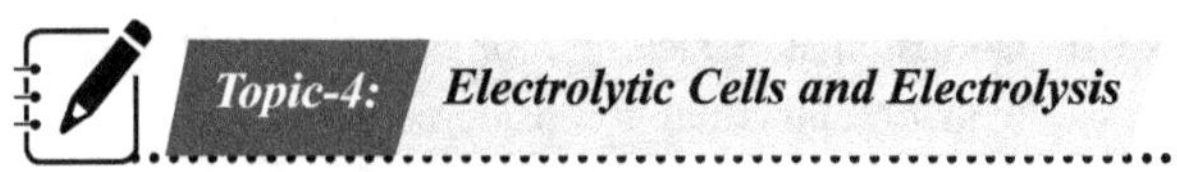

Topic-4: *Electrolytic Cells and Electrolysis*

1. **(b)** Brine solution is an aqueous solution of NaCl.

   Electrolysis of NaCl (aq.):

   $$NaCl\ (aq.) \xrightarrow{H_2O} Na^+\ (aq.) + Cl^-\ (aq.)$$

   Now, we have the following reactions occurring at cathode and anode:

   Cathode:

   $$Na^+ + e^- \longrightarrow Na\ (E^0 = -2.71\ V)$$

   $$H^+ + e^- \longrightarrow \frac{1}{2}H_2\ (E^0 = 0.00\ V)$$

   Thus, reduction of H^+ to H_2 is preferred due to higher E° value.

   Anode:

   $$Cl^- \longrightarrow \frac{1}{2}Cl_2 + e^-\ (E^0 = 1.36\ V)$$

   $$2H_2O \longrightarrow O_2 + 4H^+ + 4e^-\ (E^0 = 1.23\ V)$$

   Thus, oxidation of H_2O should be preferred but due to the over potential of O_2, oxidation of Cl^- is preferred.

   Therefore, reactions I and IV are preferred with brine solution and option **(b)** is correct. **(1 Mark)**

2. **(d)** A is false but R is true. **(1 Mark)**

   Cu will deposit at cathode

3.

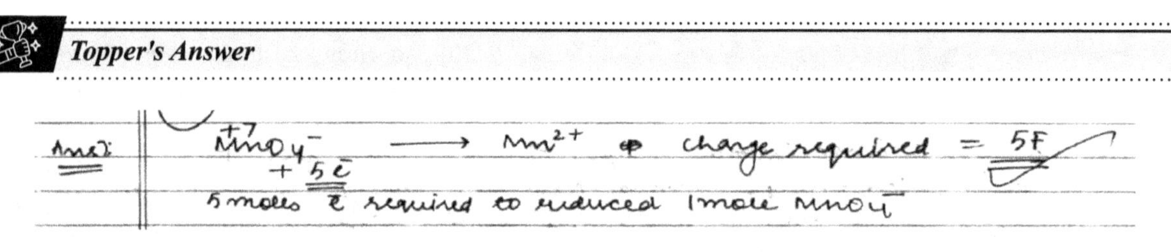

Topper's Answer

4. The electrode reaction is $Zn^2 + 2e^- \rightarrow Zn$

   Number of electrons involved $= 2$

   ∴ Quantity of charge required for reduction of 1 mol of Zn^{2+} $= 2 \times F = 2 \times 96500\ C$

   $$= 193000\ C \quad \textbf{(1 Mark)}$$

5. **(i)** For a spontaneous reaction, the change in the standard Gibbs free energy is negative.

   Thus, $\Delta G° < 0$ for a spontaneous reaction **(Negative)**

   Since, $\Delta G° = -nFE°_{cell}$, $E°_{cell}$ should be **positive**. **(1 Mark)**

   (ii) Faraday's First Law of Electrolysis:

   The amount of chemical reaction occurring at an electrode because of electrolysis, is directly proportional to the amount of current passed in the electrolytic solution. **(1 Mark)**

6. From the cell representation:

   Anode: $Fe\ (S) \longrightarrow Fe^{2+}\ (0.01\ M) + 2e^-$

   Cathode: $2H^+\ (1\ M) + 2e^- \longrightarrow H_2\ (g)\ (1\ bar)$

   $$E°_{cell} = +0.44\ V$$

   Thus, $E_{cell} = E°_{cell} - \dfrac{0.059}{n} \log \dfrac{[Fe^{2+}]}{[H^+]^2}$ **(1 Mark)**

   $$= (+0.44\ V) - \left[\dfrac{0.059}{2} \log \dfrac{(0.01\ M)}{1^2} \right]$$

   $$= +0.44\ V - [0.0295 \times \log (0.01)]$$

   $$= +0.44\ V - [0.0295 \times (-2)]$$

   $$= \textbf{0.50 V} \quad \textbf{(1 Mark)}$$

7. $Cd^{2+}(aq) + Zn(s) \longrightarrow Zn^{2+} + Cd(s)$

$E^\circ_{cell} = E^\circ_{Cd^{2+}/Cd} - E^\circ_{Zn^{2+}/Zn}$ **(½ Mark)**

$\quad = -0.403 - (-0.763) = 0.36\,V$ **(½ Mark)**

$\Delta G^\circ = -nFE^\circ_{cell}$

$\quad n = 2$

$\Delta G^\circ = -2 \times 96500 \times 0.36 = -69480\,J\,mol^{-1}$

$\quad = -69.480\,kJ\,mol^{-1}$ **(1 Mark)**

$\Delta G^\circ = -2.303\,RT\log K_c$ **(½ Mark)**

$\dfrac{\Delta G^\circ}{-2.303\,RT} = \log K_c$

$\dfrac{-69480}{-2.303 \times 8.314 \times 298} = \log K_c$

$12.17 = \log k_c$ **(½ Mark)**

Note

Relation between E°_{cell} and K_c might be calculated as given below which can used to determine the value of K_c directly from given value of E°_{cell}.

$\because \quad \Delta G = -nF\,E^\circ_{cell}$

$\because \quad \Delta G = -2.303\,RT\log K_c$

Now, $nF\,E^\circ_{cell} = 2.303\,RT\log K_c$

$\quad n\,E^\circ_{cell} = \dfrac{2.303\,RT}{F}\cdot \log K_c$

$\quad = \dfrac{2.303 \times 8.314 \times 298}{96500}\log K_c$

$\quad = 0.059\log K_c$

$\quad n\,E^\circ_{cell} = 0.059\log K_c$

8.

Topper's Answer

$i = 2A, \quad W_{Cu} = 2g$

$E_{Cu} = \dfrac{63.5}{2}, \quad E_{Zn} = \dfrac{65}{2}$ **(½ Mark)**

$E = F \times Z$ **(½ Mark)**

$Z_{Cu} = \dfrac{E_{Cu}}{F}$

$Z_{Cu} = \dfrac{63.5}{2} \times \dfrac{1}{96500}$ **(½ Mark)**

$W_{Cu} = Z_{Cu} \cdot i \cdot t$ **(½ Mark)**

$t = \dfrac{W_{Cu}}{Z_{Cu} \cdot i} = \dfrac{2 \times 2 \times 96500}{63.5 \times 2} = \mathbf{3039\ seconds}$ **(½ Mark)**

$\dfrac{W_{Zn}}{W_{Cu}} = \dfrac{E_{Zn}}{E_{Cu}}$

$W_{Zn} = \dfrac{E_{Zn} \times W_{Cu}}{E_{Cu}} = \dfrac{65}{2} \times 2 \times \dfrac{2}{63.5} = \mathbf{2.05\ g}$ **(½ Mark)**

9.

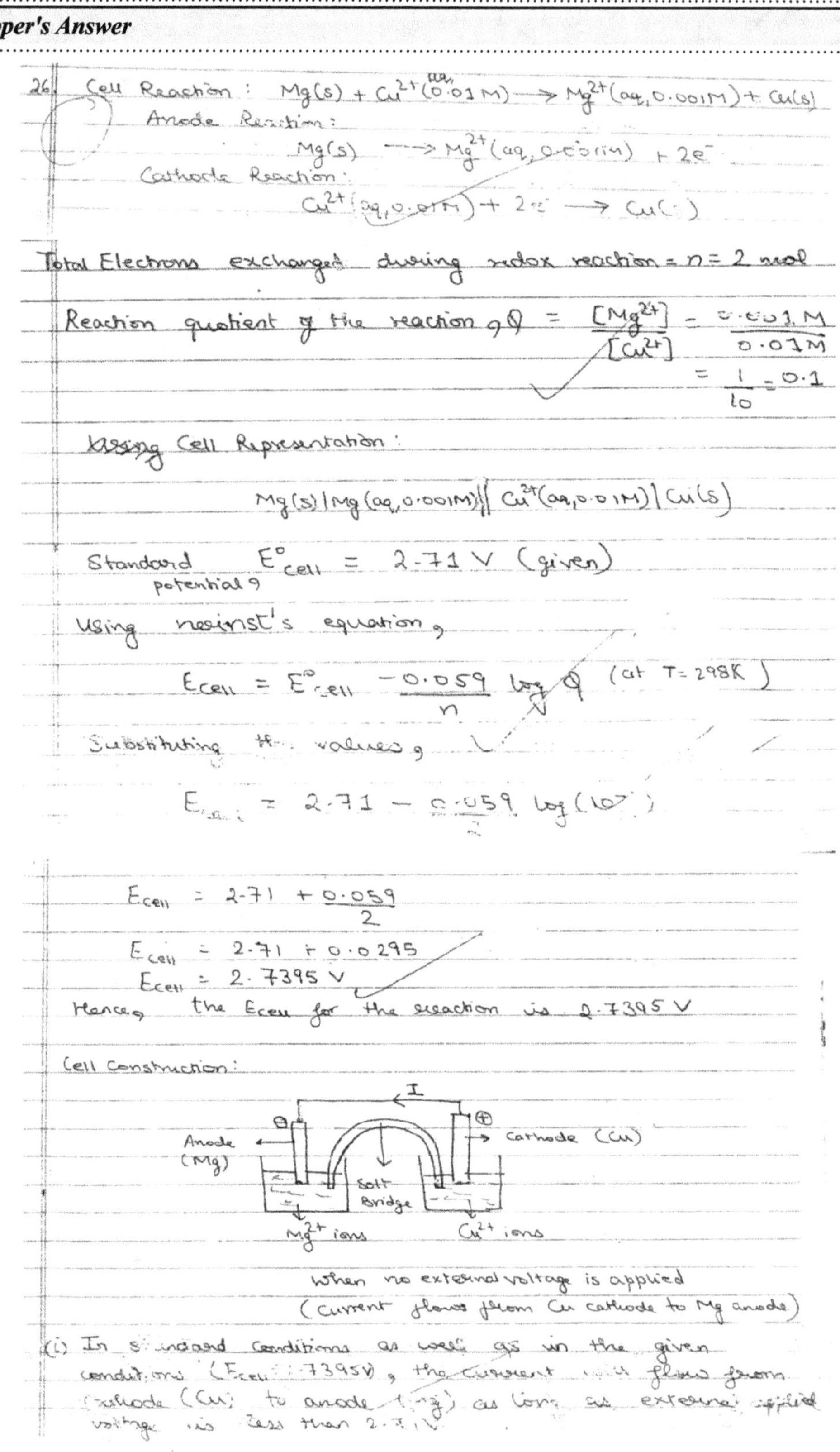

26. Cell Reaction : $Mg(s) + Cu^{2+}(aq, 0.01 M) \longrightarrow Mg^{2+}(aq, 0.001M) + Cu(s)$

Anode Reaction :
$$Mg(s) \longrightarrow Mg^{2+}(aq, 0.001M) + 2e^-$$

Cathode Reaction :
$$Cu^{2+}(aq, 0.01M) + 2e^- \longrightarrow Cu(s)$$

Total Electrons exchanged during redox reaction $= n = 2$ mol

Reaction quotient of the reaction, $Q = \dfrac{[Mg^{2+}]}{[Cu^{2+}]} = \dfrac{0.001 M}{0.01 M}$

$$= \dfrac{1}{10} = 0.1$$

Using Cell Representation :

$$Mg(s)|Mg(aq, 0.001M) \| Cu^{2+}(aq, 0.01M)|Cu(s)$$

Standard potential, $E^\circ_{cell} = 2.71$ V (given)

Using nernst's equation,

$$E_{cell} = E^\circ_{cell} - \dfrac{0.059}{n} \log Q \quad (\text{at } T = 298K)$$

Substituting the values,

$$E_{cell} = 2.71 - \dfrac{0.059}{2} \log(10^{-1})$$

$$E_{cell} = 2.71 + \dfrac{0.059}{2}$$

$$E_{cell} = 2.71 + 0.0295$$
$$E_{cell} = 2.7395 V$$

Hence, the E_{cell} for the reaction is 2.7395 V

Cell Construction :

When no external voltage is applied
(Current flows from Cu cathode to Mg anode)

(i) In standard conditions as well as in the given conditions ($E_{cell} = 2.7395V$), the current will flow from cathode (Cu) to anode (Mg) as long as external applied voltage is less than 2.71V

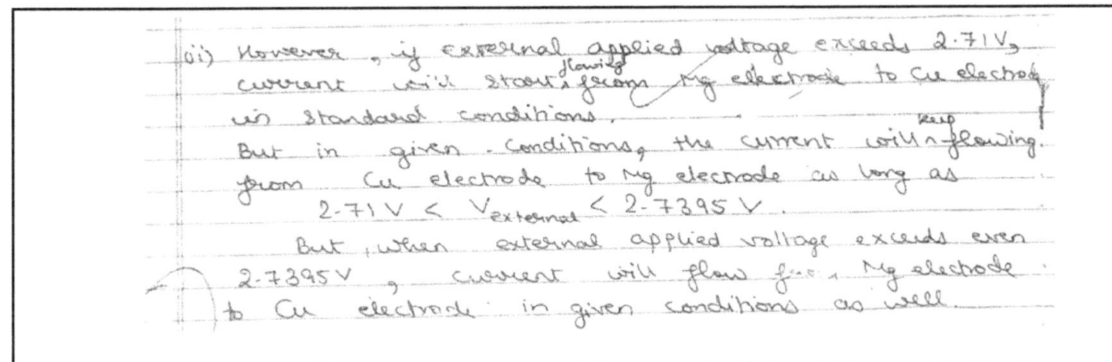

$Mg(s) + Cu^{2+}(0.01M) \longrightarrow Mg^{2+}(0.001M) + Cu(s)$

$$E_{cell} = E^{\circ}_{cell} - \frac{0.0591}{n}\log\frac{\left[Mg^{2+}\right]}{\left[Cu^{2+}\right]}$$ **(1 Mark)**

$$= 2.71 - \frac{0.0591}{2}\log\frac{[0.001]}{[0.01]}$$

$$= 2.71 - 0.0295\log\frac{10^{-3}}{10^{-2}}$$ **(1 Mark)**

$= 2.71 + 0.0295 = 2.7395$ V

$E_{cell} = 2.7395$ V **(1 Mark)**

(i) When an external opposite potential applied is less than 2.71 V, then current will flow from Cu to Mg, i.e., cathode to anode (same direction) **(1 Mark)**

(ii) When an external opposite potential applied is greater than 2.71 V, then current will flow from Mg to Cu, i.e., anode to cathode (opposite direction) **(1 Mark)**

10. $$m = \frac{\text{Atomic mass}}{n \times F} \times Q$$ **(½ Mark)**

where   m = mass deposited

t = time

Atomic mass = 52 g mol^{-1}

Q = 24000 C

F = 96500 C mol^{-1}

$$\overset{+6}{CrO_3} \xrightarrow{n=6} \overset{0}{Cr}$$ **(½ Mark)**

$$m = \frac{52 \times 24000}{6 \times 96500} = \frac{12480}{5790} = 2.15 \text{ g}$$ **(½ Mark)**

2.15 g of Cr will be electroplated by 24000 C

$Q = i \times t$ **(½ Mark)**

$$m = \frac{\text{Atomic mass}}{n \times F} \times i \times t$$

$m = 1.5$ g; $i = 12.5$ A, $t = ?$

$$1.5 = \frac{52}{6 \times 96500} \times 12.5 \times t$$

$$t = \frac{1.5 \times 6 \times 96500}{52 \times 12.5}$$ **(½ Mark)**

$= 1336.15$ sec **(½ Mark)**

11. The cell potential remains constant during its life as the overall reaction does not involve any ion in solution whose concentration can change during its life time. **(1 mark)**

(b) KCl (aq) à K$^+$ (aq) + Cl$^-$ (aq)

cathode: $H_2O(l) + e^- à \frac{1}{2}H_2 (g) + OH^- (aq)$ **(1/2 mark)**

anode: $Cl^- (aq) à \frac{1}{2}Cl_2 (aq) + e^-$ **(1/2 mark)**

net reaction:

$KCl (aq) + H_2O (l) à K^+ (aq) + OH^- (aq) + \frac{1}{2}H_2 (g) + \frac{1}{2}Cl_2 (g)$ **(1 mark)**

(c) Given, potential of hydrogen gas electrode
= –0.59 V

Electrode reaction: $H^+ + e^- \rightarrow 0.5 H_2$

Applying Nernst equation,

$$E (H^+/H_2) = E^{\circ} (H^+/H_2) - \frac{0.059}{n}\log\frac{[H_2]^{1/2}}{[H^+]}$$ **(1 mark)**

$E^{\circ} (H^+/H_2) = 0$ V

$E (H^+/H_2) = -0.59$ V

$n = 1$

$[H_2] = 1$ bar

$-0.59 = 0 - 0.059 (-\log [H^+])$ **(1/2 mark)**

$-0.59 = -0.059$pH

$\therefore$ pH = 10 **(1/2 mark)**

12. (a) "A" is copper, metals are conductors thus have high value of conductivity. **(1 mark)**

(b) $Mg^{2+} + 2e^- à Mg$

1 mole of magnesium ions gains two moles of electrons or 2F to form 1 mole of Mg

24 g Mg requires 2 F electricity

4.8 g Mg requires $2 \times 4.8/24 = 0.4$ F $= 0.4 \times 96500$
$= 38600C$ **(1 mark)**

$Ca^{2+} + 2e^- \rightarrow Ca$

2 F electricity is required to produce 1 mole $= 40$ g Ca

0.4 F electricity will produce 8 g Ca **(1 mark)**

(c) F = 96500C, n=2,

Sn^{2+} (aq) $+ 2e^- \rightarrow Sn(s) - 0.14V$

Cu^{2+}(aq) $+ e^- \rightarrow Cu^+$ (aq) 0.15 V

$E°cell = E°cathode - E°anode$
$= 0.15 - (-0.14) = 0.29V$ **(1 mark)**

$\Delta G° = -nFE°_{cell}$
$= -2 \times 96500 \times 0.29 = 55970$ J/mol **(1 mark)**

13. (a) (i) Electrical conduction of metals decreases with increase in temperature. Thus, silver wire at 30°C will show greater conduction of electricity. **(1 Mark)**

(ii) Conductance of solution increases on increase in dilution. Hence, 0.1 M CH_3COOH solution will allow greater conduction of electricity. **(1 Mark)**

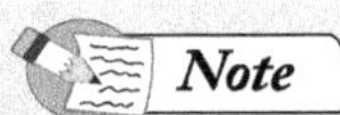

Note

As the number of ions per litre of electrolyte increases with dilution, conductance also increases with dilution which implies less concentrated solution has greater conductance.

(iii) Increase in temperature increases the dissociation of an ionic compound. Thus, KCl solution at 50°C will show greater conduction of electricity. **(1 Mark)**

(b)

Electrochemical cell		Electrolytic cell	
(i)	It generates electricity by chemical reactions.	(i)	Chemical reactions takes place by consuming electricity.
(ii)	Anode has negative and cathode has positive potential with respect to solution.	(ii)	Anode has positive and cathode has negative potential with respect to solution.

(1 + 1 = 2 Marks)

14. (a) According to Faraday's first law

$w = z \times I \times t$

$w = \dfrac{E \times I \times t}{F}$ Where $(z = E/F)$ **(1 Mark)**

For, Fe, $w = 2.8$ g, E of Fe $= 56/2 = 28$

$w = \dfrac{28 \times 2 \times t}{96500} \Rightarrow 2.8 = \dfrac{28 \times 2 \times t}{96500}$

$t = 4825$ sec **(1 Mark)**

For, Zn, $w = ?$, E of Zn $= 65.3/2$

$w = \dfrac{65.3 \times 2 \times 4825}{2 \times 96500} = 3.265$ g **(1 Mark)**

The current flow for 4825 sec and weight of Zn deposited at cathode is 3.265 g

(b)

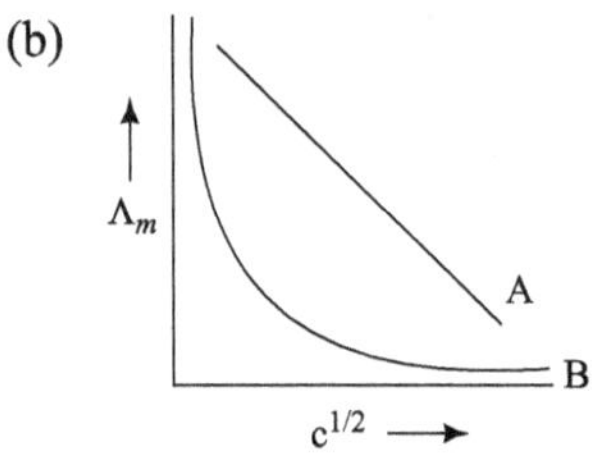

(i) A represents the strong electrolytes whereas B represents the weak electrolytes. **(½ Mark)**

(ii) It can be found from the graph that for a strong electrolyte A, as the concentration approaches the zero value, the molar conductance approaches a limiting value called molar conductance at infinite dilution.

The curve for a weak electrolyte B is a rectangular hyperbola and does not intercept the y-axis. Even though the concept of molar conductance at infinite dilution exists for a weak electrolyte, graphically the value cannot be evaluated. **(1½ Marks)**

15. (a) According to Faraday's first law of electrolysis, the amount of chemical reaction which occurs at any electrode during electrolysis by a current is proportional to the quantity of electricity passed through the electrolyte.

Reduction of 1 mol of Cu^{2+} of Cu is given by :

$Cu^{2+} + 2e^- \longrightarrow Cu$

∴ The charge required for 1 mole of $Cu^{2+} = 2F$ **(2 Marks)**

(b) Given:

Mg (s)$| Mg^{2+}$ (0.1M)) $|| Cu^{2+}$ (0.01M) $| Cu(s)$

$E°_{cell} = 2.71$ V, 1F = 96500 C mol^{-1}

To find : $E_{cell} = ?$

Solution : Using Nernst equation,

$$E_{cell} = E^\circ_{cell} - \left[\frac{0.059}{n} \log \frac{[P]}{[R]}\right] \quad \textbf{(½ Mark)}$$

The redox equation for the above cell is :

$$Mg(s) + Cu^{2+}(aq) \longrightarrow Mg^{2+}(aq) + Cu(s)$$

$$\therefore \quad E_{cell} = E^\circ_{cell} - \left[\frac{0.059}{n} \log \frac{[Mg^{2+}]}{[Cu^{2+}]}\right]$$

$$= 2.71 - \left[\frac{0.059}{2} \log \frac{[0.1]}{[0.01]}\right] \quad \textbf{(½ Mark)}$$

$$= 2.71 - \left[\frac{0.059}{2} \log 10\right] \quad \textbf{(½ Mark)}$$

$$= 2.71 - \left[\frac{0.059}{2} \times 1\right] \quad (\because \log 10 = 1)$$
$$\textbf{(½ Mark)}$$

$$= 2.68 \text{ V} \quad \textbf{(1 Mark)}$$

Topic-5: Batteries, Fuel Cells, Corrosion

1. **(c)** The Apollo space programme had used a fuel cell that would convert chemical energy into electrical energy and it was an $H_2 - O_2$ fuel cell.

   Overall reaction : $2H_2 (g) + O_2 (g) \longrightarrow 2H_2O (l)$

   Cathode : $O_2 (g) + 2H_2O (l) + 4e^- \longrightarrow 4OH^- (aq)$

   Anode : $2H_2 (g) + 4OH^- (aq) \longrightarrow 4H_2O (l) + 4e^-$

   Thus, option **(c)** is correct. **(1 Mark)**

2. Zn coating is better to protect iron objects. **(1 Mark)**

3. Fuel Cell: The galvanic cells which are designed to convert the energy of combustion of fuels like hydrogen, methane, methanol etc. directly into electrical energy are called fuel cells. **(1 Mark)**

   Advantages:

   (a) It produces electricity with an efficiency of about 70% compared to thermal plants whose efficiency is about 40%.

   (b) Fuel cells are pollution free.

   (c) The $H_2–O_2$ fuel cell produces water vapour which can be, further, condensed and reused as a drinking water. **(1 Mark)**

4. (i) Mercury cell delivers a constant potential, ~1.35 V during its life time as the overall reaction does not involve any ion in solution whose concentration can change during its life time. **(1 Mark)**

   (ii) Passing the direct current (DC) in the electrolyte changes the composition of the solution. **(1 Mark)**

5. Anode: $Zn (s) \rightarrow Zn^{2+} (aq) + 2 e^-$ **(1/2 Mark)**

   Cathode: $O_2(g) + 2H_2O(l) + 4e^- \rightarrow 4OH^- (aq)$. **(1/2 Mark)**

   Overall: $2 Zn (s) + O_2(g) + 2H_2O(l) \rightarrow$
   $$2 Zn^{2+}(aq) + 4OH^- (aq)$$
   $$2 Zn(s) + O_2(g) + 2H_2O(l) \rightarrow 2 Zn(OH)_2 \text{ (ppt)}$$
   (1 Mark)

6.

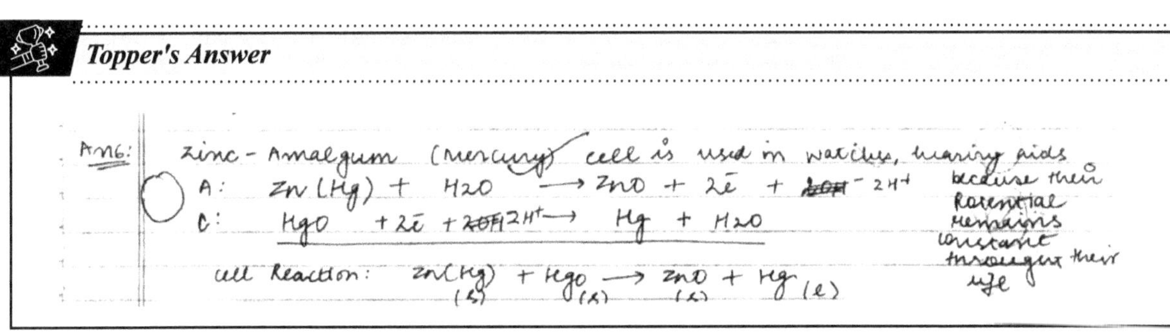

Topper's Answer

7. Corrosion is basically a process of oxidation, so oxidation potential is considered here.

   Oxidation potential of Fe = 0.44 V

   Oxidation potential of X = 2.36 V

   Oxidation potential of Y = 0.14 V

   Since, X has a higher oxidation potential than that of iron, so it will oxidise faster than Fe. Therefore, X is better for coating. **(2 Marks)**

8. The dry cell also known as Leclanche cell is used in transistors.

   The reactions taking place at the anode and cathode are given below.

   Cathode Reaction :

   $$MnO_2 + NH_4^+ + e^- \longrightarrow MnO(OH) + NH_3$$

   Anode Reaction:

   $$\underline{Zn - 2e^- \longrightarrow Zn^{2+}}$$
   $$Zn^{2+} + 2NH_3 \longrightarrow [Zn(NH_3)_2]^{2+}$$

   (1 + 1 = 2 Marks)

9. (a) Reaction of cathode

   $$Ag + e^- \longrightarrow Ag(s)$$

   $$W = z \times I \times t \quad \text{where } z = \frac{E}{F} \qquad \text{(½ Mark)}$$

   $$W = \frac{E}{F} \times It$$

   where E of $Ag = 108$

   $$W = \frac{108 \times 2 \times 15 \times 60}{96500} \qquad \text{(½ Mark)}$$

   $$= 2.015 \text{ g} \qquad \text{(1 Mark)}$$

   (b) Fuel cells are the cells that are designed to convert the energy of combustion of fuel directly into electrical energy. The most common fuel cell is the hydrogen oxygen fuel cell. **(1 Mark)**

10. (i) Mercury cell is used in hearing aids. **(½ Mark)**

    (ii) Fuel cell was used in Apollo space Programme.

    (½ Mark)

    (iii) Lead storage cell is used in automobiles and inverters. **(½ Mark)**

    (iv) Dry cell does not have long life. **(½ Mark)**

11. (a) $Mg(s) + Cu^{2+}(aq) \longrightarrow Mg^+(aq) + Cu(s)$

    Given: $E^\circ_{cell} = 2.71V$

    $1 F = 96500 \text{ C mol}^{-1}$

    To find: $\Delta G^\circ = ?$

    $\Delta G^\circ = -nFE^\circ_{cell}$ **(½ Mark)**

For this reaction, $n = 2$

$\therefore \ \Delta G^\circ = -2 \times 96500 \times 2.71$ **(½ Mark)**

$= -523030 \text{ J}$

$\therefore \ \Delta G^\circ = -523030 \text{ J} = -523.03 \text{ kJ}.$ **(1 Mark)**

(b) The hydrogen-oxygen fuel cell was used in Apollo space programme for providing electrical power.

(1 Mark)

> **Note**
>
> *The usage of hydrogen itself is purely CO_2 emission free system since hydrogen is used as a fuel and results only in H_2O without CO_2, unlike in fossil fuel engines.*

12. (a) $Zn(s) + Cu^{2+}(aq) \longrightarrow Zn^{2+}(aq) + Cu(s)$

    $E^o_{Cu^{2+}/Cu} = E^o_{cathode} = +0.34 \text{ V}$

    $E^o_{Zn^{2+}/Zn} = E^o_{anode} = -0.76 \text{ V}$

    $E^o_{cell} = E^o_{cathode} - E^o_{anode}$

    $\quad = 0.34 - (-0.76) = 1.1 \text{ V}$ **(1 Mark)**

    $n = 2$ **(½ Mark)**

    $F = 96500 \text{ C mol}^{-1}$

    $\Delta G^o = -nF \, E^o_{cell}$ **(½ Mark)**

    $\quad = -2 \times 96500 \times 1.1$

    $\quad = -212.27 \text{ kJ mol}^{-1}$ **(1 Mark)**

    (b) (i) Fuel cells produce electricity with an efficiency of about 70% as compared to thermal plants whose efficiency is about 40%.

    (ii) Fuel cells are pollution free because the by-product of H_2–O_2 fuel cell is H_2O.

    (1 + 1 = 2 Marks)

13. (a) Given :

    $2AgCl(s) + H_2(g)\ (1 \text{ atm}) \rightarrow 2Ag(s) + 2H^+ + 2Cl^-$

    $\Delta G^\circ = -43600 \text{ J}$

    $T = 25°C = 298 \text{ K}$

    To find : $E_{cell} = ?$

    Solution : $\Delta G^\circ = -nFE^\circ_{cell}$

    $n = 2$

    $\therefore \ E^\circ_{cell} = \dfrac{-\Delta G^\circ}{nF}$

    $\quad = \dfrac{-(-43600)}{2 \times 96500} = 0.226 \text{ V}$ **(1 Mark)**

    $E_{cell} = E^\circ_{cell} - \dfrac{0.059}{n} \log$

    $\dfrac{[H^+]^2[Cl^-]^2[Ag]}{[AgCl]^2[H_2]} = 0.226 - \dfrac{0.059}{2} \log[H^+]^2[Cl^-]^2$

    (1 Mark)

$$= 0.226 - \frac{0.059}{2} \log (0.1)^2 (0.1)^2$$

$$= 0.226 - \frac{0.059}{2} \log 10^{-4}$$

$$= 0.226 - \frac{0.059}{2} (-4)$$

$$= 0.226 + 0.118$$

$$E_{cell} = 0.344 \text{ V} \qquad \textbf{(1 Mark)}$$

(b) Fuels cells are the cells which convert energy of combustion of fuels like hydrogen, methane, methanol, etc directly into electrical energy.

Advantages of fuel cell :

1. They have a high efficiency of about 70%.

2. They are pollution free and run continuously as long as reactants are supplied. **(2 Marks)**

14. (a) $\lambda_m = \dfrac{\kappa \times 1000}{\text{Molarity}}$ **(½ Mark)**

Molarity = 0.20 mol L^{-1},

$\kappa = 2.48 \times 10^{-2}$ S cm^{-1}

$$\lambda_m = \frac{2.48 \times 10^{-2} \times 1000}{0.20} \text{ S cm}^2 \text{mol}^{-1}$$
$$= 124 \text{ S cm}^2 \text{ mol}^{-1} \qquad \textbf{(1 Mark)}$$

Degree of dissociation,

$$\alpha = \frac{\lambda_m^c}{\lambda_m^\infty}$$

$$\lambda_m^\infty = \lambda_{(K^+)}^\circ + \lambda_{(Cl^-)}^\circ$$

$$= (73.5 + 76.5) \text{ S cm}^2 \text{ mol}^{-1}$$
$$= 150.0 \text{ S cm}^2 \text{ mol}^{-1} \qquad \textbf{(½ Mark)}$$

$$\alpha = \frac{124}{150} = 0.826$$

or 82.6 % **(1 Mark)**

(b) Mercury cell is a type of primary battery. In primary batteries, the charging reaction occurs only once and after it has been used over a period of time, the battery becomes dead and cannot be reused.

Mercury cell is more advantageous than dry cell because dry cell has a very short life span due to the conversion of zinc to zinc chloride that makes the zinc casing porous. Due to this porous casing, the substance inside the cell leaks out and corrodes the metal, reducing the lifespan of the cell. While, in the case of mercury cell, the overall reaction does not involve formation of any ion in the solution whose concentration can change during its life time.

(1 + 1 = 2 Marks)

15. (a) (i) **Limiting molar conductivity :** It is that value of molar conductivity which is obtained at infinite dilution i.e. when the concentration of the solution approaches zero. It is denoted by Λ_m^0. **(1 Mark)**

(ii) **Fuel cell :** Galvanic cells that are designed to convert the energy of combustion of fuels like hydrogen, methane, methanol etc. directly into other form of energy are called fuel cells.

(1 Mark)

(b) **Given :**

$$R_1 = 100\Omega \qquad R_2 = 520 \ \Omega$$
$$C_1 = 0.1 \text{ mol L}^{-1} \quad C_2 = 0.02 \text{ mol L}^{-1}$$
$$\kappa_1 = 1.29 \times 10^{-2} \ \Omega^{-1} \text{ cm}^{-1}$$

To find: κ and $\wedge_m$ of 0.02 mol^{-1} KCl solution.

Sol : Cell constant $= R\kappa_1 = 100 \times 1.29 \times 10^{-2}$
$$= 1.29 \text{ cm}^{-1} \qquad \textbf{(½ Mark)}$$

As cell constant will be same,

$$\therefore \quad \kappa = \frac{\text{Cell constant}}{R} = \frac{1.29 \text{cm}^{-1}}{520\Omega} \qquad \textbf{(½ Mark)}$$

$$= 2.48 \times 10^{-3} \ \Omega^{-1} \text{ cm}^{-1} \text{ and,} \qquad \textbf{(½ Mark)}$$

$$\wedge_m = \frac{\kappa \times 1000}{C_2} = \frac{1.29}{520} \Omega^{-1} \text{cm}^{-1} \times \frac{1000}{0.02 \text{mol}^{-1}}$$

(½ Mark)

$$= 124.038 \ \Omega^{-1} \text{ cm}^{-1} \qquad \textbf{(1 Mark)}$$

16. (a) 2mol e$^-$ (or 2F) have been transferred from anode to cathode to consume 2 mol of H_2SO_4 therefore, one mole H_2SO_4 requires one faraday of electricity or 96500 coulombs.

(b) $W_{max} = -nFE^\circ = -2 \times 96500 \times 2.0 = 386000$ J of work can be extracted using lead storage cell when the cell is in use.

(c) Both yes and no should be accepted as correct answers depending upon what explanation is provided.

Yes, Hydrogen is a fuel that on combustion gives water as a byproduct. There are no carbon emissions and no pollutions caused.

However, at present the means to obtain hydrogen are electrolysis of water which use electricity obtained from fossil fuels and increase carbon emissions.

Inspite of the problems faced today in the extraction of hydrogen, we cannot disagree on the fact that hydrogen is a clean source of energy. Further research can help in finding solutions and greens ways like using solar energy for extraction of hydrogen. **(2 Marks)**

No. It is true that Hydrogen is a fuel that on combustion gives water as a byproduct. There are no carbon emissions and no pollutions caused.

However, at present the means to obtain hydrogen are electrolysis of water which use electricity obtained from fossil fuels and increase carbon emissions.

Hydrogen is no doubt a green fuel, but the process of extraction is not green as of today. At present, looking at the process of extraction, hydrogen is not a green fuel. **(2 Marks)**

OR

Both answers will be treated as correct

(i) Lead batteries are currently the most important and widely used batteries. These are rechargeable. The problem is waste management which needs research and awareness. Currently, these are being thrown into landfills and there is no safe method of disposal or recycling. Research into safer method of disposal will reduce the pollution and health hazards caused to a great extent.

(1 mark for importance, 1 for need for the research)

(ii) Fuel cell is a clen source of energy. Hydrogen undergoes combustion to produce water. The need of the hour is green fuel and hydrogen is a clean fuel. The current problem is obtaining hydrogen. Research that goes into this area will help solve the problem of pollution and will be a sustainable solution.

(1 mark for importance, 1 for need for the research)

Chapter 3

Chemical Kinetics

 **Multiple Choice Questions**

1. For the reaction $3A \rightarrow 2B$, rate of reaction $-\dfrac{d[A]}{dt}$ is equal to **[All India 2023, Set-I, U]**

(a) $\dfrac{+3}{2}\dfrac{d[B]}{dt}$

(b) $\dfrac{+2}{3}\dfrac{d[B]}{dt}$

(c) $\dfrac{+1}{3}\dfrac{d[B]}{dt}$

(d) $\dfrac{+1}{2}\dfrac{d[B]}{dt}$

2. If the initial concentration of substance A is 1.5 M and after 120 seconds the concentration of substance A is 0.75 M, the rate constant for the reaction if it follows zero – order kinetics is:

[CBSE Sample 2023-24, Ap]

(a) 0.00625 mol $L^{-1}s^{-1}$ (b) 0.00625 s^{-1}

(c) 0.00578 mol $L^{-1}s^{-1}$ (d) 0.00578 s^{-1}

 **Short Answer Questions (2 or 3 Marks)**

3. For the reaction **[All India 2018, Ap]**

$$2N_2O_5\,(g) \longrightarrow 4\,NO_2\,(g) + O_2\,(g),$$

the rate of formation of NO_2 (g) is 2.8×10^{-3} M s^{-1}. Calculate the rate of disappearance of N_2O_5 (g).

4. In the given reaction **[All India 2022, Term-II]**

$$N_2\,(g) + 3H_2\,(g) \longrightarrow 2NH_3\,(g)$$

the rate of formation of NH_3 is $3\cdot6\ 10^{-4}$ mol $L^{-1}\ s^{-1}$. Calculate the

(i) rate of reaction, and

(ii) rate of disappearance of H_2 (g).

 **Multiple Choice Questions**

1. Which of the following statement is true?

[CBSE Sample 2023-24, K]

(a) molecularity of reaction can be zero or a fraction.

(b) molecularity has no meaning for complex reactions.

(c) molecularity of a reaction is an experimental quantity

(d) reactions with the molecularity three are very rare but are fast.

2. The slope in the plot of $\log \dfrac{[R]_o}{[R]}$ vs. time for a first order reaction is **[All India 2023, Set-I, U]**

(a) $\dfrac{+k}{2.303}$

(b) $+k$

(c) $\dfrac{-k}{2.303}$

(d) $-k$

3. The slope in the plot [R] vs. time for a zero order reaction is **[All India 2023, Set-II, K]**

(a) $\dfrac{+k}{2.303}$

(b) $-k$

(c) $\dfrac{-k}{2.303}$

(d) $+k$

4. The following experimental rate data were obtained for a reaction carried out at 25°C: **[Delhi 2023, Set-III, Ap]**

$$A(g) + B(g) \rightarrow C(g) + D(g)$$

Initial [A(g)]/ Mol/dm^{-3}	Initial [B(g)]/ Mol/dm^{-3}	Initial rate/ Mol/dm^{-3} g^{-1}
3.3×10^{-2}	2.0×10^{-2}	1.89×10^{-4}
3.0×10^{-2}	4.0×10^{-2}	1.89×10^{-4}
6.0×10^{-2}	4.0×10^{-2}	7.56×10^{-4}

What are the orders with respect to $A_{(g)}$ and $B_{(g)}$?

	Order with respect to A(g)	Order with respect to B(g)
(a)	Zero	Second
(b)	First	Zero
(c)	Second	Zero
(d)	Second	First

5. Which radioactive isotope would have the longer half-life ^{15}O or ^{19}O? (Given rate constants for ^{15}O and ^{19}O are 5.63×10^{-3} s^{-1} and k = 2.38×10^{-2}s^{-1} respectively.)

[CBSE Sample 2022-23, U]

(a) ^{15}O

(b) ^{19}O

(c) Both will have the same half-life

(d) None of the above, information given is insufficient

6. For the reaction, $A + 2B \rightarrow AB_2$, the order w.r.t. reactant A is 2 and w.r.t. reactant B. What will be change in rate of reaction if the concentration of A is doubled and B is halved? **[CBSE Sample 2022-23, U]**

(a) increases four times

(b) decreases four times

(c) increases two times

(d) no change

7. The unit of rate constant for the reaction

$$2A + 2B \rightarrow A_2B_2$$

which has rate = k $[A]^2[B]$ is:

[CBSE Sample 2022-23, U]

(a) mol L^{-1}s^{-1} (b) s^{-1}

(c) mol L^{-1} (d) mol^{-2} L^2 s^{-1}

8. In a chemical reaction X $\rightarrow$ Y, it is found that the rate of reaction doubles when the concentration of X is increased four times. The order of the reaction with respect to X is

[Delhi 2020, Ap]

(a) 1   (b) 0

(c) 2   (d) $\dfrac{1}{2}$

Given below are two statements labelled as Assertion (A) and Reason (R). Select the most appropriate answer from the options given below:

(a) Both (A) and (R) are true and (R) is the correct explanation of (A).

(b) Both (A) and (R) are true, but (R) is not the correct explanation of (A).

(c) (A) is true, but (R) is false.

(d) (A) is false, but (R) is true.

9. **Assertion (A) :** The half life of a reaction is the time in which the concentration of the reactant is reduced to one half of its initial concentration.

Reason (R) : In first order kinetics when concentration of reactant is doubled, its half life is doubled.

[Delhi 2023, Set-II, K]

10. **Assertion (A):** Order of reaction is applicable to elementary as well as complex reactions.

Reason (R): For a complex reaction molecularity has no meaning. **[Delhi 2023 Set-III, U]**

11. **Assertion (A):** For a zero order reaction the unit of rate constant and rate of reaction are same.

[Delhi 2023 Set-I, K]

Reason (R): Rate of reaction for zero order reactions is independent of concentration of reactant.

12. **Assertion (A) :** The molecularity of the reaction $H_2 + Br_2 \rightarrow 2HBr$ appears to be 2.

Reason (R) : Two molecules of the reactants are involved in the given elementary reaction.

[All India 2020, K]

13. Write the slope value obtained in the plot of log [R$_0$] / [R] Vs. time for a first order reaction.

[Delhi 2020, Set-I]

14. For a reaction R $\rightarrow$ P, half-life (t$_{1/2}$) is observed to be independent of the initial concentration of reactants. What is the order of reaction ? **[Delhi 2017, K]**

5   *Short Answer Questions (2 or 3 Marks)*

15. (a) Radioactive decay follows first – order kinetics. The initial amount of two radioactive elements X and Y is 1 gm each. What will be the ratio of X and Y after two days if their half–lives are 12 hours and 16 hours respectively? **[CBSE Sample 2023-24, Ap]**

(b) The hypothetical reaction P + Q → R is half order w.r.t. 'P' and zero order w.r.t 'Q'. What is the unit of rate constant for this reaction?

[CBSE Sample 2023-24, Ap]

16. (a) For the reaction **[Delhi 2023, Set-I, Ap]**

$2N_2O_5(g) \rightarrow 4NO_2(g) + O_2(g)$ at 318 K

calculate the rate of reaction if rate of disappearance of $N_2O_5(g)$ is 1.4×10^{-3} ms^{-1}.

(b) For a first order reaction derive the relationship $t_{99\%} = 2t_{90\%}$. **[Delhi 2023, Set-I, Ap]**

17. (a) For the reaction **[Delhi 2023 Set-I, Ap]**

$2N_2O_5(g) \rightarrow 4NO_2(g) + O_2(g)$ at 318 K

calculate the rate of reaction if rate of disappearance of $N_2O_5(g)$ in 1.4×10^{-3} ms^{-1}.

(b) For a first order reaction derive the relationship $t_{99\%} = 2t_{90\%}$ **[Delhi 2023 Set-I, U]**

18. (a) The conversion of molecule A to B followed second order kinetics. If concentration of A increased to three times, how will it affect the rate of formation of B? **[All India 2023, Set-I, U]**

(b) Define Pseudo first order reaction with an example. **[All India 2023, Set-I, K]**

19. A first-order reaction takes 69.3 min for 50% completion. What is the time needed for 80% of the reaction to get completed?

(Given: log 5 =0.6990, log 8 = 0.9030, log 2 = 0.3010) **[CBSE Sample 2022-23, Ap]**

20. Explain how and why will the rate of reaction for a given reaction be affected when **[CBSE Sample 2022-23, U]**

(a) a catalyst is added

(b) the temperature at which the reaction was taking place is decreased

21. A first order reduction takes 30 minutes for 75% decomposition. Calculate $t_{1/2}$. **[All India 2022, Term-II]**

Given : [log 2 = 0·3, log 3 = 0·48, log 4 = 0·6, log 5 = 0·7]

22. Analyse the given graph, drawn between concentration of reactant vs. time. **[All India 2020, A]**

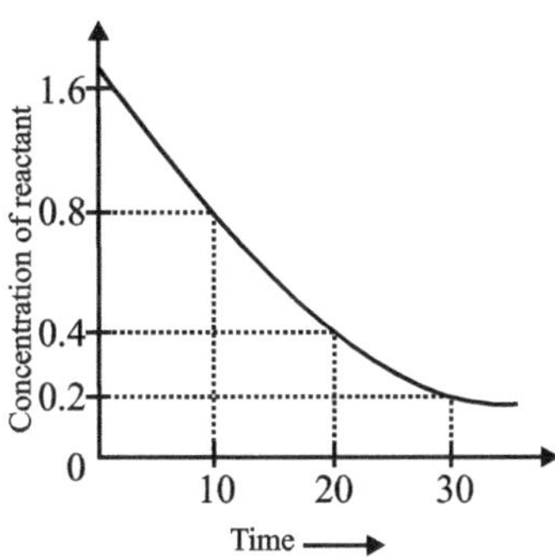

(a) Predict the order of reaction.

(b) Theoretically, can the concentration of the reactant reduce to zero after infinite time? Explain

23. For a reaction **[Delhi 2019, U]**

$$2H_2O_2 \xrightarrow[\text{alkaline medium}]{I^-} 2H_2O + O_2$$

the proposed mechanism is as given below:

(1) $H_2O_2 + I^- \rightarrow H_2O + IO^-$ (slow)

(2) $H_2O_2 + IO^- \rightarrow H_2O + I^- + O_2$ (fast)

(i) Write rate law for the reaction.

(ii) Write the overall order of reaction.

(iii) Out of steps (1) and (2), which one is rate determining step?

24. The decomposition of NH_3 on platinum surface is zero order reaction. If rate constant (k) is 4×10^{-3} Ms^{-1}, how long will it take to reduce the initial concentration of NH_3 from 0.1 M to 0.064 M. **[Delhi 2019, Ap]**

25. A first order reaction takes 20 minutes for 25% decomposition. Calculate the time when 75% of the reaction will be completed. (Given : log 2 = 0.3010, log 3 = 0.4771, log 4 = 0.6021) **[All India 2017, Ap]**

26. Following data are obtained for the reaction :

$N_2O_5 \rightarrow 2NO_2 + \frac{1}{2}O_2$ **[Delhi 2017, Ap]**

t/s	0	300	600
$[N_2O_5]$/ mol L^{-1}	1.6×10^{-2}	0.8×10^{-2}	0.4×10^{-2}

(a) Show that it follows first order reaction.

(b) Calculate the half-life.

(Given log 2 = 0.3010 log 4 = 0.6021)

27. For a reaction : $H_2 + Cl_2 \xrightarrow{hv} 2HCl$

Rate = k

(i) Write the order and molecularity of this reaction.

(ii) Write the unit of k. **[All India 2016, K]**

28. For the first order thermal decomposition reaction, the following data were obtained : **[All India 2016, Ap]**

$$C_2H_5Cl(g) \longrightarrow C_2H_4(g) + HCl(g)$$

Time/sec	**Total pressure/atm**
0	0.30
300	0.50

Calculate the rate constant.

(Given : log 2 = 0.301, log 3 = 0.4771, log 4 = 0.6021)

29. For a reaction : $2NH_3(g) \xrightarrow{Pt} N_2(g) + 3H_2(g)$

Rate = k   **[Delhi 2016, K]**

(i) Write the order and molecularity of this reaction.

(ii) Write the unit of k.

30. Define rate of reaction ? Write two factors that affect the rate of reaction.   **[All India 2015, K]**

31. For a chemical reaction R $\longrightarrow$ P, the variation in the concentration (R) vs. time (t) plot is given as

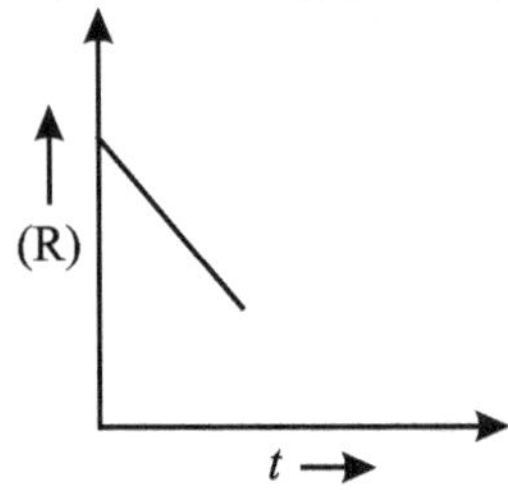

(i) Predict the order of the reaction.

(ii) What is the slope of the curve? **[All India 2014, K]**

32. The following data were obtained during the first order thermal decomposition of SO_2Cl_2 at a constant volume.

$$SO_2Cl_2(g) \longrightarrow SO_2(g) + Cl_2(g)$$

Experiment	**Times/s**	**Total pressure/atm**
1	0	0.4
2	100	0.7

Calculate the rate constant.   **[Delhi 2014, Ap]**

(Given : log 4 = 0.06021; log 2 = 0.3010)

33. (a) For a reaction A + B → P, the rate law is given by, $r = k [A]^{1/2} [B]^2$.   **[All India 2013, Ap]**

What is the order of this reaction?

(b) A first order reaction is found to have a rate constant $k = 5.5 \times 10^{-14}$ s^{-1}. Find the half life of the reaction.

34. The rate of a reaction becomes four times when the temperature changes from 293 K to 313 K. Calculate the energy of activation (E_a) of the reaction assuming that it does not change with temperature.

[R = 8.314 J K^{-1} mol^{-1}, log 4 = 0.6021]

[All India 2013, Ap]

35. (a) A first order reaction is 25% complete in 40 minutes. Calculate the value of rate constant. In what time will the reaction be 80% completed?

(b) Define order of reaction. Write the condition under which a bimolecular reaction follows first order kinetics.   **[Delhi 2020, Ap]**

36. (a) A first order reaction is 50% complete in 30 minutes at 300 K and in 10 minutes at 320 K. Calculate activation energy (E_a) for the reaction.

[R = 8.314 J K^{-1} mol^{-1}] [Given: log 2 = 0.3010, log 3 = 0.4771, log 4 = 0.6021, log 5 = 0.6991]

[Delhi 2020, Ap]

(b) Write the two conditions for collisions to be effective collisions.   **[Delhi 2020, K]**

(c) How order of reaction and molecularity differ towards a complex reaction?   **Delhi 2020, K]**

37. Read the following passage and answer the questions that follow :   **[All India 2022, Term-II, A]**

The rate of reaction is concerned with decrease in concentration of reactants or increase in the concentration of products per unit time. It can be expressed as instantaneous rate at a particular instant of time and average rate over a large interval of time. A number of factors such as temperature, concentration of reactants, catalyst affect the rate of reaction. Mathematical representation of rate of a reaction is given by rate law :

$$Rate = k[A]^x [B]^y$$

x and y indicate how sensitive the rate is to the change in concentration of A and B. Sum of $x + y$ gives the overall order of a reaction.

When a sequence of elementary reactions gives us the products, the reactions are called complex reactions. Molecularity and order of an elementary, reaction are same. Zero order reactions are relatively uncommon but they occur under special conditions. All natural and artificial radioactive decay of unstable nuclei take place by first order kinetics.

(a) What is the effect of temperature on the rate constant of a reaction?

(b) for a reaction A + B → Product, the rate law is given by, Rate = $k[A]^2 [B]^{1/2}$. What is the order of the reaction?

(c) How order and molecularity are different for complex reactions ?

(d) A first order reaction has a rate constant $2 \times 10^{-3} s^{-1}$. How long will 6g of this reactant take to reduce to 2g?

OR

The half life for radioactive decay of ^{14}C is 6930 years. An archaeological artifact containing wood had only 75% of the ^{14}C found in a living tree. Find the age of the sample.

[$\log 4 = 0.6021$ $\log 3 = 0.4771$ $\log 2 = 0.3010$ $\log 10 = 1$]

38. Read the passage given below and answer the questions that follow.

Are there nuclear reactions going on in our bodies?

There are nuclear reactions constantly occurring in our bodies, but there are very few of them compared to the chemical reactions, and they do not affect our bodies much. All of the physical processes that take place to keep a human body running are chemical processes. Nuclear reactions can lead to chemical damage, which the body may notice and try to fix. The nuclear reaction occurring in our bodies is radioactive decay. This is the change of a less stable nucleus to a more stable nucleus. Every atom has either a stable nucleus or an unstable nucleus, depending on how big it is and on the ratio of protons to neutrons. The ratio of neutrons to protons in a stable nucleus is thus **around 1:1** for small nuclei ($Z < 20$). Nuclei with too many neutrons, too few neutrons, or that are simply too big are unstable. They eventually transform to a stable form through radioactive decay. Wherever there are atoms with unstable nuclei (radioactive atoms), there are nuclear reactions occurring naturally. The interesting thing is that there are small amounts of radioactive atoms everywhere: in your chair, in the ground, in the food you eat, and yes, in your body.

The most common natural radioactive isotopes in humans are carbon-14 and potassium-40. Chemically, these isotopes behave exactly like stable carbon and potassium. For this reason, the body uses carbon-14 and potassium-40 just like it does normal carbon and potassium; building them into the different parts of the cells, without knowing that they are radioactive. In time, carbon-14 atoms decay to stable nitrogen atoms and potassium-40 atoms decay to stable calcium atoms.

Chemicals in the body that relied on having a carbon-14 atom or potassium-40 atom in a certain spot will suddenly have a nitrogen or calcium atom. Such a change damages the chemical. Normally, such changes are so rare, that the body can repair the damage or filter away the damaged chemicals.

The natural occurrence of carbon-14 decay in the body is the core principle behind carbon dating. As long as a person is alive and still eating, every carbon-14 atom that decays into a nitrogen atom is replaced on average with a new carbon-14 atom. But once a person dies, he stops replacing the decaying carbon-14 atoms. Slowly the carbon-14 atoms decay to nitrogen without being replaced, so that there is less and less carbon-14 in a dead body. The rate at which carbon-14 decays is constant and follows first order kinetics. It has a half - life of nearly 6000 years, so by measuring the relative amount of carbon-14 in a bone, archeologists can calculate when the person died. All living organisms consume carbon, so carbon dating can be used to date any living organism, and any object made from a living organism. Bones, wood, leather, and even paper can be accurately dated, as long as they first existed within the last 60,000 years. This is all because of the fact that nuclear reactions naturally occur in living organisms.

(source: The textbook Chemistry: The Practical Science by Paul B. Kelter, Michael D. Mosher and Andrew Scott states) **[All India 2021-22, Term-II, A]**

a. Why is Carbon -14 radioactive while Carbon -12 not? (Atomic number of Carbon: 6)

b. Researchers have uncovered the youngest known dinosaur bone, dating around 65 million years ago. How was the age of this fossil estimated?

c. Which are the two most common radioactive decays happening in human body?

d. Suppose an organism has 20 g of Carbon -14 at its time of death. Approximately how much Carbon -14 remains after 10,320 years?

(Given antilog 0.517 = 3.289)

OR

Approximately how old is a fossil with 12 g of Carbon -14 if it initially possessed 32 g of Carbon – 14? (Given log 2.667 = 0.4260)

(1+1+1+2 Marks)

Topic-3: Temperature Dependence of the Rate of a Reaction and Collision Theory

 **1**   *Multiple Choice Questions*

1. Arrhenius equation can be represented graphically as follows: **[CBSE Sample 2022-23, Ap]**

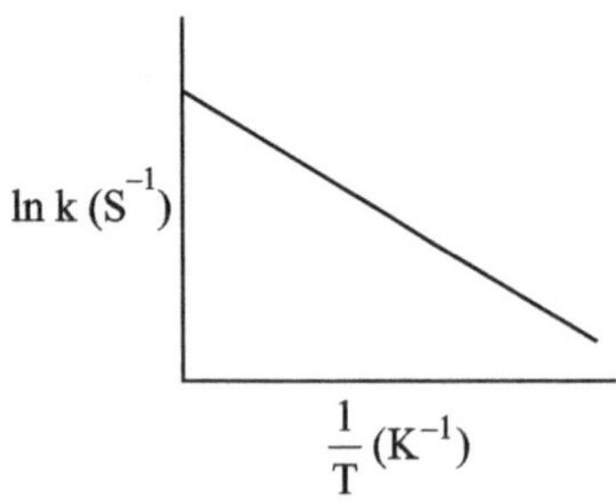

The (i) intercept and (ii) slope of the graph are:

(a) (i) $\ln A$ (ii) E_a/R

(b) (i) A (ii) E_a

(c) (i) $\ln A$ (ii) $-E_a/R$

(d) (i) A (ii) $-E_a$

 **4**   *Very Short Answer Questions (1 Mark)*

2. Will the rate constant of the reaction depend upon T if the E_{act} (activating energy) of the reaction is zero?

[All India 2020, U]

3. What is the effect of adding a catalyst on

[All India 2017, U]

(a) Activation energy (E_a), and

(b) Gibbs energy (ΔG) of a reaction?

5   *Short Answer Questions (2 or 3 Marks)*

4. The rate constants of a reaction at 200K and 500K are $0.02 s^{-1}$ and $0.20 s^{-1}$ respectively. Calculate the value of E_a (Given $2.303R = 19.15$ JK^{-1} mol^{-1})

[CBSE Sample 2023-24, Ap]

5. A first order reaction is 50% complete in 30 minutes at 300 K and in 10 minutes at 320 K. Calculate activation energy (E_a) for the reaction. $[R = 8.314$ J K^{-1} $mol^{-1}]$
[Given : $\log 2 = 0.3010$. $\log 3 = 0.4771$. $\log 4 = 0.6021$]

[All India 2023, Set-I, Ap]

6. What happens to the rate constant k and activation energy E_a as the temperature of a chemical reaction is increased? Justify. **[Delhi 2023, Set-I, K]**

7. A first order reaction is 50% completed in 40 minutes at 300 K and in 20 minutes at 320 K. Calculate the activation energy of the reaction. **[All India 2018, Ap]**
(Given : $\log 2 = 0.3010$, $\log 4 = 0.6021$, $R = 8.314$ JK^{-1} mol^{-1})

8. The rate constant for the first order decomposition of H_2O_2 is given by the following equation :

[Delhi 2016, Ap]

$$\log k = 14.2 - \frac{1.0 \times 10^4}{T} K$$

Calculate E_a for this reaction and rate constant k if its half-life period be 200 minutes.
(Given: $R = 8.314$ J K^{-1} mol^{-1})

9. The rate constant of a first order reaction increases from 2×10^{-2} to 4×10^{-2} when the temperature changes from 300 K to 310 K. Calculate the energy of activation (E_a).
($\log 2 = 0.301$, $\log 3 = 0.4771$, $\log 4 = 0.6021$)

[All India 2015, Ap]

6   *Long Answer Questions*

10. How will the rate of the reaction be affected when

[All India 2020, U]

(a) Surface area of the reactant is reduced,

(b) Catalyst is added in a reversible reaction, and

(c) Temperature of the reaction is increased?

11. (a) Consider the reaction $R \rightarrow P$ for which the change in concentration of R with time is shown by the following graph: **[All India 2019, U]**

(i) Predict the order of reaction.

(ii) What does the slope of the curve indicate?

(b) The rate of reaction quadruples when temperature changes from 293 K to 313 K. Calculate E_a assuming that it does not change with time.

$[R = 8.314$ JK^{-1} $mol^{-1}]$ **[All India 2019, Ap]**

12. (a) Draw the plot of *ln k* vs 1/T for a chemical reaction. What does the intercept represent? What is the relation between slope and E_a? **[All India 2019, K]**

(b) A first order reaction takes 30 minutes for 20% decomposition. Calculate $t_{1/2}$ [log 2 = 0·3010] **[All India 2019, Ap]**

13. For the hydrolysis of methyl acetate in aqueous solution, the following results were obtained : **[Delhi 2015]**

t/s	0	30	60
$[CH_3COOCH_3]$/mol L^{-1}	0.60	0.30	0.15

(i) Show that it follows pseudo first order reaction, as the concentration of water remains constant. **[Delhi 2015, U]**

(ii) Calculate the average rate of reaction between the time interval 30 to 60 seconds. **[Delhi 2015, Ap]** (Given log 2 = 0.3010, log 4 = 0.6021)

14. (a) For a reaction A + B $\longrightarrow$ P, the rate is given by

Rate = k[A] [B]^2 **[Delhi 2015, U]**

(i) How is the rate of reaction affected if the concentration of B is doubled ?

(ii) What is the overall order of reaction if A is present in large excess ?

(b) A first order reaction takes 30 minutes for 50% completion. Calculate the time required for 90% completion of this reaction.

(log 2 = 0.3010) **[Delhi 2015, Ap]**

15. (a) A reaction is second order in A and first order in B. **[Delhi 2013]**

(i) Write the differential rate equation. **[Delhi 2013, K]**

(ii) How is the rate affected on increasing the concentration of A three times? **[Delhi 2013, U]**

(iii) How is the rate affected when the concentrations of both A and B are doubled? **[Delhi 2013, U]**

(b) A first order reaction takes 40 minutes for 30% decomposition. Calculate $t_{1/2}$ for this reaction. (Given log 1.428 = 0.1548) **[Delhi 2013, Ap]**

16. (a) For a first order reaction, show that time required for 99% completion is twice the time required for the completion of 90% of reaction. **[Delhi 2013, U]**

(b) Rate constant 'k' of a reaction varies with temperature 'T' according to the equation :

$$\log k = \log A - \frac{E_a}{2.303R}\left(\frac{1}{T}\right)$$

Where E_a is the activation energy. When a graph is plotted for log k Vs. $\frac{1}{T}$, a straight line with a slope of -4250 K is obtained. Calculate 'E_a' for the reaction. **[Delhi 2013, Ap]**

(R = 8.314 JK^{-1} mol^{-1})

Solutions

Topic-1: *Rate of a Chemical Reaction*

1. **(a)** $\dfrac{+3}{2}\dfrac{d[B]}{dt}$;

$$3A \longrightarrow 2B$$

Rate of the reaction $= -\dfrac{1}{3}\dfrac{d[A]}{dt} = \dfrac{1}{2}\dfrac{d[B]}{dt}$

$\therefore \ -\dfrac{d[A]}{dt} = \dfrac{3}{2}\dfrac{d[B]}{dt}$ **(1 Mark)**

2. **(a)** for zero order k = [Ro] – [R] / t = 1.5 – 0.75 / 120 = 0.00625 mol L^{-1}s^{-1} **(1 Mark)**

3. Given : $2N_2O_5(g) \rightarrow 4NO_2\ (g) + O_2\ (g)$

Rate of formation of $NO_2(g) = 2.8 \times 10^{-3}\ Ms^{-1}$

Rate of reaction $= -\dfrac{1}{2}\dfrac{d[N_2O_5]}{dt} = +\dfrac{1}{4}\dfrac{d[NO_2]}{dt}$

(1 Mark)

$\therefore \quad -\dfrac{d[N_2O_5]}{dt} = \dfrac{2}{4}\dfrac{d[NO_2]}{dt}$

$= \dfrac{1}{2} \times 2.8 \times 10^{-3}\,Ms^{-1}$

$\Rightarrow \quad -\dfrac{d[N_2O_5]}{dt} = 1.4 \times 10^{-3}\ Ms^{-1}$ **(1 Mark)**

4.

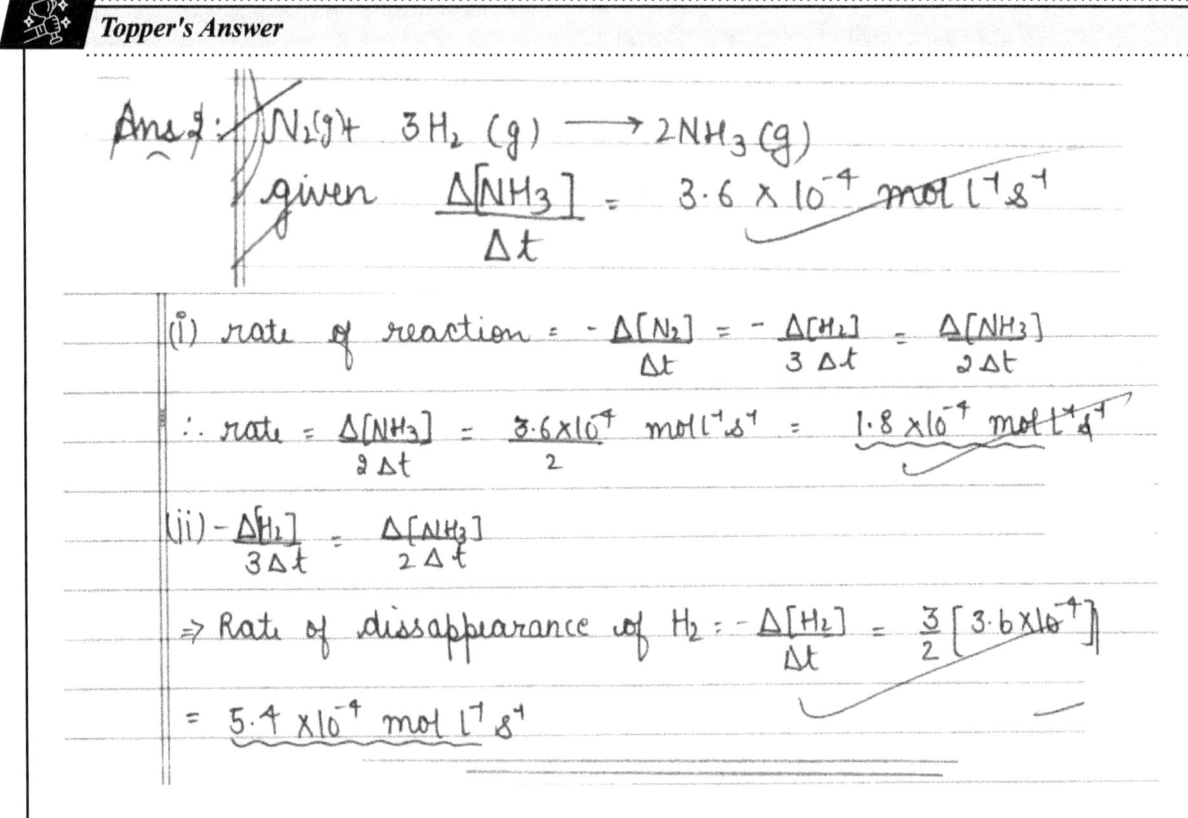

Topper's Answer

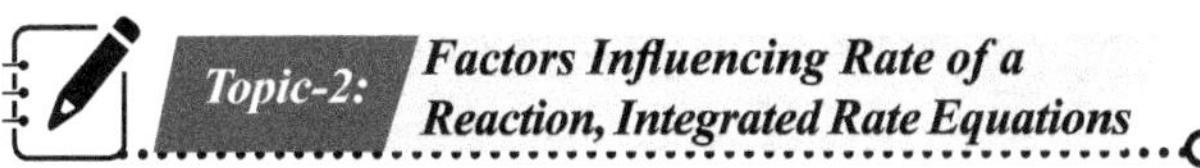

Topic-2: *Factors Influencing Rate of a Reaction, Integrated Rate Equations*

1. **(b)** molecularity has no meaning for complex reactions.

(1 Mark)

2. **(a)** $\dfrac{+k}{2.303}$;

For 1st order reaction, $[R] = [R]_0\, e^{-kt}$

or, $\dfrac{[R]_0}{[R]} = e^{kt}$

or, $2.303 \log \dfrac{[R]_0}{[R]} = kt$

or, $\log \dfrac{[R]_0}{[R]} = \dfrac{k}{2.303} t$ **(1 Mark)**

3. **(b)** Plot of [R] vs. time for a zero order reaction is given below:

For zero order, $[R] = -kt + [R]_0$

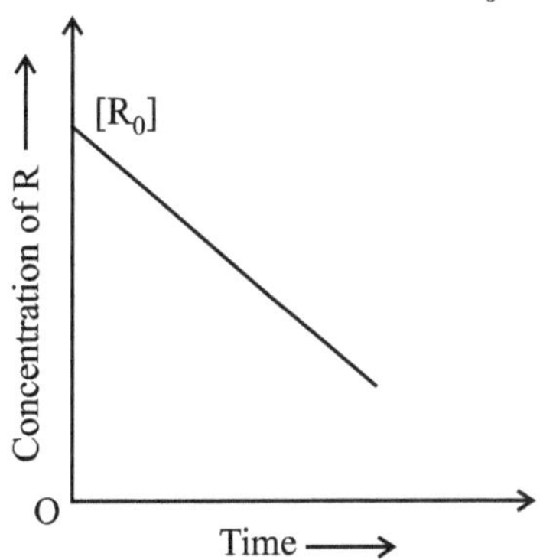

Hence, its slope will be $-k$. **(1 Mark)**

4. **(c)** From the given data, it is apparent that when the concentration of A(g) is kept constant and that of B(g) is doubled, the rate of the reaction **does not change**. Thus, the reaction is of **zero order** with respect to B(g). When the concentration of B(g) is kept constant and that of A(g) is doubled, the rate of the reaction is **quadrupled**. Thus, the reaction is of **second order** with respect to A(g).

Therefore, option **(c)** is correct. **(1 Mark)**

5. **(a)** ^{15}O **(1 Mark)**

The rate constant for the decay of O-15 is less than that for O-19. Therefore , the rate of decay of O-15 will be slower and will have a longer half life .

6. **(a)** increases 4 times

$r = [A]^2$

If [A] is doubled then $r' = [2A]^2 = 4\,[A]^2 = 4 \times r$

(1 Mark)

7. **(d)** $mol^{-2}\,L^2\,s^{-1}$ since the order of reaction is 3.

(1 Mark)

8. **(d)** $X \longrightarrow Y$

$r_1 = R \propto [X]^n$

$r_2 = 2R \propto [4X]^n$

$\Rightarrow \dfrac{2R}{R} = \dfrac{[4X]^n}{[X]^n}$

$\Rightarrow 2 = 4^n$

$\Rightarrow n = \dfrac{1}{2}$ **(1 Mark)**

9. **(c)** The half life of a reaction is defined as the time taken for the initial concentration of a reactant to be reduced to half of its value.

Thus, Assertion (A) is **true**.

For, a first order reaction, $t_{1/2} = \dfrac{0.693}{k}$ which shows that the half-life is independent of the concentration of the reactant.

Thus, Reason (R) is **false**.

Therefore, option **(c)** is correct. **(1 Mark)**

10. **(a)** Order of a reaction is applicable to elementary as well as complex reactions because it is determined by the slowest step in its mechanism.

Molecularity has no meaning in complex reaction because complex reaction proceeds through several elementary reactions. Number of molecules involved in each elementary reaction may be different i.e. molecularity of each step may be different. Thus, molecularity of overall reaction is meaningless.

(1 Mark)

11. **(a)** For zero order reaction, the rate law expression is given as,

Rate $= K\,[A]^0 = K$

i.e., the rate of reaction is entirely independent of the concentration of reactants.

Hence, for a zero order reaction, the unit of rate constant and rate of reaction are same. **(1 Mark)**

12. (i) The molecularity of a reaction depends only on the stoichiometry of the reaction. Hence, molecularity of the reaction $H_2 + Br_2 \rightarrow 2HBr$ is two.

Hence, reason is the correct explanation of given assertion. **(1 Mark)**

13.

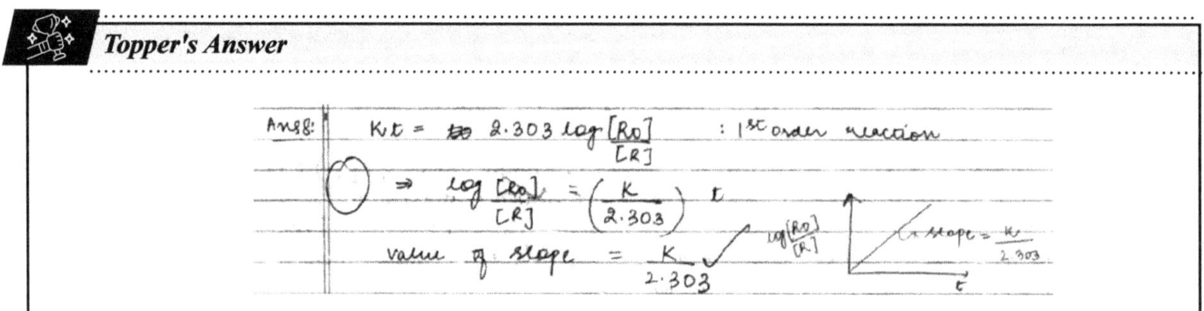

14. First Order Reaction. **(1 Mark)**

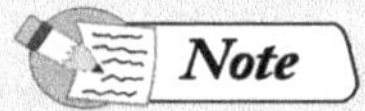

Half life period of first order reaction is independent of the initial concentration of the reactant.

15. (a) for first order reaction

half life of X = 12 hours

2 days = 48 hours means 4 half lives, amount of X left = 1/16 of initial value

half life of Y = 16 hours **(1/2 Mark)**

2 days = 48 hours means 3 half lives, amount left = 1/8 of initial value

Ratio of X : Y = 1 : 2 **(1/2 Mark)**

(b) $mol^{1/2}L^{-1}s^{-1}$ as Rate = k $[P]^{1/2}$ **(1 Mark)**

16. (a) For the given reaction:

$$\text{Rate of reaction} = -\frac{1}{2}\frac{d[N_2O_5]}{dt} \qquad \textbf{(½ Mark)}$$

$$= -\frac{1}{2} \times (1.4 \times 10^{-3}\ Ms^{-1})$$

$$= -7.0 \times 10^{-4}\ Ms^{-1}$$

or $\quad 7.0 \times 10^{-4}\ Ms^{-1}$ **(½ Mark)**

(b) For a first order reaction:

$$t = \frac{2.303}{k} \log \frac{a_0}{a} \qquad \textbf{(½ Mark)}$$

Now, $\quad t_{99\%} \Rightarrow a = \dfrac{1}{100} a_0$

$$t_{90\%} \Rightarrow a = \frac{10}{100} a_0 = \frac{1}{10} a_0 \qquad \textbf{(½ Mark)}$$

Thus,

$$t_{99\%} = \frac{2.303}{k} \log \frac{\cancel{a_0}}{\frac{1}{100}\cancel{a_0}} = \frac{2.303}{k} \log 100$$

$$= \frac{2.303}{k} \times 2$$

$$t_{90\%} = \frac{2.303}{k} \log \frac{\cancel{a_0}}{\frac{1}{10}\cancel{a_0}} = \frac{2.303}{k} \log 10 = \frac{2.303}{k}$$

(½ Mark)

Therefore, $t_{99\%} = 2 \times t_{90\%}$ **(½ Mark)**

17. (a) $2\,N_2O_5(g) \rightarrow 4\,NO_2(g) + O_2(g)$

Rate of reaction $= -\dfrac{1}{2}$ Rate of disappearance of $N_2O_5(g)$

$$= -\frac{1}{2}\frac{\Delta[N_2O_5]}{\Delta t} \qquad \textbf{(½ Mark)}$$

$$= (-)\frac{1}{2} \times 1.4 \times 10^{-3}\ m/s$$

$$= (-)\,7 \times 10^{-4}\ m/s \qquad \textbf{(½ Mark)}$$

Negative sign indicates that concentration of reactant decreases with time.

(b) For a first order reactant,

Time required for 99% completion is

$$t_{99\%} = \frac{2.303}{K} \log \frac{100}{100-99} \qquad \textbf{(½ Mark)}$$

$$t_{99\%} = \frac{2.303}{K} \log 100$$

$$t_{99\%} = 2 \times \frac{2.303}{K} \qquad ....(i) \qquad \textbf{(½ Mark)}$$

Time required for 90% completion is

$$t_{90\%} = \frac{2.303}{K} \log \frac{100}{100-90}$$ (½ Mark)

$$t_{90\%} = \frac{2.303}{K} \log 10$$

$$t_{90\%} = \frac{2.303}{K} \quad ....(ii)$$

From equation (i) and (ii), (½ Mark)

$$t_{99\%} = 2\, t_{90\%}$$

18. (a) $A \longrightarrow B$

Rate of the reaction : $r_1 = k[A]^2$

(2nd order kinetics)

Increasing concentration of A by 3 times:

$$r_2 = k(3[A])^2$$
$$= 9k[A]^2$$
$$= 9r_1$$

$\therefore$ Rate of the reaction enhances by 9 times.

The formation of 'B' enhances by 9 times. **(1 Mark)**

(b) The order of the reaction is sometimes, of higher order but appears as a first order reaction due to the presence of one of the components in excess. Such reactions are known as pseudofirst order reaction. e.g. Acid catalysed hydrolysis of ester, (½ Mark)

$$CH_3COOC_2H_5 + H_2O \xrightarrow{H^+} CH_3COOH + C_2H_5OH$$

Rate = $k[CH_3COOC_2H_5]\,[H_2O]$

H_2O is present in the reaction mixture in excess. Therefore, there is hardly any change happens in the concentration of water in the end of reaction.

$\therefore$ Rate = $k'[CH_3COOC_2H_5]$

Rate becomes dependent on the concentration of ester. **(½ Mark)**

19. Half life $t_{1/2} = 0.693\,/k$

$k = 0.693/69.3 = 1/100 = 0.01$ min^{-1} **(1/2 mark)**

For first order reaction

$$k = \frac{2.303}{t} \log \frac{[Ro]}{[R]}$$ **(1 mark)**

$$t = \frac{2.303}{0.01} \log \frac{100}{20}$$

$t = 230.3 \log 5$ (log 5 = 0.6990)

$t = 160.9$ min **(1/2 mark)**

20. (a) The rate of reaction will increase. The catalyst decreases the activation energy of the reaction therefore the reaction becomes faster.

(1/2+1/2 = 1 mark)

(b) The rate of reaction will decrease. At lower temperatures the kinetic energy of molecules decreases thereby the collisions decrease resulting in a lowering of rate of reaction. **(1/2+1/2 = 1 mark)**

21.

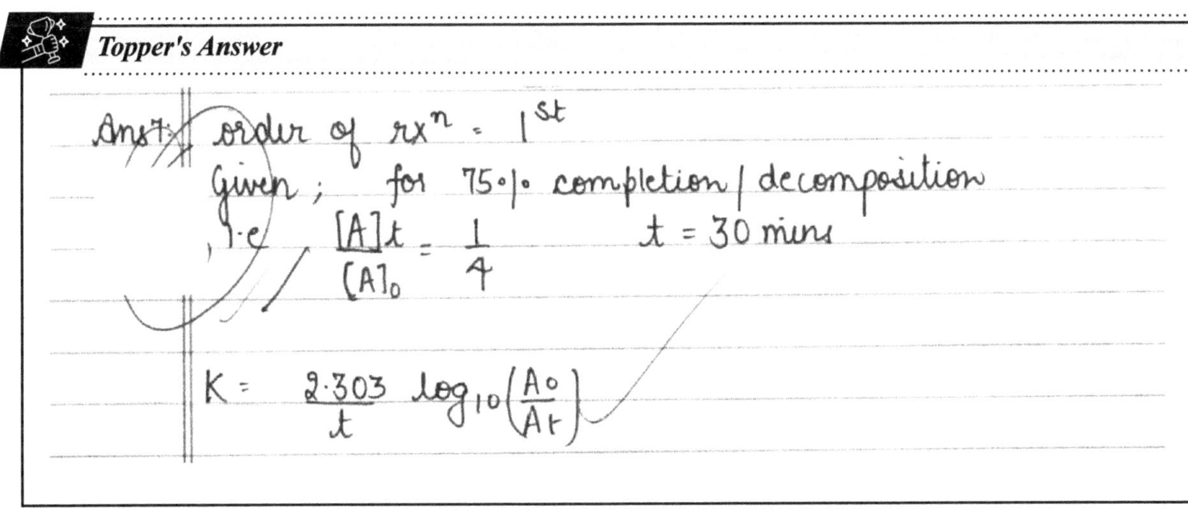

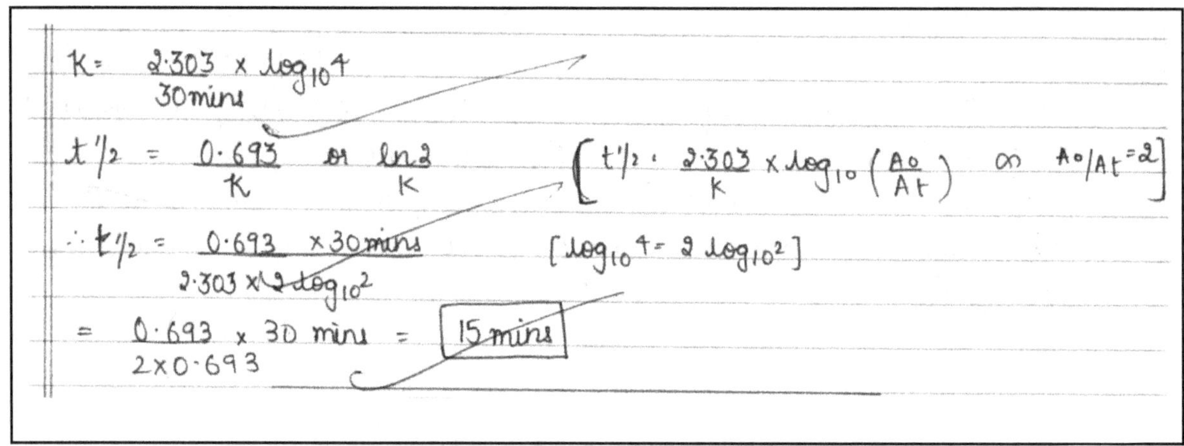

22. (a) Half-life calculation from the given graph: Concentration of reactant reduces from 0.8 to 0.4 in $(20-10) = 10$ seconds. Again the concentration reduces to half (0.4 to 0.2) in $(30-20) = 10$ seconds.

Thus, the half-life of reaction remains constant or we can say that order of reaction is one. **(1 Mark)**

(b) For a first order reaction, concentration never reduces to zero. For first order reaction $\ln \dfrac{[A]}{[A]_0} = -kt$

$$[A] = [A]_0\, e^{-kt}$$

where $[A]_0$ is the initial concentration of the reactant. Mathematically, $[A] > 0$ for all $t < \infty$ **(1 Mark)**

23. (i) Rate law for the reaction **(1 Mark)**

Rate $= k[H_2O_2]\,[I^-]$

(ii) Order of reaction is 2. **(½ Mark)**

(iii) Step 1 is rate determining step because it is the slowest step. **(½ Mark)**

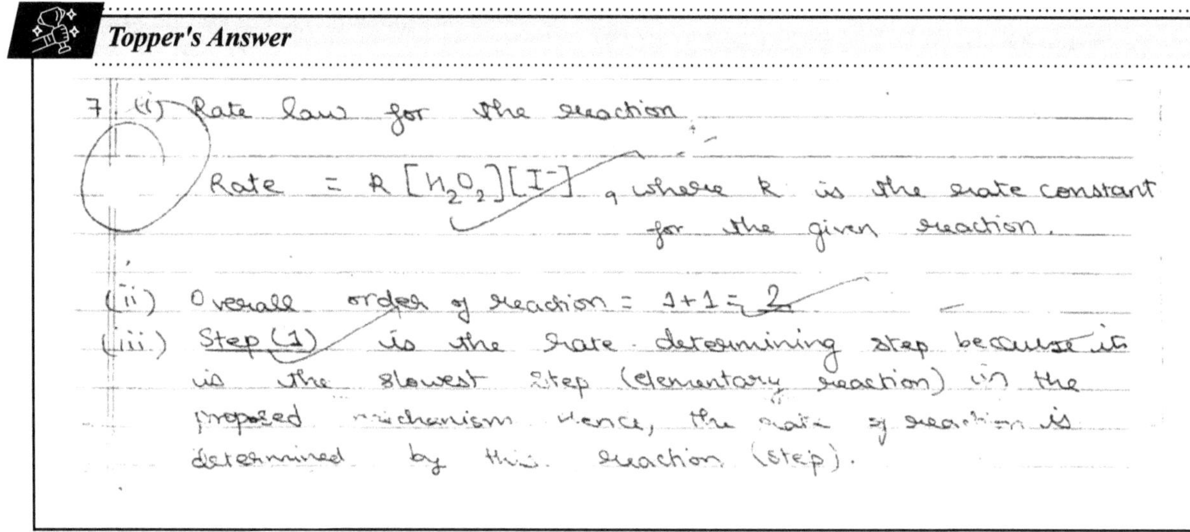

Topper's Answer

24.

> **Topper's Answer**
>
> 15. Reaction: $NH_3(g) \rightleftharpoons \frac{1}{2} N_2(g) + \frac{3}{2} H_2(g)$
>
> Rate of reaction $= -\dfrac{d[NH_3]}{dt} = k[NH_3]^0$
>
> where $k = 4 \times 10^{-3} \, Ms^{-1}$ (given)
>
> So, differential rate equation becomes,
>
> $-\dfrac{d[NH_3]}{dt} = k$
>
> $\int d[NH_3] = -\int k \, dt$
>
> $[NH_3] = -kt + C \quad —①$
>
> At $t = 0$, $[NH_3] = [NH_3]_0$ (initial concentration)
>
> So, $[NH_3]_0 = C$
>
> $\therefore$ ① becomes,
>
> $[NH_3] = [NH_3]_0 - kt$
>
> Now, $[NH_3]_0 = 0.1 \, M$
>
> $[NH_3] = 0.064 \, M$
>
> and $k = 4 \times 10^{-3} \, Ms^{-1}$
>
> So,
>
> $0.064 \, M = 0.100 \, M - kt$
>
> $kt = 0.036 \, M$
>
> $t = \dfrac{0.036 \, M}{4 \times 10^{-3} \, M} \, s = 36 \, s = 9s$
>
> Hence, it will take 9s to reduce the initial concentration of NH_3 from $0.1 \, M$ to $0.064 \, M$.

Initial concentration of $NH_3 = [A]_0 = 0.1$ M	$kt = [A]_0 - [A]$ **(1 Mark)**
Final concentration $[A] = 0.064$ M	$4 \times 10^{-3} \times t = 0.1 - 0.064$
$k = 4 \times 10^{-3}$ Ms^{-1}	$t = \xrightarrow[443K]{H_2SO_4}$ **(1 Mark)**
For zero order reaction	$= 0.009 \times 10^{-3} = 9$ sec **(1 Mark)**

25. For a first order reaction

$$t = 20 \text{ min. (given)}$$

$$t = \frac{2.303}{k} \log \frac{[R]_0}{[R]} \qquad \text{(½ Mark)}$$

$$\Rightarrow \quad k = \frac{2.303}{20} \log \frac{100}{100-25}$$

$$= \frac{2.303}{20}\left(\log 4 - \log 3\right)$$

$$= \frac{2.303}{20}\left(0.6021 - 0.4771\right)$$

$$= 1.44 \times 10^{-2} \text{ min}^{-1} \qquad \text{(1 Mark)}$$

The time when 75% of the reaction completed can be calculated as

$$t = \frac{\frac{2.303}{k} \log \frac{100}{100-75}}{} \qquad \text{(½ Mark)}$$

$$= \frac{2.303}{1.44 \times 10^{-2}} \log 4 = \frac{2.303}{1.44 \times 10^{-2}}(0.6021)$$

$$= 96.3 \text{ min (approximately)} \qquad \text{(1 Mark)}$$

Note

Some useful relationships between times for different fraction of reaction of Ist order are

$$t_{3/4} \text{ or } 75\% = 2\, t_{1/2}$$
$$t_{87.5\%} = 3\, t_{1/2}$$
$$t_{99.9\%} = 10\, t_{1/2}$$

These relations can be used to determined $t_{1/2}$ for different time intervals directly.

26. (a) At 300 s

For the first order reaction

$$k = \frac{2.303}{t} \log \frac{[A]_\circ}{[A]}, \qquad \text{(½ Mark)}$$

where $[A]_0$ is initial concentration & $[A]$ is final concentration

$$= \frac{2.303}{300} \log \frac{1.6 \times 10^{-2}}{0.8 \times 10^{-2}}$$

$$= \frac{2.303}{300} \log 2$$

$$= 2.31 \times 10^{-3} \text{ sec}^{-1} \qquad \text{(½ Mark)}$$

At 600 s

$$k = \frac{2.303}{t} \log \frac{[A]_\circ}{[A]}$$

$$= \frac{2.303}{600} \log \frac{1.6 \times 10^{-2}}{0.4 \times 10^{-2}}$$

$$= \frac{2.303}{600} \log 4$$

$$= \frac{2.303}{600} \times 0.6021$$

$$= 2.31 \times 10^{-3} \text{ sec}^{-1} \qquad \text{(1 Mark)}$$

In equal time interval, k is constant when using first order reaction, therefore it follows first order kinetics.

(b) $t_{1/2} = \dfrac{0.693}{k}, \; k = 2.31 \times 10^{-3}$

$$= \frac{0.693}{2.31 \times 10^{-3}} = 300 \text{ sec} \qquad \text{(1 Mark)}$$

half life is 300 sec.

27. (i) As the rate of the reaction does not depends on concentration of the reaction, its order will be zero whereas molecularity will be two. **(1 Mark)**

(ii) Since it is a zero-order reaction, the unit of rate constant is mole L^{-1} sec^{-1}. **(1 Mark)**

28. Given :

$P_i = 0.30$ atm

$P_t = 0.50$ atm

$$C_2H_5Cl(g) \longrightarrow C_2H_4(g) + HCl(g)$$

P_i	0	0	(At $t = 0$ s)
$P_i - x$	x	x	(At $t = 300$ s)

$$\therefore \quad P_i - x + x + x = P_t$$

$$0.30 + x = 0.50$$

$$x = 0.20$$

$$P_i - x = 0.30 - 0.20$$

$$= 0.10 \text{ atm} \qquad \text{(1 Mark)}$$

For a first-order decomposition reaction, we know that

$$k = \frac{2.303}{t} \log\left(\frac{P_i}{P_i - x}\right) \qquad \text{(½ Mark)}$$

$$= \frac{2.303}{300} \log\left(\frac{0.30}{0.10}\right) \qquad \text{(½ Mark)}$$

$$= \frac{2.303 \times \log 3}{300}$$

$$= \frac{2.303 \times 0.4771}{300}$$

$$k = 0.0037 \text{ s}^{-1} \qquad \text{(1 Mark)}$$

29. (i) Rate = k, i.e Rate = $k[A]^0$

so order of reaction is zero order. **(½ Mark)**

Molecularity = 2 **(½ Mark)**

(ii) Unit of k = mol L^{-1}s^{-1} **(1 Mark)**

30. Rate of reaction is defined as the change in concentration of reactant or product per unit time.

$$\text{Rate of reaction} = \frac{\text{Total change in concentration of reactant or product}}{\text{change in time}}$$

Factors affecting rate of reaction are

(a) Concentration of reactants

(b) Temperature **(1 + 1 = 2 Marks)**

31. 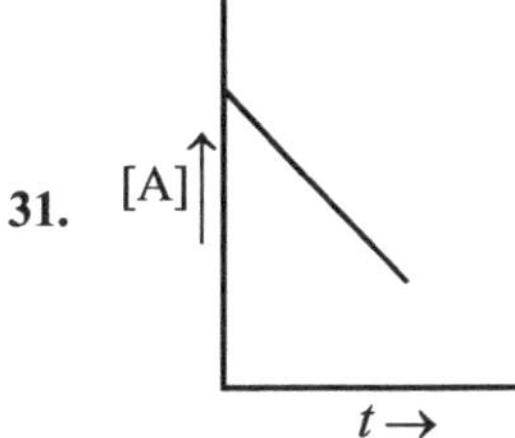

For zero order,

$$k = \frac{1}{t}\left\{[A]_0 - [A]\right\} \text{ or } [A] = -kt + [A]_0$$

∴ (i) Order of reaction = zero

(ii) Slope of the curve = $-k$ **(1 + 1 = 2 Marks)**

32. $$SO_2Cl_2(g) \longrightarrow SO_2(g) + Cl_2(g)$$

Initial	P_0	0	0
after time t	$P_0 - P$	P	P

Total pressure after time t

$(P_t) = P_0 - P + P + P = P_0 + P$

or, $P = P_t - P_0$

∴ $a = P_0$ and $(a - x) = P_0 - P = P_0 - (P_t - P_0)$

$\qquad\qquad = 2P_0 - P_t$ **(½ Mark)**

$$k = \frac{2.303}{t} \log \frac{a}{a - x}$$ **(½ Mark)**

$$= \frac{2.303}{t} \log \frac{P_0}{2P_0 - P_t}$$

$$= \frac{2.303}{100} \log \frac{0.4}{(2 \times 0.4) - 0.7}$$

$\Rightarrow \quad k = \frac{2.303}{100} \log \frac{0.4}{0.8 - 0.7}$ **(½ Mark)**

$$= \frac{2.303}{100} \log \frac{0.4}{0.1} = \frac{2.303}{100} \log(2^2)$$

$\Rightarrow \quad k = \frac{2.303}{100} \times 2 \log 2$ **(½ Mark)**

$$= \frac{2.30 \times 2 \times 0.3010}{100}$$

$k = 1.38 \times 10^{-2}$ sec^{-1} **(1 Mark)**

33. (a) Order $= \frac{1}{2} + 2 = \frac{5}{2} = 2.5$ **(1 Mark)**

(b) For a first order reaction,

$$t_{\frac{1}{2}} = \frac{0.693}{k} = \frac{0.693}{5.5 \times 10^{-14}s^{-1}} = 1.26 \times 10^{13} \text{ sec.}$$ **(1 Mark)**

34. Let $k_1 = k$, $T_1 = 293$ K

∴ $k_2 = 4k_1$, $T_2 = 313$ K

$$\log \frac{k_2}{k_1} = \frac{E_a}{2.303R}\left[\frac{T_2 - T_1}{T_1T_2}\right]$$ **(½ Mark)**

$$\log \frac{4k_1}{k_1} = \frac{E_a}{2.303 \times 8.314}\left[\frac{313 - 293}{293 \times 313}\right]$$ **(½ Mark)**

$$\log 4 = \frac{E_a}{2.303 \times 8.314}\left[\frac{20}{91709}\right]$$

$$0.6021 = \frac{E_a \times 20}{2.303 \times 8.314 \times 91709}$$ **(½ Mark)**

∴ $E_a = \frac{0.6021 \times 2.303 \times 8.314 \times 91709}{20}$ **(½ Mark)**

$= 52863.33$ J mol^{-1}

$= 52.863$ kJ mol^{-1} **(1 Mark)**

35.

Ans 37:

(a) for 1st order reaction:

$$K_t = 2.303 \log\left(\frac{A_0}{A_t}\right) \checkmark$$

$$A_0 = A_0 \qquad A_t = \frac{75}{100} A_0 = \frac{3}{4} A_0$$

$$\Rightarrow K \times 40 = 2.303 \cdot \log\left(\frac{A_0}{3A_0} \times 4\right)$$

$$\Rightarrow K = \frac{2.303}{40}\left(\log 4 - \log 3\right)$$

$$= \frac{2.303}{40} \times 0.1250$$

$$= 0.0071968875 \ min^{-1}$$

$$\approx 0.0072 \ min^{-1} \checkmark$$

Now, 80% complete $\qquad A_t = \frac{20}{100} A_0$

$$K_t = 2.303 \log\left(\frac{A_0}{20 A_0} \times 100\right) \checkmark$$

$$t = \frac{2.303 \times 40 \times \log 5}{2.303 \times 0.125}$$

$$= \frac{40 \times 0.6991 \times 1000}{0.125}$$

$$= 223.712 \ minutes.$$

(Side calculations)

$$\begin{array}{r}0.6021\\0.4771\\\hline 0.1250\end{array}$$

$$\begin{array}{r}2.303\\ \cdot 125\\\hline 11515\\46060\\230300\\\hline .287875\end{array}$$

$$4\overline{)0.287875}$$

$$223.712$$

(b) Order of the reaction is the sum of powers of the concentrations in molarity (or atm) of the reactants in the rate law expression. $\checkmark$

They may be or not be equal to sum of stochiometric coefficient in balanced chemical reaction.

$$R = K[A]^x [B]^y \qquad \text{Rate law expression}$$

$$order = x + y$$

A biomolecular reaction can be made to follow first order kinetics if one of the reactant is taken in large excess, by which there will be no effect in the rate of reaction by changing the concentration of this excess reactant.

For eg: Hydrolysis of ester.

$$CH_3COOCH_3 + H_2O \underset{}{\overset{H^+}{\rightleftharpoons}} CH_3COOH + CH_3-OH$$

water is taken is huge amount and hence have no effect on rate of reaction.

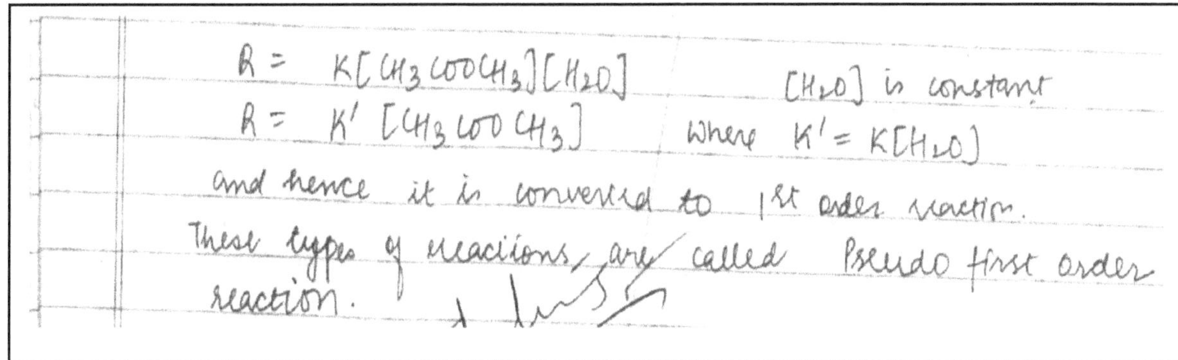

(a) For a first order reaction,

$$k = \frac{2.303}{t} \log\left(\frac{a}{a-x}\right) \qquad \text{(½ Mark)}$$

when $t = 40$ minutes, $x = 0.25a$

$$k = \frac{2.303}{40} \log\left(\frac{a}{a-0.25a}\right) \qquad \text{(½ Mark)}$$

$$\frac{2.303}{40} \log\left(\frac{1}{0.75}\right)$$

$$= 0.058 \times \log\left(\frac{4}{3}\right) \qquad \text{(½ Mark)}$$

$$= 0.058(0.6021 - 0.4771)$$

$$= 7.25 \times 10^{-3} \text{ min}^{-1} \qquad \text{(½ Mark)}$$

Now, when reaction is 80% completed, $x = 0.8a$

$$t = \frac{2.303}{k} \log\left(\frac{a}{a-x}\right)$$

$$t = \frac{2.303}{7.25 \times 10^{-3}} \log\left(\frac{a}{a-0.8a}\right) \qquad \text{(½ Mark)}$$

$$= \frac{2.303}{7.25 \times 10^{-3}} \log\left(\frac{1}{0.2}\right)$$

$$= 317.66 \log 5$$

$$= 317.66 \times 0.6991$$

$$= 222.08 \text{ min} \qquad \text{(½ Mark)}$$

(b) The sum of powers of the concentration of the reactants in the rate law expression is called the order of that chemical reaction.

In a bimolecular reaction, when one reactant is in large excess, the concentration of it does not alter, and the rate of reaction depends only on the other reactant. In these conditions, a bimolecular reaction follows first order kinetics. **(2 Marks)**

36. (a)

$$k = \frac{0.693}{t_{1/2}} \qquad \text{(½ Mark)}$$

at $\quad T_1 = 300$ K, $\quad t_{1/2} = 30$ min

at $\quad T_2 = 320$ K, $\quad t_{1/2} = 10$ min

Thus, $k_1 = \dfrac{0.693}{30}$ and $k_2 = \dfrac{0.693}{10}$ **(½ Mark)**

$$\Rightarrow \quad \frac{k_2}{k_1} = \frac{0.693}{10} \times \frac{30}{0.693} = 3 \qquad \text{(½ Mark)}$$

$$\log\frac{k_2}{k_1} = \frac{E_a}{2.303R}\left(\frac{1}{T_1} - \frac{1}{T_2}\right) \qquad \text{(½ Mark)}$$

$$\Rightarrow \quad \log 3 = \frac{E_a}{2.303 \times 8.314}\left(\frac{1}{300} - \frac{1}{320}\right)$$

$$\text{(½ Mark)}$$

$$\Rightarrow \quad 0.4771 = \frac{E_a}{19.147} \times \frac{(320-300)}{300 \times 320}$$

$$\Rightarrow \quad E_a = 43848 \text{ J/mol} = 43.848 \text{ kJ/mol} \quad \text{(½ Mark)}$$

(b) Conditions for effective collisions are:

(i) Molecules should collide with sufficient kinetic energy i.e. equal to or more than threshold energy.

(ii) Molecules should collide with proper orientation. **(1 Mark)**

(c) Complex reactions are the reactions in which there is a sequence of reactions which leads to product. Order of the reaction is given by the slowest step of the mechanism. In a complex reaction, the order of reaction is equal to the molecularity of the slowest step. **(1 Mark)**

37. **(a)** Rate constant depends on the temperature and directly proportional to each other. On increasing the temperature, the rate constant of reaction increases according to Arrhenius Equation.

$$K = Ae^{-E_a/RT}$$

As temperature increases, the exponential part of the equation becomes less negative and value of rate constant increases. **(1 Mark)**

(b) A + B $\longrightarrow$ Product

Rate = k[A]^2 [B]$^{1/2}$

$$\text{Order} = 2 + \frac{1}{2} = \frac{5}{2} \qquad \textbf{(1 Mark)}$$

(c) For complex reaction, order is given by the slowest step and molecularity of the slowest step is same as the order of the overall reaction. **(1 Mark)**

(d) For first order reaction;

$$t = \frac{2.303}{k} \log \frac{[R]_0}{[R]} \qquad \textbf{(1 Mark)}$$

$$= \frac{2.303}{2 \times 10^{-3}} \log \frac{[6]}{[2]}$$

$$= 550 \text{ s} \qquad \textbf{(1 Mark)}$$

OR

For first order reaction;

$$k = \frac{0.693}{t_{1/2}} = \frac{0.693}{6930} = 0.0001 \text{ years}^{-1} \qquad \textbf{(1 Mark)}$$

It is known that,

$$t = \frac{2.303}{k} \log \frac{[R]_0}{[R]}$$

$$= \frac{2.303}{0.0001} \log \frac{100}{75}$$

$$= 2875 \text{ years} \qquad \textbf{(1 Mark)}$$

38. **(a)** Ratio of neutrons to protons is 2.3 which is not the stable ratio of 1:1 **(1 Mark)**

(b) Age of fossils can be estimated by C-14 decay. All living organisms have C-14 which decays without being replaced back once the organism dies. **(1 Mark)**

(c) carbon-14 atoms decay to stable nitrogen atoms and potassium-40 atoms decay to stable calcium **(1 Mark)**

(d) $t = \dfrac{2.303}{k} \log (C_0/C_t)$ **(½ Mark)**

$C_0 = 20$ g, $C_t = ?$

$t = 10320$ years, $k = \dfrac{0.693}{6000}$ (half-life given in passage)

substituting in equation:

$$10320 = \left[\frac{2.303}{(0.693/6000)} \right] \log \frac{20}{C_t} \qquad \textbf{(½ Mark)}$$

$$0.517 = \frac{\log 20}{C_t} \quad \text{antilog } (0.517) = \frac{20}{C_t}$$

$$3.289 = \frac{20}{C_t} \qquad \textbf{(½ Mark)}$$

$$C_t = 6.17 \text{ g} \qquad \textbf{(½ Mark)}$$

OR

$$t = \frac{2.303}{k} \log (C_0/C_t) \qquad \textbf{(½ Mark)}$$

$C_0 = 32$ g; $C_t = 12$ g

$t = ?, k = \dfrac{0.693}{6000}$ (half life given in passage)

substituting in equation:

$$t = \left[\frac{2.303}{(0.693/6000)} \right] \log \frac{32}{12} \qquad \textbf{(½ Mark)}$$

$$t = \left[\frac{2.303 \times 60000}{0.693} \right] \log 2.667 \qquad \textbf{(½ Mark)}$$

$$t = \left[\frac{2.303 \times 6000 \times 0.4260}{0.693} \right]$$

$$= 8494 \text{ years} \qquad \textbf{(½ Mark)}$$

Temperature Dependence of the Rate of a Reaction and Collision Theory

1. **(c)** (i) ln A (ii) - E$_a$/R **(1 Mark)**

2. No **(1 Mark)**

3. **(a)** Catalyst lowers the activation energy.

(b) There is no effect on Gibbs free energy.

$$(½ + ½ = 1 \text{ Mark})$$

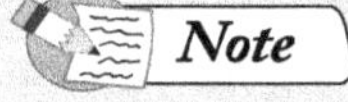

The catalyst provides an alternate pathway for the reaction by lowering the activation energy (E_a) between reactants and products.

Since the energy of reactants or products are not affected by the catalyst, so there will be no effect of catalyst on Gibbs energy.

4. $\log\left(\dfrac{k_2}{k_1}\right) = \dfrac{E_a}{2.303R}\left[\dfrac{1}{T_1} - \dfrac{1}{T_2}\right]$ **(1 Mark)**

$\log\dfrac{0.20}{0.05} = \dfrac{E_a}{2.303R}\left[\dfrac{1}{200} - \dfrac{1}{500}\right]$

$\log 10 = \dfrac{E_a}{19.15}\left(\dfrac{300}{200 \times 600}\right)$ **(1 Mark)**

$E_a = \dfrac{19.15 \times 200 \times 500}{300}$

$E_a = 6383$ J/mol **(1 Mark)**

5. For 1st order reaction, $t_{1/2} = \dfrac{0.693}{k}$

At 300k, $\left(t_{1/2}\right)_1 = \dfrac{0.693}{k_1}$; $k_1 = Ae^{-Ea/RT_1}$ **(½ Mark)**

$\therefore \; k_1 = \dfrac{0.693}{30 \times 60}$; $k_1 = Ae^{-Ea/R.320}$ ... (i) **(½ Mark)**

At 320k, $\left(t_{1/2}\right)_2 = \dfrac{0.693}{k_2}$; $k_2 = Ae^{-Ea/RT_2}$

$\therefore \; k_2 = \dfrac{0.693}{10 \times 60}$; $k_2 = Ae^{-Ea/R.320}$ ... (ii) **(½ Mark)**

$\therefore$ Eq. (ii) ÷ Eq. (i)

$\dfrac{k_2}{k_1} = \dfrac{Ae^{-Ea/R.320}}{Ae^{-Ea/R.300}} = \dfrac{\dfrac{0.693}{10 \times 60}}{\dfrac{0.693}{30 \times 60}}$ **(½ Mark)**

or $e^{\frac{Ea}{R}\left(\frac{1}{300} - \frac{1}{320}\right)} = 3$

or $\dfrac{Ea}{R} \times \dfrac{\cancel{20}}{300 \times \cancel{320}^{\,16}} = 2.303 \log 3$ **(½ Mark)**

or $Ea = 8.314 \times 4800 \times 2.303 \times 0.4771 \times 10^{-3}$ kJ

$= 43.848$ kJ ≈ 43.85 kJ **(½ Mark)**

6. An increase in the temperature of a reaction mixture increases the thermal energy of the molecules that increases the kinetic energy of the molecules.

This leads to an increase in the number of collisions between the reactant molecules that increases the rate of the chemical reaction and therefore the **rate constant K**.

Since the thermal energy increases, the average energy possessed by the molecules increases and therefore the energy required to cross the energy barrier decreases. **(1 Mark)**

Therefore, increase in the temperature decreases the activation Energy (E_a). **(1 Mark)**

7. Given : $T_1 = 300$ K, $T_2 = 320$ K

$(t_{1/2})_1 = 40$ min $\quad (t_{1/2})_2 = 20$ min

To find : activation energy, $E_a = ?$

Solution :

$k_1 = \dfrac{0.693}{(t_{1/2})_1}$; $k_2 = \dfrac{0.693}{(t_{1/2})_2}$ **(1 Mark)**

$k_1 = \dfrac{0.693}{40}$; $k_2 = \dfrac{0.693}{20}$

we know, $\log\dfrac{k_2}{k_1} = \dfrac{E_a}{2.303R}\left(\dfrac{1}{T_1} - \dfrac{1}{T_2}\right)$ **(1 Mark)**

$\therefore \quad \log\dfrac{(0.693/20)}{(0.693/40)} = \dfrac{E_a}{2.303R}\left(\dfrac{1}{300} - \dfrac{1}{320}\right)$

$\log\dfrac{40}{20} = \log 2 = \dfrac{E_a}{2.303 \times 8.314} \times \left(\dfrac{320 - 300}{320 \times 300}\right)$

$\Rightarrow \quad E_a = \dfrac{\log 2 \times 2.303 \times 8.314}{\left(\dfrac{20}{320 \times 300}\right)}$

$= 27663.79$ J mol^{-1} ≈ 27.66 kJ mol^{-1} **(1 Mark)**

8. According to Arrhenius Equation

$\log k = \log A - \dfrac{E_a}{2.303 \, RT}$ ...(i)

Given Equation is $\log k = 14.2 - \dfrac{1.0 \times 10^4}{T}\,K$ ...(ii)

On Comparing Equation (i) or (ii) we get

$\dfrac{E_a}{2.303 \, RT} = \dfrac{1.0 \times 10^4}{T}\,K$ **(1 Mark)**

$E_a = \dfrac{1.0 \times 10^4 \times 2.303 \times R \times T}{T}\,K$

$= \dfrac{1.0 \times 10^4 \times 2.303 \times 8.314 \times T}{T}\,K$

$E_a = 19.14 \times 10^4$ J/mol **(1 Mark)**

For first order reaction, half life period will be

$t_{1/2} = \dfrac{0.693}{k}$

$k = \dfrac{0.693}{t_{1/2}} = \dfrac{0.693}{200}$

$= 3.465 \times 10^{-3}$ min^{-1}

$= 5.7 \times 10^{-5}$ sec **(1 Mark)**

9. Given, $k_1 = 2 \times 10^{-2}$, $k_2 = 4 \times 10^{-2}$

$T_1 = 300K$, $T_2 = 310$ K

$$\log\left(\frac{k_2}{k_1}\right) = \frac{E_a}{2.303R}\left(\frac{T_2 - T_1}{T_1 T_2}\right)$$ **(1 Mark)**

$$\log 2 = \frac{E_a}{2.303 \times 8.314}\left(\frac{310 - 300}{300 \times 310}\right)$$

$$\Rightarrow \quad E_a = \frac{0.301 \times 2.303 \times 8.314 \times 300 \times 310}{10}$$ **(1 Mark)**

$$= 53.598 \text{ kJ mol}^{-1}$$ **(1 Mark)**

10. (a) When surface area of the reactant is reduced, the rate of reaction will also reduce. **(1 Mark)**

(b) A catalyst increases the rate of both forward and backward reactions of a reversible reaction to the same extent. **(1 Mark)**

(c) Increase in temperature reduces the activation energy and thus increases the rate of reaction.

(1 Mark)

11. (a) (i) It is a zero order reaction **(1 Mark)**

(ii)

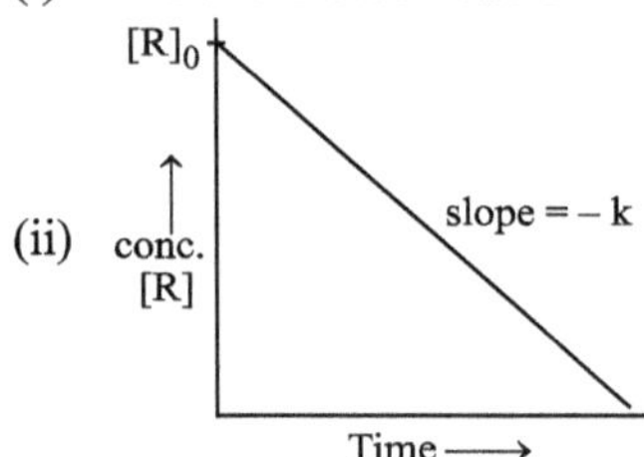

$R = -kt + [R]_0$; $y = mx + c$

The slope of the curve is negative which means concentration of reactant is decreasing with time. **(1 Mark)**

(b) $T_1 = 293$ K   ; $k_1 = k$

$T_2 = 313$ K   ; $k_2 = 4k$

$$\log\frac{k_1}{k_2} = \frac{E_a}{2.303R}\left[\frac{1}{T_2} - \frac{1}{T_1}\right]$$ **(1 Mark)**

$$\log\frac{1}{4} = \frac{E_a}{2.303 \times 8.314}\left[\frac{1}{313} - \frac{1}{293}\right]$$

$$-0.6020 = \frac{E_a}{2.303 \times 8.314}\left[\frac{293 - 313}{(313)(293)}\right]$$ **(1 Mark)**

$$E_a = \frac{-0.6020 \times 2.303 \times 8.314 \times 313 \times 293}{-20}$$

$$E_a = 52854.55 \text{ J mol}^{-1} = 52.854 \text{ kJ mol}^{-1}$$ **(1 Mark)**

12. (a) $k = Ae^{-E_a/RT}$ (Arrhenius equation)

$$\ln k = \ln A - \frac{E_a}{RT}$$

$$y = c + mx$$

$$y = \ln k \text{ ; } x = 1/T$$

$$c = \ln A$$

$$m = -E_a/R$$

A plot of *ln*k v/s $\dfrac{1}{T}$ for a chemical reaction is as straight line. **(1 Mark)**

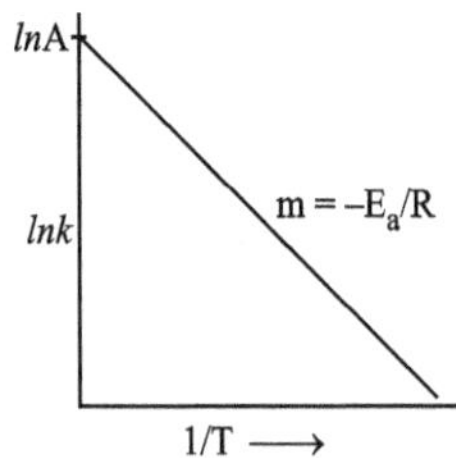

The intercept represents *ln*A, where A = frequency factor or pre-exponential factor.

$$\text{slope} = \frac{-E_a}{R}$$

$$E_a = -(\text{slope} \times R)$$ **(1 Mark)**

Note

High temperature and low activation energy favour larger rate constant, and therefore speed up the reaction. Arrhenius equation is generally a combination of the concepts of activation energy and the Maxwell-Boltzmann distribution.

(b) For first order reaction

$$k = \frac{2.303}{t}\log\frac{a}{a-x}$$ **(½ Mark)**

20% compound has been decomposed in 30 min. i.e. 80% compound is left.

$$k = \frac{2.303}{30}\log\frac{100}{100 - 20}$$ **(½ Mark)**

$$= \frac{2.303}{30}\log 1.25$$

$$= \frac{2.303}{30} \times 0.0969 = 0.0074 \text{ min}^{-1}$$ **(1 Mark)**

$$t_{1/2} = \frac{0.693}{k} = \frac{0.693}{0.0074} = 93.64 \text{ min}$$ **(1 Mark)**

13. (i) For the hydrolysis of methyl acetate to be a pseudo first-order reaction, the reaction should be first order with respect to ester when $[H_2O]$ is constant.

For first order reaction (rate constant is)

$$k = \frac{2.303}{t} \log \frac{a}{a-x} \qquad \text{(½ Mark)}$$

Let $t_1 = 30$ sec, $t_2 = 60$ sec

$$k_1 = \frac{2.303}{30} \log \frac{0.60}{0.30} \qquad \text{(½ Mark)}$$

$$= \frac{2.303}{30} \log 2$$

$$= \frac{2.303}{30} \times 0.3010 = 0.0231 \text{ sec}^{-1} \qquad \text{(1 Mark)}$$

Now, $t_2 = 60$, $k_2 = ?$

$$k_2 = \frac{2.303}{t_2} \log \frac{0.60}{0.15}$$

$$= \frac{2.303}{60} \log 4 = \frac{2.303}{60} \times 0.6021 = 0.0231 \text{ sec}^{-1}$$

So $k_1 = k_2$ **(1 Mark)**

Hence the reaction is pseudo first order reaction.

(ii) Rate $= \dfrac{\Delta x}{\Delta t}$ **(½ Mark)**

$$= \frac{0.30 - 0.15}{60 - 30} = \frac{0.15}{30} \qquad \text{(1 Mark)}$$

$$= 0.005 \text{ mol L}^{-1} \text{ sec}^{-1} \qquad \text{(½ Mark)}$$

14. (i) It is given that the reaction is first order w.r.t reactant A and second order w.r.t reactant B.

$$\therefore \qquad r = k[A][B]^2 \qquad \text{...(i)}$$

Where r is the rate of reaction and k is the rate constant of the reaction.

When concentration of B is doubled, then, let the new rate be r_1

$$r_1 = k[A][2B]^2 \qquad \text{...(ii)}$$

Divide eqns (ii) by (i)

$$\frac{r_1}{r} = \frac{k[A][2B]^2}{k[A][B]^2}$$

$$\frac{r_1}{r} = 4$$

$$\Rightarrow r_1 = 4r$$

thus if the concentration of B is doubled, rate of reaction increased by 4 times. **(1 Mark)**

(ii) If A is present in large excess, then the reaction will be independent of the concentration of A and will be dependent only on the concentration of B. As $[B]^2$ will be the only determining factor in the rate equation the overall order of the reaction will be two. **(1 Mark)**

(b) $t_1 = 30$ min, $a = 50\%$

Rate for 50%

$$k = \frac{2.303}{t_1} \cdot \log \frac{100}{100 - 50}$$

$$k = \frac{2.303}{30} \log 2 \qquad \text{...(i)} \qquad \text{(1 Mark)}$$

For 90% completion, time required $t_2 = ?$, $a = 100$

$a - x = 100 - 90 = 10$

$$k = \frac{2.303}{t_2} \log \frac{a}{a-x} \qquad \text{...(ii)}$$

$$k = \frac{2.303}{t_2} \log \frac{100}{100 - 90} = \frac{2.303}{t_2} \log 10$$

$$= \frac{2.303}{t_2} \qquad \text{(1 Mark)}$$

Put the value of k from eqn (i)

$$t_2 = \frac{2.303}{2.303} \times \frac{30}{\log 2} = \frac{30}{0.3010}$$

$$t_2 = 99.6 \text{ min} = 5.98 \times 10^3 \text{ sec.} \qquad \text{(1 Mark)}$$

15. (a) (i) Differential equation for the respective reaction will be, $\dfrac{dx}{dt} = k[A]^2[B]$ **(1 Mark)**

(ii) Now since,

Rate $= k[A]^2[B]$

$\therefore$ If conc. of A is increased three times.

The rate will increase nine times. **(1 Mark)**

(iii) Rate $= k[A^2][B]$

New rate $= k'[2A]^2[2B]$

$= k'8[A]^2[B]$

When conc. of both A and B are doubled, then the rate will become eight time. **(1 Mark)**

(b) 30% decomposition means x = 30% of a = 0.30 a.

Now, for a first order reaction

$$k = \frac{2.303}{t} \log \frac{a}{a-x}$$ (½ Mark)

$$= \frac{2.303}{40} \log \frac{a}{a-0.30a}$$ (½ Mark)

$$= \frac{2.303}{40} \log \frac{10}{7} \, min^{-1}$$

$$= \frac{2.303}{40} \log 1.428 \, min^{-1}$$

$$= \frac{2.303}{40} \times 0.1548 \, min^{-1}$$

$$= 8.91 \times 10^{-3} \, min^{-1}$$ (½ Mark)

For a first order reaction

$$t_{1/2} = \frac{0.693}{k} = \frac{0.693}{8.91 \times 10^{-3} \, min^{-1}}$$

$$= 77.7 \, min$$ (½ Mark)

16. **(a)** For a first order reaction, show that time required for 99% completion is twice the time required for the completion of 90% of reaction.

(b) Rate constant 'k' of a reaction varies with temperature 'T' according to the equation :

$$\log k = \log A - \frac{E_a}{2.303R} \left(\frac{1}{T} \right)$$

Where E_a is the activation energy. When a graph is plotted for log k Vs. $\frac{1}{T}$, a straight line with a slope of -4250 K is obtained. Calculate 'E_a' for the reaction.

$(R = 8.314 \, JK^{-1} \, mol^{-1})$

4 Chapter — The *d* and *f*-Block Elements

1   *Multiple Choice Questions*

1. The trend of which property is represented by the following graph? **[CBSE Sample 2023-24, U]**

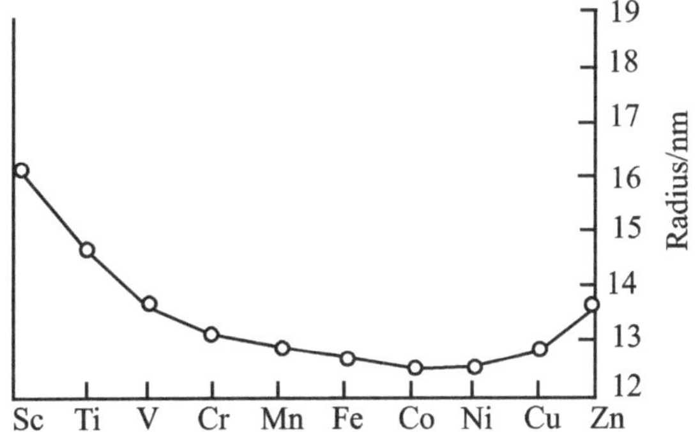

(a) ionization enthalpy

(b) atomic radii

(c) enthalpy of atomization

(d) melting point

2. Which of the following is not considered a transition element? **[CBSE Sample 2023-24, K]**

(a) Scandium

(b) Silver

(c) Vanadium

(d) Zinc

3. Which of the following transition metals shows 4.1 and 4.2 oxidation states? **[All India 2023, Set-I, K]**

(a) Mn   (b) Zn

(c) Sc   (d) Cu

4. Which one among the following metals of 3d series has the lowest melting point? **[All India 2023 Set-II, K]**

(a) Fe   (b) Mn

(c) Zn   (d) Cu

5. Which of the following ions has the electronic configuration $3d^6$? (Atomic number : Mn = 25, Co = 27, Ni = 28) **[Delhi 2023, Set-I, K]**

(a) Ni^{3+} (b) Co^{3+}

(c) Mn^{2+} (d) Mn^{3+}

6. Which property of transition metals enables them to behave as catalysts? **[Delhi 2023, Set-I, K]**

(a) High melting point

(b) High ionisation enthalpy

(c) Alloy formation

(d) Variable oxidation states

7. Which of the following is the reason for Zinc not exhibiting variable oxidation state **[CBSE Sample 2020-21, U]**

(a) inert pair effect

(b) completely filled 3d subshell

(c) completely filled 4s subshell

(d) common ion effect

8. Which of the following is a diamagnetic ion: (Atomic numbers of Sc, V, Mn and Cu are 21, 23, 25 and 29 respectively) **[CBSE Sample 2020-21, U]**

(a) V^{2+} (b) Sc^{3+}

(c) Cu^{2+} (d) Mn^{3+}

9. Which set of ions exhibit specific colours? (Atomic number of Sc = 21, Ti = 22, V=23, Mn = 25, Fe = 26, Ni = 28 Cu = 29 and Zn =30) **[CBSE Sample 2020-21, K]**

(a) $Sc^{3+}, Ti^{4+}, Mn^{3+}$

(b) $Sc^{3+}, Zn^{2+}, Ni^{2+}$

(c) V^{3+}, V^{2+}, Fe^{3+}

(d) $Ti^{3+}, Ti^{4+}, Ni^{2+}$

2 *Assertion Reason/Two Statement Type Questions*

Given below are two statements labelled as Assertion (A) and Reason (R). Select the most appropriate answer from the options given below:

(a) Both (A) and (R) are true and (R) is the correct explanation of (A).

(b) Both (A) and (R) are true, but (R) is not the correct explanation of (A).

(c) (A) is true, but (R) is false.

(d) (A) is false, but (R) is true.

10. **Assertion (A) :** Transition metals show their highest oxidation state with oxygen. **[All India 2023, Set-I, K]**

Reason (R) : The ability of oxygen to form multiple bonds to metals.

11. **Assertion (A):** Transition metals have high enthlpy of atomisation. **[All India 2023 Set-II, U]**

Reason (R): Greater number of unpaired electrons in transition metals results in weak metallic bonding.

3 *Matching Based Questions*

12. Match the properties with the elements of 3d series:

[CBSE Sample 2023-24, K]

(i) lowest enthalpy of atomisation	(p)	Sc
(ii) shows maximum number of oxidation states	(q)	Mn
(iii) transition metal that does not form coloured compounds	(r)	Zn
	(s)	Ti

(a) (i) (r), (ii) (q), (iii) (p)

(b) (i) (r), (ii) (s), (iii) (p)

(c) (i) (p), (ii) (q), (iii) (r)

(d) (i) (s), (ii) (r), (iii) (p)

13. Out of the following transition elements, the maximum number of oxidation states are shown by

[All India 2020, K]

(a) Sc(Z = 21)   (b) Cr(Z = 24)

(c) Mn(Z = 25)   (d) Fe(Z = 26)

4 *Very Short Answer Questions (1 Mark)*

14. Zn^{2+} salts are white while Cu^{2+} salts are coloured. Why?

[All India 2015, K]

15. **[All India 2022, Term-II]**

$E^{\ominus}_{M^{2+}/M}$	Cr	Mn	Fe	Co	Ni	Cu	Zn
	−0.91	−1.18	−0.44	−0.28	−0.25	+0.34	−0.76

From the given $E^{\ominus}$ values of the first row transition elements, answer the following questions :

(i) Why is $E^{\ominus}_{M^{2+}/Mn}$ value highly negative as compared to other elements ?

(ii) What is the reason for the irregularity in the above $E^{\ominus}$ values ?

(iii) Why is $E^{\ominus}_{Cu^{2+}/Cu}$ value exceptionally positive ?

5 *Short Answer Questions (2 or 3 Marks)*

16. (i) Why are melting points of transition metals high?

[All India 2022, Term-II, U]

(ii) Why the transition metals generally form coloured compounds? **[All India 2022, Term-II, U]**

(iii) Why E° value for Mn^{3+}/Mn^{2+} couple is highly positive? **[All India 2022, Term-II, U]**

17. Define transition metals. Why Zn, Cd and Hg are not called transition metals ? How is the variability in oxidation states of transition metals different from that of *p*-block elements? **[All India 2022, Term-II, K]**

18. Account for the following:

a. Ti(IV) is more stable than the Ti (II) or Ti(III).

[All India 2022, Term-II, K]

b. In case of transition elements, ions of the same charge in a given series show progressive decrease in radius with increasing atomic number.

[All India 2022, Term-II, K]

c. Zinc is a comparatively a soft metal, iron and chromium are typically hard.

[CBSE Sample 2021-22, Term-II, U]

19. a. Why are fluorides of transition metals more stable in their higher oxidation state as compared to the lower oxidation state?

[CBSE Sample 2021-22, Term-II, U]

b. Which one of the following would feel attraction when placed in magnetic field: Co^{2+}, Ag^+, Ti^{4+}, Zn^{2+} **[CBSE Sample 2021-22, Term-II, U]**

c. It has been observed that first ionization energy of 5 d series of transition elements are higher than that of 3d and 4d series, explain why?

[CBSE Sample 2021-22, Term-II, U]

20. On the basis of the figure given below, answer the following questions:

[CBSE Sample 2021-22, Term-II, U]

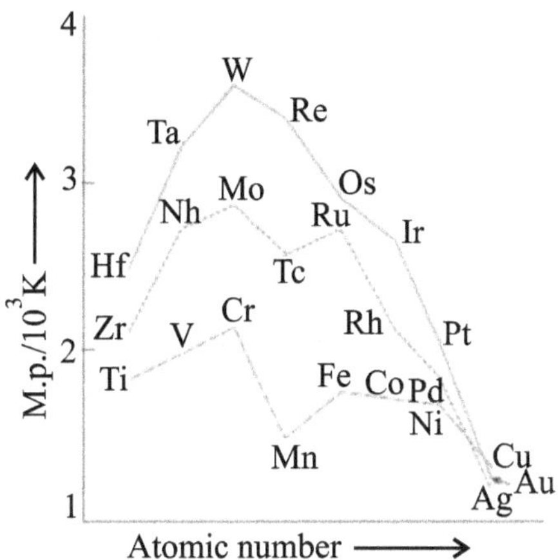

a. Why Manganese has lower melting point than Chromium? **[CBSE Sample 2021-22, Term-II, U]**

b. Why do transition metals of $3d$ series have lower melting points as compared to $4d$ series?

[CBSE Sample 2021-22, Term-II, U]

c. In the third transition series, identify and name the metal with the highest melting point.

[CBSE Sample 2021-22, Term-II, K]

21. Use the data to answer the following and also justify giving reason: **[All India 2019, U]**

	Cr	Mn	Fe	Co
$E^0_{M^{2+}/M}$	-0.91	-1.18	-0.44	-0.28
$E^0_{M^{3+}/M^{2+}}$	-0.41	$+1.57$	$+0.77$	$+1.97$

(a) Which is a stronger reducing agent in aqueous medium, Cr^{2+} or Fe^{2+} and why?

[All India 2019, U]

(b) Which is the most stable ion in +2 oxidation state and why? **[All India 2019, U]**

22. Give reasons : **[All India 2018, U]**

(a) E° value for Mn^{3+}/Mn^{2+} couple is much more positive than that for Fe^{3+}/Fe^{2+}. **[All India 2018, U]**

(b) Iron has higher enthalpy of atomization than that of copper. **[All India 2018, U]**

(c) Sc^{3+} is colourless in aqueous solution whereas Ti^{3+} is coloured. **[All India 2018, U]**

23. What are the transition elements? Write two characteristics of the transition elements.

[Delhi 2015, K]

24. (a) Which metal in the first transition series ($3d$ series) exhibits +1 oxidation state most frequently and why? **[Delhi 2013, K]**

(b) Which of the following cations are coloured in aqueous solutions and why?
Sc^{3+}, V^{3+}, Ti^{4+}, Mn^{2+}
(At. nos. Sc = 21, V = 23, Ti = 22, Mn = 25)

[Delhi 2013, K]

Topic-2: *Some Important Compounds of Transition Elements*

---

1 *Multiple Choice Questions*

1. In the two tetrahedral structures of dichromate ion **[Delhi 2023 Set-I, K]**

(a) 4 Cr – O bond are equivalent in length.

(b) 6 Cr – O bond are equivalent in length.

(c) All Cr – O bond are equivalent in length.

(d) All Cr – O bond are non-equivalent.

2. $KMnO_4$ is coloured due to: **[CBSE Sample 2022-23, K]**

(a) d-d transitions

(b) charge transfer from ligand to metal

(c) unpaired electrons in d orbital of Mn

(d) charge transfer from metal to ligand

4 *Very Short Answer Questions (1 Mark)*

3. Write the formula of an oxo-anion of Manganese (Mn) in which it shows the oxidation state equal to its group number. **[Delhi 2017, K]**

5 *Short Answer Questions (2 or 3 Marks)*

4. Explain the method, of preparation of sodium dichromate from chromite ore. Give the equation representing oxidation of ferrous salts by dichromate ion.

[All India 2019, U]

5. Complete the following reactions: **[All India 2019, U]**

(a) $MnO_2 + KOH + O_2 \longrightarrow$

(b) $I^- + MnO_4^- + H^+ \longrightarrow$

(c) $Cr_2O_7^{2-} + Sn^{2+} + H^+ \longrightarrow$

6. When MnO_2 is fused with KOH in the presence of KNO_3 as an oxidizing agent, it gives a dark green compound (A). Compound (A) disproportionates in acidic solution to give purple compound (B). An alkaline solution of compound (B) oxidises KI to compound (C) whereas an acidified solution of compound (B) oxidises KI to (D). Identify (A), (B), (C), and (D). **[Delhi 2019, A]**

7. Complete and balance the following chemical equations:

(a) $Fe^{2+} + MnO_4^- + H^+ \longrightarrow$ **[All India 2018, U]**

(b) $MnO_4^- + H_2O + I^- \longrightarrow$

8. When chromite ore $FeCr_2O_4$ is fused with NaOH in presence of air, a yellow coloured compound (A) is obtained which on acidification with dilute sulphuric acid gives a compound (B). Compound (B) on reaction with KCl forms a orange coloured crystalline compound (C). **[Delhi 2016, K]**

(i) Write the formulae of the compounds (A), (B) and (C). **[Delhi 2016, K]**

(ii) Write one use of compound (C). **[Delhi 2016, K]**

9. Complete the following chemical equations:

[Delhi 2016, K]

(i) $8MnO_4^- + 3S_2O_3^{2-} + H_2O \rightarrow$

(ii) $Cr_2O_7^{2-} + 3Sn^{2+} + 14H^+ \rightarrow$

---

6   *Long Answer Questions*

10. (I) Account for the following: **[All India 2023, U]**

(i) E^o value for Mn^{3+}/Mn^{2+} couple is much more positive than that for Cr^{3+}/Cr^{2+}.

[All India 2023, U]

(ii) Sc^{3+} is colourless whereas Ti^{3+} is coloured in an aqueous solution. **[All India 2023, U]**

(iii) Actinoids show wide range of oxidation states.

[All India 2023, K]

(II) Write the chemical equations for the preparation of $KMnO_4$ from MnO_2. **[All India 2023, U]**

11. (a) Write the number of unpaired electrons in Cr^{3+}.

(Atomic number of Cr = 24)**[Delhi 2023 Set-III, U]**

(b) Complete the reaction mentioning all the products formed:

$Cr_2O_7^{2-} + 3H_2S + 8H^+ \rightarrow$ **[Delhi 2023 Set-III, K]**

(c) Account for the following:

(i) Mn^{2+} is more stable than Fe^{2+} towards oxidation to +3 state. **[Delhi 2023 Set-III, U]**

(ii) Copper has exceptionally positive value.

[Delhi 2023 Set-III, K]

(iii) Eu^{2+} with electronic configuration [Xe] $4f^7 6s^2$ is a strong reducing agent.

[Delhi 2023 Set-III, K]

12. Answer the following: **[CBSE Sample 2022-23, U]**

(a) Why are all copper halides known except that copper iodide? **[CBSE Sample 2022-23, U]**

(b) Why is the $E^o_{(V^{3+}/V^{2+})}$ value for vanadium comparatively low? **[CBSE Sample 2022-23, U]**

(c) Why HCl should not be used for potassium permanganate titrations?

[CBSE Sample 2022-23, U]

(d) Explain the observation, at the end of each period, there is a slight increase in the atomic radius of d block elements. **[CBSE Sample 2022-23, U]**

(e) What is the effect of pH on dichromate ion solution.

[CBSE Sample 2022-23, U]

13. (a) Account for the following : **[All India 2016, K]**

(i) Mn shows the highest oxidation state of +7 with oxygen but with fluorine, it shows the highest oxidation state of +4. **[All India 2016, U]**

(ii) Cr^{2+} is a strong reducing agent.

[All India 2016, K]

(iii) Cu^{2+} salts are coloured, while Zn^{2+} salts are white. **[All India 2016, U]**

(b) Complete the following equations :

[All India 2016, K]

(i) $2MnO_2 + 4KOH + O_2 \xrightarrow{\Delta}$

(ii) $Cr_2O_7^{2-} + 14H^+ + 6I^- \longrightarrow$

14. The elements of $3d$ transition series are given as :

Sc Ti V Cr Mn Fe Co Ni Cu Zn

Answer the following : **[All India 2016, K]**

(i) Write the element which shows maximum number of oxidation states. Give reason.**[All India 2016, K]**

(ii) Which element has the highest m.p ?

[All India 2016, K]

(iii) Which element shows only + 3 oxidation state ?

[All India 2016, K]

(iv) Which element is a strong oxidizing agent in +3 oxidation state and why ? **[All India 2016, K]**

Topic-3: **The Lanthanoids, The Actinoids**

2 *Assertion Reason/Two Statement Type Questions*

Given below are two statements labelled as Assertion (A) and Reason (R). Select the most appropriate answer from the options given below:

(a) Both (A) and (R) are true and (R) is the correct explanation of (A).

(b) Both (A) and (R) are true, but (R) is not the correct explanation of (A).

(c) (A) is true, but (R) is false.

(d) (A) is false, but (R) is true.

1. **Assertion (A) :** Magnetic moment values of actinides are lesser than the theoretically predicted values.

   Reason (R) : Actinide elements are strongly paramagnetic. **[CBSE Sample 2022-23, U]**

5 *Short Answer Questions (2 or 3 Marks)*

2. Account for the following : **[All India 2022, Term-II]**

   (i) Transition metals and their compounds show catalytic activities.

   (ii) Zn, Cd and Hg are non-transition elements.

   (iii) Zr and Hf are of almost identical atomic radii.

3. Give reasons for the following: **[Delhi 2019, U]**

   (i) Transition elements and their compounds act as catalysts. **[Delhi 2019, K]**

   (ii) $E°$ value for (Mn^{2+} |Mn) is negative whereas for (Cu^{2+} |Cu) is positive. **[Delhi 2019, U]**

   (iii) Actinoids show irregularities in their electronic configuration. **[Delhi 2019, K]**

4. Give reasons : **[Delhi 2016, K]**

   (i) Mn shows the highest oxidation state of +7 with oxygen but with fluorine it shows the highest oxidation state of +4. **[Delhi 2016, K]**

   (ii) Transition metals show variable oxidation states. **[Delhi 2016, K]**

   (iii) Actinoids show irregularities in their electronic configurations. **[Delhi 2016, K]**

5. (a) How would you account for the following **[Delhi 2015, K]**

   (i) Actinoid contraction is greater than lanthanoid contraction. **[Delhi 2015, K]**

   (ii) Transition metals form coloured compounds. **[Delhi 2015, K]**

   (b) Complete the following equation :
   $$2MnO_4^- + 6H^+ + 5NO_2^- \longrightarrow$$ **[Delhi 2015, K]**

6. How would you account for the following ? **[Delhi 2013, K]**

   (i) Transition metals exhibit variable oxidation states. **[Delhi 2013, K]**

   (ii) Zr (Z = 40) and Hf (Z = 72) have almost identical radii. **[Delhi 2013, K]**

   (iii) Transition metals and their compounds act as catalyst. **[Delhi 2013, K]**

7. Complete the following chemical equations :

   (i) $Cr_2O_7^{2-} + 6Fe^{2+} + 14H^+ \longrightarrow$

   (ii) $2CrO_4^{2-} + 2H^+ \longrightarrow$

   (iii) $2MnO_4^- + 5C_2O_4^{2-} + 16H^+ \longrightarrow$ **[Delhi 2013, K]**

6 *Long Answer Questions*

8. Attempt any five of the following: **[CBSE Sample 2023-24, U]**

   (a) Which of the following ions will have a magnetic moment value of 1.73 BM.
   $Sc^{3+}, Ti^{3+}, Ti^{2+}, Cu^{2+}, Zn^{2+}$ **[CBSE Sample 2023-24, U]**

   (b) In order to protect iron from corrosion, which one will you prefer as a sacrificial electrode, Ni or Zn? Why? (Given standard electrode potentials of Ni, Fe and Zn are −0.25 V, −0.44 V and −0.76 V respectively.) **[CBSE Sample 2023-24, U]**

   (c) The second ionization enthalpies of chromium and manganese are 1592 and 1509 kJ/mol respectively. Explain the lower value of Mn. **[CBSE Sample 2023-24, U]**

   (d) Give two similarities in the properties of Sc and Zn. **[CBSE Sample 2023-24, K]**

   (e) What is actinoid contraction? What causes actinoid contraction? **[CBSE Sample 2023-24, K]**

   (f) What is the oxidation state of chromium in chromate ion and dichromate ion? **[CBSE Sample 2023-24, K]**

   (g) Write the ionic equation for reaction of KI with acidified $KMnO_4$. **[CBSE Sample 2023-24, K]**

9. (I) Account for the following: [All India 2023, U]

(i) Transition metals form alloys.

[All India 2023, K]

(ii) Ce^{4+} is a strong oxidising agent.

[All India 2023, U]

(II) Write one similarity and one difference between chemistry of Lanthanoids and Actinoids.

[All India 2023, K]

(III) Complete the following ionic equation:

$$Cr_2O_7^{2-} + 2OH^- \longrightarrow$$ [All India 2023, K]

10. (a) Why is chemistry of actinoids complicated as compared to lanthanoids? [Delhi 2023 Set-I, K]

(b) Complete the following reaction and justify that it is a disproportionation reaction: [Delhi 2023 Set-I, K]

$$3\,MnO_4^{2-}\,4H^+ \rightarrow \underline{\quad} + \underline{\quad} + 2\,H_2O.$$

(c) The given graph shows the trends in melting points of transition metals: [Delhi 2023 Set-I, U]

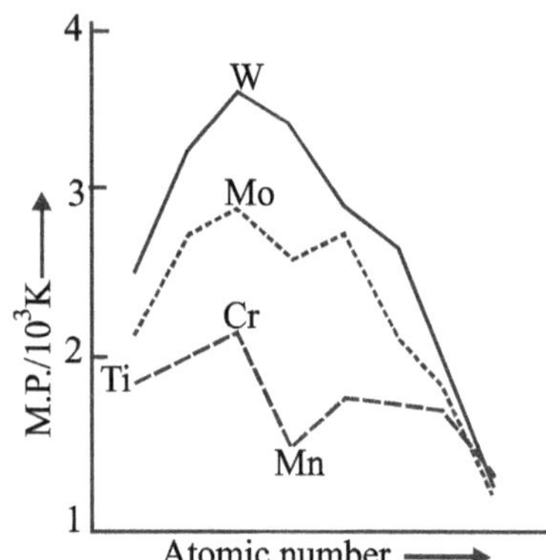

Explain the reason why Cr has highest melting point manganese (Mn) a lower melting point.

11. (a) A transition element X has electronic configuration $[Ar]\,4s^2\,3d^3$. [Delhi 2023, Set-I, U]

Predict its likely oxidation states.

(b) Complete the reaction mentioning all the products formed: [Delhi 2023, Set-I, K]

$$2KMnO_4 \xrightarrow{\Delta}$$

(c) Account for the following:

(i) In the 3d transition series, zinc has the lowest enthalpy of atomisation. [Delhi 2023, Set-I, K]

(ii) Cu^+ ion is unstable in aqueous solution.

[Delhi 2023, Set-I, K]

(iii) Actinoids show more number of oxidation states than lanthanoids. [Delhi 2023, Set-I, K]

12. (a) Account for the following: [All India 2020, U]

(i) Copper (I) compounds are white whereas copper (II) compounds are coloured.

[All India 2020, U]

(ii) Chromates change their colour when kept in an acidic solution. [All India 2020, U]

(iii) Zn, Cd, Hg are considered as *d*-block elements but not as transition elements.

[All India 2020, K]

(b) Calculate the spin-only moment of Co^{2+} (Z = 27) by writing the electronic configuration of Co and Co^{2+}.

[All India 2020, U]

13. (a) Give three points of difference between lanthanoids and actinoids. [All India 2020, K]

(b) Give reason and select one atom/ion which will exhibit asked property:

(i) Sc^{3+} or Cr^{3+} (Exhibit diamagnetic behaviour)

[All India 2020, U]

(ii) Cr or Cu (High melting and boiling point)

[All India 2020, U]

14. (a) Give reasons: [Delhi 2020, U]

(i) Transition metals and their compounds show catalytic activities. [Delhi 2020, K]

(ii) Separation of a mixture of lanthanoid elements is difficult. [Delhi 2020, U]

(iii) Zn, Cd and Hg are soft and have low melting point. [Delhi 2020, U]

(b) Write the preparation of the following:

(i) $Na_2Cr_2O_7$ from Na_2CrO_4 [Delhi 2020, K]

(ii) K_2MnO_4 from MnO_2

15. (a) Account for the following: [Delhi 2020, U]

(i) Ti^{3+} is coloured, whereas Sc^{3+} is colourless in aqueous solution. [Delhi 2020, U]

(ii) Cr^{2+} is a strong reducing agent.

[Delhi 2020, U]

(b) Write two similarities between chemistry of lanthanoids and actinoids. [Delhi 2020, K]

(c) Complete the following ionic equation:

$$3MnO_4^{2-} + 4H^+ \longrightarrow$$ [Delhi 2020, K]

16. (a) Account for the following: [All India 2017, K]

(i) Transition metals show variable oxidation states. [All India 2017, K]

(ii) Zn, Cd and Hg are soft metals.

[All India 2017, K]

(iii) $E°$ value for the Mn^{3+}/Mn^{2+} couple is highly positive $(+1.57 V)$ as compared to Cr^{3+}/Cr^{2+} **[All India 2017, K]**

(b) Write one similarity and one difference between the chemistry of lanthanoid and actinoid elements. **[All India 2017, K]**

17. (a) Following are the transition metal ions of $3d$ series: $Ti^{4+}, V^{2+}, Mn^{3+}, Cr^{3+}$ **[All India 2017, K]** (Atomic numbers: $Ti = 22, V = 23, Mn = 25, Cr = 24$) Answer the following:

(i) Which ion is most stable in an aqueous solutions and why? **[All India 2017, K]**

(ii) Which ion is a strong oxidising agent and why? **[All India 2017, K]**

(iii) Which ion is colourless and why? **[All India 2017, K]**

(b) Complete the following equations:

(i) $2MnO_4^- + 16 H^+ + 5S^{2-} \longrightarrow$

(ii) $KMnO_4 \xrightarrow{\text{heat}}$ **[All India 2017, K]**

18. (a) Account for the following : **[Delhi 2017, K]**

(i) Transition metals form large number of complex compounds. **[Delhi 2017, K]**

(ii) The lowest oxide of transition metal is basic whereas the highest oxide is amphoteric or acidic. **[Delhi 2017, U]**

(iii) $E°$ value for the Mn^{3+}/Mn^{2+} couple is highly positive $(+1.57 V)$ as compare to Cr^{3+}/Cr^{2+}. **[Delhi 2017, U]**

(b) Write one similarity and one difference between the chemistry of lanthanoid and actinoid elements. **[Delhi 2017, K]**

19. (a) (i) How is the variability in oxidation states of transition metals different from that of the p-block elements ? **[Delhi 2017, K]**

(ii) Out of Cu^+ and Cu^{2+}, which ion is unstable in aqueous solution and why? **[Delhi 2017, K]**

(iii) Orange colour of $Cr_2O_7^{2-}$ ion changes to yellow when treated with an alkali. Why ? **[Delhi 2017, K]**

(b) Chemistry of actinoids is complicated as compared to lanthanoids. Give two reasons. **[Delhi 2017, K]**

20. (a) Account for the following. **[All India 2015, K]**

(i) Zr and Hf have almost similar atomic radii. **[All India 2015, K]**

(ii) Transition metals show variable oxidation states. **[All India 2015, K]**

(iii) Cu^+ ion is unstable in aqueous solution. **[All India 2015, K]**

(b) Complete the following equations.

(i) $2 MnO_2 + 4 KOH + O_2 \rightarrow$

(ii) $2 Na_2CrO_4 + 2H^+ \rightarrow$ **[All India 2015, K]**

21. (a)

$E°_{M^{2+}/M}$	Cr	Mn	Fe	Co	Ni	Cu
	-0.91	-1.81	-0.44	-0.28	-0.25	$+0.34$

From the given data of $E°$ values, answer the following questions. **[All India 2015, U]**

(i) Why is $E°_{(Cu^{2+}/Cu)}$ value exception-ally positive? **[All India 2015, U]**

(ii) Why is $E°_{(Mn^{2+}/Mn)}$ value highly negative as compared to other elements? **[All India 2015, U]**

(iii) Which is a stronger reducing agent Cr^{2+} or Fe^{2+} ? Give reason. **[All India 2015, U]**

(b) Why do actinoids show a wide range of oxidation states? Write on similarity between the chemistry of lanthanoids and actinoids. **[All India 2015, K]**

22. (a) Complete the following equations :

(i) $Cr_2O_7^{2-} + 2OH^- \longrightarrow$ **[All India 2014, K]**

(ii) $MnO_4^- + 4H^+ + 3e^- \longrightarrow$

(b) Account for the following :

(i) Zn is not considered as a transition element. **[All India 2014, K]**

(ii) Transition metals form a large number of complexes. **[All India 2014, K]**

(iii) The $E°$ value for the Mn^{3+}/Mn^{2+} couple is much more positive than that for Cr^{3+}/Cr^{2+} couple. **[All India 2014, K]**

23. (i) With reference to structural variability and chemical reactivity, write the differences between lanthanoids and actinoids. **[All India 2014, K]**

(ii) Name a member of the lanthanoid series which is well known to exhibit +4 oxidation state. **[All India 2014, K]**

(iii) Complete the following equation : $MnO_4^- + 8H^+ + 5e^- \longrightarrow$ **[All India 2014, K]**

(iv) Out of Mn^{3+} and Cr^{3+}, which is more paramagnetic and why? **[All India 2014, U]** (Atomic nos. : $Mn = 25, Cr = 24$)

24. (a) How do you prepare : **[Delhi 2014, K]**

    (i) K_2MnO_4 from MnO_2 ?

    (ii) $Na_2Cr_2O_7$ from Na_2CrO_4 ?

  (b) Account for the following :

    (i) Mn^{2+} is more stable than Fe^{2+} towards oxidation to +3 state. **[Delhi 2014, U]**

    (ii) The enthalpy of atomization is lowest for Zn in $3d$ series of the transition elements.

     [Delhi 2014, U]

    (iii) Actinoid elements show wide range of oxidation states. **[Delhi 2014, K]**

25. (i) Name the element of $3d$ transition series which shows maximum number of oxidation states. Why does it show so ? **[Delhi 2014, K]**

  (ii) Which transition metal of $3d$ series has positive $E°$ (M^{2+}/M) value and why ? **[Delhi 2014, K]**

  (iii) Out of Cr^{3+} and Mn^{3+}, which is a stronger oxidizing agent and why ? **[Delhi 2014, K]**

  (iv) Name a member of the lanthanoid series which is well known to exhibit +2 oxidation state.

    [Delhi 2014, K]

  (v) Complete the following equation :

$$MnO_4^- + 8H^+ + +5e^- \longrightarrow$$ **[Delhi 2014, K]**

26. (a) Give reasons for the following : **[All India 2013, U]**

    (i) Mn^{3+} is a good oxidising agent.

     [All India 2013, U]

    (ii) $E°_{M^{2+}/M}$ values are not regular for first row transition metals ($3d$ series).

     [All India 2013, U]

    (iii) Although 'F' is more electronegative than 'O', the highest Mn fluoride is MnF_4, whereas the highest oxide is Mn_2O_7. **[All India 2013, U]**

  (b) Complete the following equations :

    (i) $2CrO_4^{2-} + 2H^+ \longrightarrow$ **[All India 2013, K]**

    (ii) $KMnO_4 \xrightarrow{\text{heat}}$

27. (a) Why do transition elements show variable oxidation states? **[All India 2013, K]**

    (i) Name the element showing maximum number of oxidation states among the first series of transition metals from Sc $(Z = 21)$ to Zn $(Z = 30)$.

     [All India 2013, K]

    (ii) Name the element which shows only +3 oxidation state. **[All India 2013, K]**

  (b) What is lanthanoid contraction ? Name an important alloy which contains some of the lanthanoid metals.

    [All India 2013, K]

Solutions

Topic-1: *Position in the Periodic Table, Electronic Configurations of the d-Block Elements, General Properties of the Transition Elements (d-Block)*

1. **(b)** atomic radii **(1 Mark)**

2. **(d)** Zinc **(1 Mark)**

3. **(d)** Cu;
   Cu shows (+1) and (+2) oxidation states **(1 Mark)**

4. **(c)** Zinc(Zn) has lowest melting point in the 3d series due to absence of unpaired d electrons.

5. **(b)** $Mn = 4s^2\,3d^5$, so $Mn^{2+} = 3d^5$ and $Mn^{3+} = 3d^4$
   $CO = 4s^2\,3d^7$, so $CO^{3+} = \mathbf{3d^6}$
   $Ni = 4s^2\,3d^8$, so $Ni^{3+} = 3d^7$
   Thus, option **(b)** is correct. **(1 Mark)**

6. **(d)** Transition metals act as good catalysts due to their ability to exhibit variable oxidation states.
   This property allows them to bond with and form different compounds and therefore participation in various chemical reactions.
   Therefore, option **(d)** is correct. **(1 Mark)**

7. **(b)** **(1 Mark)**

8. **(b)** **(1 Mark)**

9. **(c)** **(1 Mark)**

10. **(a)** Oxygen forms double bonds to metals in order to stabilize the highest oxidation states of metal. e.g.
   $$[MnO_4^-] \longrightarrow Mn \text{ in } (+7) \text{ oxidation state.}$$
   Structure ::
   $$\begin{bmatrix} & O & \\ & \| & \\ & Mn & \diagdown O^- \\ O \diagup & \diagdown & \\ O & & O \end{bmatrix}$$ **(1 Mark)**

11. **(c)** Transition metals have high enthalpy of atomisation due to presence of unpaired electrons in d-orbital. Generally, greater the number of valence electrons, stronger is the resultant metallic bonding.

12. **(a)** (i) (r), (ii) (q), (iii) (p)
   Zinc has no unpaired electrons in 3d or 4s orbitals, so enthalpy of atomization is low $Mn = 3d^5 4s^2$ shows + 2, +3, +4, +5, +6 and +7 oxidation state, maximum number in 3d series

13. **(c)** $Mn(25) = 1s^2\,2s^2\,2p^6\,3s^2\,3p^6\,3d^5\,4s^2$
   Mn has maximum number of oxidation states from +1 to +7 due to $3d^5 4s^2$.

14. Zn^{2+} salts are white due to the presence of completely filled *d*-orbitals, while Cu^{2+} has incompletely filled *d*-orbitals. **(1 Mark)**

15.

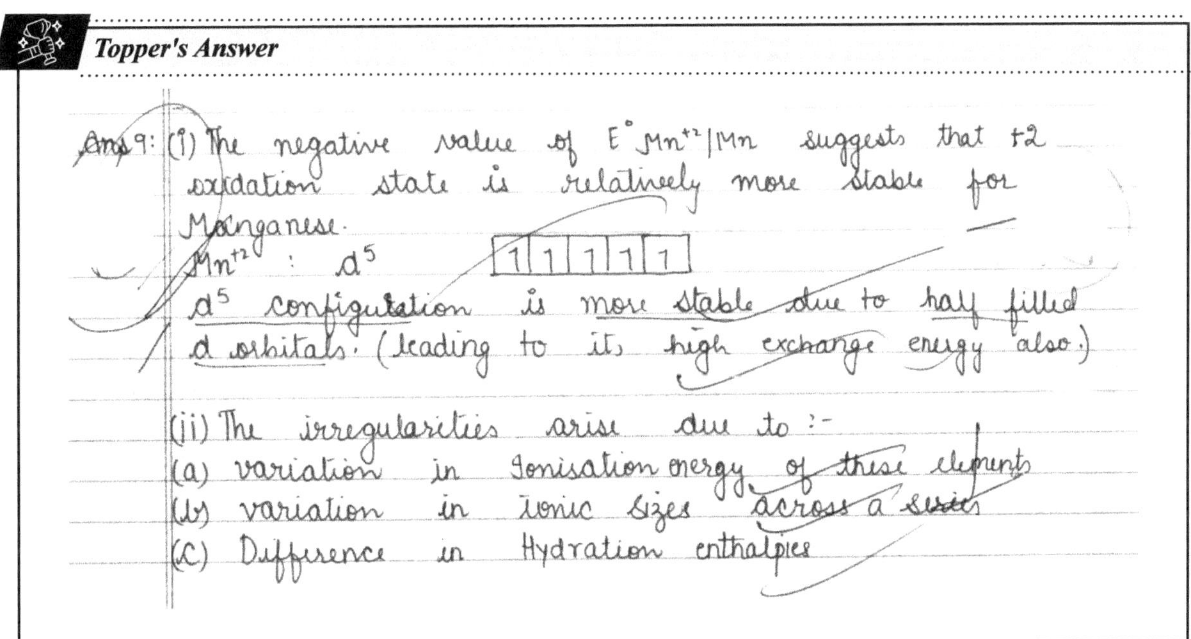

Topper's Answer

Ans 9: (i) The negative value of $E^\circ\, Mn^{+2}/Mn$ suggests that +2 oxidation state is relatively more stable for Manganese.
Mn^{+2} : d^5 [↑|↑|↑|↑|↑]
d^5 configuration is more stable due to half filled d orbitals. (leading to its high exchange energy also.)

(ii) The irregularities arise due to :-
(a) variation in Ionisation energy of these elements
(b) variation in ionic sizes across a series
(c) Difference in Hydration enthalpies

> (iii) The electrode potential values involve :-
>
> $$Cu(s) \longrightarrow Cu(g)$$
> $$Cu(g) \longrightarrow Cu^+(g) + e^- \qquad \Delta H_{IE_1}$$
> $$Cu^+(g) \longrightarrow Cu^{+2}(g) + e^- \qquad \Delta H_{IE_2}$$
> $$Cu^{+2}(g) + H_2O \longrightarrow Cu^{+2} \, aq \qquad \Delta H_{Hyd}$$
>
> For Copper, The second ionisation enthalpy is very high and thus Hydration enthalpy does not compensate for the stablisation of Cu^{+2} aq
>
> $\therefore \quad Cu^{+2}(aq) \longrightarrow Cu(s)$ has a +ve $E°$

16. (i) Transition metals have high melting point due to presence of unpaired electrons which are responsible for high strength of metallic bond. **(1 Mark)**

   (ii) Transition metals generally form coloured compounds due to absorption of radiation from visible light region to excite the electrons from its one position to another position in d-orbitals. (d-d transition) **(1 Mark)**

   (iii) The outer electronic configuration in case of Mn^{3+} is $3d^4$ while in case of Mn^{2+} is $3d^5$ which is more stable as compare to $3d^4$ due to which it shows highly positive E° value for Mn^{3+}/Mn^{2+}. **(1 Mark)**

17. Those elements which have d subshell, partially filled with electrons and has ability to form cations with an incompletely filled d orbitals are known as Transition Metals.

Zn, Hg and Cd have completely filled orbitals in their ground state due to which they are not called as transition metals.

In case of p-block the lower oxidation states are favoured by the heavier members due to inert pair effect while in case of d-block the higher oxidation states are favoured by the heavier members. **(3 Marks)**

18. (a) Ti is having electronic configuration [Ar] $3d^2 \, 4s^2$. Ti (IV) is more stable as Ti^{4+} acquires nearest noble gas configuration on loss of 4 e^-. **(1 Mark)**

   (b) In case of transition elements, ions of the same charge in a given series show progressive decrease in radius with increasing atomic number. **(1 Mark)** As the new electron enters a d-orbital each time the nuclear charge increases by unity. The shielding effect of a d-electron is not that effective, hence the net electrostatic attraction between the nuclear charge and the outermost electron increases and the ionic radius decreases.

   (c) Iron and Chromium are having high enthalpy of atomization due to the presence of unpaired electrons, which accounts for their hardness. However, Zinc has low enthalpy of atomization as it has no unpaired electron. Hence zinc is comparatively a soft metal. **(1 Mark)**

19. (a) The ability of fluorine to stabilize the highest oxidation state is attributed to the higher lattice energy or high bond enthalpy. **(1 Mark)**

   (b) Co^{2+} has three unpaired electrons so it would be paramagnetic in nature, hence Co^{2+} ion would be attracted to magnetic field. **(1 Mark)**

   (c) The transition elements of $5d$ series have intervening $4f$ orbitals. There is greater effective nuclear charge acting on outer valence electrons due to the weak shielding by $4f$ electrons. Hence first ionisation energy of $5d$ series of transition elements are higher than that of $3d$ and $4d$ series. **(1 Mark)**

20. (a) Manganese is having lower melting point as compared to chromium, as it has highest number of unpaired electrons, strong interatomic metal bonding, hence no delocalisation of electrons. **(1 Mark)**

   (b) There is much more frequent metal – metal bonding in compounds of the heavy transition metals i.e $4d$ and $5d$ series, whixh accounts for lower melting point of $3d$ series. **(1 Mark)**

   (c) Tungsten **(1 Mark)**

21. (a) Cr^{2+} is a stronger reducing agent because the more negative the electrode potential, greater is the reducing power of the electrode.

$$E^\circ_{Cr^{2+}/Cr} = -0.91 > E^\circ_{Fe^{2+}/Fe} = -0.44$$

(½ + ½ = 1 Mark)

(b) Mn^{2+} is the most stable ion because it ($Mn^{2+} - d^5$)

[1][1][1][1][1] has half filled electronic configuration and it has most negative reduction

potential $E^\circ_{Mn^{2+}/Mn} = -1.18V$ **(½ + ½ = 1 Mark)**

22. (a) E° value for $Mn^{3+} \mid Mn^{2+}$ couple is much more positive than that of $Fe^{3+} \mid Fe^{2+}$. This is explained as below : **(1 Mark)**

$$Mn(Z=25) \longrightarrow Mn^{2+} \longrightarrow Mn^{3+}$$
$$[Ar]3d^5\,4s^2 \qquad [Ar]3d^5 \qquad [Ar]3d^4$$

$$Fe(Z=26) \longrightarrow Fe^{2+} \longrightarrow Fe^{3+}$$
$$[Ar]3d^6\,4s^2 \qquad [Ar]3d^6 \qquad [Ar]3d^5$$

We see that Mn is more stable in Mn^{2+} state due to extra stable half-filled configuration of the d-orbital. In Mn^{3+}, the stability is less. As a results, Mn^{3+} readily gets reduced to Mn^{2+}.

On the other hand, Fe is more stable in +3 state due to stable d^5 configuration. Thus it does not reduce to Fe^{2+} easily. **(1 Mark)**

(b) Iron has higher enthalpy of atomization than copper. Enthalpy of atomisation depends on the number of metallic bonds which in turn depends on the number of unpaired electrons. Iron ([Ar] $3d^64s^2$) has 4 unpaired e^-s while copper ([Ar] $3d^{10}4s^1$) has only one unpaired electron. Thus, iron forms stronger metallic bonds and thus has higher enthalphy of atomisation. **(1 Mark)**

(c) Sc^{3+} is colourless in aqueous solution whereas Ti^{3+} is coloured. The colour of transition metal ions is due to d-d transitions. Sc^{3+} is [Ar] $3d^0$ i.e., a stable noble gas configuration thus no d-d transition and hence, no colour. Ti^{3+} has one unpaired e^- which results in d-d transition and hence colour. **(1 Mark)**

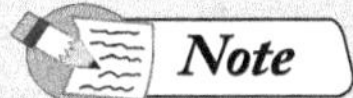

Color in octahedral complexes:

Weak field ligand	*Strong field ligand*
• Δ_0 *small*	• *Δ0 large*
• *High spin complex*	• *Low spin complex*
• *Absorb yellow / orange / red end of spectra*	• *Absorb violet / blue / green end of spectra*
• *Transmit violet / blue / green end of spectra*	• *Transmit yellow / orange/redendofspectra*

23. The elements having incomplete $(n-1)d$-sub-shell are called d-block element or transition element.

The name transition given to the elements of d-block because they are placed between s-block and p-block elements. **(1 Mark)**

Characteristic of transition metal (element) are as follows.

1. Transition elements show variable oxidation state.

2. Transition elements have tendency to form complex.

(1 Mark)

24. (a) Copper exhibits + 1 O.S. because after loss of one electron, it acquire $3d^{10}$ configuration and becomes fully filled and hence stable. **(1 Mark)**

(b) V^{3+} ($3d^2$), Mn^{2+} ($3d^5$) ions are coloured in aqueous solution because they have unpaired electrons in d-subshell. **(1 Mark)**

Topic-2: **Some Important Compounds of Transition Elements**

1. (b) In the structure of dichromate ion, it consists of two tetrahedra sharing one corner with Cr – O – G bond angle of 126°. The six terminal Cr – O bonds have same bond length (163 pm) due to resonance.

(1 Mark)

2. (b) charge transfer from ligand to metal

The Mn atom in $KMnO_4$ has $+7$ oxidation state with electron configuration $[Ar]3d^04s^0$ Since no unpaired electrons are present, d–d transitions are not possible. The molecule should, therefore, be colourless.

Its intense purple due to L→M (ligand to metal) charge transfer 2p(L) of O to 3d(M) of Mn. **(1 Mark)**

3. The formula of an oxo-anion of Manganese in which it shows the oxidation state equal to it's group number is permanganate MnO_4^- or $KMnO_4$. **(1 Mark)**

4. Chromite ore $\longrightarrow$ sodium dichromate

STEPS

- Chromite ore is fused with sodium carbonate in excess of air to give yellow solution of Na_2CrO_4 (sodium chromate). **(1 Mark)**

$$4FeCr_2O_4 + 8Na_2CO_3 + 7O_2 \longrightarrow$$
Chromite ore

$$8Na_2CrO_4 + 2Fe_2O_3 + 8CO_2$$
Sod. chromate
(yellow)

- Yellow sodium chromate is filtered and acidified with sulphuric acid to give orange coloured sodium dichromate. **(1 Mark)**

$$2Na_2CrO_4 + 2H^+ \longrightarrow Na_2Cr_2O_7 + H_2O + 2Na^+$$
Sod. dichromate
(orange colour)

Ferrous salts (Fe^{2+}) are oxidised to ferric (Fe^{3+}) salts when they are treated with acidified $K_2Cr_2O_7$.

$$Cr_2O_7^{2-} + 6Fe^{2+} + 14H^+ \longrightarrow 2Cr^{3+} + 6Fe^{3+} + 7H_2O$$

(1 Mark)

5. (a) $2MnO_2 + 4KOH + O_2 \rightarrow 2K_2MnO_4 + 2H_2O$

(1 Mark)

(b) $10I^- + 2MnO_4^- + 16H^+ \rightarrow 2Mn^{2+} + 8H_2O + 5I_2$

(1 Mark)

(c) $Cr_2O_7^{2-} + 3Sn^{2+} + 14H^+ \rightarrow 2Cr^{3+} + 3Sn^{4+} + 7H_2O$

(1 Mark)

6.

Topper's Answer

A — K_2MnO_4

Potassium manganate

B — $KMnO_4$

Potassium permanganate

C — KIO_3 (or IO_3^-)

Potassium iodate

D — I_2

Iodine

$$MnO_2 \xrightarrow[KNO_3]{KOH} \underset{\underset{(A)}{Green}}{K_2MnO_4} \xrightarrow{H^+} \underset{\underset{(B)}{Purple}}{KMnO_4} + MnO_2$$

$$\underset{(B)}{KMnO_4} \xrightarrow[H^+]{KI} \underset{(D)}{Mn^{2+} + I_2,}$$

$$\underset{(B)}{KMnO_4} \xrightarrow[OH^-]{KI} \underset{(C)}{MnO_2 + IO_3 + OH^-}$$

$$(½ + ½ + ½ + ½ = \textbf{2 Marks})$$

7. (a) $MnO_4^- + 8H^+ + 5e^- \rightarrow Mn^{2+} + 4H_2O$

$Fe^{2+} \rightarrow Fe^{3+} + 1e^- \times 5$

$\overline{MnO_4^- + 5\,Fe^{2+} + 8H^+ \rightarrow Mn^{2+} + 5\,Fe^{3+} + 4H_2O}$

(1 Mark)

(b) $[MnO_4^- + 2H_2O + 3e^- \rightarrow MnO_2 + 4OH^-] \times 2$

$I^- + 6OH^- \rightarrow IO_3^- + 3H_2O + 6e^-$

$\overline{2MnO_4^- + I^- + H_2O \rightarrow 2MnO_2 + IO_3^- + 2OH^-}$

(1 Mark)

8. (i) On fusing chromite ore $FeCr_2O_4$ with NaOH in presence of air it give yellow coloured compound(A)

$4FeCr_2O_4 + 16NaOH + 7O_2 \longrightarrow$

$\qquad\qquad 8Na_2CrO_4 + 2Fe_2O_3 + 5H_2O$

$\qquad\qquad\qquad\qquad (A)$

On acidification with dil. H_2SO_4 it forms sodium dichromate (B)

$2\underset{(B)}{Na_2CrO_4} + 2H^+ \longrightarrow Na_2Cr_2O_7 + 2Na^+ + H_2O$

$\underset{(B)}{Na_2Cr_2O_7} + 2KCl \longrightarrow \underset{(C)}{K_2Cr_2O_7} + 2NaCl$

So, the formula of compounds are

(A) Sodium chromate – Na_2CrO_4

(B) Sodium dichromate – $Na_2Cr_2O_7$

(C) Potassium dichromate – $K_2Cr_2O_7$ **(1 Mark)**

(ii) potassium dichromate $K_2Cr_2O_7$ is used as an oxidizing agent   **(1 Mark)**

9. (i) $8MnO_4^- + 3S_2O_3^{2-} + H_2O \longrightarrow$

$\qquad\qquad 8MnO_2 + 6SO_4^{2-} + 2OH^-$ **(1 Mark)**

(ii) $Cr_2O_7^{2-} + 3Sn^{2+} + 14H^+ \longrightarrow$

$\qquad\qquad 3Sn^{4+} + 2Cr^{3+} + 7H_2O$

(1 Mark)

10. (a) (I) (i) The third ionization energy of Mn is very large compare to Cr. The 3rd ionization of Mn corresponds to Mn^{2+} (d^5) $\longrightarrow$ Mn^{3+} (d^4) which implies the stability of d^5 (half - filled) system, hence, more positive Mn^{3+}/Mn^{2+} reduction potential.   **(1 Mark)**

(ii) Sc (21) $\longrightarrow 3d^1 4s^2$; $Sc^{3+} \longrightarrow 3d^0\,4s^0$

Ti (22) $\longrightarrow 3d^2 4s^2$; $Ti^{3+} \longrightarrow 3d^1\,4s^0$

Ti^{3+} shows the d-d transition in its aqueous complex, $[Ti(H_2O)_6]^{3+}$ and this is responsible for colour of the aqueous solution.   **(1 Mark)**

(iii) Actinoids show in general (+3) oxidation state. The elements, in the first half of the series frequently exhibit higher oxidation states because they have 5f, 6d, 7s orbitals of comparable energies.   **(1 Mark)**

(II) $KMnO_4$ is prepared by fusion of MnO_2 with an alkali metal hydroxide and an oxidizing agent like KNO_3.

$2MnO_2 + 4KOH + O_2 \longrightarrow \underset{(dark\ green)}{2K_2MnO_4} + 2H_2O$

$3K_2MnO_4 + 4H^+ \longrightarrow 2KMnO_4 + MnO_2 + 2H_2O$

(2 Marks)

11. (a) Electronic configuration of Cr (24) = [Ar] $3d^5\,4\,s^1$

Electronic configuration of Cr^{3+} = [Ar] $3d^3$

(1 Mark)

Hence, there are three unpaired electrons in Cr^{3+}.

(b) $Cr_2O_7^{2-} + 3\,H_2S + 8\,H^+ \rightarrow 2\,Cr^{3+} + 3\,S + 7\,H_2O$

(1 Mark)

(c) (i) Electronic configuration of Mn^{2+} = [Ar] $3d^5$ (half filled)

Electronic configuration of Fe^{2+} = [Ar] $3d^6$

Since, Mn^{2+} has half filled configuration. So, it is stable. While Fe^{2+} has 6 electrons in the outermost shell. It tends to loose one electron to attain stable half filled configuration.

(1 Mark)

(ii) $E^{\circ}_{M^{2+}/M}$ value of any metal depends on the atomization enthalpy, ionisation enthalpy and hydration enthalpy. It is related to sum of enthalpy changes taking place in the following steps:

$M\,(s) + \Delta_a H \rightarrow M\,(g)$

$M\,(g) + \Delta_i H \rightarrow M^{2+} + 2\,e^-$

$M^{2+}(g) + aq \rightarrow M^{2+}(aq) + \Delta_{hyd}H$

Copper has high value of and low hydration enthalpy.

Hence, the $E^{\circ}_{M^{2+}/M}$ value for copper is positive.   **(1 Mark)**

(iii) Electronic configuration of Eu = [Xe] $4f^7 6s^2$

Electronic configuration of Eu^{2+} = [Xe] $4f^7$

Eu^{2+} has half filled f^7 configuration. It acts as a strong reducing agent to attain common +3 oxidation state. **(1 Mark)**

12. **(a)** Cu^{2+} oxidizes iodide ion to iodine. **(1 Mark)**

(b) The low value for V is related to the stability of V^{2+} (half-filled t_{2g} level) **(1 Mark)**

(c) Permanganate titrations in presence of hydrochloric acid are unsatisfactory since hydrochloric acid is oxidised to chlorine. **(1 Mark)**

(d) The d orbital is full with ten electrons and shield the electrons present in the higher s-orbital to a greater extent resulting in increase in size. **(1 Mark)**

(e) The chromates and dichromates are interconvertible in aqueous solution depending upon pH of the solution. Increasing the pH (in basic solution) of dichromate ions a colour change from orange to yellow is observed as dichromate ions change to chromate ions. **(1 Mark)**

13. **(a)** **(i)** Mn shows the highest oxidation states of +7 with oxygen because it can form $p\pi - d\pi$ multiple bonds involving 2p-orbitals of oxygen and 3d orbitals of Mn. On the other hand, Mn shows the highest oxidation state of +4 with F because it forms single bond with F due to unavailability of 2p-orbitals in F for multiple bonding. **(1 Mark)**

(ii) Cr^{2+} has d^4 configuration while Cr^{3+} has d^3 configuration with half filled t_{2g} orbitals which makes Cr^{3+} more stable than Cr^{2+}. Cr^{2+} easily lose electron to attain stability and form Cr^{3+} and act as a reducing agent. **(1 Mark)**

(iii) Cu^{2+} has one unpaired e^- in d-orbitals, thereby allowing for the d-d transition and forming coloured salts, whereas Zn^{2+} has fully filled d-orbitals and does not form coloured salts. **(1 Mark)**

(b) **(i)** $2MnO_2 + 4KOH + O_2 \longrightarrow 2K_2MnO_4 + 2H_2O$ **(1 Mark)**

(ii) $Cr_2O_7^{2-} + 14H^+ + 6I^- \longrightarrow 2Cr^{3+} + 3I_2 + 7H_2O$ **(1 Mark)**

14. **(i)** Mn shows maximum number of oxidation states. This is because the valence shell electronic configuration of Mn is $3d^5 4s^2$. In Mn, d-orbitals are half-filled so that it can lose all seven valence electrons. **(1½ Marks)**

(ii) Cr has the highest melting point due to availability of maximum number of unpaired electrons, which results an increase in strength of metallic bond. **(1 Mark)**

(iii) Sc shows only the +3 oxidation state because it has one $3d$ and two $4s$ electrons. So, it can lose maximum of three electrons. **(1 Mark)**

(iv) Mn shows strong oxidising character in the +3 oxidation state because it acquires highly stable $3d^5$ configuration in the +2 oxidation state. **(1½ Marks)**

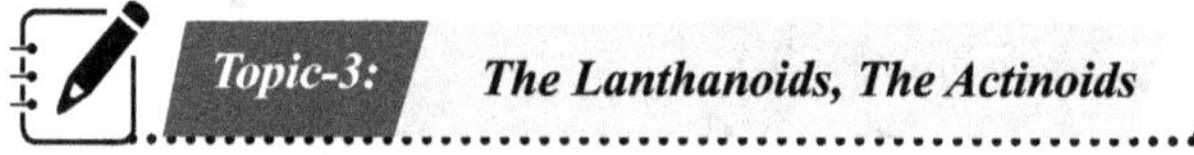
Topic-3: **The Lanthanoids, The Actinoids**

1. **(b)** Both A and R are true but R is not the correct explanation of A. **(1 Mark)**

The magnetic moment is less as the 5f electrons of actinides are less effectively shielded which results in quenching of orbital contributions , they are strongly paramagnetic due to presence of unpaired electrons.

2.

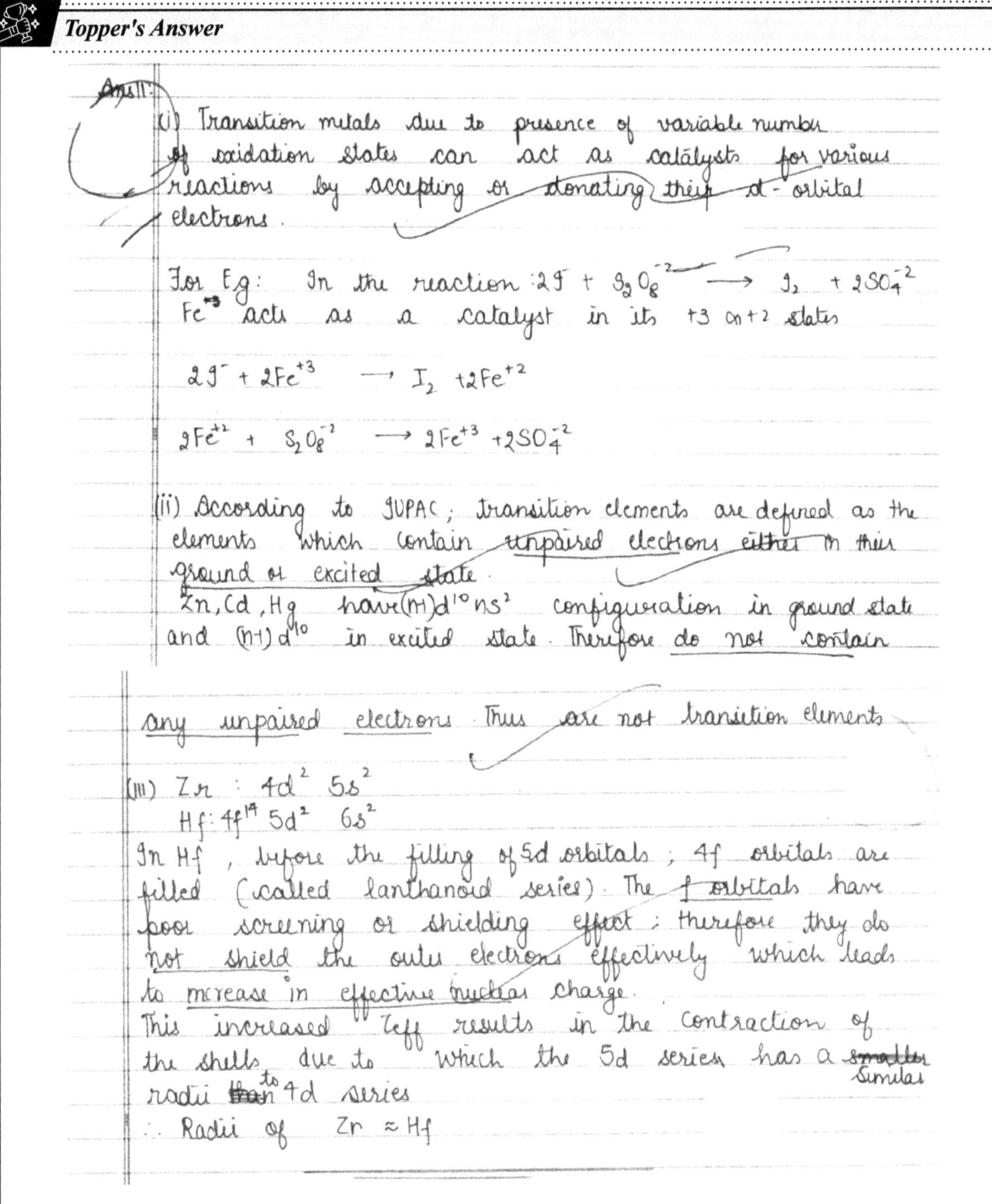

Topper's Answer

Ans:

(i) Transition metals due to presence of variable number of oxidation states can act as catalysts for various reactions by accepting or donating their d-orbital electrons.

For Eg: In the reaction: $2I^- + S_2O_8^{-2} \longrightarrow I_2 + 2SO_4^{-2}$
Fe^{+3} acts as a catalyst in its +3 or +2 states

$2I^- + 2Fe^{+3} \longrightarrow I_2 + 2Fe^{+2}$

$2Fe^{+2} + S_2O_8^{-2} \longrightarrow 2Fe^{+3} + 2SO_4^{-2}$

(ii) According to IUPAC; transition elements are defined as the elements which contain unpaired electrons either in their ground or excited state.
Zn, Cd, Hg have $(n-1)d^{10}ns^2$ configuration in ground state and $(n-1)d^{10}$ in excited state. Therefore do not contain any unpaired electrons. Thus are not transition elements.

(iii) $Zr : 4d^2 5s^2$
$Hf : 4f^{14} 5d^2 6s^2$
In Hf, before the filling of 5d orbitals; 4f orbitals are filled (called lanthanoid series). The f-orbitals have poor screening or shielding effect; therefore they do not shield the outer electrons effectively which leads to increase in effective nuclear charge.
This increased Z_{eff} results in the contraction of the shells, due to which the 5d series has a similar radii to 4d series
∴ Radii of $Zr \approx Hf$

3. (i) Transition elements and their compounds act as catalyst because

    (1) They have ability to show variable oxidation state and form complexes.

    (2) Transition metal also provide large surface area for the reaction to occur. **(1 Mark)**

(ii) $E^\circ_{(M^{2+}/M)}$ for any metal is related to the sum of ethalpy changes taking place in following steps :

$$M(s) + \Delta_a H \rightarrow M(g)$$
$$M(g) + \Delta_i H \rightarrow M^{2+}(g)$$
$$M^{2+}(g) + aq \rightarrow M^{2+}(aq) + \Delta_{hyd.} H$$

Cu has high enthalpy of atomisation $\Delta_a H$ and low enthalpy of hydration ($\Delta_{hyd.} H$). The high energy required to transform Cu(s) to Cu^{2+} (aq) is not balanced by its hydration enthalpy.

$\therefore$ E° value for Cu^{2+}/Cu is positive. **(1 Mark)**

(iii) Actinoids show irregularities in their electronic configuration because the energy difference between $5f$, $6d$, $7s$ subshell of the actinides is very small and hence electrons can be accommodated in any of them. **(1 Mark)**

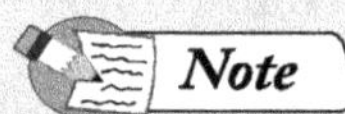

Actinoid contraction is more pronounced than lanthanoid contraction in the series due to poor sheilding effect of 5f electrons. Consequently energy of 5f, 6d, 7s subshells nearly become comparable.

4. (i) Mn shows the highest oxidation state of +7 with oxygen because it can form $p\pi - d\pi$ multiple bonds using $2p$ orbitals of oxygen and $3d$ orbitals of Mn. On the other hand with fluorine, Mn shows the highest oxidation state of +4 because it can form only single bond. **(1 Mark)**

(ii) The variable oxidation state of transition metal are due to the participation of ns and $(n-1)d$ electrons in bonding. **(1 Mark)**

(iii) Actinoids show irregularities in their electronic configuration because there are very less energy difference in $6d$, $7s$, and $5f$ subshell, hence an electron can be occupied in any of the subshells. **(1 Mark)**

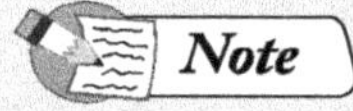

Due to contraction in size in Actinoid Series, energies of 6d, 7s and 5f orbitals become comparable. Therefore actinoid shows number of oxidation state and irregularity in their electronic configuration.

5. (a) (i) In actinoids, $5f$-orbitals are filled. So these element show actinoid contraction due to poor shielding effect of $5f$-subshells. So the effective nuclear charge experienced by electrons in valence shells in case of actinoids is much more than that experienced by electrons in valence shells in case of lanthanoids. Hence, the size contraction in actinoids is greater than that in lanthanoids. **(1 Mark)**

(ii) Transition metals form coloured compounds because under the influence of magnetic effect of ligands, d-subshell of metal is split into two groups name t_{2g} and e_g or t_{2g} this is called d-d-splitting, *these two subsets* have different energies and the difference between energies is equivalent to energy of visible light. Thus in a d-d-transition some wavelength of visible region are absorbed by the ion and complementary colour of reflected wavelength is seen. Hence they are coloured compound. **(1 Mark)**

(b) $$2MnO_4^- + 6H^+ + 5NO_2^- \longrightarrow 2\,Mn^{2+} + 5\,NO_3^- + 3H_2O$$ **(1 Mark)**

6. (i) The energy difference between $(n-1)\,d$ and ns orbitals of transition metal atoms is very small, so the electrons from both these orbitals can participate in bonding and hence they show variable oxidation states. **(1 Mark)**

(ii) Due to Lanthanoid contraction, Hf has size similar to that of Zr. **(1 Mark)**

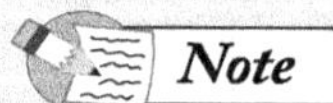

Lanthanoid contraction is due to the poor shielding of one 4f electron by another in the same sub-shell. Lanthanoid contraction causes the radii of the members of the third transition series to be very similar to those of the corresponding members of the second series.

(iii) The transition metals and their compounds behave as catalyst due to the presence of partly filled d-orbitals and exhibiting various oxidation states. They form unstable intermediate complex with reactants and thus lowering the energy of activation. They also provide a suitable surface for the reaction to occur. **(1 Mark)**

7. (i) $$Cr_2O_7^{2-} + 6Fe^{2+} + 14H^+ \longrightarrow$$
$$2Cr^{3+} + 6Fe^{3+} + 7H_2O$$ **(1 Mark)**

(ii) $2CrO_4^{2-} + 2H^+ \longrightarrow Cr_2O_7^{2-} + H_2O$ **(1 Mark)**

(iii) $2MnO_4^- + 5C_2O_4^{2-} + 16H^+ \longrightarrow$

$$2Mn^{2+} + 8H_2O + 10CO_2$$ **(1 Mark)**

8. (a) Both Ti^{3+} and Cu^{2+} have 1 unpaired electron, so the magnetic moment for both will be 1.73 BM

(b) Zn, it has a more negative electrode potential so will corrode itself in place of iron.

(c) Mn^+ has $3d^5 4s^1$ configuration and configuration of Cr^+ is $3d^5$, therefore, ionisation enthalpy of Mn^+ is lower than Cr^+.

(d) Sc and Zn both form colourless compound and are diamagnetic.

(e) The decrease in the atomic and ionic radii with increase in atomic number of actinoids due to poor shielding effect of 5f electron.

(f) In both chromate and dichromate ion the oxidation state of Cr is +6

(g) $10I^- + 2MnO_4^- + 16H^+ \rightarrow 2Mn^{2+} + 8H_2O + 5I_2$
        (1 each, any 5)

9. (I) (i) Alloys are solid solutions. The transition elements have minimal difference in their atomic sizes. So, the lattice points are replaceable by atoms of different elements in solid states.   **(1 Mark)**

(ii) Ce^{4+} $(4f^0)$ has a tendency to form Ce^{3+} $(4f^1)$.

$$\left(E^0_{Ce^{4+}/Ce^{3+}} = +1.74\ V \right)$$

It has very high positive standard electrode potential which favours the formation of Ce^{3+}. However, $Ce^{4+} \longrightarrow Ce^{3+}$ conversion is slow enough to use as oxidizing agent in analytical chemistry.   **(1 Mark)**

[**Note:** $4f^0 \rightarrow$ the empty orbital gets extra stability like half-filled and full filled subshells]

(II) **Similarities:**

(i) Both series of elements experience contraction in atomic sizes from left to right.

(ii) The general oxidation state shown by these elements (+3).   **(1 Mark)**

Differences:

(i) Most of the actinoids are radioactiars in comparison to lanthanoids.

(ii) Actinoids are highly reactive metals why they are finely divided.

(iii) Magnetic properties of actinoids are more complex than lanthanoids.   **(1 Mark)**

(III) $Cr_2^{+6} O_7^{2-} + 2OH^- \longrightarrow 2Cr^{+6} O_9^{2-} + H_2O$
      (dichromate)   (chromate)

This reaction is dependent on pH.   **(1 Mark)**

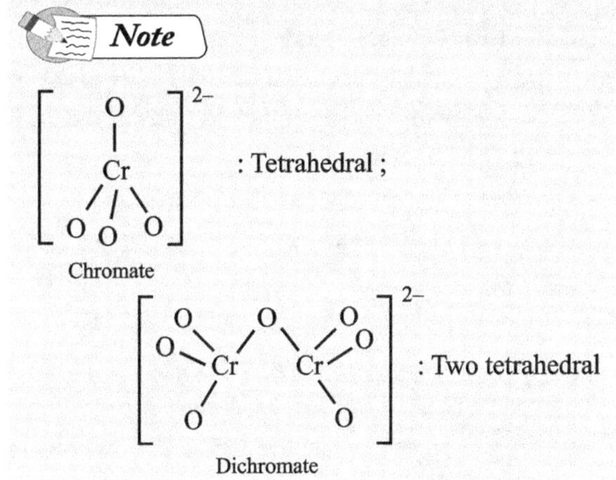

10. (a) Actinoids show wide range of oxidation states. They have strong tendency towards complex formation in comparison to lanthanoids. Furthermore, many of the actinoid elements are radioactive which make the study of actinoids complicated.   **(1 Mark)**

(b) $3 MnO_4^{2-} + 4H^+ \rightarrow 2 MnO_4^- + MnO_2 + 2 H_2O$
In this reaction, MnO_4^{2-} is reduced to MnO_2 as well as oxidised to MnO_4^-. Hence, it is a disproportionation reaction.   **(2 Marks)**

(c) Generally, transition metals have high melting and boiling points. Manganese has half-filled stable configuration, its enthalpy of atomization is low and hence its melting point is also low. Also, greater the number of valence electrons, stronger is the resultant bonding. As, chromium has more number of unpaired electrons than manganese so it has strong bonding and hence, has high melting point than manganese.
        (2 Marks)

11. (a) The given electronic configuration has two electrons in 4s and three electrons in 3d subshell.

So, it can lose two 4s-electrons to exhibit +2 and also one or two electrons from the 3d-subshell to exhibit +3 and +4 states.

So, the species X = V (Vanadium) can exhibit V^{2+}, V^{3+} and V^{4+} states.   **(1 Mark)**

(b) Heating of $KMnO_4$ at 513 K causes it to decompose into potassium manganate, manganese oxide and dioxygen.

$$2KMnO_4 \xrightarrow{\Delta} K_2MnO_4 + MnO_2 + O_2 \quad \textbf{(1 Mark)}$$

(c) **(i)** Zinc has the lowest enthalpy of atomization due to the absence of unpaired electrons that results in weak interatomic forces. **(1 Mark)**

(ii) Cu^+ ion is unstable in aqueous solution because its hydration enthalpy is smaller than that of Cu^{2+} ion which is smaller than Cu^+. **(1 Mark)**

(iii) Actinoids show more number of oxidation states than lanthanoids because of the participation of the electrons of the 5f, 6d and 7s - subshells.

This is due to the poor shielding of these electrons and small energy gap between them. **(1 Mark)**

12. **(a)** **(i)** $_{29}Cu = 1s^2\ 2s^2\ 2p^6\ 3s^23p^63d^{10}\ 4s^1$

$Cu^+ = 1s^2\ 2s^2\ 2p^6\ 3s^23p^63d^{10}$

$Cu^{2+} = 1s^2\ 2s^2\ 2p^6\ 3s^23p^63d^9$

Due to unpaired electron, Cu^{2+} is coloured and due to all paired electrons, Cu^+ is white. **(1 Mark)**

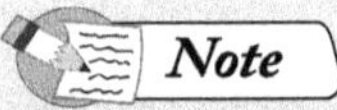

> **Note**
>
> *d–d transition impart colouration to certain compounds which have unpaired electrons.*

(ii) In acidic solution, yellow coloured chromate ions change to orange coloured dichromate ions.

$$2CrO_4^{2-} + 2H^+ \longrightarrow Cr_2O_7^{2-} + H_2O \text{ (1 Mark)}$$

(iii) Zn, Cd and Hg are in d-block of modern periodic table but they have fully filled (d^{10}) d-orbitals, hence they are not considered as transition elements. **(1 Mark)**

> **Note**
>
> *General electronic configuration of transition elements is $(n-1)d^{1-9}ns^2$. Elements which have partially filled d-orbital are considered as transition elements.*

(b) $_{27}Co = 1s^2\ 2s^2\ 2p^6\ 3s^2\ 3p^6\ 3d^7\ 4s^2$

$Co^{2+} = 1s^2\ 2s^2\ 2p^6\ 3s^2\ 3p^6\ 3d^7$ **(1 Mark)**

$3d$

Unpaired electrons, $n = 3$

Spin only magnetic moment $= \sqrt{n(n+2)}$ B.M.

$= \sqrt{3(3+2)}$ B.M. $= \sqrt{15}$ B.M. $= 3.87$ B.M. **(1 Mark)**

> **Note**
>
> *Spin only magnetic moment is given by unpaired electrons only.*

13. **(a)**

	Lanthanoids		Actinoids
(i)	Lanthanoid contraction is the consequence of poor shielding by 4*f*-electrons.	(i)	Actinoid contraction is greater from element to element resulting from poorer shielding by 5*f*-electrons.
(ii)	Most common oxidation state in lanthanoids is +3.	(ii)	There is a greater range of oxidation states because 5*f*, 6*d* and 7*s* levels are of comparable energies.
(iii)	Less tendency of complex formation. Lanthanoids are non-radioactive, except promethium.	(iii)	These are more reactive metals. Actinoids are radioactive.

(1 + 1 + 1 = 3 Marks)

(b) **(i)** $_{21}Sc = 1s^2\ 2s^2\ 2p^6\ 3s^23p^63d^1\ 4s^2$

$Sc^{3+} = 1s^2\ 2s^22p^6\ 3s^23p^6$

Because of no unpaired electrons, Sc^{3+} is diamagnetic. **(1 Mark)**

> **Note**
>
> *When a magnetic field is applied to substance, diamagnetic substances are repelled by the applied field.*
>
> $Cr^{3+} = 1s^2\ 2s^2\ 2p^6\ 3s^2\ 3p^6\ 3d^3$
>
> *It has 3 unpaired electrons, hence paramagnetic.*

(ii) $_{24}Cr = 1s^2\ 2s^2\ 2p^6\ 3s^23p^63d^5\ 4s^1$

$3d$ $\qquad\qquad$ $4s$

$_{29}Cu = 1s^2\ 2s^2\ 2p^6\ 3s^2\ 3p^6\ 3d^{10}\ 4s^1$

$3d$ $\qquad\qquad$ $4s$

Due to greater number of unpaired electrons which lead to metallic bonding, Cr has high melting point than Cu.

Due to high enthalpy of atomisation, Cr has high boiling point than that of Cu. **(1 Mark)**

> **Note**
>
> _Greater number of unpaired electrons leads to stronger interatomic interaction resulting in higher enthalpy of atomisation._

14. **(a)** **(i)** The catalytic activity of transition metals is due to their characteristic of multiple oxidation states and formation of complex compounds. **(1 Mark)**

Transition metals utilise vacant orbitals to form bond between reactant molecules and atoms on the surface of catalyst. This increases the concentration of reactants at the catalyst surface and also weakens the bonds in the reacting molecules.

(ii) Lanthanoid elements have similar chemical properties, therefore separation of a mixture of lanthanoid elements is difficult. **(1 Mark)**

> **Note**
>
> _Lanthanoid contraction in 4f series causes similarities in the properties of the elements._

(iii) Zn, Cd and Hg are soft and have low melting point due to completely filled orbitals. Their electrons are not involved in the interatomic metallic bonding. **(1 Mark)**

(b) **(i)** $2Na_2CrO_4 + H_2SO_4 \longrightarrow$
$$Na_2Cr_2O_7 + Na_2SO_4 + H_2O \quad \textbf{(1 Mark)}$$

(ii) $2MnO_2 + 4KOH + O_2 \xrightarrow{\Delta}$
$$2K_2MnO_4 + 2H_2O \quad \textbf{(1 Mark)}$$

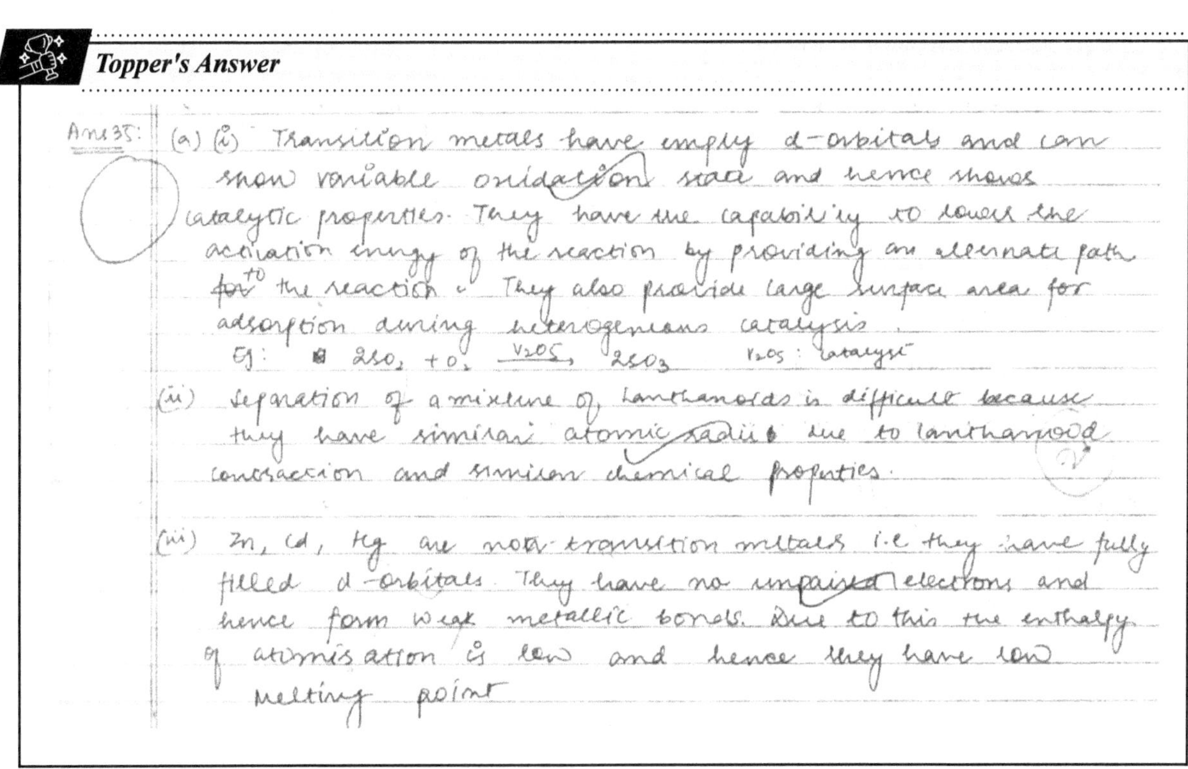

Topper's Answer

(Sodium chromate)

(b) (i) Na_2CrO_4 is converted to sodium dichromate $Na_2Cr_2O_7$ by reacting it in an acidic medium like in dil H_2SO_4

$$2Na_2CrO_4 + 2H^+ \longrightarrow Na_2Cr_2O_7 + 2Na^+ + H_2O$$

(ii) Potassium manganate K_2MnO_4 is prepared by pyrolusite ore (MnO_2) by fusing it with KOH followed with oxidation by atmospheric oxygen or HNO_3.

$$2MnO_2 + 4KOH + O_2 \longrightarrow 2K_2MnO_4 + 2H_2O$$

15. (a) (i) Ti^{3+} has an unpaired electron ($3d^1$), whereas Sc^{3+} has no unpaired electron, therefore d-d transition is possible in Ti^{3+}.

Hence, Ti^{3+} is coloured and Sc^{3+} is colourless. **(1 Mark)**

Note

When white light falls on the transition metal compounds, some wave length is absorbed and promotes electrons from t_{2g} to e_g within the same d-subshell. The remainder light is reflected which imparts, particular colour to the compound.

(ii) Upon oxidation Cr^{2+} becomes Cr^{3+}

$$Cr^{3+}: \quad 3d \quad \uparrow\ \uparrow\ \uparrow\ \ \ \ \ \ 4s\ \square$$
$$\underbrace{\quad}_{t_{2g}}\ \underbrace{\quad}_{e_g}$$

In Cr^{3+}, the t_{2g} level is half-filled which makes it very stable. Hence, Cr^{2+} can easily oxidise to Cr^{3+} or we can say that Cr^{2+} is a strong reducing agent. **(1 Mark)**

(b) (i) Both (lanthanoids and actinoids) show +3 as the most common oxidation state. **(1 Mark)**

(ii) As the atomic number increases, both show a contraction of radii. **(1 Mark)**

(c) $3MnO_4^{2-} + 4H^+ \longrightarrow 2MnO_4^- + MnO_2 + 2H_2O$ **(1 Mark)**

16. (a) (i) Transition metals exhibit a variety of oxidation states. The variable oxidation states of transition metals are due to involvement of ns and $(n-1)$ d-electrons in bonding. The lower oxidation state is generally exhibited when only ns-electrons are involved in bonding and higher oxidation states when ns as well as $(n-1)$ d electrons are involved. **(1 Mark)**

(ii) Zn, Cd and Hg are soft metals due to presence of completely filled orbitals. Therefore absence of any unpaired electrons results into weak metal-metal bonding. **(1 Mark)**

(iii) Mn^{2+} exists in half-filled d^5 state which is very stable while Mn^{3+} has d^4 configuration which is not so stable. Conversion from Mn^{3+} to Mn^{2+} will be quick and have negative ΔG value. Hence because of the stability factor the $E°$ value is high for this process. **(1 Mark)**

(b) Similarity : They both show contraction of radii, and progressive decrease in the radii of atoms of the lanthanoid and actionoid elements as the atomic number increases. **(1 Mark)**

Difference : Actionids show a large number of oxidation states whereas lanthanoids primarily show only three oxidation states $+2, +3, +4$. **(1 Mark)**

17. (a)

Transition Metal ion	Number of unpaired electrons
$Ti^{4+}[Ar]3d^0$	0
$V^{2+}[Ar]3d^3$	3
$Mn^{3+}[Ar]3d^4$	4
$Cr^{2+}[Ar]3d^3$	3

(i) V^{2+} and Cr^{3+} are the most stable ions in aqueous solutions owing to stable t_{2g}^3 configuration. **(1 Mark)**

(ii) Mn^{3+} ion are the strongest oxidising agents in aqueous solutions and itself reduced to Mn^{2+} state which has stable d^5 configuration.

(1 Mark)

(iii) Those ions which have unpaired electrons in *d*-orbital and in which *d-d* transition is possible will be coloured while the ions in which *d*-orbitals are empty or completely filled will be colourless as no *d-d* transition is possible in those configuration.

Only Ti^{4+} has an empty *d*-orbital so it is colourless ion among these metal ions.

(1 Mark)

(b) (i)

$$2MnO_4^- + 16H^+ + 5S^{2-} \longrightarrow 2Mn^{2+} + 8H_2O + 5S$$

(1 Mark)

(ii) $2KMnO_4 \xrightarrow{\text{heat}} K_2MnO_4 + MnO_2 + O_2$

(1 Mark)

18. (a) (i) Due to small atomic radii and presence of high positive nuclear charge, transition metal have strong tendency to form complexes. Secondly these metal have vacant d-orbital in which the electron pair donated by ligands donor atom can be accommodated. Transition metals, therefore show strong tendency to form complexes and complex ions. **(1 Mark)**

(ii) In case of a lower oxides of a transition metal, the metal atom has a low oxidation state. This means that some of the valance electrons of the metal atom are not involved in bonding. As a result it can donate electron and behave as a basic metal oxides whereas highest oxide is acidic or amphoteric due to highest oxidation state. **(1 Mark)**

(iii) Mn^{2+} exists in $3d^5$ configuration which is a half-filled configuration which provides extra stability to the metal ion while Mn^{3+} will exist in $3d^4$ configuration which is less stable than $3d^5$. Hence the conversion from 3+ to 2+ is very feasible. Hence E° value is more, while in Cr^{3+}, it exist in $3d^3$ half-filled *d* orbital ($3e^-$, electron in t_{2g}) extra stability is attain by Cr^{3+} than Cr^{2+}. Hence Cr^{3+} to Cr^{2+} is less feasible

and hence it has less reduction potential as compare to Mn^{3+}/Mn^{2+}. **(1 Mark)**

(b) *Similarity:*

- Both show common oxidation state of +3.
- Both are electropositive elements
- Lanthenides and actinides show magnetic properties.

Difference: Lanthanoide have less tendency to form complex whereas actinoid have more tendency (great tendency) to form complex. Lanthanoids are colourless where as, actinoids are colourful.

(2 Marks)

19. (a) (i) The variability in oxidation state of transition metal is due to partially filled *d*-orbitals. Their oxidation state differ from each other by +1 *i.e.* Fe^{+2} and Fe^{3+}. In case of *p* block elements the oxidation state differ from each other by +2 for example: +3 and +5. **(1 Mark)**

(ii) Cuprous (Cu^+) ions are not stable in aqueous solution and get converted into Cu and Cu^{2+} due to self reduction and disproportion.

$$2Cu^+(aq) \longrightarrow Cu^{2+}(aq) + Cu$$

2nd ionisation enthalpy of copper is large but hydration enthalpy for Cu^{2+} is much more negative than that for Cu^+. So Cu^{2+} is stable than Cu^+. **(1 Mark)**

(iii) Orange colour of $Cr_2O_7^{2-}$ ion changes to yellow when treated with an alkali due to the formation of CrO_4^{2-} ion, which is yellow in colour.

$$\underset{\substack{\text{Dichromate ion}\\\text{(orange)}}}{Cr_2O_7^{2-}} + 2OH^- \longrightarrow \underset{\substack{\text{Chromate ion}\\\text{(yellow)}}}{2CrO_4^{2-}} + H_2O$$

(1 Mark)

(b) Chemistry of actinoids is complicated as compared to lanthanoids. The two reasons are as follows.

(i) Actinoids are radioactive and the radioactive decay gives out extremely energetic particles which may break bonds and distrupt crystal structure.

(ii) The breaking up of bonds by emitted particles due to higher energy associated with them also develops the process of self oxidation and it is therefore difficult to decides the more stable oxidation state. **(2 Marks)**

20. (a) (i) Zr and Hf have similar atomic radii due to lanthanide contraction. In lanthanoid series, with increasing atomic number, there is a progressive decrease in atomic as well as ionic radii of trivalent ions from La^{3+} to Lu^{3+}. This regular decrease in the atomic and the ionic radii of lanthanoids with increasing atomic number is known as lanthanoid contraction. Lanthanoid contraction, causes the radii of the members of the 3rd transition series to be very similar to those of the corresponding members of the 2nd series. **(1 Mark)**

(ii) The transition elements show variable oxidation states because the energies of $(n-1)d$ orbitals and ns orbitals are very close. Hence, electrons from both of these orbitals can participate in bonding. **(1 Mark)**

(iii) Copper (I) compound are unstable in aqueous solution and undergo disproportionation to give more stable Cu^{2+} and Cu.

$$2Cu^+ \longrightarrow Cu^{2+} + Cu$$

The high stability of Cu^{2+} (aq) rather than Cu^+ (aq) is due to the much more negative $\Delta_{hyd}H$ of Cu^{2+} (aq) than Cu^+ (aq), which is more than that compensates for the second ionisation enthalpy of Cu. **(1 Mark)**

(b) (i) $$2MnO_2 + 4KOH + O_2 \longrightarrow \quad \textbf{(1 Mark)}$$
$$2K_2MnO_4 + 2H_2O$$

(ii) $$2Na_2CrO_4 + 2H^+ \longrightarrow Na_2Cr_2O_7$$
$$+ 2Na^+ + H_2O$$
(1 Mark)

21. (a) (i) $E^{\circ}_{M^{2+}/M}$ for any metal is related to the sum of enthalpy changes taking place in following steps:

$M(s) + \Delta_a H \rightarrow M(g)$

$M(g) + \Delta_i H \rightarrow M^{2+}(g)$

$M^{2+}(g) \rightarrow M^{2+}(aq) + \Delta_{hyd}H$

Cu has a high enthalpy of atomisation ($\Delta_a H$) and a low enthalpy of hydration ($\Delta_{hyd}H$). The high energy required to transform Cu(s) to Cu^{2+}(aq) is not balanced by its hydration enthalpy. Hence, $E^{\circ}(Cu^{2+}/Cu)$ is positive.

(1 Mark)

(ii) $E^{\circ}_{Mn^{2+}/Mn}$ is highly negative because it is difficult to reduce Mn^{2+} to Mn as it has already half-filled d-orbital which leads to extra stability. However, Mn can be easily oxidized to Mn^{2+}. **(1 Mark)**

(iii) Cr^{2+} is a stronger reducing agent than Fe^{2+}. This is because $E^{\circ}(Cr^{3+}/Cr^{2+})$ is negative ($-0.41V$) whereas $E^{\circ}(Fe^{3+}/Fe^{2+})$ is positive ($+0.77V$). Thus, Cr^{2+} is easily oxidised to Cr^{3+} but Fe^{2+} cannot be easily oxidised to Fe^{3+}.

(1 Mark)

(b) Actinoid elements show wide range of oxidation states due to comparable energies of $5f$, $6d$ and $7s$ levels.

(i) Electronic configuration: In both lathanoids and actionoids, f-orbitals are progressively filled. In lanthanoids $4f$- orbitals are progressively filled, whereas in actinoids $5f$-orbitals are progressively filled.

(ii) Oxidation states : Common oxidation state of lanthanoids and actinoids is +3. Some lanthanoids show +2 and +4 oxidation state also. Actinoids shows +3, +4, +5 +6, +7 oxidation states. Although +3 and +4 are most common.

(iii) Lanthanoids and actinoids both shows atomic/ionic size contraction.

(iv) Chemical reactivity: Both are highly reactive and exhibit similar chemical properties.

(1 + 1 = 2 Marks)

22. (a) (i) $$Cr_2O_7^{2-} + 2OH^- \longrightarrow 2CrO_4^{2-} + H_2O$$
(1 Mark)

(ii) $$MnO_4^- + 4H^+ + 3e^- \longrightarrow MnO_2 + 2H_2O$$
(1 Mark)

(b) (i) Zinc is not considered as a transition element because it does not contain vacant d-orbitals in either the ground state or its common oxidation state (+2) **(1 Mark)**

(ii) Transition elements form a large number of complexes because of:
(a) smaller size of their ions
(b) high ionic charges
(c) availability of vacant d-orbitals.

(1 Mark)

(iii) $\underset{3d^5 4s^2}{\text{Mn}(25)} \xrightarrow{-e^-} \underset{3d^5 4s^1}{\text{Mn}^+} \xrightarrow{-e^-} \underset{3d^5 4s^0}{\text{Mn}^{2+}} \xrightarrow{-e^-} \underset{3d^4 4s^0}{\text{Mn}^{3+}}$

$\underset{3d^5 4s^1}{\text{Cr}(24)} \xrightarrow{-e^-} \underset{3d^5 4s^0}{\text{Cr}^+} \xrightarrow{-e^-} \underset{3d^4 4s^0}{\text{Cr}^{2+}} \xrightarrow{-e^-} \underset{3d^3 4s^0}{\text{Cr}^{3+}}$

The reduction of $\text{Mn}^{3+} \longrightarrow \text{Mn}^{2+}$ gives stable half-filled configuration of $3d^5$, which is not the case when $\text{Cr}^{3+} \longrightarrow \text{Cr}^{2+}$. Thus, E° value for $\text{Mn}^{3+}/\text{Mn}^{2+}$ couple is more positive than $\text{Cr}^{3+}/\text{Cr}^{2+}$ couple. **(1 Mark)**

23. (i) **Lanthanoids :**

1. They are non-radioactive.
2. Their compounds are less basic.
3. They show only one O.S, 3. This is due to large energy gap between $4f$ and $5d$ subshells.
4. They are less reactive chemically.

Actinoids :

1. They are radioactive.
2. Their compounds are more basic.
3. They show many O.S. like,

   $+ 3, + 4, + 5, + 6, + 7$ due to small energy gap between $5d, 6s$ and $7s$ subshells.
4. They are highly reactive. **(2 marks)**

(ii) Cerium (Ce) shows $+ 4$ O.S. due to stable configuration $[\text{Xe}]4f^0$ **(1 Mark)**

(iii) $\text{MnO}_4^- + 8\text{H}^+ + 5e^- \longrightarrow \text{Mn}^{2+} + 4\text{H}_2\text{O}$

   (1 Mark)

(iv) $\underset{3d^5 4s^2}{\text{Mn}(25)} \xrightarrow{-3e^-} \underset{3d^4 4s^0}{\text{Mn}^{3+}}$

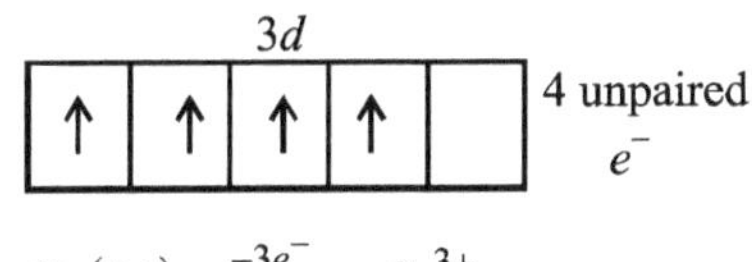

Cr$(24) \xrightarrow{-3e^-} \underset{3d^3 4s^0}{\text{Cr}^{3+}}$
$\underset{3d^5 4s^1}{}$

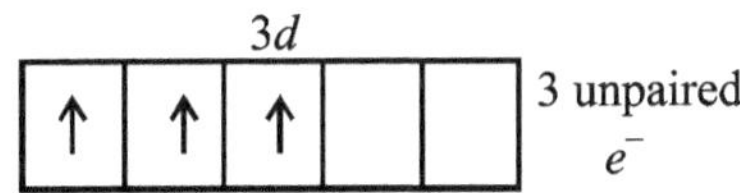

Due to presence of 4 unpaired, e^- in Mn^{3+} as compared to 3 in Cr^{3+}, Mn^{3+} is more paramagnetic than Cr^{3+}. **(1 Mark)**

24. (a) (i) $2\text{MnO}_2 + 4\text{KOH} + \text{O}_2 \longrightarrow$

   $2\text{K}_2\text{MnO}_4 + 2\text{H}_2\text{O}$

   (1 Mark)

(ii) $\text{Na}_2\text{CrO}_4 + 2\text{H}^+ \longrightarrow$

   $\text{Na}_2\text{Cr}_2\text{O}_7 + 2\text{Na}^+ + \text{H}_2\text{O}$

   (1 Mark)

(b) (i) Mn is stable in +2 state with $3d^5$ half-filled configuration. So, it does not tend to get oxidised to +3 state. On the other hand, Fe in +2 state has $3d^6$ configuration and in +3 state, it has $3d^5$ stable configuration hence Fe^{2+} readily gets oxidised to Fe^{3+}. **(1 Mark)**

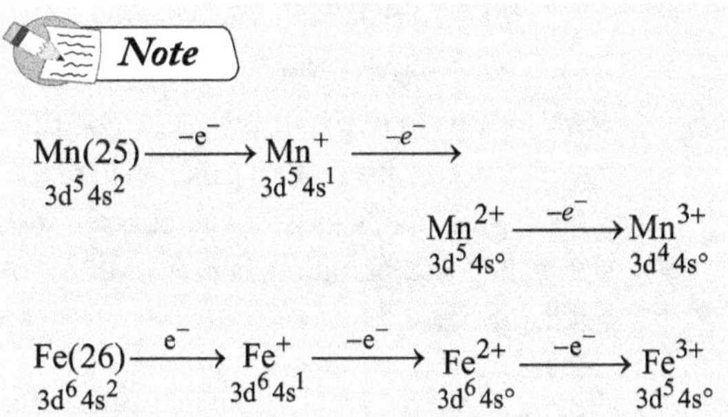

> **Note**
>
> $\underset{3d^5 4s^2}{\text{Mn}(25)} \xrightarrow{-e^-} \underset{3d^5 4s^1}{\text{Mn}^+} \xrightarrow{-e^-}$
>
> $\underset{3d^5 4s^0}{\text{Mn}^{2+}} \xrightarrow{-e^-} \underset{3d^4 4s^0}{\text{Mn}^{3+}}$
>
> $\underset{3d^6 4s^2}{\text{Fe}(26)} \xrightarrow{e^-} \underset{3d^6 4s^1}{\text{Fe}^+} \xrightarrow{-e^-} \underset{3d^6 4s^0}{\text{Fe}^{2+}} \xrightarrow{-e^-} \underset{3d^5 4s^0}{\text{Fe}^{3+}}$

(ii) Enthalpy of atomization depends upon the number of unpaired electrons. More the number of unpaired electrons, more the number of bonds formed and hence more is the enthalpy of atomization. Zn has $3d^{10}\ 4s^2$ configuration. So it has no unpaired electrons and so it has lowest enthalpy of atomization. **(1 Mark)**

(iii) Actinoid elements shows wide range of oxidation states due to comparable energies of $5f$, $6d$ and $7s$ levels. **(1 Mark)**

25. (i) Mn shows the maximum no. of oxidation states in $3d$-series. This is because variability of oxidation states depends upon the no. of unpaired electrons in d-orbitals. As Mn has maximum no. of unpaired electrons ($3d^5$), so it shows maximum number of oxidation states. **(1 Mark)**

(ii) Cu has positive E° (M^{2+}/M) value. This is because standard reduction potential depends upon three factors :

1. Enthalpy of atomization.
2. Enthalpy of submination
3. Hydration enthalpy

The sum of the above three gives E° value. For copper, enthalpy of atomization is very high while its hydration enthalpy is low. As a result, E° comes to be +ve. **(1 Mark)**

(iii) $\underset{3d^4 4s^0}{Cr^{2+}} \xrightarrow{-e^-} \underset{3d^3 4s^0}{Cr^{3+}} \quad \underset{3d^5 4s^0}{Mn^{2+}} \xrightarrow{-e^-} \underset{3d^4 4s^0}{Mn^{3+}}$

Reduction of $Mn^{3+} \longrightarrow Mn^{2+}$ gives stable configuration of $3d^5$. Hence, Mn^{3+} is a stronger oxidising agent than Cr^{3+}. **(1 Mark)**

(iv) Europium (Eu) shows + 2 oxidation state because of formation of stable f^7 configuration after loss of two s-electrons. **(1 Mark)**

(v) $MnO_4^- + 8H^+ + 5e^- \longrightarrow Mn^{2+} + 4H_2O$ **(1 Mark)**

26. (a) (i) $_{25}Mn = [Ar]\, 3d^5 4s^2$

$\qquad _{25}Mn^{+3} = [Ar]\, 3d^4 4s^0$

Mn^{3+} is a good oxidizing agent. A good oxidising agent reduces itself i.e. gains electron(s) from others. Mn^{3+} tends to gain one electron to acquire stable $3d^5$ configuration hence Mn^{3+} is a good oxidizing agent. **(1 Mark)**

(ii) $E^{\circ}_{M^{2+}/M}$ values are the sum of sublimation enthalpy, ionisation enthalpy, hydration enthalpy etc. The irregularity in the E° values is, because of irregular variation of ionisation enthalpies $(IE_1 + IE_2)$ and also the sublimation enthalpies. **(1 Mark)**

(iii) Oxygen stabilises the highest oxidation state even more than fluorine, e.g., the highest fluoride of Mn is MnF_4 whereas highest oxide is Mn_2O_7. The reason for this is the ability of oxygen to form multiple bonds with metal atoms. **(1 Mark)**

(b) (i) $2CrO_4^{2-} + 2H^+ \longrightarrow Cr_2O_7^{2-} + H_2O$ **(1 Mark)**

(ii) $2KMnO_4 \xrightarrow{513K} K_2MnO_4 + MnO_2 + O_2$ **(1 Mark)**

27. (a) The transition elements show variable oxidation states because the energies of $(n-1)d$ orbitals and ns orbitals are very close. Hence, electrons from both of these orbitals can participate in bonding. **(1 Mark)**

(i) In the first series of transition elements, Mn shows maximum number of oxidation states. **(1 Mark)**

(ii) Scandium shows only +3 O.S. **(1 Mark)**

(b) In lanthanoid series, with increasing atomic number, there is a progressive decrease in atomic as well as ionic radii of trivalent ions from La^{3+} to Lu^{3+}. This regular decrease in the atomic and the ionic radii of lanthanoids with increasing atomic number is known as lanthanoid contraction.

'Mischmetal' is an alloy which contains some of the lanthanoid metals. **(2 Marks)**

Note

Lanthanoid contraction is a unique feature in the chemistry of lanthanoids, lanthanoid contraction, results due to improper shielding of 4f electrons. Similar effect is also observe in actinoid series which is due to improper shielding of 5f electrons. However effect is more pronounced in actionoid series due to greater deshielding effect of 5f electrons in comparison to 4f electrons.

Chapter 5: Coordination Compounds

1 — Multiple Choice Questions

1. Which of the following ligands is an ambidentate ligand?
[All India 2023, Set-I, K]

(a) CO   (b) NO_2

(c) NH_3 (d) H_2O

2. What is the secondary valency of Cobalt in $[Co(en_2)Cl_2]^+$? **[All India 2023 Set-II, K]**

(a) 6   (b) 4

(c) 2   (d) 8

3. The number of ions formed on dissolving one molecule of $FeSO_4 \cdot (NH_4)_2SO_4 \cdot 6H_2O$ in water is:
[CBSE Sample 2022-23, U]

(a) 3   (b) 4

(c) 5   (d) 6

4. Ambidentate ligands like NO_2^- and SCN^- are :
[CBSE Sample 2020-21, K]

(a) unidentate

(b) didentate

(c) polydentate

(d) has variable denticity

5. The formula of the coordination compound Tetraammineaquachloridocobalt(III) chloride is
[CBSE Sample 2020-21, K]

(a) $[Co(NH_3)_4(H_2O)Cl]Cl_2$

(b) $[Co(NH_3)_4(H_2O)Cl]Cl_3$

(c) $[Co(NH_3)_2(H_2O)Cl]Cl_2$

(d) $[Co(NH_3)_4(H_2O)Cl]Cl$

6. Which of the following will give a white precipitate upon reacting with $AgNO_3$? **[Delhi 2020, U]**

(a) $K_2[Pt(en)_2Cl_2]$ (b) $[Co(NH_3)_3Cl_3]$

(c) $[Cr(H_2O)_6]Cl_3$ (d) $[Fe(H_2O)_3Cl_3]$

2 — Assertion Reason/Two Statement Type Questions

(a) Both Assertion (A) and Reason (R) are true and Reason (R) is the correct explanation of the Assertion (A).

(b) Both Assertion (A) and Reason (R) are true, but Reason (R) is not the correct explanation of the Assertion (A).

(c) Assertion (A) is true, but Reason (R) is false.

(d) Assertion (A) is false, but Reason (R) is true.

7. **Assertion (A) :** EDTA is a hexadentate ligand.

Reason (R) : EDTA has 2 nitrogen and 4 oxygen donor atoms. **[Delhi 2023, Set-I, K]**

8. **Assertion (A):** $[Co(NH_3)_5\ SO_4]$ Cl gives a white precipitate with silver nitrate solution.
[Delhi 2023 Set-III, U]

Reason (R): The complex dissociates to give Cl^- and SO_4^{2-} ions.

4 — Very Short Answer Questions (1 Mark)

9. When a coordination compound $CrCl_3 \cdot 6H_2O$ is mixed with $AgNO_3$, two moles of AgCl are precipitated per mole of the compound. What is the structural formula of the coordination compound? **[All India 2019, U]**

10. What is the difference between a complex and a double salt? **[All India 2019, U]**

11. Write the coordination number and oxidation state of Platinum in the complex $[Pt(en)_2Cl_2]$.
[All India 2018, K]

12. Which of the following is more stable complex and why?
$[Co(NH_3)_6]^{3+}$ and $[Co(en)^3]^{3+}$ **[Delhi 2014, U]**

Topic-2: *Nomenclature of Coordination Compounds*

1   *Multiple Choice Questions*

1. The formula of the complex Iron (III) hexacyanidoferrate (II) is   **[All India 2023, Set-I, K]**

(a) $Fe_2[Fe(CN)_6]_3$

(b) $Fe_1[Fe(CN)_6]_3$

(c) $Fe[Fe(CN)_6]$

(d) $Fe_3[Fe(CN)_6]_2$

2. The formula of the complex dichloridobis (ethane – 1, 2-diamine) pltinum (IV) nitrate is

[All India 2023 Set-II, K]

(a) $Pt(Cl_2(en)_2(NO_3)_2]$

(b) $[Pt\,Cl_2\,(en_2)]\,(NO_3)_2$

(c) $[Pt\,Cl_2(en_2)\,(NO_3)]\,NO_3$

(d) $[Pt\,(en)_2\,(NO_3)_2]Cl_2$

5   *Short Answer Questions (2 or 3 Marks)*

3. Write the IUPAC names of the following:

[All India 2023, Set-I, K]

(i) $[Co(NH_3)_5(ONO)]^{2+}$

(ii) $K_2[NiCl_4]$

4. (i) What is a chelate complex? Give one example.

(ii) What are heterolptic complex? Give one example.

[All India 2023, Set-I, K]

5. Give the formulae of the following compounds:

[All India 2020, K]

(a) Potassium tetrahydroxidozincate (II)

(b) Hexaammineplatinum (IV) chloride

6. (a) Write the IUPAC name and hybridisation of the complex $[Fe(CN)_6]^{3-}$.   **[Delhi 2020, Set-I]**

(Given : Atomic number of Fe = 26)

(b) What is the difference between an ambidentate ligand and a chelating ligand ?

7. Write IUPAC name of the complex $[Pt(en)_2Cl_2]$. Draw structures of geometrical isomers for this complex.

[Delhi 2019, U]

8. Using IUPAC norms write the formulae for the following:

(i) Hexaamminecobalt(III) sulphate   **[Delhi 2019, U]**

(ii) Potassium trioxalatochromate(III)

9. When a coordination compound $CoCl_3.6NH_3$ is mixed with $AgNO_3$, 3 moles of AgCl are precipitated per mole of the compound. Write

(i) Structural formula of the complex

(ii) IUPAC name of the complex   **[All India 2016, K]**

10. When a co-ordination compound $CrCl_3.6H_2O$ is mixed with $AgNO_3$, 2 moles of AgCl are precipitated per mole of the compound. Write   **[Delhi 2016, K]**

(i) Structural formula of the complex.

(ii) IUPAC name of the complex.

11. Write down the IUPAC name of the complex $[Pt(en)_2Cl_2]^{2+}$. What type of isomerism is shown by this complex?   **[All India 2015, K]**

12. Using IUPAC norms write the formulae for the following coordination compounds.   **[All India 2015, K]**

(i) Hexaamminecobalt (III) chloride

(ii) Potassium tetrachloridonickelate (II)

13. (i) Write down the IUPAC name of the following complex: **[Delhi 2015, K]**

$[Cr(NH_3)_2Cl_2(en)]Cl$ (en = ethylenediamine)

(ii) Write the formula for the following complex :

Pentaamminenitrito-o-Cobalt (III).

14. Write the IUPAC names of the following coordination compounds :

(i) $[Cr(NH_3)_3Cl_3]$ (ii) $K_3[Fe(CN)_6]$

(iii) $[CoBr_2(en)_2]^+$, (en = ethylenediamine)

[Delhi 2013, K]

Topic-3: *Isomerism in Coordination Compounds*

1 *Multiple Choice Questions*

1. The magnetic moment of $[NiCl_4]^{2-}$.

   [Delhi 2023, Set-I, Ap]

   (a) 1.82 BM   (b) 2.82 BM

   (c) 4.42 BM   (d) 5.46 BM

   (Atomic number : Ni = 28)

2 *Assertion Reason/Two Statement Type Questions*

   (a) Both Assertion (A) and Reason (R) are true and Reason (R) is the correct explanation of the Assertion (A).

   (b) Both Assertion (A) and Reason (R) are true, but Reason (R) is not the correct explanation of the Assertion (A).

   (c) Assertion (A) is true, but Reason (R) is false.

   (d) Assertion (A) is false, but Reason (R) is true.

2. **Assertion (A):** Trans $[Cr\ Cl_2(ox)_2]^{3-}$ shows optical isomerism. **[Delhi 2023 Set-I, K]**

   Reason (R): Optical isomerism is common in octahedral complexes involving didentate ligands.

3. **Assertion (A) :** Linkage isomerism arises in coordination compounds because of ambidentate ligand.

   Reason (R) : Ambidentate ligand like NO_2 has two different donor atoms i.e., N and O. **[All India 2020, K]**

5  *Short Answer Questions (2 or 3 Marks)*

4. (a) Which of the following species cannot act as a ligand? Give reason. **[Delhi 2023, Set-I, U]**

   OH^-, NH_4^+, CH_3NH_2, H_2O

   (b) The complex $[Co(NH_3)_5(NO_2)]Cl_2$ is red in colour. Give IUPAC name of its linkage isomer.

   [Delhi 2023, Set-I, K]

5. The formula $Co(NH_3)_5CO_3Cl$ could represent a carbonate or a chloride. Write the structures and names of possible isomers. **[CBSE Sample 2022-23, U]**

6. Write IUPAC name of the complex $[Cr(NH_3)_4Cl_2]^+$. Draw structures of geometrical isomers for this complex.

   [All India 2019, Set-II]

7. Write the IUPAC name of the complex $[Cr\ (NH_3)_4\ Cl_2]^+$. What type of isomerism does it exhibit ?

   [Delhi 2014, K]

Topic-4: *Bonding in Coordination Compounds*

1 *Multiple Choice Questions*

1. The CFSE of $[CoCl_6]^{3-}$ is 18000 cm^{-1} the CFSE for $[CoCl_4]^-$ will be: **[CBSE Sample 2022-23, Ap]**

   (a) 18000 cm^{-1} (b) 8000cm^{-1}

   (c) 2000 cm^{-1} (d) 16000 cm^{-1}

4 *Very Short Answer Questions (1 Mark)*

Given below are two statements labelled as Assertion (A) and Reason (R). Select the most appropriate answer from the options given below:

(a) Both (A) and (R) are true and (R) is the correct explanation of (A).

(b) Both (A) and (R) are true, but (R) is not the correct explanation of (A).

(c) (A) is true, but (R) is false.

(d) (A) is false, but (R) is true.

2. **Assertion (A):** Low spin tetrahedral complexes are rarely observed.

   Reason (R): Crystal field splitting energy is less than pairing energy for tetrahedral complexes.

   [Delhi 2020, U]

5  *Short Answer Questions (2 or 3 Marks)*

3. (a) Write the formula for the following coordination compound **[CBSE Sample 2023-24, K]**

   Bis(ethane–1, 2–diamine) dihydroxidochromium (III) chloride

   (b) Does ionization isomer for the following compound exist? Justify your answer.

   $Hg[Co(SCN)_4]$ **[CBSE Sample 2023-24, U]**

   (c) Is the central metal atom in coordination complexes a Lewis acid or a Lewis base? Explain.

   [CBSE Sample 2023-24, U]

4. (a) Draw of geometrical isomers of $[Co(en)_2Cl_2]^{2+}$. Which geometrical isomer of $[Co(en)_2Cl_2]^{2+}$ is not optically active and why? **[All India 2023, Set-I, U]**

   (b) Write the hybridisation and magnetic behaviour of $[CoF_6]^3$. **[All India 2023, Set-I, K]**

   [**Given** : Atomic number of Co = 27]

5. (a) On the basis of crystal field theory write the electronic configuration for d^5 ion with a weak ligand for which $\Delta_0 < P$. **[Delhi 2023, Set-I, K]**

   (b) Explain $[Fe(CN)_6]^{3-}$ is an inner orbital complex whereas $[FeF_6]^{3-}$ is an outer orbital complex.

   [Atomic number : Fe = 26] **[Delhi 2023, Set-I, K]**

6. (a) Using valence bond theory, predict the hybridization and magnetic character of the complex : $[Ni(CO)_4]$ (Atomic number : Ni = 28)

   [All India 2022, Term-II, U]

   (b) Write IUPAC name of $[Pt(NH_3)_2 Cl(NO_2)]$

   [All India 2022, Term-II, K]

   (c) Why $[Co(en)_3]^{3+}$ is a more stable complex than $[Co(NH_3)_6]^{3+}$? **[All India 2022, Term-II, U]**

7. Using Valence bond theory, explain the following in relation to the paramagnetic complex $[Mn(CN)_6]^{3-}$

   [CBSE Sample 2022-23, U]

   (a) type of hybridization

   (b) magnetic moment value

   (c) type of complex – inner, outer orbital complex

8. Answer the following questions:

   (a) $[Ni(H_2O)_6]^{2+}$ (aq) is green in colour whereas $[Ni(H_2O)_4 (en)]^{2+}$(aq)is blue in colour, give reason in support of your answer.

   [All India 2021-22, Term-II, U]

   (b) Write the formula and hybridization of the following compound: tris(ethane-1,2–diamine) cobalt(III) sulphate **[All India 2021-22, Term-II, K]**

9. In a coordination entity, the electronic configuration of the central metal ion is $t_{2g}^3 e_g^1$

   (a) Is the coordination compound a high spin or low spin complex? **[All India 2021-22, Term-II, U]**

   (b) Draw the crystal field splitting diagram for the above complex. **[All India 2021-22, Term-II, K]**

10. (i) Write the IUPAC name of the following complex: $[Co(NH_3)_4(H_2O)Cl]Cl_2$ **[All India 2022, Term-II]**

    (ii) What is the difference between an Ambidentate ligand and a Bidentate ligand ?

(iii) Out of $[Fe(NH_3)_6]^{3+}$ and $[Fe(C_2O_4)_3]^{3-}$, which complex is more stable and why?

11. Write the hybridisation and magnetic character of the following complexes: **[All India2019, U]**

    (i) $[Fe(H_2O)_6]^{2+}$

    (ii) $[Ni(CN)_4]^{2-}$

    [Atomic number : Fe = 26, Ni = 28]

12. Out of $[CoF_6]^{3-}$ and $[Co(en)_3]^{3+}$, which one complex is

    (i) paramagnetic **[Delhi 2019, U]**

    (ii) more stable

    (iii) inner orbital complex and

    (iv) high spin complex

    (Atomic no. of Co = 27)

13. Out of $[CoF_6]^{3-}$ and $[Co(C_2O_4)_3]^{3-}$, which one complex is

    (i) diamagnetic **[All India 2019, Set-II]**

    (ii) more stable

    (iii) outer orbital complex and

    (iv) low spin complex ?

    (Atomic no. of Co = 27)

14. (a) Write the formula of the following coordination compound: **[All India 2018, K]**

    Iron (III) hexacyanoferrate (II)

    (b) What type of isomerism is exhibited by the complex $[Co(NH_3)_5Cl]SO_4$? **[All India 2018, U]**

    (c) Write the hybridisation and number of unpaired electrons in the complex $[CoF_6]^{3-}$.

    (Atomic No. of Co = 27) **[All India 2018, U]**

15. (i) What type of isomerism is shown by the complex $[Co(NH_3)_6] [Cr(CN)_6]$? **[Delhi 2017, K]**

    (ii) Why a solution of $[Ni(H_2O)_6]^{2+}$ is green while a solution of $[Ni(CN)_4]^{2-}$ is colourless? (At. no. of Ni = 28) **[Delhi 2017, U]**

    (iii) Write the IUPAC name of the following complex : $[Co(NH_3)_5(CO_3)]Cl$. **[Delhi 2017, K]**

16. (a) What type of isomerism is shown by the complex $[Co(NH_3)_5(SCN)]^{2+}$? **[All India 2017, K]**

    (b) Why is $[NiCl_4]^{2-}$ paramagnetic while $[Ni(CN)_4]^{2-}$ is diamagnetic? (Atomic number of Ni = 28)

    [All India 2017, U]

    (c) Why are low spin tetrahedral complexes rarely observed? **[All India 2017, K]**

17. (a) For the complex $[Fe(H_2O)_6]^{3+}$, write the hybridisation, magnetic character and spin of the complex.

    (At. number : Fe = 26) **[All India 2016, U]**

(b) Draw one of the geometrical isomers of the complex $[Pt(en)_2Cl_2]^{2+}$ which is optically inactive.

[All India 2016, K]

18. (a) For the complex $[Fe(CN)_6]^{3-}$, write the hybridization type, magnetic character and spin nature of the complex. (At. number : Fe = 26).   **[Delhi 2016, K]**

(b) Draw one of the geometrical isomers of the complex $[Pt(en)_2Cl_2]^{2+}$ which is optically active.

[Delhi 2016, U]

19. (a) Write the hybridisation and shape of the following complexes.   **[All India 2015, K]**

(i) $[CoF_6]^{3-}$

(ii) $[Ni (CN)_4]^{2-}$

(Atomic number : Co = 27, Ni = 28)

(b) Out of NH_3 and CO, which ligand forms a more stable complex with a transition metal and why?

[All India 2015, K]

20. (i) Draw the geometrical isomers of complex $[Pt(NH_3)_2Cl_2]$.   **[Delhi 2015, K]**

(ii) On the basis of crystal field theory, write the electronic configuration for d^4 ion if $\Delta_0 < P$.

[Delhi 2015, K]

(iii) Write the hybridisation and magnetic behaviour of the complex $[Ni(CO)_4]$.

(At.no. of Ni = 28)   **[Delhi 2015, U]**

21. (i) Write the IUPAC name of the complex $[Cr(NH_3)_4Cl_2]Cl$.   **[All India 2014, K]**

(ii) What type of isomerism is exhibited by the complex $[Co(en)_3]^{3+}$?   **[All India 2014, K]**
(en = ethane-1,2-diamine)

(iii) Why is $[NiCl_4]^{2-}$ paramagnetic but $[Ni(CO)_4]$ is diamagnetic?

(At. nos. : Cr = 24, Co = 27, Ni = 28)

[All India 2014, K]

22. For the complex $[NiCl_4]^{2-}$, write   **[All India 2013, K]**

(i) the IUPAC name.

(ii) the hybridization type.

(iii) the shape of the complex.

(atomic no. of Ni = 28)

23. What is meant by crystal field splitting energy? On the basis of crystal field theory, write the electronic configuration of d^4 in terms of t_{2g} and e_g in an octahedral field when   **[All India 2013, K]**

(i) $\Delta_0 > P$ (ii) $\Delta_0 < P$

7   *Case Based Questions*

24. Crystal field splitting by various ligands

Metal complexes show different colours due to d–d transitions. The complex absorbs light of specific wavelength to promote the electron from t2g to eg level. The colour of the complex is due to the transmitted light, which is complementary of the colour absorbed.

[CBSE Sample 2023-24, A]

The wave number of light absorbed by different complexes of Cr ion are given below:

Complex	Wavenumber of light absorbed (cm^{-1})	Energy of light absorbed (kJ/mol)
$[CrA_6]^{3-}$	13640	163
$[CrB_6]^{3+}$	17830	213
$[CrC_6]^{3+}$	21680	259
$[CrD_6]^{3-}$	26280	314

Answer the following questions:

(a) Out of the ligands "A", "B", "C" and "D", which ligand causes maximum crystal field splitting? Why?

OR

Which of the two, "A" or "D" will be a weak field ligand? Why?

(b) Which of the complexes will be violet in colour? $[CrA_6]^{3-}$ or $[CrB_6]^{3+}$ and why? (Given: If 560 – 570 nm of light is absorbed, the colour of the complex observed is violet.)

(c) If the ligands attached to Cr3+ ion in the complexes given in the table above are water, cyanide ion, chloride ion, and ammonia (not in this order)

Identify the ligand, write the formula and IUPAC name of the following:

(i) $[CrA_6]^{3-}$ (ii) $[CrC_6]^{3+}$

Topic-5: *Bonding in Metal Carbonyls, Importance and Applications of Coordination Compounds*

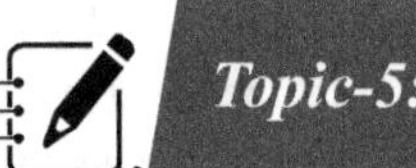   *Multiple Choice Questions*

1. The oxidation state of Ni in $[Ni(CO)_4]$ is

   [Delhi 2020, Set-I]

   (a) 0   (b) 2

   (c) 3   (d) 4

5   *Short Answer Questions (2 or 3 Marks)*

2. (a) On the basis of crystal field theory, write the electronic configuration for d^4 with a strong field ligand for which $\Delta_0 > P$. **[Delhi 2023 Set-III, K]**

   (b) A solution of $[Ni(H_2O)_6]^{2+}$ is green but a solution of $[Ni(CO)_4]$ is colourless. Explain.

   [Atomic number: Ni = 28] **[Delhi 2023 Set-III, K]**

3. Discuss the nature of bonding in metal carbonyls.

   [Delhi 2020, K]

4. Using IUPAC norms write the formula for the following:

   [All India 2017, K]

   (a) Potassium trioxalatoaluminate (III)

   (b) Dichloridobis (ethane-1, 2-diamine) cobalt (III)

Solutions

Topic-1: *Werner's Theory of Coordination Compounds, Definitions of Some Important Terms pertaining to Coordination Compounds*

1. **(b)** NO_2; $M \longleftarrow N \overset{O}{\underset{O}{\Big\langle}}$ and $M \longleftarrow O - N = O$

Two donor atoms of NO_2 are 'O' and 'N' are ligating with central metal atom (M) at a time. **(1 Mark)**

2. **(a)** The secondary valency of a metal is equal to its coordination number. In $[Co(en)_2 Cl_2]^+$, the coordination number of Co is 6. So, its secondary valency will also be 6.

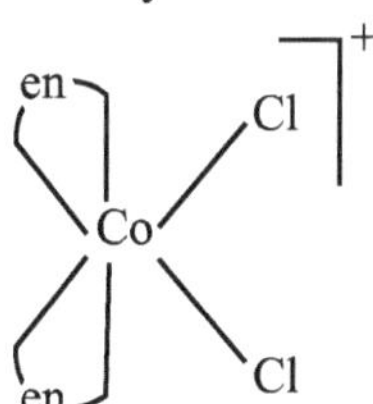

(1 Mark)

3. **(c)** 5
$1Fe^{2+}$, $2 SO_4^{2-}$ and $2 NH_4^+$ ions **(1 Mark)**

4. **(a)** **(1 Mark)**

5. **(a)** **(1 Mark)**

6. **(c)** $[Cr(H_2O)_6]Cl_3$
This compound dissociates to $[Cr(H_2O)_6]^{3+}$ and $3Cl^-$ ions. Thus, it will give white precipitate of $AgCl$ on reacting with $AgNO_3$. **(1 Mark)**

7. **(a)** EDTA stands for Ethyline Diamine Tetra Acetate which is a **hexadentate ligand** indicating that it has **six** donor atoms.

The donor atoms are two N-atoms and four O-atoms.

$$HOOC - H_2C \diagdown \diagup CH_2 - COOH$$
$$N - CH_2 - CH_2 - N$$
$$HOOC - H_2C \diagup \diagdown CH_2 - COOH$$

Therefore, both, Assertion and Reason are **true** and Reason correctly explains the assertion.

Therefore, option **(a)** is correct. **(1 Mark)**

8. **(c)** $[Co(NH_3)_5 SO_4]Cl + AgNO_3 \rightarrow$
$$[Co(NH_3)_5 SO_4] NO_3 + AgCl\downarrow$$
$$\text{(White ppt)}$$
The complex $[Co(NH_3)_5 SO_4]Cl$ dissociates to give $[Co(NH_3)_5 SO_4]^+$ and Cl^- ions. **(1 Mark)**

9. Structural formula: $[Cr(H_2O)_5 Cl] Cl_2 . H_2O$ **(1 Mark)**

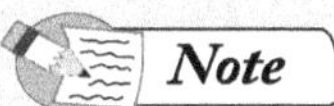

Note

Since 2 moles of AgCl get precipitated, two Cl^- ions are present outside the coordination sphere. While five H_2O molecules and one Cl^- ion are present in the coordination sphere, making the coordination number 6.

10. The main difference between a double salt (like alums, Mohr's salt, etc.) and a complex (like ferrocyanide ion) is that the former dissociates completely into ions in aqueous solution and gives tests of the constituent ions, while latter does not dissociate into ions and thus do not give positive test of the constituent ions. **(1 Mark)**

11. $[Pt (en)_2 Cl_2]$
Co-ordination number = 6
Oxidation number = +2 **(1 Mark)**

12. Out of $[Co(NH_3)_6]^{3+}$ and $[Co(en)_3]^{3+}$, $[Co(en)_3]^{3+}$ is more stable because of the formation of a chelate (i.e. ring) which makes it more stable.

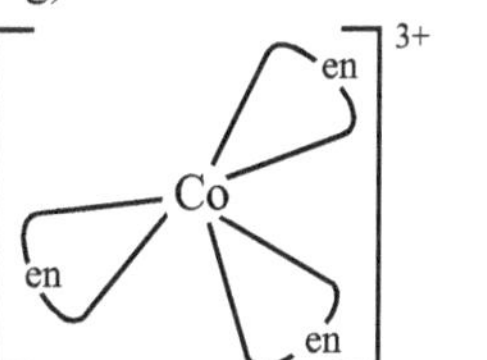

(1 Mark)

Topic-2: *Nomenclature of Coordination Compounds*

1. **(b)** $\overset{III}{Fe_4}[\overset{II}{Fe}(CN)_6]_3$;
Counter ion : 4Fe (III) $\longrightarrow$ (+3) × 4 = +12
Complex ion :
$$\overset{II}{[Fe(CN)_6]_3} \longrightarrow [(+2) + \{(-6) \times 1\}] \times 3 = -12$$
↑
Unidentate
ligand (CN^-)

(1 Mark)

2. **(b)** The formula of the complex dichloridobis (ethane –1, 2 – diamine) platinum (IV) nitrate is [Pt Cl$_2$ (en)$_2$] (NO$_3$)$_2$. **(1 Mark)**

3. **(a)** (i) [Co(NH$_3$)$_5$ (ONO)]$^{2+}$ ⇒ Pentaamminenitrito-O-Cobalt(III) **(1 Mark)**

    (ii) K$_2$(NiCl$_4$) ⇒ Potassium tetrachloridonickelate (II) **(1 Mark)**

4. (i) The complex which is formed by ligating more than one donor sites of a multidentate ligand simultaneously to the metal centre is known as chelating complex. e.g. **(1 Mark)**

⇒ Ethylenediamminetetraacetate ion (EDTA^{4-}) is a hexadentate ligand. It uses all 6 donor site to form a chelating complex. **(1 Mark)**

5. (a) Potassium tetrahydroxidozincate(II), K$_2$[Zn(OH)$_4$] **(1 Mark)**

    (b) Hexaammineplatinum(IV) chloride, [Pt(NH$_3$)$_6$]Cl$_4$ **(1 Mark)**

6.

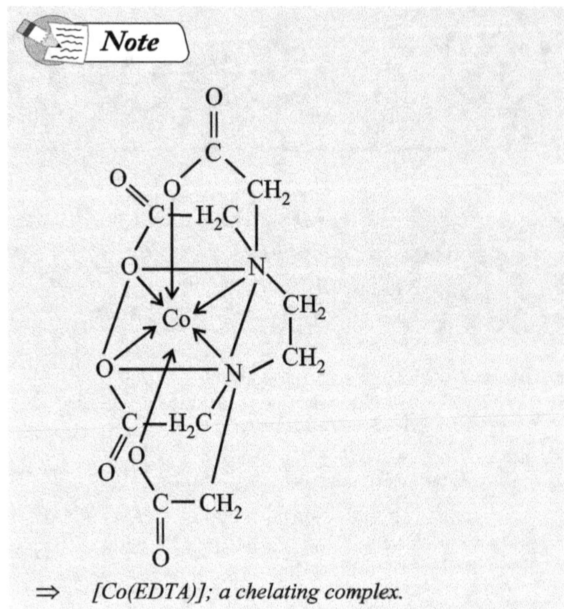

Note

⇒ *[Co(EDTA)]; a chelating complex.*

(ii) The complexes in which a metal is bound to more than one kind of donor groups, are known as heteroleptic complex. **(1 Mark)**

e.g. [Co(NH$_3$)$_4$ Cl$_2$]$^+$ **(1 Mark)**

Topper's Answer

Ans 24. (a) [Fe^{+3}(CN)$_6$]$^{3-}$

IUPAC: Hexacyanidoferrate (III) ion

hybridization:

Fe$_{26}$ = [Ar]^{18} 4s^2 3d^6

Fe^{3+} = [Ar]^{18} 4s^0 3d^5

as CN$^-$ is a strong field ligand and causes pairing up of e

    3d   4s   4p

↑ 6 CN$^-$

hence its hybridisation is d^{2}sp^3

shape: octahedral

(b) Ambidentate ligand : ligands having two different atoms through which it can act as a ligand.

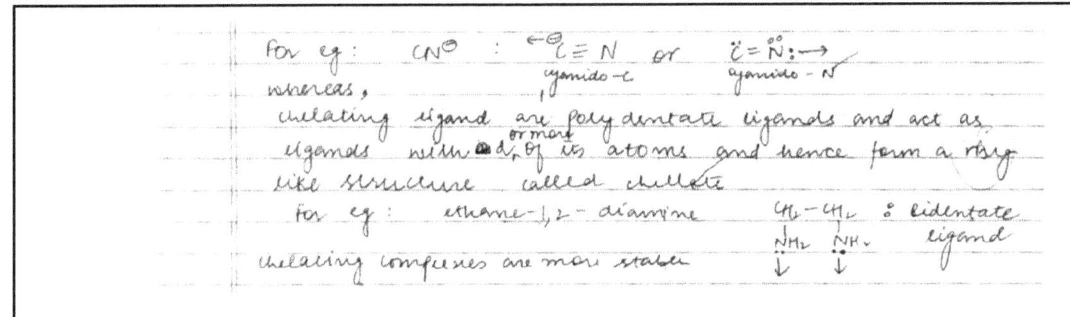

7. Bis(ethylene diamine) dichloro platinum (II)

Geometrical isomers

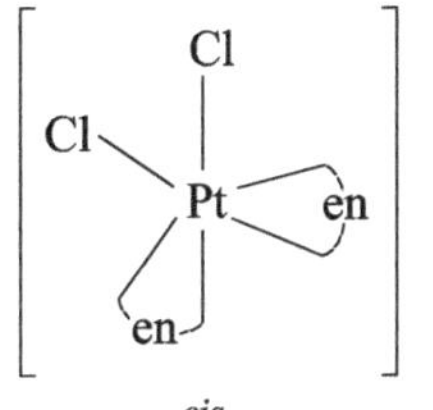
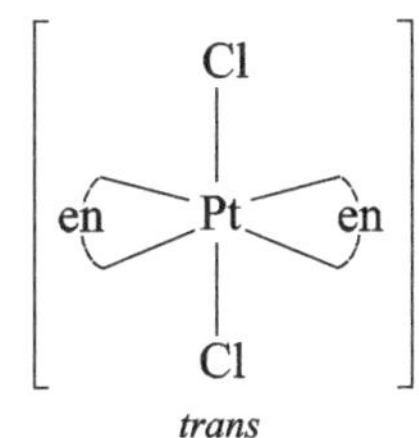

cis   *trans*

(1 + 1 = 2 Marks)

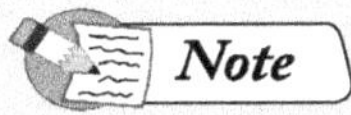 **Note**

cis-isomer of [Pt(en)₂Cl₂] has enantiomer pair i.e., d and l form while trans-isomer is optically inactive due to plane of symmetry in the molecule.

8. (i) Hexaamminecobalt (III) sulphate **(1 Mark)**

$[Co(NH_3)_6]_2 (SO_4)_3$

(ii) Potassium trioxalatochromate (III) **(1 Mark)**

$K_3[Cr(C_2O_4)_3]$

9. (i) Since 3 moles of AgCl get precipitated, therefore 3 Cl^- ions in the coordination compound are present outside the coordination sphere. Thus structural formula of the complex is $[Co(NH_3)_6]Cl_3$. **(1 Mark)**

(ii) The IUPAC name of the complex is hexaamminecobalt (III) chloride. **(1 Mark)**

10. (i) $[CrCl(H_2O)_5] Cl_2 . H_2O$ **(1 Mark)**

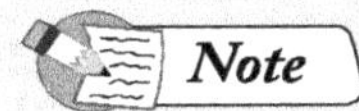 **Note**

As 2 moles of AgCl are precipitated per mole of the compound so the structural formula would contain two Cl^- ion satisfying the primary valencies, while $5H_2O$ molecules and one Cl^- ion are present inside the co-ordination sphere, making the co-ordination no. 6. One H_2O molecule will be present as the molecule of hydration.

(ii) IUPAC name - pentaaquachloridochromium(iii) Chloride **(1 Mark)**

11. IUPAC name:

Dichloridobis (ethylenediamine) platinum (IV)

Geometrical isomerism is shown by this complex.

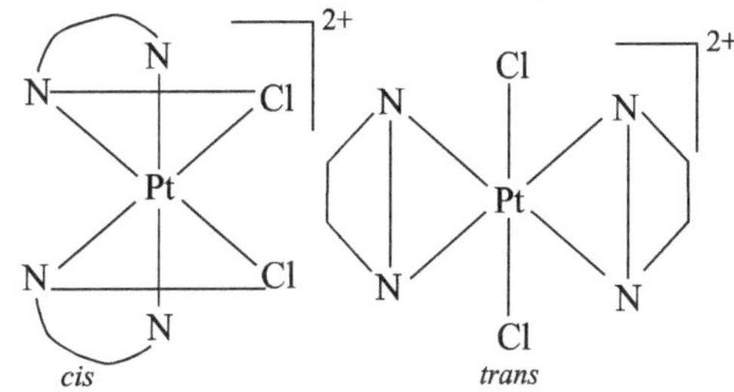

cis   *trans*

(1 + 1 = 2 Marks)

12. (i) $[Co(NH_3)_6]Cl_3$ **(1 Mark)**

(ii) $K_2[NiCl_4]$ **(1 Mark)**

13. (i) $[Cr(NH_3)_2 Cl_2(en)]Cl$ diammindichloridoethylenediamine chromium (III) Chloride. **(1 Mark)**

(ii) Pentaaminenitrito o-cobalt(III) $[(Co(NH_3)_5 (ONO)]^{2+}$ **(1 Mark)**

14. (i) Triamminetrichloridochromium (III). **(1 Mark)**

(ii) Potassiumhexacyanoferrate (III). **(1 Mark)**

(iii) Dibromidobis(ethylenediamine) cobalt (III) ion. **(1 Mark)**

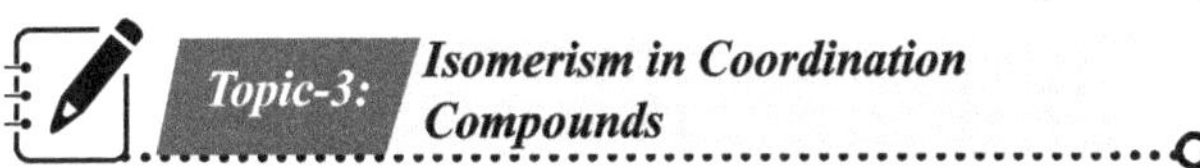

Topic-3: *Isomerism in Coordination Compounds*

1. (b) Ni in $[NiCl_4]^{2-}$ exists as Ni^{2+} ion as there are four Cl^- ligands and the net charge on the complex is –2. The configuration for Ni^{2+} is $4s^0 3d^8$ or just $3d^8$. The weak Cl^- ligands are unable to pair up the electrons in the 3d - subshell of Ni^{2+} and therefore its configuration will be ⇅ ⇅ ⇅ ↑ ↑ that has **two** unpaired electrons.

Thus, magnetic moment $(M_s) = \sqrt{n(n+2)}$ B.M.

$= \sqrt{2(2+2)}$ B.M.

$= \sqrt{8}$ B.M. $= \textbf{2.82 B.M.}$

Therefore, option **(b)** is correct. **(1 Mark)**

2. (d) Optical isomers are mirror images that cannot be superimposed on one another. Trans $[Cr\,Cl_2(ox)_2]^{3-}$ does not show optical isomerism because it has plane of symmetry.

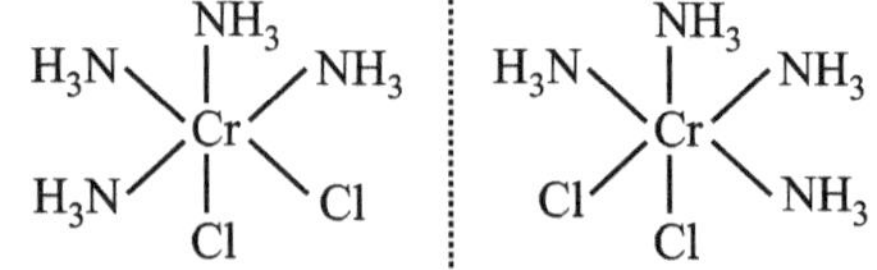

Optical isomerism is common in octahedral complexes involving didentate ligands. **(1 Mark)**

3. Ambidentate ligand like NO_2 has two different donor atoms *i.e.* N and O. Thus, it can form coordinate bonds through N and O both or we can say that it can form linkage isomers. **(1 Mark)**

4. (a) The species that does not have an atom with a lone pair (donor atom), cannot act as a ligand. Among the given choices, NH_4^+ is the species that cannot act as a ligand. **(1 Mark)**

(b) The linkage isomerism results in two complexes with the same molecular formula but different linkages of an ambidentate ligand to the central metal atom or ion.

In the given complex, $-NO_2^-$ is an ambidentate ligand that gives red $[CO(NH_3)_5\,(NO_2)]Cl_2$ complex and yellow $[Co(NH_3)_5\,(ONO)]Cl_2$ complex.

(½ Mark)

The IUPAC name of $[CO(NH_3)_5\,(ONO)]Cl_2$ is:

Pentaamminenitrito-o-Cobalt (III) chloride.

(½ Mark)

5. $[Co(NH_3)_5CO_3]Cl$ and $[Co(NH_3)_5Cl]CO_3$

(1/2 + 1/2 = 1 Mark)

Pentaaminecarbonatocobalt(III)chloride **(1/2 Mark)**

Pentaaminechloridocobalt(III)carbonate **(1/2 Mark)**

6.

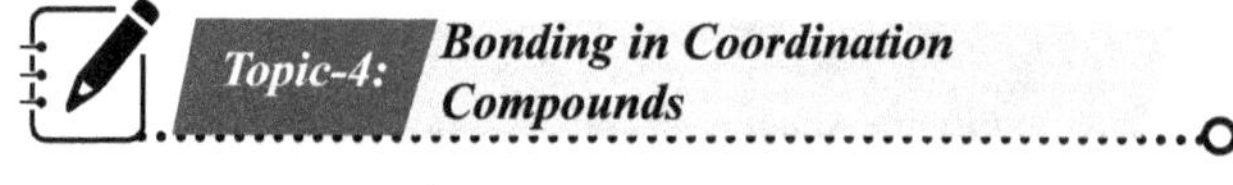

7. IUPAC name : Tetrammine dichloridochrominium (III) ion. It shows geometrical and optical isomerism as shown below : **(1 Mark)**

Geometrical isomers

Trans   *Cis*

(ii) The *cis* form is optically active. **(1 Mark)**

<hr>

Topic-4: *Bonding in Coordination Compounds*

1. (b) $8000\ cm^{-1}$

$\Delta t = (4/9) \times 18000\,cm^{-1} = 8000\ cm^{-1}$ **(1 Mark)**

2.

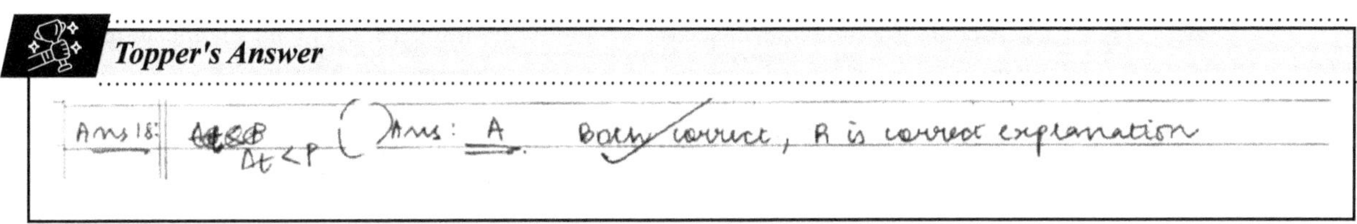

(a) For tetrahedral complexes, the orbital splitting energy is not sufficiently large for forcing pairing of electrons. Therefore, low spin tetrahedral configurations are rarely observed. **(1 Mark)**

3. **(a)** $[Cr(en)_2(OH)_2]Cl$ or $[Cr(H_2NCH_2CH_2NH_2)_2(OH)_2]$ Cl **(1 Mark)**

(b) No, ionization isomers are possible by exchange of ligand with counter ion only and not by exchange of central metal ion. **(1 Mark)**

(c) The central atom is electron pair acceptor so it is a Lewis acid. **(1 Mark)**

4. **(a)**

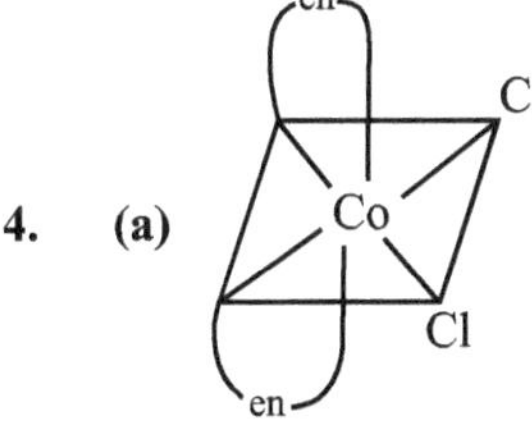

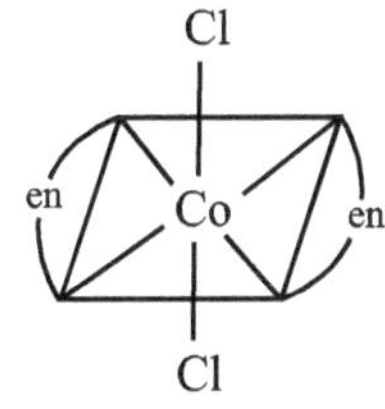

(1 Mark)

Trans - isomer is not optically active as it has plane of symmetry and axis of symmetry. **(1 Mark)**

(b) $[CoF_6]^{3-} \Rightarrow$ Co is in (+3) oxidation state.

$$Co^{3+}(24) \Rightarrow 3d^6\,4s^0 \Rightarrow \underset{3d}{\boxed{1\!\downarrow}\;\boxed{1}\;\boxed{1}\;\boxed{1}\;\boxed{1}}\;\underset{4s}{\underline{\quad}}$$

Since F^- is a weak field ligand, the outer d-orbital participates in the hybridization to form 6 equivalent bonds. Hence, the hybridization of the central metal atomic orbitals is $\textbf{sp}^3\textbf{d}^2$.

Co^{3+} has 4 unpaired electrons which imparts the spin magnetic moment of the complex. Therefore $[CoF_6]^{3-}$ is a paramagnetic complex.

$$\mu_{s.o} = \sqrt{n(n+2)} = \sqrt{4(4+2)} = 2\sqrt{6} \approx 4.9\,B.M.$$

(1 Mark)

5. **(a)** According to crystal field theory (CFT), when the ligands approach the central metal atom or ion, the five degenerate d-orbitals split into two different sets; e_g and t_{2g} according to the number of ligands present around the central atom/ion.

The e_g set has two orbitals and t_{2g} has three orbitals. For the d^5-configuration with a weak field ligand:

$$d^5 = e_g^2\,t_{2g}^3 \quad \text{or} \quad t_{2g}^3\,e_g^2 \qquad \textbf{(1 Mark)}$$

(b) $[Fe(CN)_6]^{3-}$ is an inner orbital complex because it has CN^- ligands that are strong field ligands that pair up the electrons in the Fe^{3+} ion and donate an electron pair in the inner d-orbital (3d-orbital). **(1 Mark)**

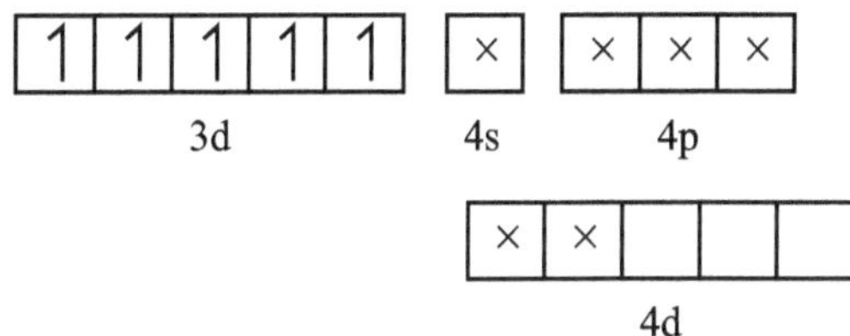

$[FeF_6]^{3-}$ is an outer orbital complex because it has F^- ligands that are weak field ligands that are unable to pair the electrons in the Fe^{3+} ion and therefore donate their electron-pairs to the outer d-orbitals (4d). **(1 Mark)**

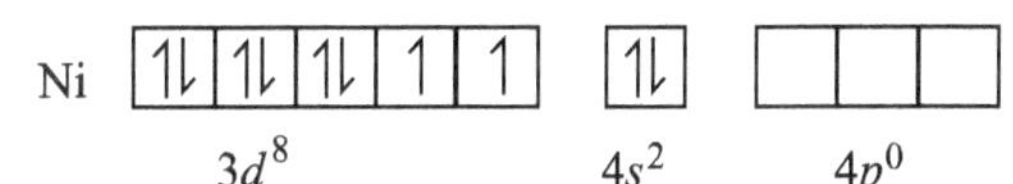

6. **(a)** Electronic configuration of Ni in ground state

Ni
$$\underset{3d^8}{\boxed{1\!\downarrow}\,\boxed{1\!\downarrow}\,\boxed{1\!\downarrow}\,\boxed{1}\,\boxed{1}}\quad\underset{4s^2}{\boxed{1\!\downarrow}}\quad\underset{4p^0}{\boxed{\quad}}$$

Electronic configuration of Ni atom in $Ni\,(CO)_4$

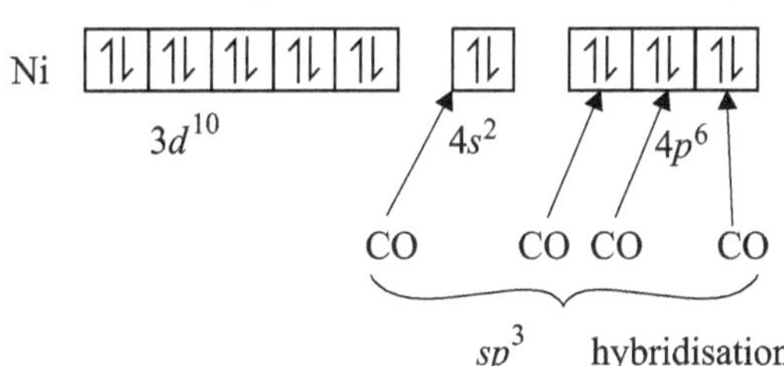

(1 Mark)

∴ Hybridisation of $Ni\,(CO)_4$ is sp^3 and diamagnetic in nature.

(b) IUPAC name of $[Pt(NH_3)_2Cl(NO_2)]$ is diamminechloridonitrito-N-platinum (II). **(1 Mark)**

(c) Ethylene diammine is a bidentate ligand and forms a stable chelate i.e. $[Co(en)_3]^{3+}$ chelating ligands form more stable complexes as compared to non-chelating ligands. Therefore; $[Co(en)_3]^{3+}$ is more stable complex than $[Co(NH_3)_6]^{3+}$. **(1 Mark)**

7. $[Mn(CN)_6]^{3-}$

$Mn = [Ar]\ 3d^5 4s^2$

$Mn^{3+} = [Ar]\ 3d^4$

Mn (ground state)

Mn in +3 state

Mn in $[Mn(CN)_6]^{3-}$

d^2sp^3 hybridisation

xx are electrons donated by ligand CN^-

Type of hybridization – d^2sp^3 **(1 mark)**

Magnetic moment value – $\sqrt{n(n+2)} = \sqrt{(2(2+2))} = 2.87$ BM

(n= no. of unpaired electrons) **(1 mark)**

Type of complex – inner orbital **(1 mark)**

8. (a) The colour of coordination compound depends upon the type of ligand and dd transition taking place .

H_2O is weak field ligand, which causes small splitting, leading to the *d-d* transition corresponding green colour, however due to the presence of (en) which ia strong field ligand , the splitting is increased. Due to the change in $t_{2g\text{-}eg}$ splitting the colouration of the compound changes from green to blue. **(1 Mark)**

(b) Formula of the compound is

$[Co(H_2NCH_2CH_2NH_2)_3]_2(SO_4)_3$

The hybridisation of the compound is: d^2sp^3

(1 Mark)

9. (a) As the fourth electron enters one of the e_g orbitals giving the configuration $t_{2g}^3 e_g^1$, which indicates $\Delta_o < P$ hence forms high spin complex.

(b)

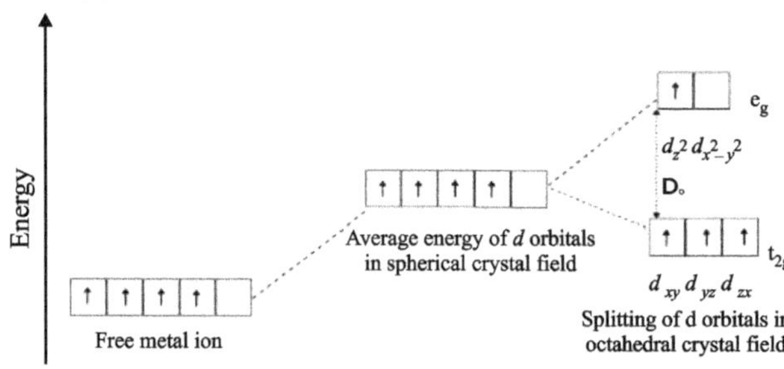

10.

Topper's Answer

Ans 4. (b) (i) $[Co(NH_3)_4(H_2O)Cl]Cl_2$

Tetraammineaqua chlorido Cobalt (III) Chloride

(ii) An ambidentate ligand has 2 ligating atoms out of which at a time only one bonds with the central metal atom

Eg : NO_2^- (Nitrite) SCN^- (thiocyanate)

nitrito-N   nitrito-O   thiocyanato S   thiocyanato N
or iso thiocyanato

whereas a bidentate ligand has 2 ligating sites with which it _simultaneously_ bonds to central metal atom

Eg : oxalate   and   ethane 1,2 diamine

$(C_2O_4)^-$ $\begin{matrix} COO^- \rightarrow \\ | \\ COO^- \rightarrow \end{matrix}$ $H_2N-CH_2-CH_2-NH_2$

(III) Although ammonia is a strong field ligand but out of $[Fe(NH_3)_6]^{+3}$ and $[Fe(C_2O_4)_3]^{-3}$; $[Fe(C_2O_4)_3]^{-3}$ is more stable because _oxalate_ is a bidentate ligand and therefore forms a _chelating_ complex, which provides it more stability as compared to the unidendated complex of similar structure.

$\therefore [Fe(C_2O_4)_3]^{+3} > [Fe(NH_3)_6]^{+3}$ in stability

---

11. (i) $[Fe(H_2O)_6]^{2+}$ complex is sp^3d^2 hybridised.

(1 Mark)

Complex is paramagnetic due to presenc of unpaired electrons **(½ Mark)**

(ii) $[Ni(CN)_4]^{2-}$ complex is dsp^2 hybridised. **(1 Mark)**

Complex is diamagnetic due to absence of unpaired electrons. **(½ Mark)**

12. (a) $[CoF_6]^{3-}$ is paramagnetic **(½ Mark)**

(b) $[Co(en)_3]^{3+}$ is more stable than $[CoF_6]^{3-}$ **(½ Mark)**

(c) $[Co(en)_3]^{3+}$ forms inner orbital complex **(½ Mark)**

(d) $[CoF_6]^{3-}$ forms high spin complex. **(½ Mark)**

Note

$[CoF_6]^{3-}$

$Co(27) \Rightarrow 1s^2\,2s^2\,2p^6\,3s^2\,3p^6\,4s^2\,3d^7$

$Co^{3+} = 3d^6\,4s^0$

F^- is a weak field ligand, therefore pairing of electron will not take place $[CoF_6]^{3-}$

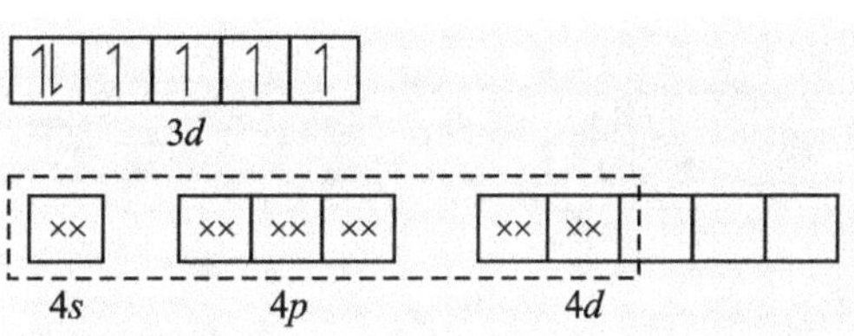

This complex has four unpaired electron. For $[Co(en)_3]^{3+}$

$Co^{3+} = 3d^6\,4s^0$

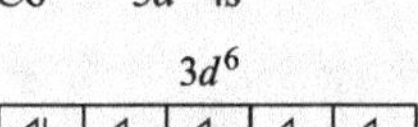

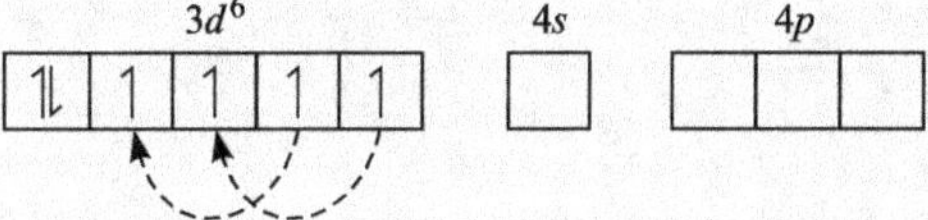

$[Co(en)_3]^{3+}$

(en) is strong field ligand, therefore pairing of electron takes place $[Co(en)_3]^{3+}$

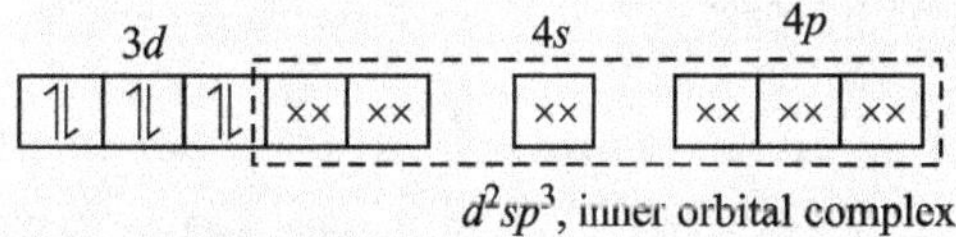

d^2sp^3, inner orbital complex

This complex does not have any unpaired electron.

13.

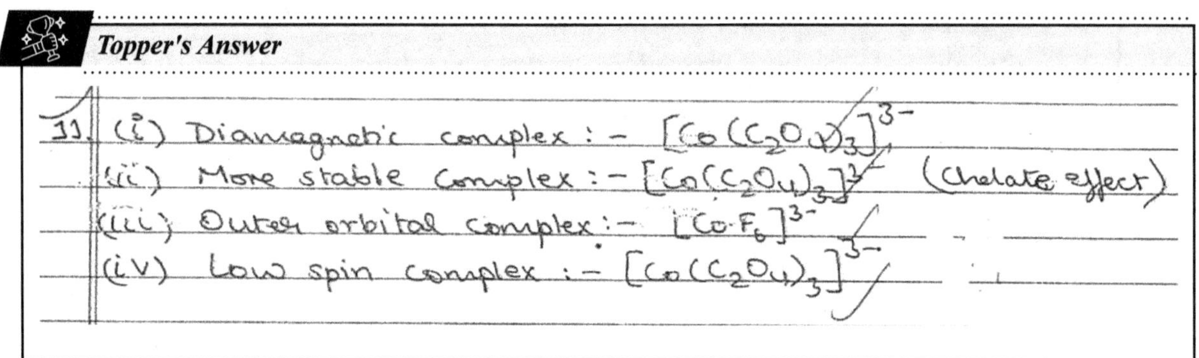

14. (a) Iron (III) hexacyanoferrate (II)

The formula is $Fe_4[Fe(CN)_6]_3$ **(1 Mark)**

(b) The complex $[Co(NH_3)_5Cl]SO_4$ exhibits ionization isomerism.

(the isomers are $[Co(NH_3)_5Cl]SO_4$ and $[Co(NH_3)_5(SO_4)]Cl$ **(1 Mark)**

(c) $[CoF_6]^{3-}$ hybridisation : sp^3d^2

number of unpaired e⁻s : 4 **(1 Mark)**

$[Co\,(27)]$: $[Ar]\,3d^7\,4s^2$

Co^{3+} : $[Ar]\,3d^6\,4s^0$

$[CoF_6]^{3-}$:

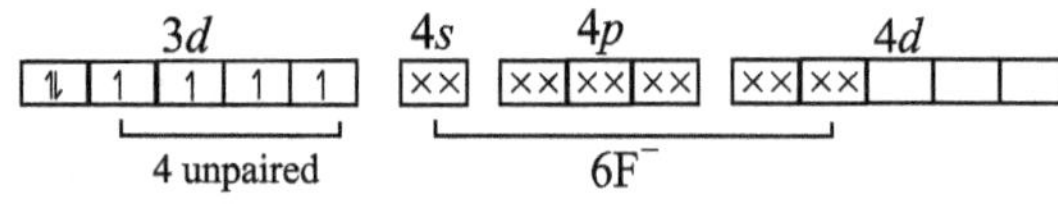

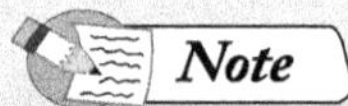

4 unpaired   6F⁻

> **Note**
>
> *Such type of problems might be asked in several wayes and are very important from compitative point of view. So in order to determine the hybridisation and no. of unpaired electrons in any complexes spectrochemical series plays a very important role. So you should memorised it always.*

15. (i) Coordination isomerism **(1 Mark)**

> **Note**
>
> *This type of isomerism arises from the inter change of ligands between cationic and anionic entities of different metal ions present in a complex.*

(ii) In case of $[Ni(H_2O)_6]^{2+}$, H_2O is weak field ligand so it does not cause the pairing of unpaired electron of Ni^{2+} ion. Thus there is possibility of intra d-d-transition. Thus light is absorbed from the visible region and colour is observed.

But in case of $[Ni(CN)_4]^{2-}$, CN⁻ is a strong field ligand. Therefore it will cause pairing of the unpaired electron of Ni^{2+} ion. There are no unpaired electron are present, so there are no d-d-transition and hence it is colourless. **(1 Mark)**

> **Note**
>
> *Some transition metal complexes are intensely coloured in solution but do not posses d-electrons. The intense colour is due to charge transfer from ligand to empty or partially filled metal d-orbitals.*

(iii) Pentamminecarbonatocobalt(III)chloride **(1 Mark)**

16. (a) Linkage isomerism is shown by the given complex.

$[CO(NH_3)_5(SCN)]^{2+}$

$[CO(NH_3)_5(NCS)^{2+}$

Therefore, it has Co-SCN and Co-NCS linkages.

  (1 Mark)

(b) $[Ni(CN)_4]^{2-}$, Ni is in +2 state

∴ Ni^{2+} : $3d^8\,4s^0$

CN⁻ ligand being a strong field ligand pairs up the electrons, thus

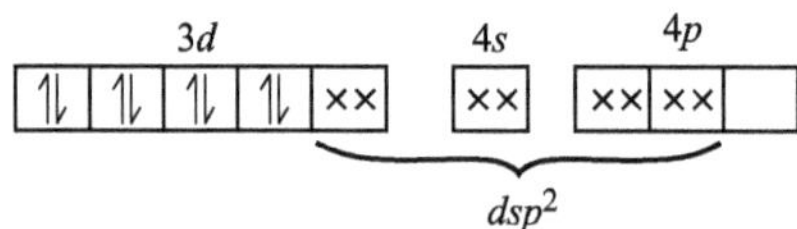

dsp^2

Since no unpaired electron is present, so $[Ni(CN)_4]^{2-}$ is diamagnetic.

$[NiCl_4]^{2-}$: Ni is in +2 state, thus Ni^{2+} : $3d^8$

Cl⁻ ligand being a weak field ligand cannot pair up the electrons

∴ $[NiCl_4]^{2-}$: 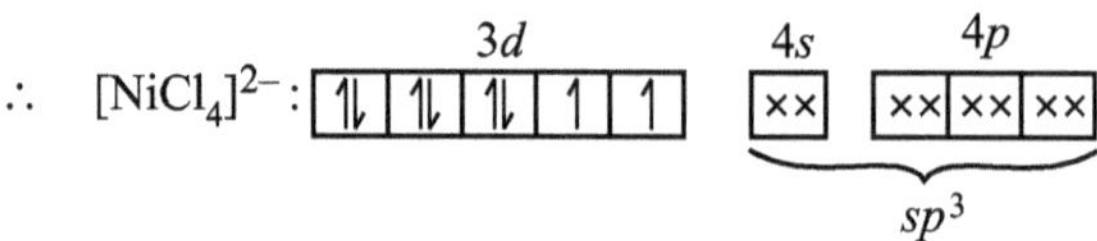

sp^3

Since it has unpaired electrons, so $[NiCl_4]^{2-}$ is paramagnetic. **(1 Mark)**

(c) In a tetrahedral complex, Δ_t is relatively small even with strong field ligands as there are fewer ligands to with. It is rare for the Δ_t of tetrahedral complexes to exceed the pairing energy. Usually, electrons will be more up to the higher energy orbitals rather than pair. Because of this low spin complexes are rarely observed. **(1 Mark)**

17. (a) Fe in ground state

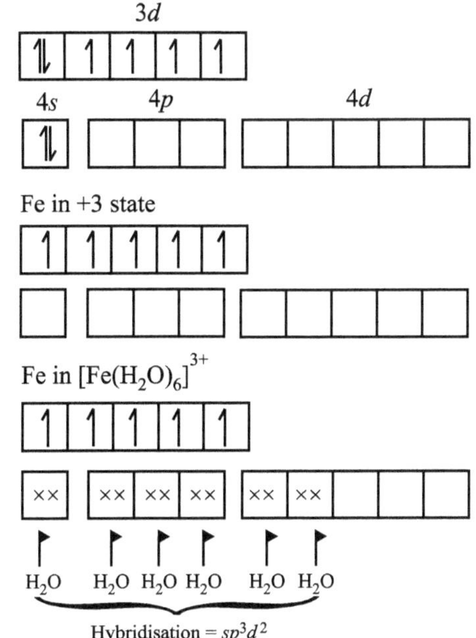

Fe in $[Fe(H_2O)_6]^{3+}$

Hybridisation: sp^3d^2

Magnetic character: Paramagnetic

Spin: High spin **(1 + 1 = 2 Marks)**

(b) *trans*-isomer of $[Pt(en)_2Cl_2]^{2+}$ is optically inactive.

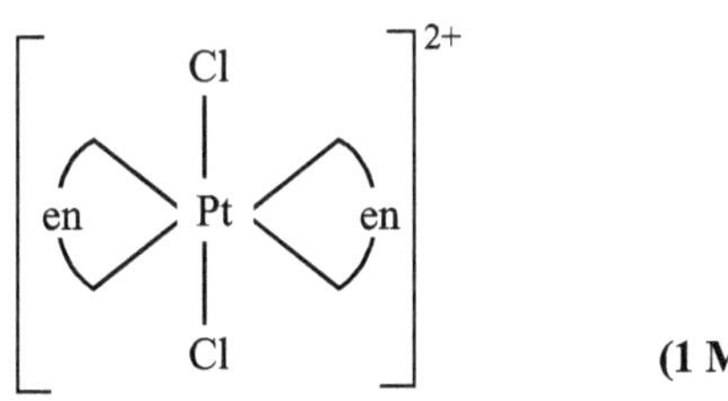

(1 Mark)

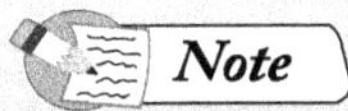 *Note*

The complexes which are non-superimposable on their mirror images are optically active and optically active complexes are asymmetric in nature. Because trans isomer contains plane of symmetry, so it is optically inactive.

18. (a) (i) Hybridisation type and shape - d^2sp^3, octahedral

(ii) Spin nature - low spin

(iii) Magnetic character - weakly paramagnetic (1 unpaired electron) **(2 Marks)**

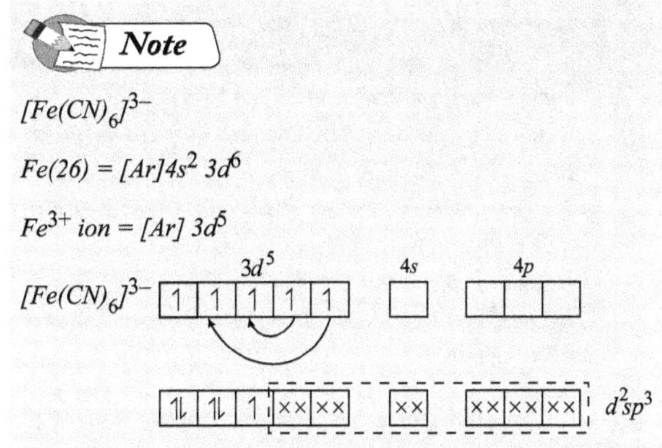 *Note*

$[Fe(CN)_6]^{3-}$

$Fe(26) = [Ar]4s^2\ 3d^6$

Fe^{3+} ion $= [Ar]\ 3d^5$

as CN^- is a strong field ligand hence pairing will take place in d-orbital.

(b)

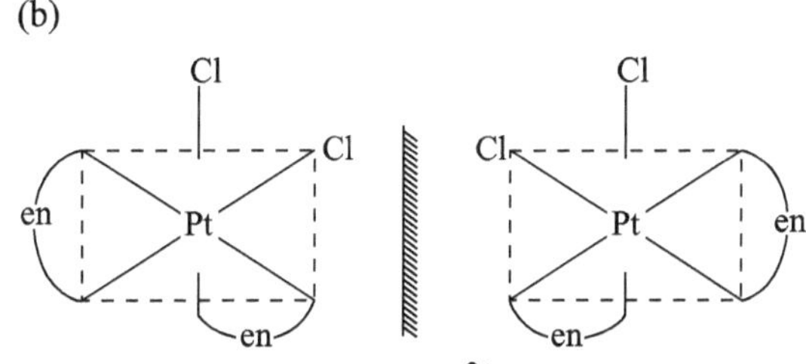

cis isomer of $[Pt(en)_2Cl_2]^{2+}$ is optically active.

(1 Mark)

19. (a) (i) $[CoF_6]^{3-}$ is sp^3d^2 hybridised, octahedral in shape and paramagnetic in nature.

Co (Z = 27) ground state :

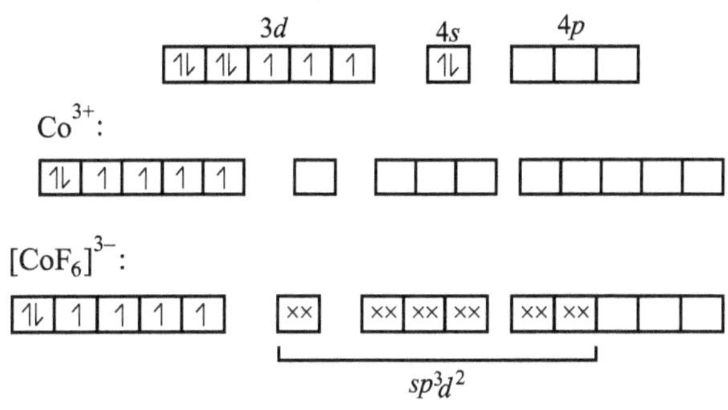

Co^{3+}:

$[CoF_6]^{3-}$:

As F^- ions are weak ligands, pairing of electrons does not take place. **(1 Mark)**

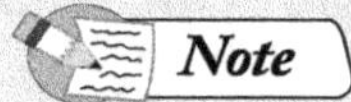

Note

The nature of ligands either weak field or strong field can be predicted by the help of spectrochemical series. Weak field ligands cause less crystal fields splitting, so they form high spin complexes. The strong field ligands cause greater crystal field splitting, so they form low spin complexes. In general, ligands can be arranged in a series which is termed as spectrochemical series in the order of increasing field strength as given below.

$I^- < Br^- < SCN^- < Cl^- < S^{2-} < F^- < OH^- < H_2O < Py < NH_3 < en < Phen < NO_2^- < H^- < CN^- = CO$

Ligands on the left are commonly referred to as weak-field ligands, and ligands on the right side are called strong filled ligands.

(ii) $[Ni(CN)_4]^{2-}$ is dsp^2 hybridised, square planar in shape and diamagnetic in nature.

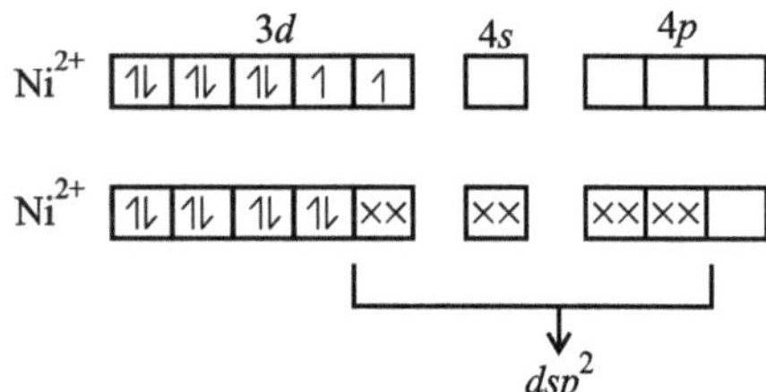

As CN^- ions are strong ligands, pairing of electrons will take place. **(1 Mark)**

(b) Since CO can form σ as well as π bond, whereas NH_3 has lone pair of electrons and can form σ bond only. Therefore, CO is better complexing reagent and forms a more stable complex than NH_3.

(1 Mark)

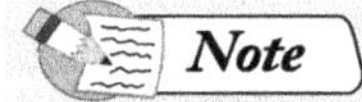

Note

σ-donor ligands : All ligands are σ-donors. The ligands lone pair that forms a bond with the metal will maximize its overlap with the metal's orbital by pointing directly at it. The more readily a ligand can share its lone pair, the higher its position on the spectrochemical series. For example hydride.

π-donor ligand : Some ligands have extra lone pairs on their bonding atom beyond the one that forms the σ-donor interaction.

These additional lone pair electrons can also interact with the metal's d-orbital in side on fasion, creating an additional bond. For examples, halides can form strong bond with metal.

π-acceptor ligand: Sometimes a ligands can donate electrons with its lone pair to form one bond, but also accept electrons from the metal with one of its empty orbitals. This phenomenon is sometime called back donation or back-bonding. The interaction is very strong, and results in very large Δ values.

20. (i) 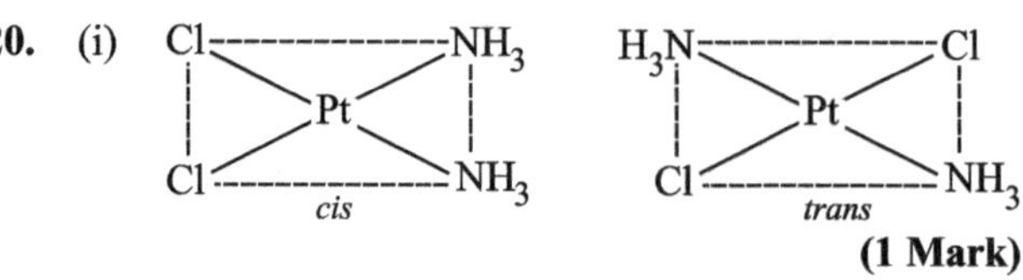

(1 Mark)

(ii) On the basis of crystal field theory, if $\Delta_o < P$, then high spin complex is formed. Therefore d^4 ion exhibit the electronic configuration as $t_{2g}^3 e_g^1$.

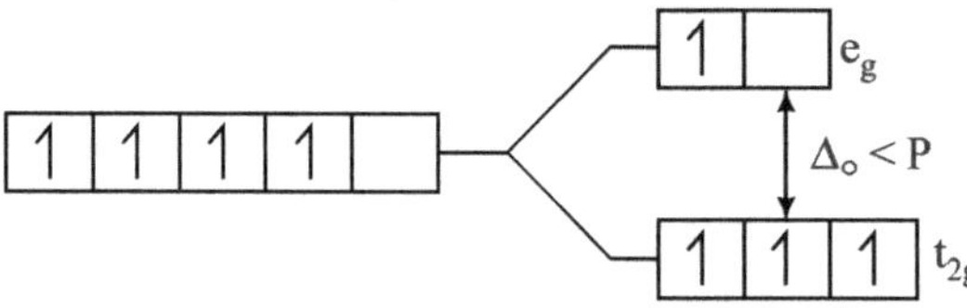

(1 Mark)

(iii) In $[Ni(CO)_4]$, Ni has zero oxidation state. **(1 Mark)** The hybridisation is sp^3 and complex is diamagnetic.

Note

$Ni (28) \Rightarrow 3d^8, 4s^2$

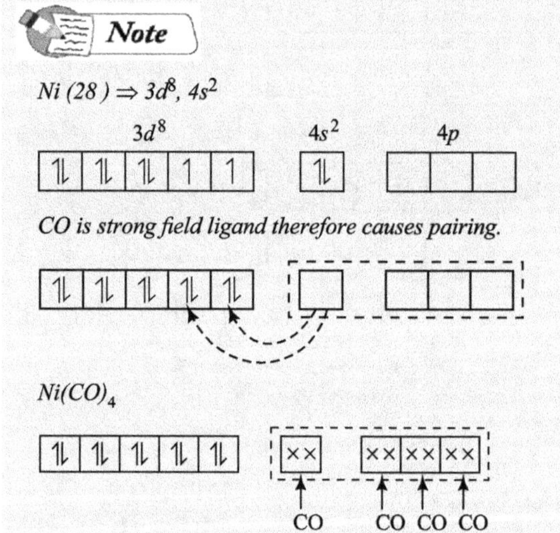

21. (i) IUPAC name of $[Cr(NH_3)_4Cl_2]Cl$ is tetraamminedichloridochromium (III) chloride

(1 Mark)

(ii) $[Co(en)_3]^{3+}$ exhibits optical isomerism as follows:

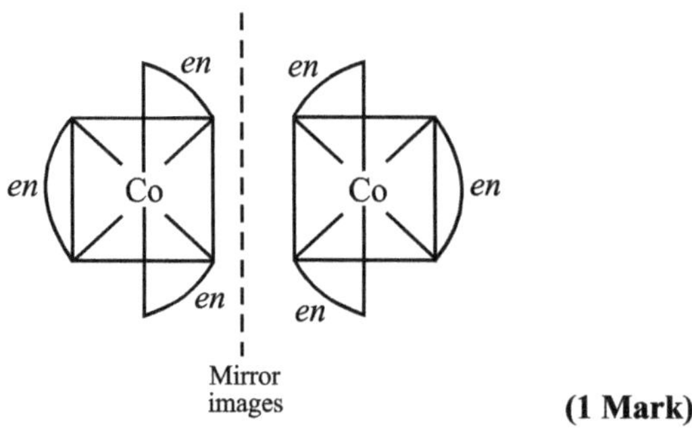

(1 Mark)

(iii) In $[NiCl_4]^{2-}$, Ni is in +2 oxidation state.

Ni (28) : $3d^84s^2$ Ni^{2+} : $3d^8\,4s^0$

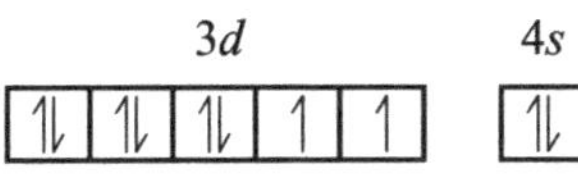

Cl^- is weak field ligand. It does not pair up electrons. Hence, it is paramagnetic.

In $[Ni\,(CO)_4]$, Ni is in 0 O.S.   Ni (28) : $3d^8\,4s^2$

CO is strong field ligand, as it pairs up the $4s$ electrons with $3d$ electrons to give $3d^{10}\,4s^0$. So, there is no unpaired electron and hence, the complex is diamagnetic. **(1 Mark)**

22. (i) Tetrachloridonickelate (II) ion

(ii) sp^3

(iii) Tetrahedral   **(1 + 1 + 1 = 3 Marks)**

23. The d-orbitals present in metal have the same energy in the free state. This is called degenerate state of d-orbital. But, when a complex is formed the ligands destroy the degeneracy of these orbitals. The d-orbitals gets split into two sets one with lower and one with higher energy. The difference of energy between two sets is called crystal field splitting energy. **(1 Mark)**

(i) When $\Delta_o > P$, the d^4 has configuration i.e., $t_{2g}^4 e_g^0$

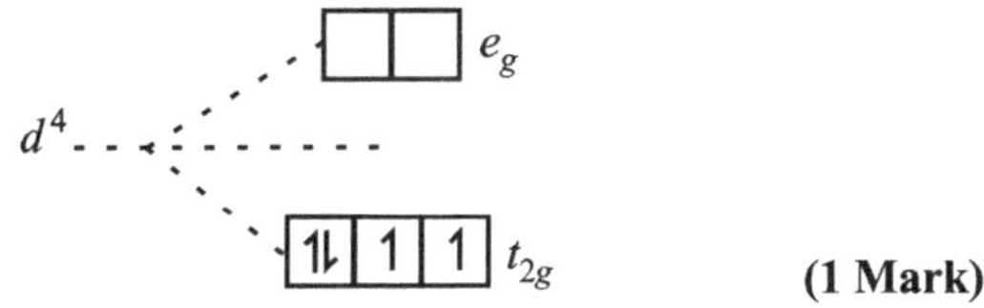

(1 Mark)

(ii) When $\Delta_o < P$, the d^4 has configuration i.e., $t_{2g}^3 e_g^1$

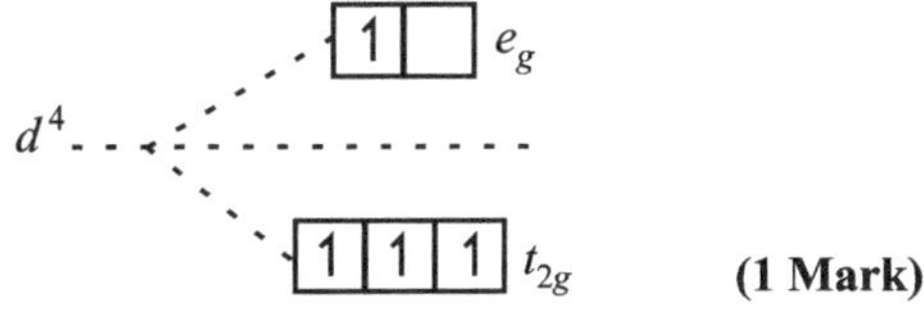

(1 Mark)

24. (a) D. Energy is directly proportional to the wave number. Maximum energy of light is required for an electron to jump from t_{2g} to eg in case of $[CrD_6]^{3-}$ **(1/2+1/2 Mark)**

OR

(a) A, The splitting caused in least in this case as the energy required for electron to jump from t_{2g} to eg., is minimum.   **(1/2 + 1/2 Mark)**

(b) $[CrB_6]^{3+}$, wavelength of light absorbed is $1/17830 = 560nm$ for the complex while $1/13640 = 733nm$ for $[CrA_6]^{3-}$ complex.   **(1/2+1/2 Mark)**

(c) (i) $[CrCl_6]^{3-}$, Hexachloridochromate(III) ion   **(1 Mark)**

(ii) $[Cr(NH_3)_6]^{3+}$, Hexaamminechromium(III) ion

$A = Cl^-$, $B = H_2O$, $C = NH_3$, $D = CN^-$

Topic-5: *Bonding in Metal Carbenyls, Importance of applications of Coordination Compounds*

1. **Topper's Answer**

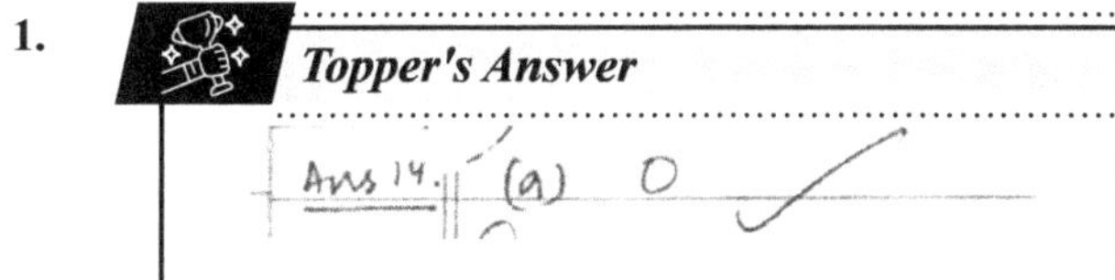

2. (a) For strong field ligands, $\Delta_0 > P$. It becomes more energetically favourable for the fourth electron to occupy α try orbital. Thus, the electronic configuration for d^4 becomes $t_{2g}^4 e_g^0$.   **(1 Mark)**

(b) In $[Ni(H_2O)_6]^{2+}$ complex, H_2O is a weak field ligand. Therefore, there are unpaired electrons in $N^{:2+}$. In this complex, the d electrons from the lower energy level can be excited to the higher energy level i.e., the possibility of d – d transition is present. Hence, $[Ni(H_2O)_6]^{2+}$ is coloured.   **(1 Mark)**

In $[Ni(CO)_4]$ complex, CO is a strong field ligand. Therefore, all the electrons are paired. The d – d transition is not possible in this complex. Hence, it is colourless.   **(1 Mark)**

108   **Chemistry**

3. The metal-carbon bond in metal carbonyls possess both σ and π character. The M–C σ bond is formed by the donation of lone pair of electrons from the carbonyl carbon into a vacant orbital of metal. The M–C π bond is formed by the donation of a pair of electrons from a filled d-orbital of metal into the vacant antibonding π^* orbital of carbon monoxide.

This type of metal to ligand bonding creates a synergic effect which strengthens the metal-carbon bond.

(1 + 1 = 2 Marks)

4. (a) $K_3[Al(C_2O_4)_3]$

(b) $[CoCl_2(en)_2]^+$ (1 + 1 = 2 Marks)

Note

Bis, tris, tetrakis etc. should not be used when ligands are arranged in alphabetical order to write the IUPAC name of the complexes or draw the formula.

6 Chapter — Haloalkanes and Haloarenes

Topic-1: *Classification, Nomenclature, Nature of C–X Bond*

1 — Multiple Choice Questions

1. Which of the following belongs to the class of Vinyl halides? **[All India 2023 Set-II, K]**

(a) $CH_2 = CHCH_2CH_2Cl$

(b) $CH_2 = \underset{\underset{Br}{|}}{C} - CH_3$

(c) $CH_2 = CH - CH_2 - Br$

(d) $CH \equiv C - Br$

2. Which one of the following halides contains $C_{sp^2} - X$ bond? **[All India 2022, Term-I, K]**

(a) Allyl halide   (b) Alkyl halide

(c) Benzyl halide   (d) Vinyl halide

4 — Very Short Answer Questions (1 Mark)

3. Write the IUPAC name of **[All India 2019, K]**

$CH_2 - CH_2 - Cl$

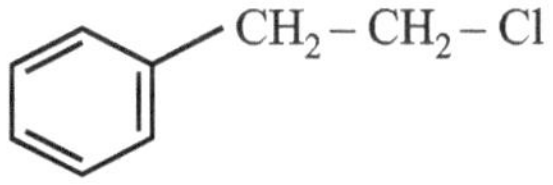

4. Write IUPAC name of the given compound : **[All India 2019, Set-II]**

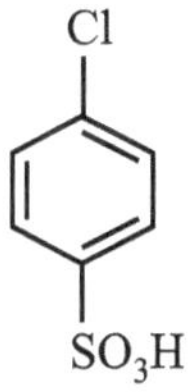

5. Which would undergo S_N1 reaction faster in the following pair? **[All India 2015, K]**

$$CH_3 - CH_2 - Br \text{ and } CH_3 - \underset{\underset{Br}{|}}{\overset{\overset{CH_3}{|}}{C}} - CH_3$$

6. Write the IUPAC name of the following compound: **[All India 2013, K]**

$$CH_3 - \underset{\underset{CH_3}{|}}{\overset{\overset{CH_3}{|}}{C}} - \underset{\underset{Cl}{|}}{CH} - CH_3$$

7. Write the IUPAC name of

$$CH_3\underset{\underset{Cl}{|}}{CH} - CH_2CH = CH_2.$$

[Delhi 2013, K]

Topic-2: *Methods of Preparation of Haloalkanes*

1 — Multiple Choice Questions

1. Which of the following isomer of pentane (C_5H_{12}) will give three isomeric monochlorides on photochemical chlorination ? **[All India 2022, Term-I, U]**

(a) $CH_3 - \underset{\underset{CH_3}{|}}{\overset{\overset{CH_3}{|}}{C}} - CH_3$

(b) $CH_3 - CH_2 - CH_2 - CH_2 - CH_3$

(c) $CH_3 - \underset{\underset{CH_3}{|}}{CH} - CH_2 - CH_3$

(d) All of the above

2. Major product obtained on reaction of 3-Phenyl propene with HBr in presence of organic peroxide : **[All India 2021-22, Term-I, U]**

(a) 3- Phenyl 1-bromopropane

(b) 1-Phenyl-3-bromopropane

(c) 1-Phenyl-2-bromopropane

(d) 3-Phenyl-2-bromopropane

3. o-hydroxy benzyl alcohol when reacted with PCl_3 gives the product as (IUPAC name)

[CBSE Sample 2021-22, ]

(a) o- hydroxy benzyl chloride

(b) 2-chloromethylphenol

(c) o-chloromethylchlorobenzene

(d) 4-hydroxymethylphenol

4. Alkenes decolourise bromine water in presence of CCl_4 due to formation of : **[CBSE Sample 2021-22, K]**

(a) allyl bromide

(b) vinyl bromide

(c) bromoform

(d) vicinal dibromide

 **Topic-3:** *Preparation of Haloarenes*

1 *Multiple Choice Questions*

1. The reaction of toluene with Cl_2 in presence of $FeCl_3$ gives 'X' while that of toluene with Cl_2 in presence of light gives 'Y'. Thus 'X' and 'Y' are:

[All India 2021-22, Term-I, U]

(a) X = benzyl chloride Y = o and p – chlorotoluene

(b) X = m – chlorotoluene Y = p – chlorotoluene

(c) X = o and p–chlorotoluene Y = trichloromethylbenzene

(d) X= benzyl chloride, Y = m-chlorotoluene

2. The reaction of toluene with Cl_2 in presence of $FeCl_3$ gives 'X' while that of toluene with Cl_2 in presence of light gives 'Y'. Thus 'X' and 'Y' are:

[CBSE Sample 2021-22, U]

5 *Short Answer Questions (2 or 3 Marks)*

5. Write the mechanism of the following reaction:

$$CH_3CH_2OH \xrightarrow{HBr} CH_3CH_2Br + H_2O$$

[All India 2014, K]

6. Draw the structure of major monohalo product in each of the following reactions : **[Delhi 2014, K]**

(i) 

(ii) 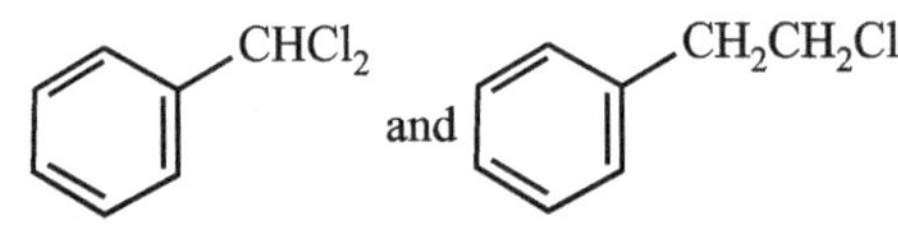

(a) X = benzyl chloride Y = o and p – chlorotoluene

(b) X = m – chlorotoluene Y = p – chlorotoluene

(c) X = o and p–chlorotoluene Y = trichloromethylbenzene

(d) X= benzyl chloride, Y = m-chlorotoluene

4 *Very Short Answer Questions (1 Mark)*

3. Out of **[All India 2017, K]**

and

which is an example of benzylic halide?

Topic-4: *Physical Properties, Chemical Reactions*

1 *Multiple Choice Questions*

1. Which of the following is not correct?

[CBSE Sample 2023-24, U]

(a) In haloarenes, the electron pairs on halogen atom are in conjugation with π–electrons of the ring.

(b) The carbon–magnesium bond is covalent and non–polar in nature.

(c) During S_N1 reaction, the carbocation formed in the slow step being sp^2 hybridised is planar.

(d) Out of $CH_2 = CH{-}Cl$ and $C_6H_5CH_2Cl$, $C_6H_5CH_2Cl$ is more reactive towards S_N1 reaction

2. Inversion of configuration occurs in

(a) S_N2 reaction **[All India 2023, Set-I, K]**

(b) S_N1 reaction

(c) Neither S_N2 nor S_N1 reaction

(d) S_N1 as well as S_N2 reaction

3. Retention of configuration is observed in

[**All India 2023 Set-II, K**]

(a) S_N1 reaction

(b) S_N2 reaction

(c) Neither S_N1 nor S_N2 reaction

(d) S_N2 reaction as well as S_N1 reaction

4. Which of the following molecules has a chiral centre correctly labelled with an asterisk (*)?

[**Delhi 2023 Set-1, U**]

(a) $CH_3C^*HBrCH_3$

(b) $CH_3C^*HClCH_2Br$

(b) $HOCH_2C^*H(OH)CH_2OH$

(d) $CH_3C^*Br_2CH_3$

5. Consider the following compounds :

[**All India 2022, Term-I, U**]

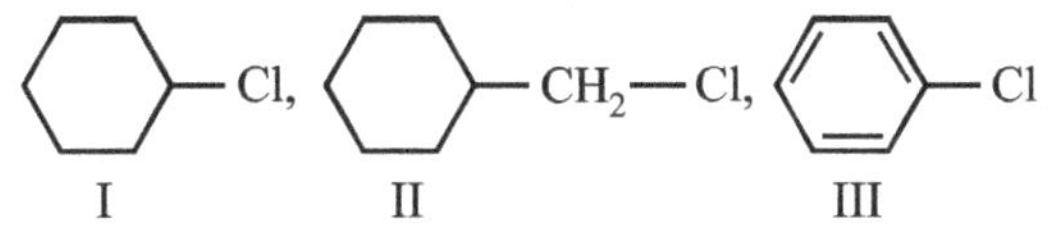

The correct order of reactivity towards S_N2 reaction

(a) I > III > II

(b) II > III > I

(c) II > I > III

(d) III > I > II

6. Major product formed in the following reaction

[**All India 2022, Term-I, U**]

$$CH_3-\underset{\underset{CH_3}{|}}{\overset{\overset{CH_3}{|}}{C}}-Br + NaOCH_3 \longrightarrow$$

(a) $CH_3-\underset{\underset{CH_3}{|}}{\overset{\overset{CH_3}{|}}{C}}-ONa$

(b) $CH_3-\underset{\underset{CH_3}{|}}{\overset{\overset{CH_3}{|}}{C}}-OCH_3$

(c) $CH_3-\underset{\underset{CH_3}{|}}{\overset{\overset{CH_3}{|}}{C}}-O-\underset{\underset{CH_3}{|}}{\overset{\overset{CH_3}{|}}{C}}-CH_3$

(d) $CH_3-\underset{\underset{CH_3}{|}}{C}=CH_2$

7. Enantiomers differ only in [**All India 2022, Term-I, K**]

(a) boiling point

(b) rotation of polarised light

(c) melting point

(d) solubility

8. In the reaction

$$\text{⬡}-Br \xrightarrow[\text{Dry ether}]{Mg} \text{'X'} \xrightarrow{H_2O} \text{'Y'}$$

compound 'Y' is [**All India 2022, Term-I, U**]

(a) ⬡—OH

(b) ⬡—OMgBr

(c) ⬡

(d) ⬡⬡

9. Which of the following is optically inactive ?

[**All India 2022, Term-I, K**]

(a) (+) – Butan–2–ol

(b) (–) – Butan–2–ol

(c) (±) – Butan–2–ol

(d) (+) – 2 – Bromobutane

10. Which of the following has highest boiling point ?

[**All India 2022, Term-I, U**]

(a) C_2H_5-F

(b) C_2H_5-Cl

(c) C_2H_5-Br

(d) C_2H_5-I

11. Which one of the following compounds is more reactive towards S_N1 reaction? [**CBSE Sample 2022-23, U**]

(a) $CH_2{=}CHCH_2Br$

(b) $C_6H_5CH_2Br$

(c) $C_6H_5CH(C_6H_5)Br$

(d) $C_6H_5CH(CH_3)Br$

12. Which of the following isomer has the highest melting point. [**CBSE Sample 2021-22, U**]

(a) 1,2-dichlorobenzene

(b) 1,3 -dichlorobenzene

(c) 1,4-dichlorobenzene

(d) all isomers have same melting points

13. Which of the following is a correct statement for C_2H_5Br?

[**CBSE Sample 2021-22, U**]

(a) It reacts with metallic Na to give ethane.

(b) It gives nitroethane on heating with aqueous solution of $AgNO_2$

(c) It gives C_2H_5OH on boiling with alcoholic potash.

(d) It forms diethylthioether on heating with alcoholic KSH.

14. Which reagents are required for one step conversion of chlorobenzene to toluene? **[CBSE Sample 2021-22, K]**

   (a) CH_3Cl / $AlCl_3$

   (b) CH_3Cl, Na, Dry ether

   (c) CH_3Cl / Fe dark

   (d) $NaNO_2$ / HCl / 0-5°C

15. Complete the following analogy:

                           [CBSE Sample 2021-22, K]

   Same molecular formula but different structures: A : : Non superimposable mirror images: B

   (a) A : Isomers : : B : Enantiomer

   (b) A : Enantiomers : : B : Racemic mixture

   (c) A : Sterioisomers : : B : Retention

   (d) A : Isomers : : B : Sterioisomers

16. The conversion of an alkyl halide into an alcohol by aqueous NaOH is classified as   **[Delhi 2020, Set-I]**

   (a) a dehydrohalogenation reaction

   (b) a substitution reaction

   (c) an addition reaction

   (d) a dehydration reaction

17. Identify A,B,C and D: **[CBSE Sample 2020-21, K]**

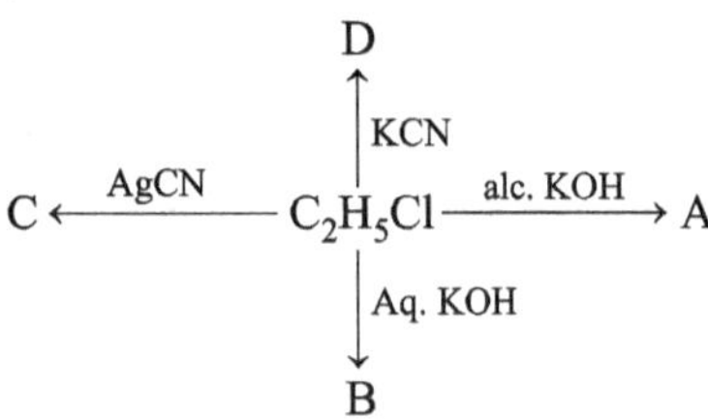

   (a) A = C_2H_4, B = C_2H_5OH, C = C_2H_5NC, D = C_2H_5CN

   (b) A = C_2H_5OH, B = C_2H_4, C = C_2H_5CN, D = C_2H_5NC

   (c) A = C_2H_4, B = C_2H_5OH, C = C_2H_5CN, D = C_2H_5NC

   (d) A = C_2H_5OH, B = C_2H_4, C = C_2H_5NC, D = C_2H_5CN

2   *Assertion Reason/Two Statement Type Questions*

Given below are two statements labelled as Assertion (A) and Reason (R). Select the most appropriate answer from the options given below:

(a) Both (A) and (R) are true and (R) is the correct explanation of (A).

(b) Both (A) and (R) are true, but (R) is not the correct explanation of (A).

(c) (A) is true, but (R) is false.

(d) (A) is false, but (R) is true.

18. **Assertion (A) :** Chlorobenzene is resistant to nucleophilic substitution reaction at room temperature.

   Reason (R) : C-Cl bond gets weaker due to resonance.

                       [All India 2023, Set-I, K]

19. **Assertion (A) :** Chlorobenzene is less reactive towards nucleophilic substitution reaction.

   Reason (R) : Nitro group in chlorobenene increases its reactivity towards nucleophilic substi-tution reaction.

                [All India 2022, Term-I, U]

20. **Assertion (A):** Alkyl halides are insoluble in water.

   Reason (R): Alkyl halides have halogen attached to sp^3 hybrid carbon.   **[CBSE Sample 2021-22, U]**

4   *Very Short Answer Questions (1 Mark)*

21. Out of ⬡Cl and ⬡CH_2–Cl , which will undergo S_N1 reaction faster with OH^- ?   **[Delhi 2020, U]**

22. Define ambidient nucleophile with an example.

                           [Delhi 2019, K]

23. Out of chlorobenzene and benzyl chloride, which one gets easily hydrolysed by aqueous NaOH and why?

                      [All India 2018, U]

24. Out of $CH_3 - \underset{\underset{CH_3}{|}}{CH} - CH_2 - Cl$ and $CH_3 - CH_2 - \underset{\underset{CH_3}{|}}{CH} - Cl$, which is more reactive towards S_N1 reaction and why ?   **[Delhi 2016, K]**

25. Which would undergo S_N2 reaction faster in the following pair and why ?   **[Delhi 2015, K]**

     $CH_3 - CH_2 - Br$ and $CH_3 - \underset{\underset{Br}{|}}{\overset{\overset{CH_3}{|}}{C}} - CH_3$

26. Identify the chiral molecule in the following pair:

                            [All India 2014, K]

5   *Short Answer Questions (2 or 3 Marks)*

27. An organic compound A with the molecular formula (+)C_4H_9Br undergoes hydrolysis to form (±) C_4H_9OH. Give the structure of A and write the mechanism of the reaction.   **[CBSE Sample 2023-24, U]**

28. Answer any 3 of the following:

[All India 2023, Set-I, U]

(a) Which isomer of C_5H_{10} gives a single monochloro compound C_5H_9Cl in bright sunlight?

(b) Arrange the following compounds in increasing order of reactivity towards S_N2 reaction:

2-Bromopentane, 1-Bromopentane, 2-Bromo-2-methylbutane **[All India 2023, Set-I, U]**

(c) Why p-dichlorobenzene has higher melting point than those of ortho-and meta-isomers?

[All India 2023, Set-I, U]

(d) Identify A and B in the following:

$$\square\!-\!Br \xrightarrow[\text{Dry ether}]{\text{Mg}} A \xrightarrow{H_2O} B$$

[All India 2023, Set-I, K]

29. Why is boiling point of o-dichlorobenzene higher than p-dichlorobenzene but melting point of para isomer is higher than ortho isomer? **[Delhi 2023 Set-I, U]**

30. Why haloarenes are not reactive towards nucleophilic substitution reaction? Give two reasons.

[Delhi 2023 Set-III, U]

31. (a) Identify the major product formed when 2-cyclohexylchloroethane undergoes a dehydrohalogenation reaction. Name the reagent which is used to carry out the reaction.

[CBSE Sample 2022-23, K]

(b) Why are haloalkanes more reactive towards nucleophilic substitution reactions than haloarenes and vinylic halides? **[CBSE Sample 2022-23, U]**

32. (a) Name the possible alkenes which will yield 1-chloro-1-methylcyclohexane on their reaction with HCl. Write the reactions involved.

[CBSE Sample 2022-23, U]

(b) Allyl chloride is hydrolysed more readily than n-propyl chloride. Why? **[CBSE Sample 2022-23, U]**

33. Give reason for the following:

[CBSE Sample 2022-23, U]

(a) During the electrophilic substitution reaction of haloarenes, para substituted derivative is the major product.

(b) The product formed during SN1 reaction is a racemic mixture.

34. (a) Name the suitable alcohol and reagent, from which 2-Chloro-2-methyl propane can be prepared.

[CBSE Sample 2022-23, U]

(b) Out of the Chloromethane and Fluoromethane, which one is has higher dipole moment and why?

[CBSE Sample 2022-23, U]

35. Identify A, B, C, D, E and F in the following:

$$E \xleftarrow{H_2O} D \xleftarrow[\text{dry ether}]{Mg} CH_3-\underset{\underset{CH_3}{|}}{CH}-CH_2-Br \xrightarrow{\text{alcoholic KOH}} A$$

$$\xrightarrow{NaOC_2H_5} F \qquad \Big| HBr$$

$$C \xleftarrow{\text{Na/dry ether}} B$$

[Delhi 2020, U]

36. Give reasons for the following : **[All India 2019, U]**

(a) The presence of $-NO_2$ group at ortho or para position increases the reactivity of haloarenes towards nucleophilic substitution reactions.

(b) p-dichlorobenzene has higher melting point than that of ortho or meta isomer.

(c) Thionyl chloride method is preferred for preparing alkyl chloride from alcohols.

37. (a) Write equation for preparation of 1-iodobutane from 1-chlorobutane. **[All India 2019, U]**

(b) Out of 2-bromopentane, 2-bromo-2-methylbutane and 1-bromopentane, which compound is most reactive towards elimination reaction and why?

[All India 2019, K]

(c) Give IUPAC name of **[All India 2019, K]**

$$CH_3-CH=CH-\underset{\underset{Br}{|}}{\overset{\overset{CH_3}{|}}{C}}-CH_3$$

38. (i) Out of $(CH_3)_3C-Br$ and $(CH_3)_3C-I$, which one is more reactive towards S_N1 and why?

[Delhi 2019, U]

(ii) Write the product formed when p-nitrochlorobenzene is heated with aqueous NaOH at 443 K followed by acidification. **[Delhi 2019, K]**

(iii) Why *dextro* and *laevo* – rotatory isomers of Butan-2-ol are difficult to separate by fractional distillation?

[Delhi 2019, U]

39. (a) Identify the chiral molecule in the following pair :

[All India 2018, U]

$$\text{(i)} \quad \underset{OH}{\diagup\!\!\diagdown} \qquad \& \qquad \text{(ii)} \quad \underset{OH}{\diagup\!\!\diagdown\!\!\diagup}$$

(b) Write the structure of the product when chlorobenzene is treated with methyl chloride in the presence of sodium metal and dry ether. **[All India 2018, K]**

(c) Write the structure of the alkene formed by dehydrohalogenation of 1-bromo-1 methylcyclohexane with alcoholic KOH. **[All India 2018, K]**

40. The following compounds are given to you:

2-Bromopentane, 2-Bromo-2-methylbutane,

1-Bromopentane **[All India 2017, K]**

(a) Write the compound which is most reactive towards S_N2 reaction.

(b) Write the compound which is optically active.

(c) Write the compound which is most reactive towards β-elimination reaction.

41. Following compounds are given to you : **[Delhi 2017, K]**

2-Bromopentane, 2-Bromo-2-methylbutane, 1-Bromopentane

(i) Write the compound which is most reactive towards S_N2 reaction.

(ii) Write the compound which is optically active.

(iii) Write the compound which is most reactive towards β-elimination reaction.

42. Write the structure of an isomer of compound C_4H_9Br which is most reactive towards S_N1 reaction.

[All India 2016, K]

43. How do you convert :

(i) Chlorobenzene to biphenyl

(ii) Propene to 1-iodopropane

(iii) 2-Bromobutane to but-2-ene **[All India 2016, K]**

44. Write the major product(s) in the following :

[All India 2016, K]

(i) O_2N—C$_6H_4$—CH$_2$—CH$_3$ $\xrightarrow{Br_2, UV\ light}$

(ii) $2CH_3 - \underset{\underset{Cl}{|}}{CH} - CH_3 \xrightarrow[dry\ ether]{Na}$

(iii) $CH_3 - CH_2 - Br \xrightarrow{AgCN}$

45. Give reasons : **[Delhi 2016, K]**

(i) C–Cl bond length in chlorobenzene is shorter than C–Cl bond length in CH_3–Cl.

(ii) The dipole moment of chlorobenzene is lower than that of cyclohexyl chloride.

(iii) S_N1 reactions are accompanied by racemization in optically active alkyl halides.

46. Write the structure of the major product in each of the following reactions. **[All India 2015, K]**

(i) $CH_3 - CH = \underset{\underset{CH_3}{|}}{C} - CH_3 + HBr \longrightarrow$

(ii) $CH_3CH_2CH_2\underset{\underset{Br}{|}}{CH} - CH_3 \xrightarrow[\Delta]{KOH\ (alc.)}$

(iii) $C_6H_5Br + CH_3Cl \xrightarrow{anhyd.AlCl_3}$

47. Give reasons : **[Delhi 2015, U]**

(a) *n*-Butyl bromide has higher boiling point than *t*-butyl bromide.

(b) Racemic mixture is optically inactive.

(c) The presence of nitro group ($-NO_2$) at o/p positions increases the reactivity of haloarenes towards nucleophilic substitution reactions.

48. (a) Draw the structures of major monohalo products in each of the following reactions :**[All India 2014, K]**

(i) cyclohexyl—$CH_2OH \xrightarrow{PCl_5}$

(ii) phenyl—$CH_2 - CH = CH_2 + HBr \longrightarrow$

(b) Which halogen compound in each of the following pairs will react faster in S_N2 reaction:

(i) CH_3Br or CH_3I

(ii) $(CH_3)_3C - Cl$ or $CH_3 - Cl$ **[All India 2014, K]**

49. (i) Which alkyl halide from the following pair is chiral and undergoes faster S_N2 reaction ? **[Delhi 2014, K]**

(a) butyl–Br (b) isobutyl–Br

(ii) Out of S_N1 and S_N2, which reaction occurs with (a) Inversion of configuration (b) Racemisation ?

50. Give reasons for the following : **[All India 2013, U]**

(i) Ethyl iodide undergoes S_N2 reaction faster than ethyl bromide

(ii) (±) 2-Butanol is optically inactive.

(iii) C – X bond length in halobenzene is smaller than C – X bond length in CH_3 – X.

51. Chlorobenzene is extremely less reactive towards a nucleophilic substitution reaction. Give two reasons for the same. **[Delhi 2013, K]**

7   *Case Based Questions*

52. Nucleophilic Substitution

Nucleophilic Substitution reaction of haloalkane can be conducted according to both S_N1 and S_N2 mechanisms. S_N1 is a two step reaction while S_N2 is a single step reaction. For any haloalkane which mechanism is followed depends on factors such as structure of haloalkane, properties of leaving group, nucleophilic reagent and solvent.

Influences of solvent polarity : In S_N1 reaction the polarity of the system increases from the reactant to the transition state, because a polar solvent has a greater effect on the transition state than the reactant, thereby reducing activation energy and accelerating the reaction, In S_N2 reaction, the polarity of the system generally does not change from the reactant to the transition state and only charge dispersion occurs. At this time, polar solvent has a great stabilizing effect on Nu than the transition state, thereby increasing activation energy and slow down the reaction rate. For example, the decomposition rate (S_N1) of tertiary chlorobutane at 25°C in water (dielectric constant 79) is 300000 times faster than in ethanol (dielectric constant 24). The reaction rate (S_N2) of 2-Bromopropane and NaOH in ethanol containing 40% water is twice slower than in absolute ethanol. Hence the level of solvent polarity has influence on both S_N1 and S_N2 reaction, but with different results. Generally speaking weak polar solvent is favourable for S_N2 reaction, while strong polar solvent is favourable for S_N1. Generally speaking the substitution reaction of tertiary haloalkane is based on S_N1 mechanism in solvents with a strong polarity (for example ethanol containing water).

Answer the following questions: **[Delhi 2023, Set-I, A]**

(a) Why racemisation occurs in S_N1

(b) Why is ethanol less polar than water ?

(c) Which one of the following in each pair is more reactive towards S_N2 reaction?

(i) $CH_3 - CH_2 - I$ or $CH_3CH_2 - Cl$

(ii) 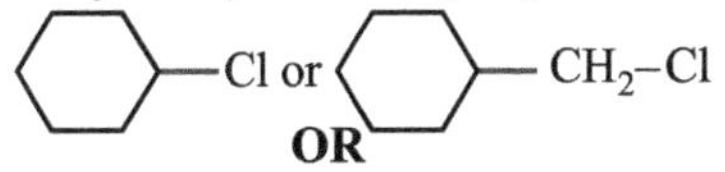   [structure]—Cl or [structure]—CH_2–Cl

OR

(c) Arrange the following in the increasing order of their reactivity towards S_N1 reactions:

(i) 2-Bromo-2-methylbutane, 1-Bromopentane, 2-Bromopentane

(ii) 1-Bromo-3-methylbutane, 2-Bromo-2-methylbutane, 2-Bromo-3-methylbutane

53. N*Read the given passage and answer the questions number 1 to 5 that follow*:

The substitution reaction of alkyl halide mainly occurs by S_N1 or S_N2 mechanism. Whatever mechanism alkyl halides follow for the substitution reaction to occur, the polarity of the carbon halogen bond is responsible for these substitution reactions. The rate of S_N1 reactions are governed by the stability of carbocation whereas for S_N2 reactions steric factor is the deciding factor. If the starting material is a chiral compound, we may end up with an inverted product or racemic mixture depending upon the type of mechanism followed by alkyl halide. Cleavage of ethers with HI is also governed by steric factor and stability of carbocation, which indicates that in organic chemistry, these two major factors help us in deciding the kind of product formed.

(i) Predict the stereochemistry of the product formed if an optically active alkyl halide undergoes substitution reaction by S_N1 mechanism. **[All India 2020, A]**

(ii) Name the instrument used for measuring the angle by which the plane polarised light is rotated. **[All India 2020, A]**

(iii) Predict the major product formed when 2-bromopentane reacts with alcoholic KOH. **[All India 2020, A]**

(iv) Give one use of CHI_3. **[All India 2020, A]**

(v) Write the structures of the products formed when anisole is treated with HI. **[All India 2020, A]**

Topic-5: *Polyhalogen Compounds*

1   *Multiple Choice Questions*

1. Auto oxidation of chloroform in air and sunlight produces a poisonous gas known as **[All India 2023, Set-I, K]**

(a) Tear gas   (b) Mustard gas

(c) Phosgene gas   (d) Chlorine gas

5   *Short Answer Questions (2 or 3 Marks)*

2. Write equations for the following:**[Delhi 2023, Set-I, K]**

(a) Oxidation of chloroform by air and light

(b) Reaction of chlorobenzene with CH_3Cl/anhyd. $AlCl_3$.

Solutions

Topic-1: Classification, Nomenclature, Nature of C–X Bond

1. (b) Vinyl halides are the compounds in which the halogen atom is bonded to a sp^2 – hybridised carbon atom of a carbon-carbon double bond (C = C)

So, $CH_2 = C - CH_3$ belongs to the class of vinyl
$\quad\quad\quad\quad |$
$\quad\quad\quad Br$
halides. **(1 Mark)**

2. (d) The vinyl halide contains (C_{sp^2} – X bond)

$$H_2C = CH—X$$
$$\downarrow$$
$$sp^2$$
Vinyl halide **(1 Mark)**

3.

$$\overset{2}{C}H_2 - \overset{1}{C}H_2 - Cl$$

1-chloro-2-Phenylethane **(1 Mark)**

4.

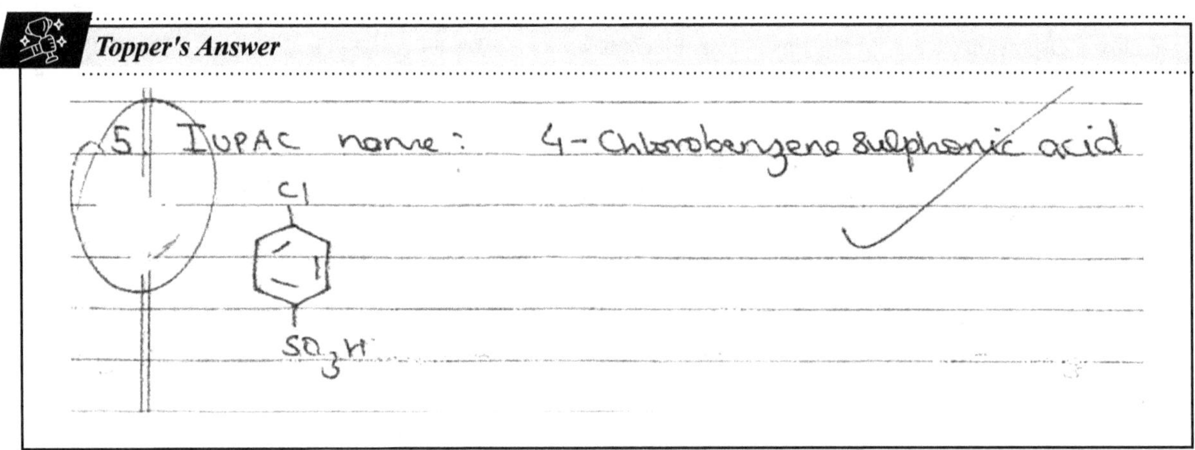

5. $(CH_3)_3C – Br$ undergoes S_N1 reaction faster in comparison to C_2H_5Br. **(1 Mark)**

6. 2-Chloro-3, 3-dimethylbutane. **(1 Mark)**

7. 4-Chloropent-1-ene **(1 Mark)**

Topic-2: Methods of Preparation of Haloalkanes

1. (b) n-Pentane will form three isomeric monochlorides on photochemical chlorination.

$$\overset{a}{C}H_3 —\overset{b}{C}H_2 —\overset{c}{C}H_2 —\overset{b}{C}H_2 —\overset{a}{C}H_3$$

$\xrightarrow[\text{hv}]{\text{Cl}_2}$

$CH_3—CH_2—CH_2—CH_2—Cl$

$CH_3—CH_2—CH_2—CH—CH_3$
$\quad\quad\quad\quad\quad\quad\quad\quad |$
$\quad\quad\quad\quad\quad\quad\quad\quad Cl$

$CH_3—CH_2—CH—CH_2—CH_3$
$\quad\quad\quad\quad\quad\quad |$
$\quad\quad\quad\quad\quad\quad Cl$ **(1 Mark)**

2. (b) $C_6H_5CH_2CH = CH_2 + HBr \xrightarrow[\text{Anti Markovnikov's Addition}]{\text{Organic peroxide}}$

$C_6H_5CH_2CH_2CH_2Br$
1-bromo-3-phenylpropane **(1 Mark)**

3. (b)

2-chloromethylphenol **(1 Mark)**

4. (d) $CH_2 = CH_2 + Br_2 \rightarrow BrCH_2 – CH_2Br$
vicinal dibromide **(1 Mark)**

5. $H^{\delta+}Br^{\delta-} \longrightarrow H^+Br^-$

$$CH_3CH_2OH \xrightarrow{H^+} CH_3CH_2\overset{+}{O}H_2$$

$$Br^- \cdots C \cdots \overset{+}{O}H_2 \longrightarrow \left[Br^{\delta-} \cdots C \cdots \overset{+}{O}H_2 \right]$$

$$\longrightarrow Br\!-\!C + H_2O$$

(2 Marks)

> **Note**
>
> *An acid protonates the most basic atom in a molecule. Primary alcohols cannot undergo S_N1 reactions because primary carbocations are too unstable to be formed even when the reaction is heated. Therefore, when a primary alcohol reacts with a hydrogen halide, it must do so in S_N2 reaction pathway.*

6. (i) ⬡—OH $\xrightarrow{SOCl_2}$ ⬡—Cl **(1 Mark)**

(ii) **(1 Mark)**

⬡—CH_2–$CH = CH_2$ + HBr $\xrightarrow{\text{Peroxide}}$

⬡—CH_2–CH_2–$\overset{|}{\underset{Br}{CH_2}}$

✏️ **Topic-3: Preparation of Haloarenes** ⭕

1. **(c)** The reaction of toluene with Cl_2 in presence of $FeCl_3$ gives 'X' due to electrophilic substitution reaction taking place at ortho and para positions and reaction in the presence of light gives 'Y', due to substitution reaction occurring via free radical mechanism.

Thus X = *o* and

p–chlorotoluene Y = trichloromethylbenzene

$$\text{toluene} + Cl_2 \xrightarrow{FeCl_3} \underbrace{\text{o-chlorotoluene} + \text{p-chlorotoluene}}_{X}$$

2. **(c)** The reaction of toluene with Cl_2 in presence of $FeCl_3$ gives 'X' due to electrophilic substitution reaction taking place at ortho and para positions and reaction in the presence of light gives 'Y', due to substitution reaction occurring via free radical mechanism. **(1 Mark)**

Thus X = *o* and *p*–chlorotoluene

  Y = trichloromethylbenzene

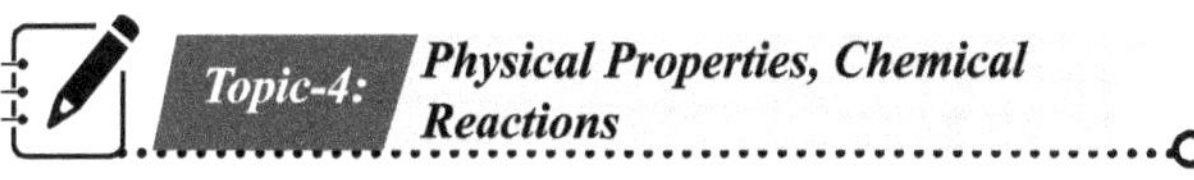

$$\text{toluene} + Cl_2 \xrightarrow{FeCl_3} \underbrace{\text{o-chlorotoluene} + \text{p-chlorotoluene}}_{X}$$

$$\text{toluene} + Cl_2 \xrightarrow{hv} \underset{Y}{\text{benzene-}CCl_3}$$

3. The example of benzylic halide is

⬡—$CHCl_2$

(1 Mark)

> **Note**
>
> *In benzylic halides the halogen atom is bonded to an sp^3-hybridised carbon atom which is directly attached with an aromatic ring.*

✏️ **Topic-4: Physical Properties, Chemical Reactions** ⭕

1. **(b)** The carbon–magnesium bond is covalent and non–polar in nature. **(1 Mark)**

2. **(a)** S_N2;

S_N2 reaction always produces the product with inversion of configuration in comparison to the reactant. **(1 Mark)**

3. **(a)** In S_N2 mechanism, inversion of configuration is observed while S_N1 mechanism are accompained by racemisation i.e. 50:50 mixture of products are obtained followed by retention as well as inversion. **(1 Mark)**

4. **(b)** The carbon atom which is attached with four different group or atom is known as chiral carbon atom. The molecule $CH_3C^*HClCH_2Br$ has a chiral centre correctly marked with asterisk (*) as this carbon atom is attached with four different groups.

$$H_3C - \overset{\displaystyle |}{\underset{\displaystyle Cl}{C}} - CH_2\,Br$$

(1 Mark)

5. **(c)** The order of reactivity towards S_N2 reaction is $1° > 2° > 3°$. Therefore, the correct order is II > I > III.

(1 Mark)

6. **(d)**

$$CH_3 - \overset{\displaystyle \overset{CH_3}{|}}{\underset{\displaystyle \underset{CH_3}{|}}{C}} - Br + NaOCH_3 \longrightarrow CH_3 - \overset{\displaystyle \overset{CH_3}{|}}{C} = CH_2$$

The tertiary alkyl halides undergo elimination reaction to give alkenes. **(1 Mark)**

> **Note**
>
> *A primary alkyl halide will prefer an S_N2 reaction, a secondary halide prefers S_N2 or elimination depending upon the strength of base/nucleophile. A tertiary alkyl halide prefers S_N1 or elimination depending upon the stability of carbocation or the more substituted alkene.*

7. **(b)** The compounds which are non-superimposable but have mirror images are known as enantiomers. They differ only in optical activity i.e. rotation of polarised light. **(1 Mark)**

8. **(c)**

$$\text{⬡} - Br \xrightarrow[\text{dry ether}]{Mg} \text{⬡} - MgBr \xrightarrow{H_2O}$$

$$\text{⬡} - H$$

(1 Mark)

9. **(c)** $(\pm)$ – butane-2-ol is a racemic mixture and behave as optically inactive. **(1 Mark)**

10. **(d)** On moving down the group, the size of halogen atoms and vander waals force of attraction increases due to which boiling point also increases. Therefore; $C_2H_5 - I$ has the highest boiling point. **(1 Mark)**

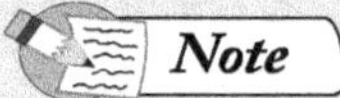

> **Note**
>
> *B. pt $\propto$ Strength of intermolecular forces*
> *$\propto$ Molar mass of compound*
> *$\propto$ Surface area*

11. **(c)** $C_6H_5CH\,(C_6H_5)Br$

$C_6H_5CH\,(C_6H_5)+$ carbocation formed is more stable **(1 Mark)**

12. **(c)** 1,4-dicholorbenzene (para isomers are more symmetric than ortho and meta isomers) **(1 Mark)**

13. **(b)** It gives nitroethane on heating with aqueous solution of $AgNO_2$.

(C_2H_5Br reacts with metallic Na to give butane, gives ethene on boiling with alcoholic potash and forms C_2H_5SH (thiol) on heating with alcoholic KSH) **(1 Mark)**

14. **(b)** 3rd excited state :

$\boxed{1}$	$\boxed{1\;1\;1}$	$\boxed{1\;1\;1\;\;}$
ns^1	np^3	nd^3

(7 unpaired electrons account for +7 oxidation state)

(1 Mark)

15. **(a)** A : Isomers : : B: Enantiomer

Isomers have Same molecular formula but different structure

Enantiomers are Non superimposable mirror images

(1 Mark)

16.

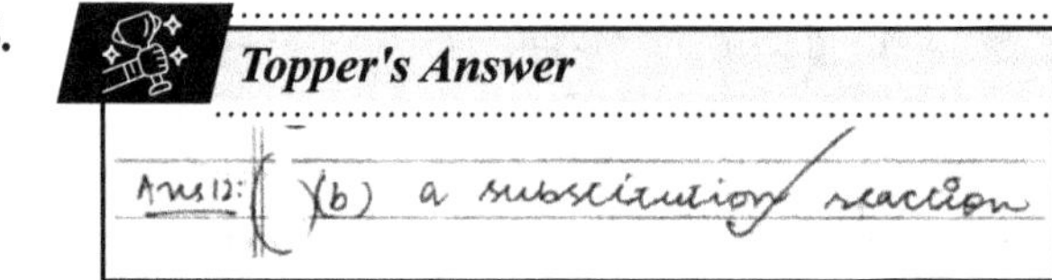

(1 Mark)

17. **(a)** $A = C_2H_4$, $B = C_2H_5OH$, $C = C_2H_5NC$, $D = C_2H_5CN$

(1 Mark)

18. **(c)**

Due to the delocalization of lone pair of 'Cl' atom in the benzene ring the electron density enhances, which is not favourable for nucleophilic substitution reaction. Further, the C – Cl bond gets stronger due to resonance. **(1 Mark)**

19. **(b)** Chlorobenzene is less reactive towards nucleophilic substitution reaction because the carbon atom on which halogen is attached is sp^2 hybridised and decreases the nucleophilic substitution whereas NO_2 group in chlorobenzene increases the reactivity by withdrawing or by making the ring deficient.

(1 Mark)

20. **(b)** Alkyl halides are insoluble in water.

Alkyl halides have halogen attached to sp^3 hybrid carbon. Alkyl halides are insoluble in water because they are unable to form hydrogen bonds with water or break pre-existing hydrogen bonds. **(1 Mark)**

21. Benzyl chloride will undergo reaction faster as compared to chlorobenzene due to the formation of more stable benzyl cation in the rate determining step. **(1 Mark)**

22. Ambidient nucleophile are those nucleophile which have more than one binding site but bind to the central atom through any one site at a time. **(½ Mark)**

Example: NO_2^- ion is an ambident nucleophile

Nitrite ion can coordinate through oxygen or nitrogen to the central metal atom. **(½ Mark)**

23. Out of chlorobenzene and benzyl chloride, benzyl chloride gets easily hydrolysed, because Cl attached to sp^3 hybridised carbon in benzyl chloride is easier to break as compared to chlorobenzene where Cl is attached to sp^2 hybridised carbon which has a partial double bond character due to resonance. **(1 Mark)**

24. CH_3—CH_2—CH—Cl will form secondary carbocation
    with CH_3 below the CH
while

CH_3—CH—CH_2—Cl will form primary carbocation,
    with CH_3 below the CH

which is less stable than secondary carbocation.

So CH_3—CH_2—CH—Cl is more reactive towards S_N^1
    with CH_3

reaction. **(1 Mark)**

25. CH_3 CH_2—Br undergo S_N2 reaction faster than
    CH_3
H_3C—C—CH_3 because tertiary alkyl halides have more
    Br

stearic hinderence as compared to primary alkyl halides.

(1 Mark)

26. 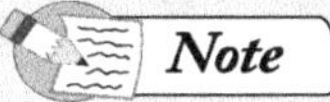

(1 Mark)

> **Note**
>
> *A chiral molecule has atleast one C-atom in which all the four groups are different (chiral carbon).*

27. C_2H_5–CH–CH_3
        |
        Br
(1 Mark)

Mechanism:

$$H_3C - \underset{Br}{\underset{|}{\overset{\overset{H}{|}}{C}}} - C_2H_5 \xrightarrow{\text{Slow step}} \underset{H_3C}{\overset{H}{\underset{}{}}}\overset{\oplus}{C}\diagdown C_2H_5 + Br^\ominus$$

$$\underset{H_3C}{}\overset{H}{\overset{\oplus}{C}}\diagdown C_2H_5 + OH^\ominus \xrightarrow{\text{Fast}} H_3C - \underset{C_2H_5}{\underset{|}{\overset{\overset{H}{|}}{C}}} - OH - H_3C - \underset{C_2H_5}{\underset{|}{\overset{\overset{H}{|}}{C}}} - OH^-$$

(1 Mark)

28. **(a)** To produce single monochloro compound all the 'H' atoms have to be equivalent. That is possible only in the following structure.

$$C_5H_{10} = \text{Cyclopentane} \xrightarrow{Cl_2,\ h\nu}$$

(1 Mark)

(b) 2-Bromopentane :

(I)

$CH_3\,CH_2\,CH_2\,CHCH_3 \Rightarrow 2°$ substrate
                         |
                         Br

1-Bromopentane :

(II)

$CH_3\,CH_2\,CH_2\,CH_2\,CH_2 \Rightarrow 1°$ substrate
                         |
                         Br

2-Bromo-2-methylbutane :

(III)
                    CH_3
                     |
$CH_3CH_2 - C - CH_3 \Rightarrow 3°$ substrate
                     |
                    Br

order of reactivity towards S_N2 reaction:

$3° < 2° < 1° \Rightarrow$ (III) < (I) < (II)   **(1 Mark)**

(c)

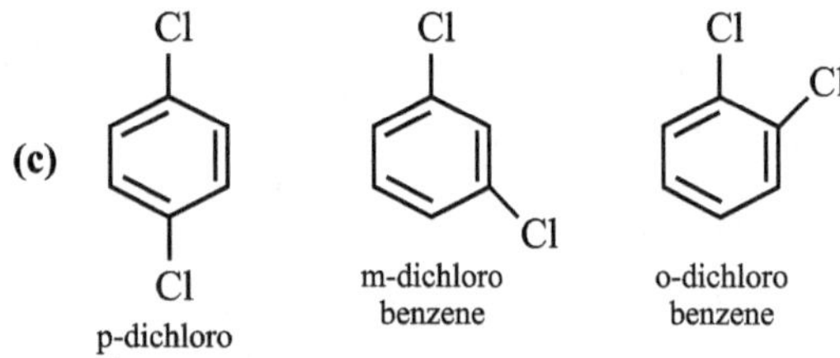

p-dichloro benzene

m-dichloro benzene

o-dichloro benzene

p-dichlorobenzene is symmetric in structure in comparison to o- or m-dichlorobenzene. Therefore, the packing of p-dichlorobenzene in crystal lattice is highly ordered and compact in comparison to other two isomers. **(1 Mark)**

(d)

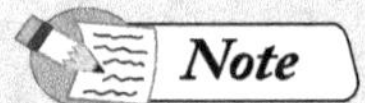

Cyclobutane

(1 Mark)

> **Note**
>
> *The 'c' atom attached to – MgBr always have more electron density as Mg is the electropositive elements. So, the Grignard agent always acts as nucleophile.*

29. Boiling point of isomeric bihalobenzenes are nearly same. Boiling point of O–dichlorobenzene is highest due to more dipole – dipole interactions.

However, the para–isomer have high melting point as compared to ortho– and meta–isomers. It is due to symmetry of para–isomer that fits in crystal lattice better as compared to ortho– and meta–isomers. **(2 Marks)**

30. Aryl halides are extremely less reactive towards nucleophilic substitution reactions due to the following reasons:

(i) Resonance effect:

In haloarenes, C – Cl acquires a partial double bond character due to resonance. Thus, the bond cleavage in haloarene is difficult than haloalkane and therefore, they are less reactive towards nucleophilic substitution reaction. **(1 Mark)**

(ii) Difference in hybridisation of carbon atom in C – X bond:

In haloalkane, the carbon atom attached to halogen is sp^3 hybridised while in haloarene, the carbon atom attached to halogen is sp^2 hybridised. Due to this, C – Cl bond length in haloalkane is longer than that

in haloarene. Since it is difficult to break a shorter bond than a longer bond. Therefore, haloarenes are less reactive than haloalkanes towards nucleophilic substitution reaction. **(1 Mark)**

31. (a) The major product formed when 2-cyclohexylchloroethane undergoes dehydrohalogenation reaction is 1-cyclohexylethene. The reagent which is used to carry out the reaction is ethanolic KOH. **(1+1 = 2 marks)**

(b) Haloalkanes are more reactive than haloarenes and vinylic halides because of the presence of partial double bond character C-X bond in haloarenes and vinylic halides. Hence they do not undergo nucleophilic reactions easily. **(1 mark)**

32. (a) Methylenecyclohexane

1-Methylcyclohexene **(1/2+1/2 = 1 mark)**

(1/2+1/2 = 1 mark)

(b) Allyl chloride shows high reactivity as the carbocation formed in the first step is stabilised by resonance while no such stabilisation of carbocation exists in the case of n-propyl chloride. **(1 mark)**

33. (a) At the ortho position, higher steric hindrance is there, hence para isomer is usually predominate and is obtained in the major amount. **(1 mark)**

(b) During the S_N1 mechanism, intermediate carbocation formed is sp^2 hybridized and planar in nature. This allows the attack of nucleophile from either side of the plane resulting in a racemic mixture. **(1 mark)**

34. (a) Tert butyl alcohol or 2-methyl propan-2-ol using Lucas reagent , mixture of conc. HCl and $ZnCl_2$ the reaction will follow the S_N1 pathway. **(1 mark)**

(b) Chloromethane is having higher dipole moment. Due to smaller size of fluorine the dipole moment of flouromethane is comparatively lesser. **(1 mark)**

35.

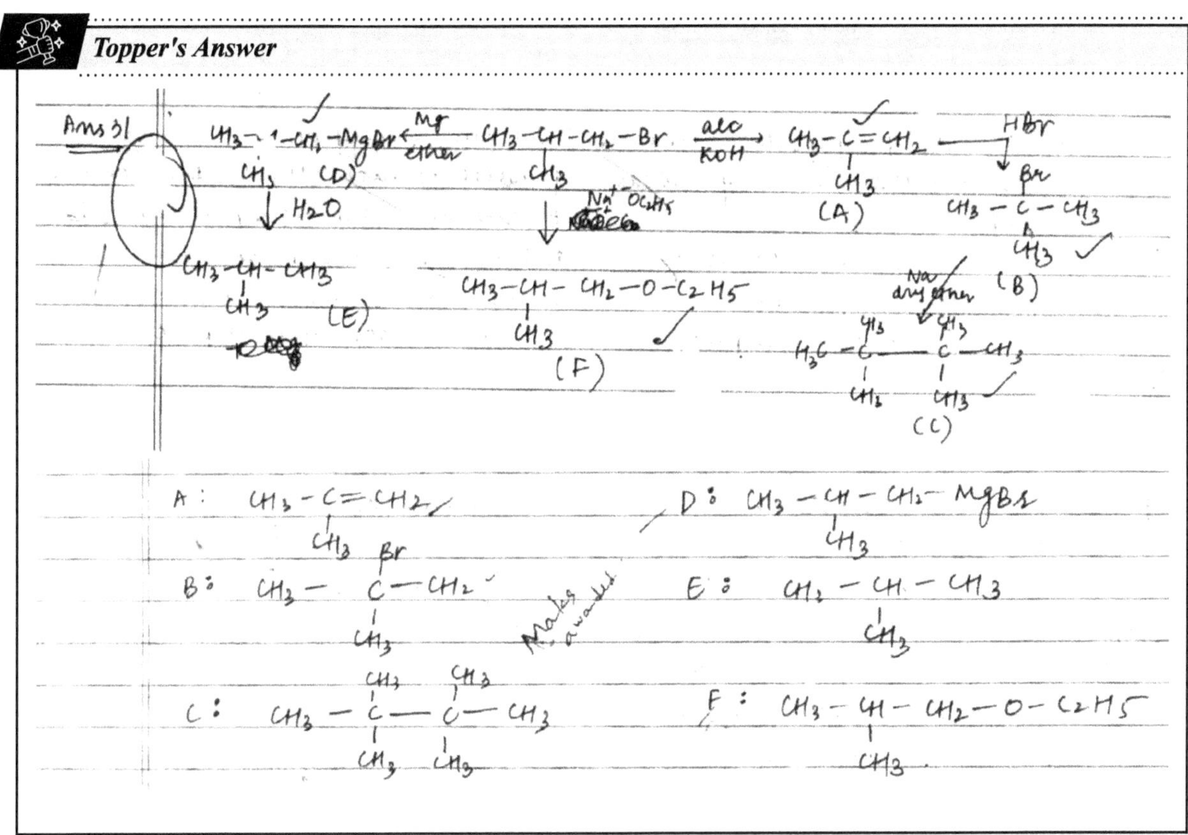

$$CH_3-CH-CH_2-Br \xrightarrow{\text{alc. KOH}} CH_3-C=CH_2$$
$$\quad\;\; |\qquad\qquad\qquad\qquad\qquad\quad |$$
$$\quad\; CH_3\qquad\qquad\qquad\qquad\quad\; CH_3$$
$$\qquad\qquad\qquad\qquad\qquad\qquad\qquad (A)$$

$\downarrow$ NaOC$_2$H$_5$

$$CH_3-CH-CH_2\,OCH_2CH_3$$
$$\qquad\;\; |$$
$$\qquad\; CH_3$$
$$\qquad\;\; (F)$$

$\downarrow$ HBr

$$CH_3\;CH_3 \qquad\qquad\qquad\qquad Br$$
$$\;\; |\qquad |\qquad\qquad\qquad\qquad\;\; |$$
$$CH_3-C-C-CH_3 \xleftarrow{\text{Na/dry ether}} CH_3-C-CH_3$$
$$\;\; |\qquad |\qquad\qquad\qquad\qquad\;\; |$$
$$\;\; CH_3\;CH_3 \qquad\qquad\qquad\qquad CH_3$$
$$\qquad (C)\qquad\qquad\qquad\qquad\qquad (B)$$

$$CH_3-CH-CH_2-Br \xrightarrow[\text{dry ether}]{Mg} CH_3-CH-CH_2MgBr$$
$$\qquad\;\; |\qquad\qquad\qquad\qquad\qquad\qquad |$$
$$\qquad\; CH_3\qquad\qquad\qquad\qquad\qquad\;\; CH_3$$
$$\qquad\qquad\qquad\qquad\qquad\qquad\qquad\qquad (D)$$

$$\xrightarrow{H_2O} CH_3-CH-CH_3 + Mg\,(OH)\,Br$$
$$\qquad\qquad\qquad\;\; |$$
$$\qquad\qquad\quad CH_3$$
$$\qquad\qquad\qquad (E)$$

(½ + ½ + ½ + ½ + ½ + ½ = 3 Marks)

36. (a) The presence of electron-withdrawing groups such as $-NO_2$, $-CN$, etc. at *o*-and *p*-positions (but not at *m*-position) w.r.t. the halogen greatly activates the halogen towards nucleophilic displacemnt. The NO_2 group at *o*- and *p*- positions withdraws electrons from the benzene ring and thus makes the ring electron deficient and facilitates the attack of the nucleophile (OH^-) on haloarenes.   **(1 Mark)**

Resonating structures

p-Nitrophenol

(b) p-Dichlorobenzene, being symmetrical, fits tightly in its crystal lattice. Thus the intermolecular forces of attraction in the p-isomer are stronger than those in the o-and m- isomers; which requires larger amount of energy to melt or dissolve the p-isomer than the o- and m-isomers. Consequently, the melting point of the p-isomer will be higher and its solubility lower than the corresponding o- and m-isomers.   **(1 Mark)**

(c) Thionyl chloride method is preferred over hydrogen chloride or phosphorus pentachloride method since both the by-products (SO_2 and HCl) in this reaction being gases escape leaving the chloro alkanes in almost pure state.

$$R-OH + \underset{\text{Thionyl chloride}}{SOCl_2} \xrightarrow{\text{Pyidine}}$$

$$\underset{\text{Haloalkane}}{R-Cl} + SO_2\uparrow + HCl\uparrow$$

(1 Mark)

37. (a) $\underset{\text{1-chlorobutane}}{CH_3CH_2CH_2CH_2Cl} + NaI \xrightarrow{\text{acetone}}$

$$\underset{\text{1-Iodobutane}}{CH_3CH_2CH_2CH_2I} + NaCl\downarrow$$

(1 Mark)

(b) 2-bromo-2-methyl butane is most reactive towards elimination reaction.

$$\underset{\text{1-Bromopentane}}{CH_3 - CH_2CH_2CH_2CH_2 - Br} \qquad \text{1° alkyl halide}$$

$$\underset{\text{2-Bromopentane}}{CH_3 - CH_2 - CH_2 - \overset{\overset{\displaystyle Br}{|}}{CH} - CH_3} \quad \text{2° alkyl halide}$$

$$\underset{\text{2-Bromo-2-methylbutane}}{CH_3CH_2 - \overset{\overset{\displaystyle Br}{|}}{\underset{\underset{\displaystyle CH_3}{|}}{C}} - CH_3} \qquad \text{3° alkyl halide}$$

3° alkyl halide is most reactive towards elimination reaction (E_1) due to the formation of more stable 3° carbocation which loses proton to form alkene.

$$CH_3CH_2 - \overset{\overset{\displaystyle +}{C}}{\underset{\underset{\displaystyle CH_3}{|}}{|}} - CH_3 \xrightarrow{-H^+}$$

3° Carbocation

$$\underset{\text{Saytzeff's product}}{CH_3 - CH = \overset{\overset{\displaystyle}{C}}{\underset{\underset{\displaystyle CH_3}{|}}{|}} - CH_3}$$

(1 Mark)

(c) 4-Bromo-4-methylpent-2-ene.   **(1 Mark)**

38.

22. i) $(CH_3)_3 C-I$ is more reactive than $(CH_3)_3 C-Br$ towards S_N1 reaction, because $I^\ominus$ is a better leaving group than $Br^\ominus$. Because of its larger size as compared to $Br^\ominus$, $I^\ominus$ is able to effectively stabilise the negative charge on itself, therefore, making the cleavage step more favourable.

Also, C-I bond is weaker than C-Br bond (i.e. C-I bond is longer than C-Br bond due to large size of $I^\ominus$ ion)

$$(CH_3)_3 C-I \underset{\substack{\text{polar protic}\\\text{solvent}}}{\overset{H^\oplus}{\rightleftharpoons}} (CH_3)_3 C^\oplus + I^\ominus$$

$$(CH_3)_3 C-Br \underset{\substack{\text{polar protic}\\\text{solvent}}}{\overset{H^\oplus}{\rightleftharpoons}} (CH_3)_3 C^\oplus + Br^\ominus$$

$I^\ominus$ is more stable and hence, cleavage takes easily

Also, we know that H-I is a stronger acid than H-Br, because of low bond-dissociation enthalpy of H-I bond as compared to H-Br.

∴ by Bronsted theory of acids and bases, the conjugate base $I^\ominus$ should be a weaker base than $Br^\ominus$, and we know that a stronger base can replace a weaker base more easily in a nucleophilic substitution anion. Hence, $I^\ominus$ is more easily replaced by other nucleophiles as compared to $Br^{\ominus}$. Thus increasing the rate of reaction.

(ii) [structure of p-nitrochlorobenzene] →(i) NaOH, 443K (ii) $H^{\oplus}, H_2O$→ [structure] **4-Nitrophenol**

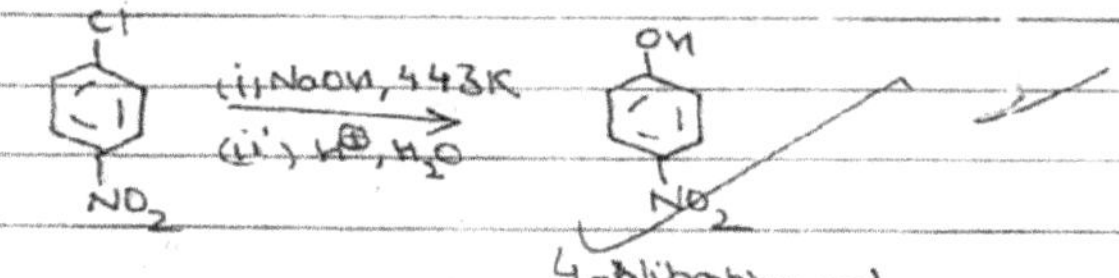

(iii) 'dextro' and 'laevo' rotatory forms of Butan-2-ol, mainly constitute the enantiomers of the same compound. i.e.

[structure with CH₃, Et, OH, H — **(R-configuration)**] and [structure with CH₃, Et, H, OH — **(S-configuration)**]

Key:
Et = ethyl group

These two forms of Butan-2-ol differ only in their spatial arrangement of molecules : Me, Et H, OH around the chiral carbon 9 and therefore have the same physical properties like – melting point, boiling point, electrical conductivity, solubility etc.

Hence, it is difficult to separate these two isomers (optical stereoisomers) of Butan-2-ol by fractional distillation, as fractional distillation makes use of difference in boiling point of two substances (which should be greater than 20–25°C). But in this case, both the isomers have identical boiling points and thus these are not separable by this method.

(i) $(CH_3)_3$ C—I is more reactive towards S_N1 than $(CH_3)_3$ C—Br because I^- is a better leaving group than Br^-. **(1 Mark)**

(ii)

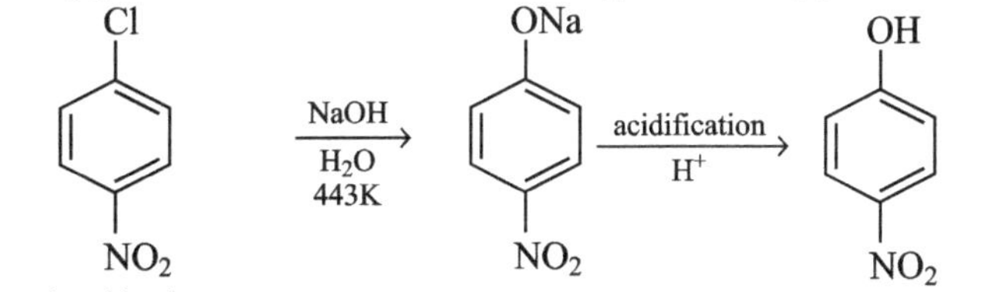

[Cl on benzene with NO₂, labeled *p*-nitrochlorobenzene] →NaOH / H_2O / 443K→ [ONa on benzene with NO₂] →acidification / H^+→ [OH on benzene with NO₂, labeled *p*-nitrophenol]

p-nitrochlorobenzene   *p*-nitrophenol   **(1 Mark)**

(iii) Dextro and laevo-rotatory isomers of butan-2-ol have identical boiling points, so they are difficult to separate by fractional distillation. **(1 Mark)**

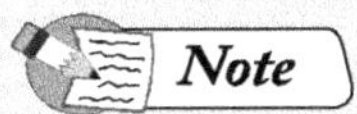
Note

Enantiomers have identical physical properties except the direction in which they rotate plane polarized light.

39. (a) 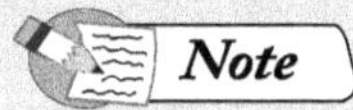 **(1 Mark)**

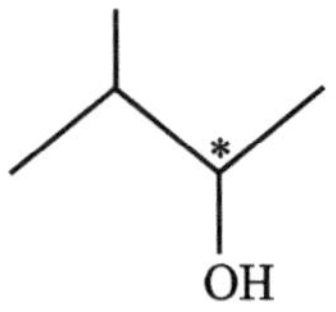

> **Note**
>
> *Chirality depends upon the pressence of asymmetric carbon atoms.*

(b) 

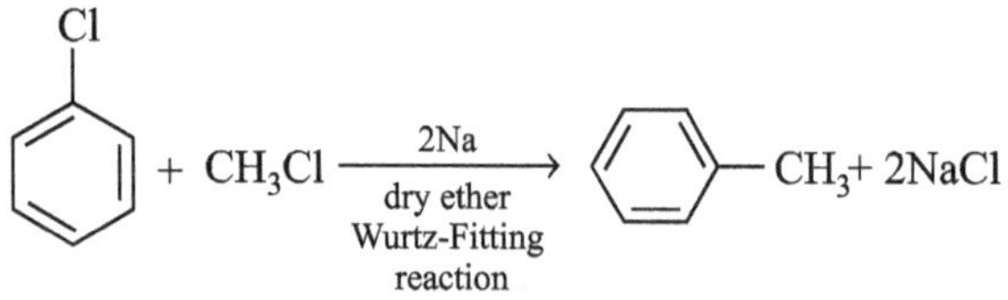

(1 Mark)

(c) 

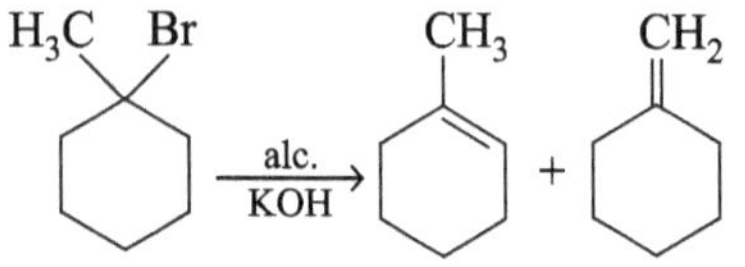

(This is in accordance with the Saytzeff's rule)**(1 Mark)**

40. Structure of the given compounds are :

$$H_3C - CH_2 - CH_2 - CH_2 - CH_2 - Br$$

1-Bromopentane
(A)

$$H_3C - CH_2 - CH_2 - \underset{|}{\overset{Br}{CH}} - CH_3$$

2-Bromopentane
(B)

$$H_3C - CH_2 - \underset{|}{\overset{Br}{\underset{CH_3}{C}}} - CH_3$$

2-Bromo-2-methylbutane
(C)

(a) As we can see in the above figures, (A), contains the least steric hindrance so towards the S_N2 reaction 1-bromopentane will be most reactive. **(1 Mark)**

(b) 2-Bromopentane (figure B) contain chiral carbon in it. So, this compound is optically active. **(1 Mark)**

(c) 2-Bromo-2-methylbutane will be most reactive towards the β-elimination since it will form most stable alkene (on account of highest no of α-hydrogens) **(1 Mark)**

> **Note**
>
> *The identity of the nucleophile or base also determines which mechanism is favoured. E_2 reactions require strong bases whereas SN^2 reactions require good nucleophiles. Therefore, a good nueleophile (i.e., weak base) will favour SN^2 while a weak nucleophile (i.e, strong base) will favour E_2.*

41. (i) 1-Bromopentane is most reactive towards S_N2 reaction. It is a primary halide. **(1 Mark)**

> **Note**
>
> *Primary halides are more reactive towards S_N2 reaction and tertiary halides are more reactive towards S_N1 reaction.*

(ii) 2-Bromopentane $CH_3 - \underset{*}{\overset{\overset{Br}{|}}{CH}} - CH_2CH_2CH_3$

(1 Mark)

(iii) 2-Bromo-2-methylbutane is most reactive towards β-elimination reaction. **(1 Mark)**

> **Note**
>
> $$CH_3 - \underset{\underset{Br}{|}}{\overset{\overset{CH_3}{|}}{C}} - CH_2 - CH_3 \xrightarrow[alc.]{KOH} CH_3 - C = CH_2CH_3$$
>
> (Highly substituted alkene)

42. The isomer of C_4H_9Br, which is most reactive towards S_N1 reaction, is the one that forms a tertiary carbocation upon the elimination of the leaving group. Its structure is shown below: **(1 Mark)**

$$H_3C - \underset{\underset{CH_3}{|}}{\overset{\overset{Br}{|}}{C}} - CH_3 \xrightarrow[(-Br^-)]{} H_3C - \underset{\underset{CH_3}{|}}{\overset{+}{C}} - CH_3$$

(C_4H_9Br) Stable carbocation

43. (i)

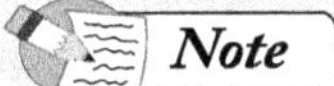

$$2 \text{ Chlorobenzene} + 2\text{Na} \xrightarrow[\text{(Fittig reaction)}]{\text{Dry ether}}$$

Chlorobenzene

Biphenyl $+ 2\text{NaCl}$

(1 Mark)

> **Note**
>
> *Wurtz reaction is just for alkyl halides, wurtz fitting for alkyl and aryl halides together whereas fitting reaction is for only aryl halides. All these reactions result in formation of a new C–C bond.*

(ii) $\underset{\text{Propene}}{H_2C = CH - CH_3} + HBr \xrightarrow[\text{(anti-Markovnikov's)}]{\text{Peroxide}}$

$$CH_3CH_2CH_2Br \xrightarrow[\text{KI/acetone}]{\text{(Finkelstein reaction)}} \underset{\text{1-Iodopropane}}{CH_3CH_2CH_2I}$$

(1 Mark)

> **Note**
>
> *Propene can not be converted directly into 1-iodopropane. The addition of HBr to a unsymmetrical alkene (e.g. propene) in the presence of peroxide is free radical. In the case of HI, the H-I bond is weaker than H-Br bond and undergoes homolysis readily to from iodine free radical. But iodine free radicals have greater trendency to combine themselves to from iodine molecules rather than add to the ethylenic bond. Hence HI does not respond to the peroxide effect.*

(iii) $\underset{\underset{\text{2-Bromobutane}}{|}}{CH_3 - \overset{|}{C}H - CH_2 - CH_3} \xrightarrow{\text{alc KOH}}$

$\underset{Br}{}$

$$\underset{\text{But-2-ene}}{CH_3 - CH = CH - CH_3}$$

(1 Mark)

44. (i)

$$O_2N-C_6H_4-CH_2CH_3 \xrightarrow[\text{UV light}]{Br_2}$$

$$O_2N-C_6H_4-\underset{Br}{\overset{|}{C}H-CH_3}$$

(1 Mark)

(ii) $2CH_3CH(Cl)CH_3 \xrightarrow[\substack{\text{dry ether} \\ \text{(Wurtz reaction)}}]{2\text{Na}}$

$$\begin{array}{c} CH_3 - \overset{|}{C}H - CH_3 \\ | \\ CH_3 - \overset{|}{C}H - CH_3 \end{array} \quad \textbf{(1 Mark)}$$

(iii) $CH_3 - CH_2 - Br \xrightarrow{\text{AgCN}} CH_3 - CH_2 - NC$

(1 Mark)

> **Note**
>
> *Haloalkanes react with KCN to form RCN as major product while AgCN forms iso-cyanide (RNC) as the major product. Because, KCN is ionic in nature, so provides CN^- ions in solution while AgCN is mainly covalent in nature and nitrogen is free to donate electron pair forming RNC as the major product.*

45. (i) C – Cl bond in chlorobenzene has partial double bond character due to which it has shorter bond length than C – Cl bond in CH_3Cl. **(1 Mark)**

(ii) In cyclo-hexyl chloride, the carbon in C – Cl bond is sp^3 hybridized whereas in chlorobenzene C – Cl bond carbon is sp^2 hybridized. sp^2 carbon is more electronegative than sp^3 carbon. So C – Cl bond of chlorobenzene is less polar.

(1 Mark)

(iii) In S_N^1 reaction, formation of carbocation as an intermediate takes place. This carbocation has sp^2 hybridization and planar structure. This planar carbocation is attacked by nucleophile from both sides equally to form *d* and *l* isomers in equal proportion (50 : 50) such products are called racemic mixture. Hence S_N^1 reaction are accompanied by racemisation in optically active alkyl halides. **(1 Mark)**

> **Note**

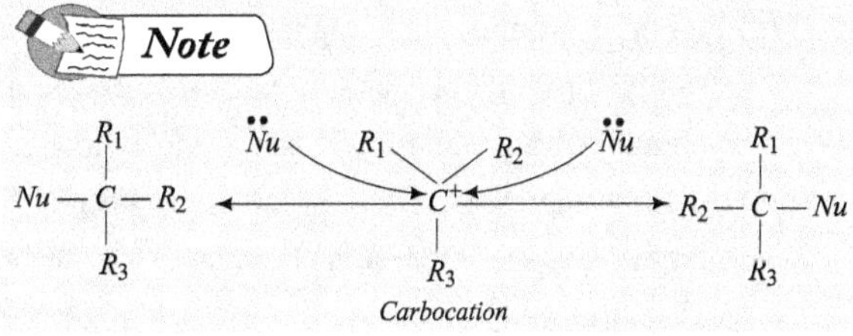

46. (i)

$$CH_3 - CH = \underset{\underset{CH_3}{|}}{C} - CH_3 + HBr \longrightarrow$$

2-Methylbut-2-ene

$$CH_3 - CH_2 - \underset{\underset{Br}{|}}{\overset{\overset{CH_3}{|}}{C}} - CH_3$$

2-Bromo-2-methylbutane

(1 Mark)

(ii) $CH_3 - CH_2 - CH_2 - \underset{\underset{Br}{|}}{CH} - CH_3 \xrightarrow[\Delta]{KOH(alc.)}$

2-Bromopentane

$$CH_3 - CH_2 - CH = CH - CH_3$$

Pent-2-ene
(Major)

(1 Mark)

> **Note**
>
> *Alcoholic KOH, specially in ethanol, produces C_2H_5O–ions. Which is a stronger base than the OH^-. Thus, the former abstract the β-hydrogen of an alkyl halide to produce alkenes while aqueous KOH is alkaline in nature i.e., it dissociates to produce a hydroxide ion, which acts as a strong nucleophile and replaces the halogen atom in an alkyl halide.*

(iii)  + CH₃Cl $\xrightarrow{anhyd.AlCl_3}$

Bromobenzene

p-Methylbromobenzene
(Major)
+
o-Methylbromobenzene

(1 Mark)

47. (a) *n*-butyl bromide has higher boiling point than *t*-butyl bromide because in case of isomeric alkyl halide boiling point decrease as the branching in carbon increases. Straight chain molecule have larger surface area and therefore has stronger intermolecular forces. **(1 Mark)**

(b) Racemic mixture contains two enantiomers (*d*- and *l*-forms) in equal proportions and thus, the rotation due to one isomer is cancelled by the rotation due to another. Therefore, it has zero optical rotation and hence, it is optically inactive. **(1 Mark)**

(c) The presence of nitro groups (—NO_2) at-*o*/-*p* positions increases the reactivity of haloarenes towards nucleophilic substitution reaction because nitro groups (—NO_2) at-*o*/-*p* position withdraw the electron density from the benzene ring facilitating the attack of the nucleophile. The negative charge in the carbanion formed, at ortho and para position with respect to halogen atom, is stabilised through resonance and by the presence of nitro group (—NO_2). **(1 Mark)**

48. (a) (i) —$CH_2OH \xrightarrow{PCl_5}$ ⬡—CH_2Cl

(1 Mark)

(ii) ⬡—$CH_2CH = CH_2 + HBr \longrightarrow$

⬡—$CH_2\underset{\underset{Br}{|}}{C}HCH_3$

(1 Mark)

(b) (i) CH_3I reacts faster by S_N2 reaction because I^- is a better leaving group than Br^- **(½ Mark)**

(ii) CH_3Cl being 1° alkyl halide reacts faster by S_N2 reaction. **(½ Mark)**

> **Note**
>
> *Primary alkyl halides react faster in S_N2 reactions. Nucleophile attack from the back side in S_N2 reaction therefore less stearic hindrance at the substrate in the transition state favoured the reaction.*

49. (i) is chiral due to presence of asymmetric carbon atom

and Br undergoes S_N2 reaction faster.

(1 Mark)

(ii) S_N2 occurs with inversion of configuration and S_N1 occurs with racemisaiton. **(1 Mark)**

Note

Primary alkyl halides undergo SN2 mechanism because primary substrates have little steric hindrance to nucleophilic attack. As more alkyl groups added to α carbon atom, the substrate becomes less susceptible to SN2 attack. In SN2 reactions nucleophile will always attack from the backside and results into inversion of configuration.

50. **(i)** Ethyl iodide undergoes S_N2 reaction faster than ethyl bromide because I^- is a better leaving group than Br^-. **(1 Mark)**

(ii) ($\pm$) 2-Butanol represents a racemic mixture of two enantiomers. Two enantiomers always show opposite optical activities. i.e., they rotate the plane of polarized light by equal amounts in opposite directions. The optical rotation of an equimolar mixture of a pair of enantiomers is zero because the optical rotations of the enantiomers cancel out.

(1 Mark)

(iii) C – X bond in haloarene acquires partial double bond character due to rasonance and also carbon atom in C – X bond in haloarene is sp^2 hybridised while in alkyl halide it is sp^3 hybridised. Therefore C–X bond length is shorter in haloarene. **(1 Mark)**

51. chloro benzene (like vinyl halides) are less reactive towards nucleophilic substitutions under ordinary conditions. This low reactivity is due to

(i) resonance effect,

(ii) sp^2 hybridisation of carbon atom holding the halogen atom and

(iii) less polarity of the C–X bond. **(2 Marks)**

52. **(a)** In S_N1 reactions, the first step involves the formation of a carbocation which is planar in structure. The second step involves the attack of the nucleophile on the planar carbocation which can occur from cither side of the plane.

This results in the formation of an equimolar mixture of the two enantiomers that is **racemic** in nature. **(1 Mark)**

(b) Ethanol is less polar than water due to the presence of an alkyl group instead of a hydrogen atom. In water, the bond dipole moments add up that result in the greater polarity while this is not the case with ethanol that has a very small contribution to the bond dipole. **(1 Mark)**

(c) The reactivity in the case of an S_N2 reaction depends on the nature of the substrate, nucleophilicity and the nature of the solvent.

(i) $CH_3CH_2 - I$ will be more reactive than $CH_3CH_2 - Cl$ due to the weaker C – I bond.

(1 Mark)

(ii) $\langle$hexyl$\rangle$— $CH_2 - Cl$ will be more reactive than

$\langle$hexyl$\rangle$— Clas there is less crowding in

$\langle$hexyl$\rangle$— $CH_2 - Cl$at the α-carbon.

(1 Mark)

OR

(c) **(i)** Among the given compounds, 2-Bromo-2-methylbutane has the highest reactivity as it forms the most stable tertiary carbocation.

1-Bromopentane is least reactive as it forms a primary carbocation which is least stable.

Thus, order will be:

1-Bromopentane < 2-bromopentane < 2-bromo-2-methylbutane **(1 Mark)**

(ii) Among the given compounds, 2-bromo-2-methylbutane has the highest reactivity as it forms a tertiary carbocation while 1-bromo-3-methylbutane is least reactive as it forms a primary carbocation.

Thus, the order will be:

1-Bromo-3-methylbutane < 2-bromo-3-methylbutane < 2-bromo-2-methylbutane

(1 Mark)

Note

Substitution Nucleophilic unimolecular (S_N1) reactions are two-step reactions in which the slowest or rate-determining step is the formation of a carbocation from the cleavage of C–X bond.

53. (i) Inversion occurs more than retention, leading to partial racemization.

(ii) Polarimeter

(iii)

2-bromopentane $\xrightarrow{\text{alc.KOH}}$ pent-2-ene (major product)

(iv) Iodoform (CHI_3) is used as a disinfectant.

(v)

anisole + HI $\longrightarrow$ phenol + CH_3– I

1. **(c)** Phosgene gas;

$$2CHCl_3 + O_2 \xrightarrow{\text{sunlight}} 2COCl_2 + 2HCl$$

Carbonyl chloride

or Phosgene **(1 Mark)**

2. **(a)** Oxidation of chloroform by air and light:

$$2CHCl_3\,(l) + O_2\,(g) \xrightarrow{h\nu} 2COCl_2\,(g) + 2HCl(aq.)$$

Chloroform   Phosgene

(1 Mark)

(b) Electrophilic substitution of chlorobenzene with CH_3Cl in anhydrous $AlCl_3$:

(1 Mark)

7 Chapter — Alcohols, Phenols and Ethers

Topic-1: *Classification, Nomenclature, Structures of Functional Groups*

1 — Multiple Choice Questions

1. The C – O – H bond angle in alcohol is

[All India 2022, Term-I, K]

(a) slightly greater than 109°28′.

(b) slightly less than 109°28′.

(c) slightly greater than 120°.

(d) slightly less than 120°.

2. Identify the secondary alcohols from the following set:

[CBSE Sample 2021-22, K]

(i) $CH_3CH_2CH(OH)CH_3$

(ii) $(C_2H_5)_3COH$

(iii) 

(iv)

(a) (i) and (iv)

(b) (i) and (iii)

(c) (i) and (ii)

(d) (i), (iii) and (iv)

4 — Very Short Answer Questions (1 Mark)

3. Write the IUPAC name of the following:

[All India 2018, K]

$$CH_3-\underset{\underset{C_2H_5OH}{|}}{\overset{\overset{CH_3}{|}}{C}}-\underset{|}{CH}-CH_3$$

4. Write the IUPAC name of the following compound:

[All India 2017, K]

$$CH_3-O-\underset{\underset{CH_3}{|}}{\overset{\overset{CH_3}{|}}{C}}-CH_3$$

5. Write the IUPAC name of the given compound :

CH_2—CH_2—OH

[All India 2016, K]

6. Write the IUPAC name of the given compound.

$$CH_2 = \underset{\underset{CH_3}{|}}{C}-CH_2-OH$$

[All India 2015, K]

7. Write the IUPAC name of the given compound:

NO_2 —— OH —— NO_2

[Delhi 2015, K]

Topic-2: *Alcohols and Phenols, Some Commercially Important Alcohols*

1 — Multiple Choice Questions

1. Which of the following observation is shown b 2 –phenyl ethanol with Lucas Reagent?

[CBSE Sample 2023-24, U]

(a) Turbidity will be observed within five minutes

(b) No turbidity will be observed

(c) Turbidity will be observed immediately

(d) Turbidity will be observed at room temperature but will disappear after five minutes.

2. Which of the following alcohols will not undergo oxidation? **[Delhi 2023, K]**

(a) Butanol   (b) Butan-2-ol

(c) 2-Methylbutan-2-ol   (d) 3-Methylbutan-2-ol

3. The oxidation of toluene to benzaldehyde by chromyl chloride is called   [CBSE Sample 2022-23, K]
   (a) Etard reaction
   (b) Riemer-Tiemann reaction
   (c) Stephen's reaction
   (d) Cannizzaro's reaction

4. Consider the following reaction :

$$CH_3 - CH = CH_2 \xrightarrow[\text{2. aq. KOH}]{\text{1. HBr}}$$

   The major end product is   [All India 2022, Term-I, U]

   (a)   CH$_3$ — CH — CH$_3$
                  |
                  OH

   (b)   CH$_3$ — CH — CH$_3$
                  |
                  Br

   (c)   CH$_3$–CH$_2$–CH$_2$–OH

   (d)   CH$_3$–CH$_2$–CH$_2$–Br

5. In the following reaction   [All India 2022, Term-I, U]

$$CH_3 - CH = CH - CH_2 - OH \xrightarrow{\text{PCC}}$$

   the product formed is
   (a) CH$_3$ – CHO and CH$_3$CH$_2$OH
   (b) CH$_3$ – CH = CH – COOH
   (c) CH$_3$ – CH = CH – CHO
   (d) CH$_3$ – CH$_2$ – CH$_2$ – CHO

6. The major product of acid catalysed dehydration of 1-methylcyclohexanol is: [CBSE Sample 2022-23, K]
   (a) 1-methylcyclohexane
   (b) 1-methylcyclohexene
   (c) 1-cyclohexylmethanol
   (d) 1-methylenecyclohexane

7. Which of the following reactions is used to prepare salicylaldehyde?   [All India 2021-22, Term-I, K]
   (a) Kolbe's reaction
   (b) Etard reaction
   (c) Reimer-Tiemann reaction
   (d) Stephen's reduction.

8. What would be the reactant and reagent used to obtain 2, 4-dimethyl pentan-3-ol?   [CBSE Sample 2021-22, U]
   (a) Propanal and propyl magnesium bromide
   (b) 3-methylbutanal and 2-methyl magnesium iodide
   (c) 2-dimethylpropanone and methyl magnesium iodide
   (d) 2-methylpropanal and isopropyl magnesium iodide

9. During dehydration of alcohols to alkenes by heating with concentrated H$_2$SO$_4$, the initiation step is: [CBSE Sample 2021-22, U]
   (a) protonation of alcohol molecule
   (b) formation of carbocation
   (c) elimination of water
   (d) formation of an ester

10. The boiling points of alcohols are higher than those of hydrocarbons of comparable masses due to: [CBSE Sample 2021-22, U]
    (a) Hydrogen bonding
    (b) Ion – dipole interaction
    (c) Dipole-dipole interaction
    (d) Van der Waal's forces.

11. Lower molecular mass alcohols are: [CBSE Sample 2021-22, K]
    (a) miscible in limited amount of water
    (b) miscible in excess of water
    (c) miscible in water in all proportions
    (d) immiscible in water

12. Phenol does not undergo nucleophilic substitution reaction easily due to: [CBSE Sample 2021-22, U]
    (a) acidic nature of phenol
    (b) partial double bond character of C-OH bond
    (c) partial double bond character of C-C bond
    (d) instability of phenoxide ion

2   *Assertion Reason/Two Statement Type Questions*

Given below are two statements labelled as Assertion (A) and Reason (R). Select the most appropriate answer from the options given below:
(a) Both (A) and (R) are true and (R) is the correct explanation of (A).
(b) Both (A) and (R) are true, but (R) is not the correct explanation of (A).
(c) (A) is true, but (R) is false.
(d) (A) is false, but (R) is true.

13. **Assertion (A):** Alcohols react both as nucleophiles and electrophiles.

    Reason (R): The bond between C–O is broken when alcohols react as nucleophiles.

    [CBSE Sample 2023-24, U]

 **Very Short Answer Questions (1 Mark)**

14. Which of the following isomers is more volatile : *o*-nitrophenol or *p*-nitrophenol   **[Delhi 2014, K]**

15. Rearrange the following compounds in the increasing order of their boiling points :   **[All India 2013, K]**
$CH_3 - CHO, CH_3 - CH_2 - OH, CH_3 - CH_2 - CH_3$

 **Short Answer Questions (2 or 3 Marks)**

16. Write the chemical equation involved in the following reactions: **[All India 2023 Set - I, K]**
    (a) Reimer-Tiemann reaction
    (b) Acetylation of Salicylic acid

17. For the pair phenol and cyclohexanol, answer the following: **[Delhi 2023, U]**
    (a) Why is phenol more acidic than cyclohexanol?
    (b) Give one chemical test to distinguish between the two.

18. Write the reaction and IUPAC name of the product formed when 2-Methylpropanal (isobutyraldehyde) is treated with ethyl magnesium bromide followed by hydrolysis.   **[CBSE Sample 2022-23, U]**

19. (a) Arrange the following compounds in the increasing order of their acid strength: **[All India 2017, U]**
    p-cresol, *p*-nitrophenol, phenol
    (b) Write the mechanism (using curved arrow notation) of the following reaction: **[All India 2017, K]**
    $$CH_2 = CH_2 \xrightarrow{H_3O^+} CH_3 - CH_2^+ + H_2O$$

20. Write the structures of the products when Butan–2 – ol reacts with the following   **[All India 2017, K]**
    (a) CrO_3
    (b) $SOCl_2$

21. (a) Write the mechanism of the following reaction:
    $$CH_3CH_2OH \xrightarrow{HBr} CH_3CH_2Br + H_2O$$
    [Delhi 2014, K]
    (b) Write the equation involved in Reimer-Tiemann reaction.   **[Delhi 2014, K]**

22. Explain the mechanism of the following reaction: **[All India 2013, K]**
    $$CH_3 - CH_2 - OH \xrightarrow[443\,K]{H^+} CH_2 = CH_2 + H_2O$$

23. How will you convert :
    (i) Propene to Propan-2-ol?
    (ii) Phenol to 2, 4,6-trinitrophenol?   **[Delhi 2013, K]**

 **Long Answer Questions**

24. (a) How do you convert the following: **[Delhi 2019, U]**
    (i) Phenol to Anisole
    (ii) Ethanol to Propan-2-ol
    (b) Write mechanism of the following reaction:
    [Delhi 2019, U]
    $$C_2H_5OH \xrightarrow[443K]{H_2SO_4} CH_2 = CH_2 + H_2O$$
    (c) Why phenol undergoes electrophilic substitution more easily than benzene?   **[Delhi 2019, U]**

25. (a) Account for the following: **[Delhi 2019, U]**
    (i) o-nitrophenol is more steam volatile than p-nitrophenol.
    (ii) t-butyl chloride on heating with sodium methoxide gives 2-methylpropene instead of t-butylmethylether.
    (b) Write the reaction involved in the following:
    (i) Reimer-Tiemann reaction   **[Delhi 2019, K]**
    (ii) Friedal-Crafts Alkylation of Phenol
    (c) Give simple chemical test to distinguish between Ethanol and Phenol.   **[Delhi 2019, K]**

 **Case Based Questions**

Alcohols and Phenols are acidic in nature. Electron withdrawing groups in phenol increase its acidic strength and electron donating groups decrease it. Alcohols undergo nucleophilic substitution with hydrogen halides to give alkyl halides. On oxidation primary alcohols yield aldehydes with mild oxidising agents and carboxylic acids with strong oxidising agents while secondary alcohols yields ketones. The presence of – OH groups in phenols activates the ring towards electrophilic substitution. Various important products are obtained from pheonol like salicylaldehyde, salicylic acid, picric acid etc.

26. Which of the following alcohols is resistant to oxidation?   **[All India 2022, Term-I, U]**

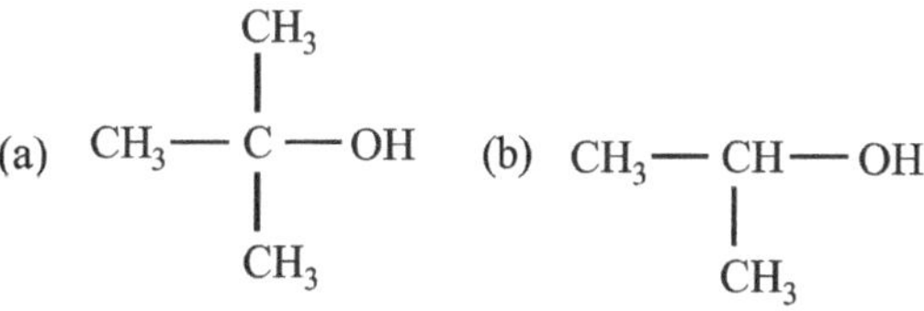

27. Which of the following group increases the acidic character of phenol ? **[All India 2022, Term-I, U]**

(a) CH_3O —

(b) CH_3 —

(c) NO_2 —

(d) All of these

28. Consider the following reaction :

$$X \xleftarrow[\text{(ii) } H^+]{\text{(i) NaOH, } CO_2} \xrightarrow[\text{(ii) } H^+]{\text{(i) } CHCl_3 + \text{aq. NaOH}} Y$$

the products X and Y are **[All India 2022, Term-I, U]**

(a) X = (phenol with COOH at ortho position, OH) Y = (benzene with CHO and OH)

(b) X = (phenol with CHO at ortho, OH) Y = (phenol with COOH at ortho, OH)

(c) X = (benzene with COOH and OH) Y = (phenol with CHO para, OH)

(d) X = (phenol with COOH at ortho, OH) Y = (phenol with CHO at ortho, OH)

29. Read the passage given below and answer the following questions: **[CBSE Sample 2020-21, A]**

An efficient, aerobic catalytic system for the transformation of alcohols into carbonyl compounds under mild conditions, copper-based catalyst has been discovered. This copper-based catalytic system utilizes oxygen or air as the ultimate, stoichiometric oxidant, producing water as the only by-product

$$R^2 \underset{H}{\overset{R_1}{\diagdown}} OH \xrightarrow[\substack{5\% \text{ DBADH}_2; O_2 \\ \text{Toluene; } 70° \text{ to } 90°C}]{\substack{5\% \text{ CuCl; } 5\% \text{ Phen;} \\ 2 \text{ equiv. } K_2CO_3;}} R^2 \underset{2}{\overset{R_1}{\diagdown}} O$$

A wide range of primary, secondary, allylic, and benzylic alcohols can be smoothly oxidized to the corresponding aldehydes or ketones in good to excellent yields. Air can be conveniently used instead of oxygen without affecting the efficiency of the process. However, the use of air requires slightly longer reaction times.

This process is not only economically viable and applicable to large-scale reactions, but it is also environmentally friendly.

(Reference: Ohkuma, T., Ooka, H., Ikariya, T., & Noyori, R. (1995). Preferential hydrogenation of aldehydes and ketones. Journal of the American Chemical Society, 117(41), 10417-10418.)

The following questions are multiple choice questions. Choose the most appropriate answer:

(i) The Copper based catalyst mention in the study above can be used to convert:

(a) propanol to propanonic acid

(b) propanone to propanoic acid

(c) propanone to propan-2-ol

(d) propan-2-ol to propanone

(ii) The carbonyl compound formed when ethanol gets oxidised using this copper-based catalyst can also be obtained by ozonolysis of:

(a) But-1-ene (b) But-2-ene

(c) Ethene (d) Pent-1-ene

OR

Which of the following is a secondary allylic alcohol?

(a) But-3-en-2-ol (b) But-2-en-2-ol

(c) Prop-2-enol (d) Butan-2-ol

(iii) Benzyl alcohol on treatment with this copper-based catalyst gives a compound 'A' which on reaction with KOH gives compounds 'B' and 'C'. Compound 'B' on oxidation with $KMnO_4$ - KOH gives compound 'C'. Compounds 'A', 'B' and 'C' respectively are:

(a) Benzaldehyde, Benzyl alcohol, potassium salt of Benzoic acid

(b) Benzaldehyde, potassium salt of Benzoic acid, Benzyl alcohol

(c) Benzaldehyde, Benzoic acid, Benzyl alcohol

(d) Benzoic acid, Benzyl alcohol, Benzaldehyde

(iv) An organic compound 'X' with molecular formula C_3H_8O on reaction with this copper based catalyst gives compound 'Y' which reduces Tollen's reagent. 'X' on reaction with sodium metal gives 'Z'. What is the product of reaction of 'Z' with 2-chloro-2-methylpropane?

(a) $CH_3CH_2CH_2OC(CH_3)_3$

(b) $CH_3CH_2OC(CH_3)_3$

(c) $CH_2 = C(CH_3)_2$

(d) $CH_3CH_2CH = C(CH_3)_2$

Topic-3: *Ethers*

<table><tr><td>**1**</td><td>*Multiple Choice Questions*</td></tr></table>

1. Anisole undergoes bromination with bromine in ethanoic acid even in the absence of iron (III) bromide catalyst
   [CBSE Sample 2023-24, U]
   (a) Due to the activation of benzene ring by the methoxy group.
   (b) Due to the de–activation of benzene ring by the methoxy group.
   (c) Due to the increase in electron density at ortho and para positions
   (d) Due to the formation of stable carbocation.

2. Which of the following reactions are feasible?
   [All India 2023 Set - I, U]
   (a) $CH_3CH_2Br + Na^+ \, O^-C(CH_3)_3 \rightarrow CH_3CH_2-O-C(CH_3)_3$
   (b) $(CH_3)_3C-Cl + Na^+ \, O^-CH_2CH_3 \rightarrow CH_3CH_2-O-C(CH_3)_3$
   (c) Both (a) and (b)
   (d) Neither (a) nor (b)

3. What would be the major product of the following reaction? **[CBSE Sample 2022-23, U]**
   $C_6H_5—CH_2—OC_6H_5 + HBr \rightarrow A + B$
   (a) $A = C_6H_5CH_2OH$, $B = C_6H_6$
   (b) $A = C_6H_5CH_2OH$, $B = C_6H_5Br$
   (c) $A = C_6H_5CH_3$, $B = C_6H_5Br$
   (d) $A = C_6H_5CH_2Br$, $B = C_6H_5OH$

4. Williamson's synthesis of preparing dimethyl ether is an:
   [All India 2021-22, Term-I, K]
   (a) S_N1 reaction
   (b) Elimination reaction
   (c) S_N2 reaction
   (d) Nucleophilic addition reaction

5. Williamson's synthesis of preparing dimethyl ether is an:
   (a) S_N1 reaction **[CBSE Sample 2021-22, U]**
   (b) Elimination reaction
   (c) S_N2 reaction
   (d) Nucleophilic addition reaction

<table><tr><td>**2**</td><td>*Assertion Reason/Two Statement Type Questions*</td></tr></table>

Given below are two statements labelled as Assertion (A) and Reason (R). Select the most appropriate answer from the options given below:
(a) Both (A) and (R) are true and (R) is the correct explanation of (A).
(b) Both (A) and (R) are true, but (R) is not the correct explanation of (A).
(c) (A) is true, but (R) is false.
(d) (A) is false, but (R) is true.

6. **Assertion (A):** An ether is more volatile than an alcohol of comparable molecular mass.
   Reason (R): Ethers are polar in nature.
   [CBSE Sample 2022-23, U]

7. **Assertion:** Methoxy ethane reacts with HI to give ethanol and iodomethane **[CBSE Sample 2020-21, U]**
   Reason: Reaction of ether with HI follows S_N2 mechanism

8. **Assertion (A) :** The C-O-C bond angle in ethers is slightly less than tetrahedral angle. **[Delhi 2020, Set-I]**
   Reason (R) : Due to the repulsive interaction between the two alkyl groups in ethers.

<table><tr><td>**5**</td><td>*Short Answer Questions (2 or 3 Marks)*</td></tr></table>

9. Write the name of the reaction, structure and IUPAC name of the product formed when:
   [CBSE Sample 2023-24, U]
   (a) phenol reacts with $CHCl_3$ in the presence of NaOH followed by hydrolysis.
   (b) $CH_3CH_2CH(CH_3)CH(CH_3)ONa$ reacts with C_2H_5Br
   [CBSE Sample 2023-24, U]

10. (i) Write the mechanism of the following reaction:
    [All India 2023, Set - I, K]

    $$2CH_3CH_2OH \xrightarrow[413K]{H^+} CH_3-CH_2-O-CH_2-CH_3 + H_2O$$
    (ii) Why ortho-nitrophenol is steam volatile while para nitrophenol is not? **[All India 2023, Set - I, K]**

11. What happens when   **[All India 2023, Set - I, K]**

   (i) Anisole is treated with CH_3Cl anhydrous $AlCl_3$?

   (ii) Phenol is oxidised with $Na_2Cr_2O_7/H^+$?

   (iii) $(CH_3)_3C – OH$ is heated with CuI 573 K ?

   Write chemical equation in support of your answer.

12. Write the chemical equation involved in the following:

        [All India 2023 Set-2, K]

   (a) Kolbe's reaction

   (b) Williamson synthesis

13. (i) Why is the C–O bond length in phenols less than that in methanol?   **[Delhi 2023, U]**

   (ii) Arrange the following in order of increasing boiling point: **[Delhi 2023, U]**

   Ethoxyethane, Butanal, Butanol, n-butane

   (iii) How can phenol be prepared from anisole? Give reaction.   **[Delhi 2023, U]**

14. (i) Give mechanism of the following reaction:

        [Delhi 2023, Set-I, U]

$$CH_3CH_2OH \xrightarrow[413K]{H_2SO_4} CH_3CH_2 – O – CH_2CH_3 + H_2O$$

   (ii) Illustrate hydroboration - oxidation reaction with an example.   **[Delhi 2023, Set-I, K]**

15. Write the equations for the following reaction:

        [CBSE Sample 2022-23, U]

   (a) Salicylic acid is treated with acetic anhydride in the presence of conc. H_2SO_4

   (b) Tert butyl chloride is treated with sodium ethoxide.

   (c) Phenol is treated with chloroform in the presence of NaOH

16. Give the structures of final products expected from the following reactions: **[Delhi 2020, U]**

   (a) Hydroboration of propene followed by oxidation with H_2O_2 in alkaline medium.

   (b) Dehydration of $(CH_3)_3C–OH$ by heating it with 20% H_3PO_4 at 358 K.

   (c) heating of ⟨C₆H₄⟩–$CH_2 – O$–⟨C₆H₅⟩ with HI.

17. How can you convert the following?   **[Delhi 2020, U]**

   (a) Phenol to o-hydroxybenzaldehyde.

   (b) Methanal to ethanol

   (c) Phenol to phenyl ethanoate.

18. What happens when   **[All India 2019, U]**

   (a) Phenol reacts with conc. HNO_3 ?

   (b) Ethyl chloride reacts with $NaOC_2H_5$?

Write the chemical equations involved in the above reactions.

19. (a) Butan-1-ol has a higher boiling point than diethyl ether. Why?   **[All India 2019, U]**

   (b) Write the mechanism of the following reaction:

$$2CH_3CH_2OH \xrightarrow[413K]{H^+} CH_3CH_2 – O – CH_2 – CH_3$$

20. Write the structures of the main products in the following reactions: **[All India 2018, U]**

   (i) cyclohexanone–CH_2–C(=O)–$OCH_3 \xrightarrow{NaBH_4}$

   (ii) C_6H_5–$CH = CH_2 + H_2O \xrightarrow{H^+}$

   (iii) C_6H_5–OC_2H_2 + HI $\longrightarrow$

21. Write the final product(s) in each of the following reactions :   **[All India 2016, K]**

   (a) $CH_3 – \underset{\underset{CH_3}{|}}{\overset{\overset{CH_3}{|}}{C}} – O — CH_3 + HI \longrightarrow$

   (b) $CH_3 — CH_2 — \underset{\underset{OH}{|}}{CH} — CH_3 \xrightarrow{Cu/573K}$

   (c) $C_6H_5 — OH \xrightarrow[(ii)\ H^+]{(i)\ CHCl_3 + aq.NaOH}$

22. Write the mechanism of the following reaction:

        [Delhi 2016, K]

$$2CH_3CH_2OH \xrightarrow[413K]{Conc.H_2SO_4} CH_3CH_2 – O – CH_2 – CH_3$$

23. Write the main product(s) in each of the following reactions :   **[Delhi 2016, K]**

   (i) $CH_3 – \underset{\underset{CH_3}{|}}{\overset{\overset{CH_3}{|}}{C}} – O – CH_3 + HI \longrightarrow$

   (ii) $CH_3 – CH = CH_2 \xrightarrow[(ii)\ 3H_2O_2/OH]{(i)\ B_2H_6}$

   (iii) $C_6H_5 – OH \xrightarrow[(ii)\ CO_2,H^+]{(i)\ aq.NaOH}$

24. Give reasons for the following.   **[All India 2015, K]**

   (i) Phenol is more acidic than ethanol.

   (ii) Boiling point of ethanol is higher in comparison to methoxymethane

   (iii) $(CH_3)_3C - O - CH_3$ on reaction with HI gives CH_3OH and $(CH_3)_3C - I$ as the main products and not $(CH_3)_3C - OH$ and CH_3I.

25. How do you convert the following :   **[Delhi 2015, U]**

   (i) Phenol to anisole

   (ii) Propan-2-ol to 2-methylpropan-2-ol

   (iii) Aniline to phenol

26. (a) Write the mechanism of the following reaction :   **[Delhi 2015, U]**

$$2CH_3CH_2OH \xrightarrow{H^+} CH_3CH_2 - O - CH_2CH_3$$

   (b) Write the equation involved in the acetylation of salicylic acid.

27. Write the equations involved in the following reactions:

   (i) Reimer – Tiemann reaction

   (ii) Williamson synthesis   **[All India 2014, K]**

28. Write the equations involved in the following reactions :

   (i) Reimer – Tiemann reaction   **[All India 2013, K]**

   (ii) Williamson's ether synthesis

29. Explain the mechanism of the following reaction:

$$2CH_3 - CH_2 - OH \xrightarrow[413K]{H^+}$$

$$CH_3CH_2\ddot{O} - CH_2 - CH_3 + H_2O$$ **[Delhi 2013, K]**

 **Long Answer Questions**

30. (a) Out of t-butyl alcohol and n-butanol, which one will undergo acid catalyzed dehydration faster and why?   **[All India 2020, U]**

   (b) Carry out the following conversions:

   (i) Phenol to salicylaldehyde

   (ii) t-Butylchloride to t-butyl ethyl ether

   (iii) Propene to propanol

31. (a) Give the mechanism for the formation of ethanol from ethene.   **[All India 2020, U]**

   (b) Predict the reagent for carrying out the following conversions:

   (i) Phenol to benzoquinone

   (ii) Anisole to p-bromoanisole

   (iii) Phenol to 2,4,6-tribromophenol

32. (a) Write the product(s) in the following reactions :   **[Delhi 2017, K]**

   (i)

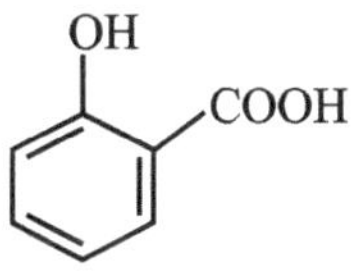

$$\text{(salicylic acid)} \xrightarrow[H^+]{(CH_3CO)_2O} ?$$

   (ii) $CH_3 - \overset{\overset{\displaystyle CH_3}{|}}{CH} - O - CH_2 - CH_3 \xrightarrow{HI} ? + ?$

   (iii) $CH_3 - CH = CH - CH_2 - OH \xrightarrow{PCC} ?$

   (b) Give simple chemical tests to distinguish between the following pairs of compounds:

   (i) Ethanol and Phenol

   (ii) Propanol and 2-methylpropan-2-ol

33. (a) Write the formula of reagents used in the following reactions :   **[Delhi 2020, U]**

   (i) Bromination of phenol to 2,4,6-tribromophenol

   (ii) Hydroboration of propene and then oxidation to propanol.

   (b) Arrange the following compound groups in the increasing order of their property indicated :

   (i) p-nitrophenol, ethanol, phenol (acidic character)

   (ii) Propanol, Propane, Propanal (boiling point)

   (c) Write the mechanism (using curved arrow notation) of the following reaction :

$$CH_3 - CH_2 - \overset{+}{O}H_2 \xrightarrow{CH_3CH_2OH} CH_3 - CH_2 - \overset{\overset{\displaystyle +}{|}}{\underset{\underset{\displaystyle H}{|}}{O}} - CH_2 - CH_3 + H_2O$$

Solutions

Topic-1: *Classification, Nomenclature, Structures of Functional Groups*

1. (b) The shape of alcohol is tetrahedral but due to presence of lone pair on oxygen atom, C—O—H bond angle decreases i.e. it will become less than 109°28′.

(1 Mark)

2. (a)

  (i) $CH_3CH_2CH(OH)CH_3$ (secondary)

  (ii) $(C_2H_5)_3COH$ (tertiary)

  (iii)   (Phenol not an alcohol)

  (iv)   (secondary)   **(1 Mark)**

3. $^5CH_3 - {}^4CH_2 - {}^3C - {}^2CH - {}^1CH_3$ with CH_3 above and CH_3, OH below

3, 3 – Dimethylpentan-2-ol.   **(1 Mark)**

4. IUPAC name of the given compound is 2-Methoxy-2-methylpropane.   **(1 Mark)**

5. $\overset{2}{C}H_2 - \overset{1}{C}H_2 - OH$

The IUPAC name of the given compound is 2-phenylethanol.   **(1 Mark)**

6. 2-Methylprop–2–ene–1– ol.   **(1 Mark)**

7. NO_2 ... OH ... NO_2

2, 5-dinitrophenol or 2, 5-dinitrohydroxy benzene

(1 Mark)

Topic-2: *Alcohols and Phenols, Some Commercially Important Alcohols*

1. (b) no turbidity will be observed, given compound is a primary alcohol   **(1 Mark)**

2. (c) Tertiary alcohols do not undergo oxidation due to the absence of an α-hydrogen atom.

Among the given options, **2-Methyl butan-2-ol** is a tertiary alcohol that would not undergo oxidation.

$$H_3C - H_2C - \underset{CH_3}{\overset{CH_3}{C}} - OH$$

3° alcohol

Therefore, option **(c)** is correct.   **(1 Mark)**

3. (a) Etard reaction   **(1 Mark)**

4. (a) Step I: Addition of HBr

$$CH_3 - CH = CH_2 \xrightarrow{HBr} CH_3 - \underset{Br}{CH} - CH_3$$

2-bromopropane

The product is formed according to markovnikov rule.

Step II: Reaction with aq. KOH

$$CH_3 - \underset{Br}{CH} - CH_3 \xrightarrow{aq.\ KOH} CH_3 - \underset{OH}{CH} - CH_3$$

The final product is formed by S_N2 reaction.

(1 Mark)

5. (c) PCC act as amild oxidising agent which converts 1° alcohol to aldehyde.

$$CH_3CH = CHCH_2OH \xrightarrow{PCC}$$
$$CH_3CH = CH - CHO \quad \textbf{(1 Mark)}$$

6. (b) 1-methylcyclohexene

According to Saytzeff rule i.e highly substituted alkene is major product. Here dehydration reaction takes place, alkene is formed due to the removal of a water molecule.   **(1 Mark)**

7. (c) Kolbe's reaction is used to prepare salicylic acid, Etard reaction for benzaldehyde, Reimer- Tiemann reaction for salicylaldehyde and Stephen's reduction for aldehyde.   **(1 Mark)**

8. (d)

$$CH_3 - CH - C = O + (CH_3)_2CHMgI \longrightarrow$$

(Isopropyl magnesium iodide)

2-Methylpropanal

$$(CH_3)_2CH - C - OMgI \xrightarrow{H_2O} (CH_3)_2CH - C - OH$$

with $CH(CH_3)_2$ substituent

2, 4-Dimethylpentan-3-ol

(1 Mark)

9. (a) Protonation of alcohol molecule

Step 1: Formation of protonated alcohol

$$H - C - C - \ddot{O} - H + H^+ \underset{\text{Fast}}{\rightleftharpoons} H - C - C - \overset{+}{\ddot{O}} - H$$

Ethanol

Protonated alcohol
(Ethyl oxonium ion)

Step 2: Formation of carbocation: It is the slowest step and hence, the rate determining step of the reaction.

$$H - C - C - \overset{+}{O} - H \underset{\text{Slow}}{\rightleftharpoons} H - C - C^+ - H_2O$$

Step 3: Formation of ethene by elimination of a proton.

$$H - C - C^+ \rightleftharpoons C = C + H^+$$

Ethene **(1 Mark)**

10. (a) Alcohols form intermolecular hydrogen bonds due to which their b.pt. is high. **(1 Mark)**

11. (c) Miscible in water in all proportions. Lower molecular mass alcohols are able to form hydrogen bonds with water **(1 Mark)**

12. (b) Due to partial double bond character of C–OH bond. **(1 Mark)**

13. (c) A is true but R is false **(1 Mark)**

14. o-Nitrophenol is more volatile than p-nitrophenol.

(1 Mark)

> **Note**
>
> *Various types of interactions present in the molecule affect the properties of that molecule. o-Nitrophenol has intramolecular H-bonding where as p-Nitrophenol has intermolecular H-bonding. Intramolecular H-bonding in o-Nitrophenol make it more volatile than p-Nitrophenol.*

15. $CH_3 - CH_2 - CH_3 < CH_3 - CHO < CH_3 - CH_2 - OH$

(1 Mark)

16. (a) Reimer-Tiemann Reaction:

Phenol (OH) $\xrightarrow{CHCl_3, \text{ aq NaOH}}$ [ONa with $CHCl_2$] $\xrightarrow{NaOH}$

Benzal Chloride

ONa with CHO $\xrightarrow{H^+}$ OH with CHO

Salicylaldehyde **(1 Mark)**

> **Note**
>
> *This reaction is specifically used for ortho-formylation.*

(b) Acetylation of Salicylic acid:

OH, COOH $\xrightarrow{(CH_3CO)_2O, \, H^+}$ OCOCH$_3$, COOH $+ CH_3COOH$

(Salicylic acid)

(Acetylacetic acid)
(Aspirin)

(1 Mark)

17. (a) Phenol is more acidic than cyclohexanol because the conjugate base of phenol, which is phenoxide ion, is much more stable than the conjugate base of cyclohexanol which is cyclohexoide ion due to resonance stabilization. **(1 Mark)**

> **Note**

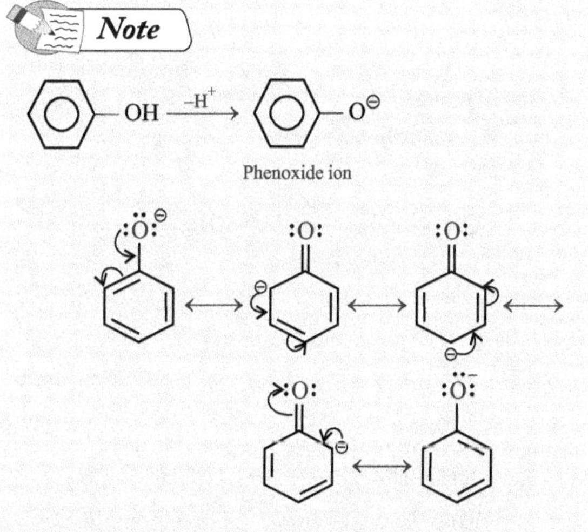

Phenoxide ion

(b) Phenol being an aromatic alcohol, gives positive FeCl$_3$ test and gives violet solution while cyclohexanol gives negative FeCl$_3$ test. **(1 Mark)**

18. $(CH_3)_2CHCHO + C_2H_5MgBr \xrightarrow{dry\ ether}$

$(CH_3)_2CHCH(C_2H_5)(OMgBr)$ **(1 mark)**

$(CH_3)_2CHCH(C_2H_5)(OMgBr) \xrightarrow{H^+/H_2O}$

$(CH_3)_2CHCH(C_2H_5)(OH)$ **(1 mark)**
2-Methylpentan-3-ol

19. (a) Increasing order of acid strength is *p*-cresol < phenol < *p*-nitrophenol **(1 Mark)**

(b) Reaction :

$$CH_2 = CH_2 \xrightarrow{H_3O^+} CH_3 - CH_2^+ + H_2O$$

Mechanism :

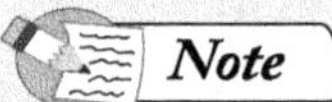

(1 Mark)

20. (a) Secondary alcohol (butan-2-ol) on reaction with chromic anhydride (CrO_3) oxidises to ketone (butan-2-one).

$$\underset{\text{Butan-2-ol}}{CH_3 - CH_2 - \overset{\overset{\displaystyle OH}{|}}{CH} - CH_3}$$

$$\xrightarrow{CrO_3} \underset{\text{Butan-2-one}}{CH_3 - CH_2 - \overset{\overset{\displaystyle O}{\|}}{C} - CH_3}$$

(1 Mark)

(b) Butan-2-ol on treating with $SOCl_2$ forms 2-chlorobutane

$$\underset{\text{Butan-2-ol}}{CH_3 - CH_2 - \overset{\overset{\displaystyle OH}{|}}{CH} - CH_3}$$

$$\xrightarrow{SOCl_2} \underset{\text{2-Chlorobutane}}{CH_3 - CH_2 - \overset{\overset{\displaystyle Cl}{|}}{CH} - CH_3}$$

(1 Mark)

21. (a) $CH_3CH_2OH \xrightarrow{HBr} CH_3CH_2Br + H_2O$

This is an example of nucleophilic substitution reaction :

As ethanol (CH_3CH_2 OH) is a primary alcohol, it will undergo substitution by S_N2 mechanism. The mechanism is shown below :

$$HBr \rightleftharpoons H^+ + Br^-$$

(2 Marks)

(b) **Reimer-Tiemann reaction**

Phenol $\xrightarrow[\text{aq. NaOH}]{CHCl_3}$ Intermediate $\xrightarrow{NaOH}$ $\xrightarrow{H^+}$ Salicylaldehyde

(1 Mark)

> **Note**
>
> *Dichlorocarbene is the reactive intermediate which form in the first step of reaction.*
>
> $H-\overset{\overset{\displaystyle Cl}{|}}{\underset{\underset{\displaystyle Cl}{|}}{C}}-Cl \xrightarrow{NaOH} \longrightarrow :C\overset{Cl}{\underset{Cl}{}}$
>
> *Dichlorocarbene act as a electrophile in the reaction.*

22. **Step 1.** Formation of protonated alcohol :

$$CH_3CH_2 - \overset{..}{\underset{..}{O}} - H + H^+ \rightleftharpoons CH_3 - CH_2 - \overset{\oplus}{\underset{..}{O}}\overset{\nearrow H}{\searrow_H}$$

(½ Mark)

Step 2. Formation of carbocation

$$CH_3 - CH_2 - \overset{\oplus}{\underset{..}{O}}\overset{H}{\underset{H}{}} \overset{slow}{\rightleftharpoons} CH_3 - \overset{\oplus}{C}H_2 + H_2O$$

(½ Mark)

It is the rate determining step.

Step 3. Elimination of a proton to form ethene

$$H-CH_2 - \overset{\oplus}{C}H_2 \overset{Fast}{\rightleftharpoons} \underset{\text{Ethene}}{CH_2 = CH_2} + H^+ \quad \textbf{(½ Mark)}$$

23. (i)
$$CH_3 - CH = CH_2 + H_2SO_4 \xrightarrow[\text{Propene}]{\text{H}_2\text{O, Boil} \atop \left(\text{Markovnikov Addition}\right)}$$

$$CH_3 - \underset{\underset{OH}{|}}{CH} - CH_3$$
Propene-2-ol   **(1 Mark)**

(ii) Phenol $\xrightarrow[\text{conc. H}_2\text{SO}_4]{\text{conc. HNO}_3}$ 2, 4, 6-Trinitrophenol

(1 Mark)

24. (a) (i) Phenol to anisole

Phenol $+ \text{NaOH} \longrightarrow$ Sodium phenoxide $\xrightarrow{CH_3Br}$ Anisole

(1 Mark)

(ii) Ethanol to propan-2-ol

$$CH_3-CH_2OH \xrightarrow[\text{oxidation}]{PCC} CH_3-\overset{\overset{O}{\|}}{C}-H + CH_3MgI$$

$$\xrightarrow[\text{ether}]{Dry} \left[CH_3-\underset{\underset{OMgI}{|}}{CH}-CH_3 \right] \xrightarrow{H^+/H_2O}$$

$$CH_3-\underset{\underset{OH}{|}}{CH}-CH_3 + Mg \overset{I}{\underset{O}{<}}$$

(1 Mark)

(b) $C_2H_5OH \xrightarrow[443K]{H_2SO_4} CH_2 = CH_2 + H_2O$

Mechanism is as follows:

Step I: $CH_3CH_2\overset{..}{\underset{..}{O}}H + H-O-\overset{\overset{O}{\|}}{\underset{\underset{O}{\|}}{S}}-O-H$

$$\rightleftharpoons CH_3CH_2\overset{+}{O}H_2 + HSO_4^-$$

Step II: $CH_3CH_2\overset{\overset{H}{|}}{\underset{+}{O}}-H \rightleftharpoons CH_3\overset{+}{C}H_2 + H_2O$

Step III: $H-\underset{\underset{H}{|}}{\overset{\overset{H}{|}}{C}}-\overset{+}{C}H_2 + \ ^-O-\overset{\overset{O}{\|}}{\underset{\underset{O}{\|}}{S}}-O-H \rightleftharpoons$

$$CH_2{=}CH_2 + H_2SO_4$$

(2 Marks)

(c) The rate of any electrophilic substitution reaction depends upon the electron density in the aromatic ring. Higher the electron density in the aromatic ring, higher is the rate of electrophilic substitution reaction. The presence of OH group in phenol, increases the electron density at ortho and para position by +R effect. Since the electron density is more in phenol than in benzene. Therefore phenol undergoes electrophilic substitution more easily than benzene.   **(1 Mark)**

25. (a) (i) Ortho nitrophenol is more steam volatile than para nitrophenol because o-Nitrophenol has intra molecular hydrogen bonding where as para nitrophenol has intermolecular H-bonding. Energy is required to overcome attractive forces in the molecules of p-nitrophenol. This means that boiling point of o-nitrophenol is less and is steam volatile while that of p-nitrophenol is more, and is non-volatile.   **(1 Mark)**

(ii) Sodium methoxides is a strong nucleophile and a strong base. Thus elimination predominates substitution. In this reaction E_1 favored over S_N1. So t-butyl chloride on heating with sodium methoxide gives 2-methylpropene instead of t-butyl methyl ether.   **(1 Mark)**

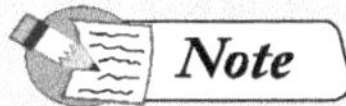

> **Note**

Elimination reaction is favored under strong base condition while substitution reaction is favored under weak nucleophile condition.

(b) (i) $2 \ \text{(Phenol, OH)} + CHCl_3 \xrightarrow{3 \ KOH}$ o-Hydroxy benzaldehyde (major)

$$+ \ 3 \ KCl + 2H_2O$$

(1 Mark)

(ii) Friedel Craft alkylation of phenol

In this reaction phenol react with alkyl halide in the presence of anhydrous $AlCl_3$ & forms o-methyl phenol, p-methyl phenol.

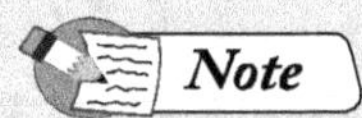

$$+ CH_3Cl \xrightarrow{\text{anhyd AlCl}_3}$$

(a p-cresol and o-cresol product structures)

(1 Mark)

Note

Phenols undergoes Friedel craft alkylation with very low yield due to the formation of complex with $AlCl_3$.

(c) Ethanol and phenol can be distinguished by iodoform test.

$$CH_3CH_2OH + 4I_2 + 6NaOH \longrightarrow$$

ethanol

$$CH I_3 \downarrow + HCOONa + 5H_2O$$

Iodoform
(yellow)

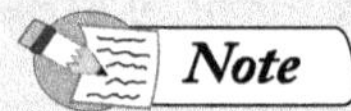

$$+ I_2 + NaOH \longrightarrow \text{No reaction}$$

(1 Mark)

26. (a) Tertiary alcohols, i.e.,

$$CH_3 - \underset{\underset{CH_3}{|}}{\overset{\overset{CH_3}{|}}{C}} - OH \text{ does not}$$

show oxidation.

Note

In tertiary alcohols, tertiary C does not have hydrogen and it is bonded to another carbon. It is difficult to break $C - C$ bond for the oxidation of C bonded to OH. Therefore it does not undergo oxidation.

27. (c) Electron withdrawing group increases the acidic character of alcohol. Therefore; ($-NO_2$) group will increases the acidic character.

28. (d)

(structure X: salicylic acid, and reaction scheme)

$$\xleftarrow[\text{(ii) H}^+]{\text{(i) NaOH, CO}_2}$$ (phenol)

$$\downarrow \begin{array}{l}\text{(i) } CHCl_3 + aq.\ NaOH \\ \text{(ii) H}^+\end{array}$$

(structure Y: salicylaldehyde)

29. (i) (d) (ii) (b) OR (a) (iii) (a) (iv) (c)

Topic-3: **Ethers**

1. (a) Due to the activation of benzene ring by the methoxy group. **(1 Mark)**

2. (b)

$$CH_3CH_2 - Br + Na^+ \, \bar{O}C(CH_3)_3 \xrightarrow{S_N2}$$

Bulky
t-butoxide

$$CH_3CH_2 - O - C(CH_3)_3 + Br^- + Na^+$$

Although primary alkyl halide favours the S_N2 reaction but the bulky t-Butoxide nucleophile acts as strong base instead of nucleophile.

$$Br - CH_2 - CH_2 + \bar{O}C(CH_3)_3 \longrightarrow$$

$$H \qquad H_2C = CH_2 + (CH_3)_3COH$$

Whereas in (b) the substrate facilitates the carbocation stability and therefore, S_N1 mechanism as the attacking nucleophile is not bulky one. **(1 Mark)**

3. (d) $A. = C_6H_5CH_2Br$, $B = C_6H_5OH$,

$C_6H_5CH_2OC_6H_5 \; H + C_6H_5CH_2OC_6H_5$ **(1 Mark)**

4. (c) Reaction since alkoxide ion reacts with primary alkyl halide in a single step to form ether. Hence, it is S_N2 reaction. **(1 Mark)**

5. (c) Reaction since alkoxide ion reacts with primary alkyl halide in a single step to form ether. Hence, it is S_N2 reaction. **(1 Mark)**

6. (b) Both A and R are true but R is not the correct explanation of A. A and R are two different statements about ethers The correct reason is that hydrogen bonding does not exist amongst ether molecules. **(1 Mark)**

7. (a)   **(1 Mark)**

8.

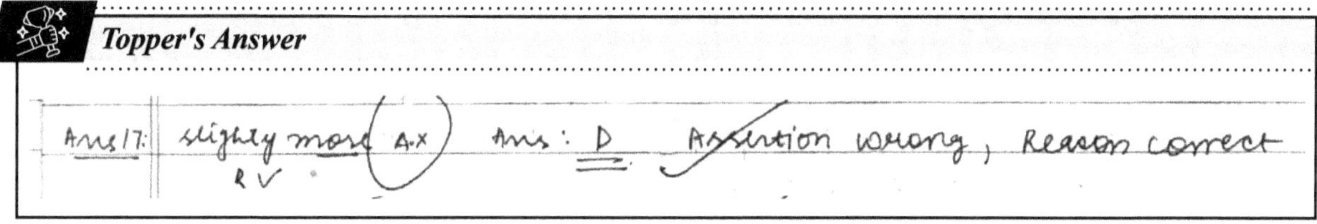

                                           (1 Mark)

9. (a) Reimer Tiemann,   **(1/2 Mark)**

2-Hydroxybenzaldehyde

                   (1/2 + 1/2 Mark)

(b) Williamson synthesis,

$CH_3CH_2CH(CH_3)CH(CH_3)O\ C_2H_5$

2– Ethoxy–2–methylpentane   **(1/2+1/2+1/2 Mark)**

10. (a) (i) $CH_3CH_2\ddot{O}H \xrightarrow{H^+} CH_3CH_2\overset{+}{O} - H$ ... H

                           (½ Mark)

$CH_3CH_2\ddot{O}H + CH_3CH_2 - \overset{+}{O} - H \longrightarrow$ ... H

$CH_3CH_2 - \overset{+}{O} - CH_2CH_3 \xrightarrow{-H^+}$ ... H

$CH_3CH_2 - O - CH_2CH_3$

                           (1 Mark)

                           (½ Mark)

(ii) Ortho-nitrophenol is steam volatile while para-nitrophenol is not due to intermolecular Hydrogen bonding present in p-nitrophenol.   **(1 Mark)**

11. (i) $\xrightarrow{CH_3Cl/Anhy.\ AlCl_3}$ **(1 Mark)**

(ii) $\xrightarrow{Na_2Cr_2O_7/H^+}$ Benzoquinone   **(1 Mark)**

(iii) $H_3C - \overset{\overset{\displaystyle CH_3}{|}}{\underset{\underset{\displaystyle CH_3}{|}}{C}} - OH \xrightarrow[\text{Dehydration}]{Cu,\ 573k} CH_3 - \overset{\overset{\displaystyle CH_3}{|}}{C} = CH_2$

                             (1 Mark)

t-alcohol gives alkene by dehydration whereas p- and s-alcohols undergo dehydrogenation resulting into aldehyde and ketone, respectively.

12. (a) Kolbe's reaction

Phenol $\xrightarrow{NaOH}$ (ONa) $\xrightarrow[\text{(ii) }H^+]{\text{(i) }CO_2}$ 2-Hydroxybenzoic acid (Salicylic acid)

                             (1 Mark)

(b) Williamson synthesis

$CH_3 - \overset{\overset{\displaystyle CH_3}{|}}{\underset{\underset{\displaystyle CH_3}{|}}{C}} - Br + Na\overset{+}{\ }\overset{-}{\ddot{O}} - CH_3 \longrightarrow CH_3 - \overset{\overset{\displaystyle CH_3}{|}}{C} = CH_2 + CH_3OH$

2-Methylpropene

                             (1 Mark)

13. (i) The C – O bond length in phenols is less than that in methanol because the carbon atom in phenol that is bonded to the oxygen atom is sp^2 - hybridized while that in methanol is sp^3 - hybridized.   **(1 Mark)**

The C–O bond in phenol has partial double bond character and therefore it is stronger and shorter.

(ii) n-butane has the lowest boiling point due to the weakest inter molecular forces (Van der Waals forces).

Butanol has the highest boiling point due to strongest inter molecular forces (Hydrogen - bonding) of attraction.

Among Ethoxyethane and butanal, butanal has a higher boiling point due to dipole-dipole interactions.   **(½ Mark)**

Thus, the increasing order of boiling point will be:

n-butane < ethoxy ethane < Butanal < Butanol

(½ Mark)

(iii) Preparation of phenol from anisole:

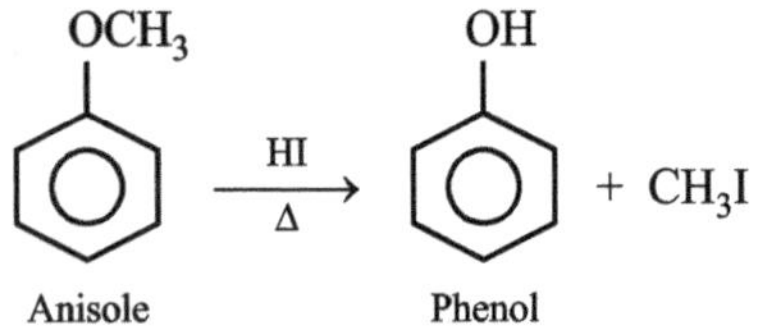

$$\underset{\text{Anisole}}{\text{C}_6\text{H}_5\text{OCH}_3} \xrightarrow[\Delta]{\text{HI}} \underset{\text{Phenol}}{\text{C}_6\text{H}_5\text{OH}} + \text{CH}_3\text{I}$$

(1 Mark)

14. (i) The given reaction is the acid-catalysed nucleophilic substitution reaction (S_N2):

$$\text{CH}_3 - \text{CH}_2 - \overset{..}{\underset{..}{\text{O}}} - \text{H} + \text{H}^+ \longrightarrow \text{CH}_3 - \text{CH}_2 - \overset{+}{\underset{\text{H}}{\text{O}}} - \text{H}$$

$$\text{CH}_3 - \text{CH}_2 - \overset{..}{\text{O}}\text{H} + \text{CH}_3 - \text{CH}_2 - \overset{+}{\text{O}} - \text{H} \longrightarrow$$

$$\text{CH}_3\text{CH}_2 - \overset{+}{\underset{\text{H}}{\text{O}}} - \text{CH}_2\text{CH}_3 + \text{H}_2\text{O}$$

(1 Mark)

$$\text{CH}_3\text{CH}_2 - \overset{+}{\underset{\text{H}}{\text{O}}} - \text{CH}_2\text{CH}_3 \longrightarrow$$

$$\underset{\text{Ether}}{\text{CH}_3\text{CH}_2 - \text{O} - \text{CH}_2\text{CH}_3} + \text{H}^+$$

(1 Mark)

(ii) **Hydroboration-oxidation:**

$$\text{CH}_3 - \text{CH} = \text{CH}_2 + (\text{H} - \text{BH}_2)_2 \longrightarrow$$
$$(\text{CH}_3 - \text{CH}_2 - \text{CH}_2)_3 \text{B}$$

$$(\text{CH}_3 - \text{CH}_2 - \text{CH}_2)_3 \text{B} \xrightarrow[3\text{H}_2\text{O}_2, \text{OH}^-]{\text{H}_2\text{O}}$$

$$3\text{CH}_3 - \text{CH}_2 - \text{CH}_2 - \text{OH} + \text{B(OH)}_3 \quad \textbf{(1 Mark)}$$

15. (a) Aspirin is formed

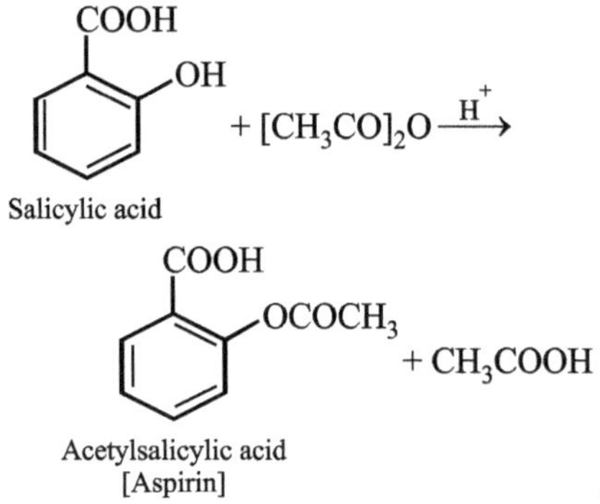

$$\underset{\text{Salicylic acid}}{\text{C}_6\text{H}_4(\text{COOH})(\text{OH})} + [\text{CH}_3\text{CO}]_2\text{O} \xrightarrow{\text{H}^+}$$

$$\underset{\substack{\text{Acetylsalicylic acid}\\ \text{[Aspirin]}}}{\text{C}_6\text{H}_4(\text{COOH})(\text{OCOCH}_3)} + \text{CH}_3\text{COOH}$$

(1 mark)

(b) $(\text{CH}_3)_3\text{CCl} \xrightarrow{\text{sodium ethoxide}} \underset{\text{2methylpropene}}{(\text{CH}_3)_2\text{C}\!=\!\text{CH}_2}$

(1 mark)

(c) o-hydroxybenzaldehyde will be formed **(1 mark)**

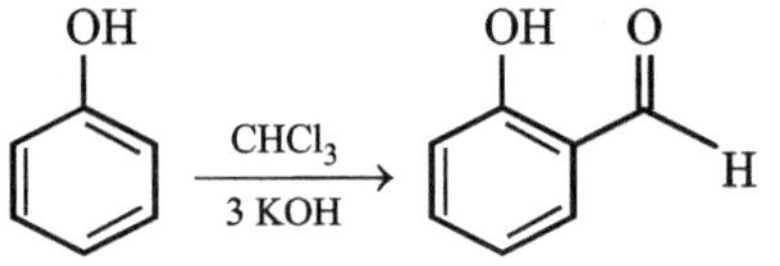

$$\underset{}{\text{C}_6\text{H}_5\text{OH}} \xrightarrow[3\text{ KOH}]{\text{CHCl}_3} \text{o-HO-C}_6\text{H}_4\text{-CHO}$$

16.

(a) $CH_3 - CH = CH_2 \xrightarrow{B_2H_6} (CH_3 - CH_2 - CH_2)_3B$

$\xrightarrow[OH^-]{H_2O_2} CH_3 - CH_2 - CH_2 - OH + B(OH)_3$

(1 Mark)

> **Note**
>
> *Hydroboration-oxidation is an anti-Markonikov addition reaction in which hydroxyl group is attached to less substituted carbon.*

(b) $H_3C - \overset{\overset{\displaystyle CH_3}{|}}{\underset{\underset{\displaystyle CH_3}{|}}{C}} - OH \xrightarrow[358\ K]{20\%\ H_3PO_4} H_3C - \overset{\overset{\displaystyle CH_2}{\|}}{\underset{\underset{\displaystyle CH_3}{|}}{C}} + H_2O$ **(1 Mark)**

(c) 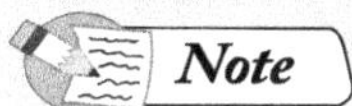 $\xrightarrow[\Delta]{HI}$

$\bigcirc\!\!-CH_2 - I + HO\!-\!\!\bigcirc$

(1 Mark)

> **Note**
>
> *In acidic cleavage of ethers, alkyl or aryl halides are formed from the more stable carbocation.*

OR

17. **(a)** Phenol $\xrightarrow[aq.\ NaOH]{CHCl_3}$ *o*-hydroxybenzaldehyde **(1 Mark)**

Reimer – Tiemann reaction

> **Note**
>
> *Dichlorocarbene is the reactive intermediate which is formed in the first step of the reaction.*

(b) $H - \overset{}{\underset{\underset{\displaystyle O}{\|}}{C}} - H + CH_3 - MgBr \longrightarrow$

Methanal

$H - \overset{\overset{\displaystyle CH_3}{|}}{\underset{\underset{\displaystyle O-MgBr}{|}}{C}} - H \xrightarrow{HOH} H - \overset{\overset{\displaystyle CH_3}{|}}{\underset{\underset{\displaystyle OH}{|}}{C}} - H + Mg(OH)Br$

Ethanol

(1 Mark)

(c) Phenol $+ CH_3COOH \rightleftharpoons$ Phenyl ethanoate $+ H_2O$

(1 Mark)

18. **(a)** Phenol $\xrightarrow[HNO_3]{Conc.}$ **(1 Mark)**

2, 4, 6 Tritritrophenol
(Picric acid)

(b) $CH_3CH_2Cl + NaOC_2H_5 \xrightarrow{S_N 2} CH_3CH_2OC_2H_5$
Diethyl ether

(1 Mark)

> **Note**
>
> *When picric acid is hydrated then it is safe to handle, but it becomes a powerful explosive when dry (less than 10% H_2O). Dry picric acid is highly sensitive to heat, shock and friction. The moistened solid is classified as a flammable solid.*

19. **(a)** Boiling point of butan-ol-1 is higher than diethyl ether because the former forms hydrogen bond among their molecules, while diethyl ether molecules do not form intermolecular hydrogen bond.

$CH_3(CH_2)_2CH_2 - O - H \cdots OH_2C(CH_2)_2CH_3$

$\overset{\vdots}{H}$

$\vdots$

$C_2H_5 - O - C_2H_5$

No H-bond because
it does not have H with O.

Thus, alcohol molecules, being polar, are associated through intermolecular hydrogen bonds and hence their boiling points are high. **(1 Mark)**

> **Note**
>
> *The hydrogen bond is an attractive interaction between a hydrogen atom from a molecule or a molecular fragment X – H in which X is more electronegative than hydrogen, and an atom on a group of atoms in the same or a different molecule.*

If it takes place between different molecules then it is intermolecular hydrogen bonding.

If it takes place in same molecule than it is intermolecular hydrogen bonding.

(b) **(i)** $CH_3CH_2OH \xrightarrow{H^+} CH_3CH_2\overset{+}{O}H_2$

(ii) $CH_3CH_2 - \overset{\cdot\cdot}{\underset{\cdot\cdot}{O}} - H + CH_3 - CH_2 \overset{+}{O}H_2 \xrightarrow{-H_2O}$

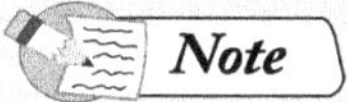

$CH_3CH_2 - \overset{+}{\underset{\underset{\displaystyle H}{|}}{O}} - CH_2CH_3$

(iii) $CH_3CH_2-\overset{+}{\underset{H}{O}}-CH_2CH_3 \xrightarrow{(-H^+)}$

$$CH_3CH_2-O-CH_2CH_3$$
Diethyl ether

(½ + 1 + ½ = 2 Marks)

20. (i)

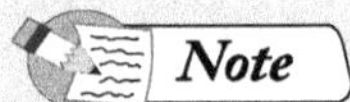

(NaBH$_4$ does not reduce the ester group, so only ketonic group gets reduced to alcohol) **(1 Mark)**

(ii)

$$+ H_2O \xrightarrow{H^+}$$

(This is in accordance with Markovnikov's rule)

(1 Mark)

(iii)

$$+ HI \longrightarrow + C_2H_5I$$

(The $O-C_2H_5$ bond breaks to give C_2H_5I. C_6H_5-O does not break due to partial double bond character)

(1 Mark)

21. The final products of the given reactions are :

(a) $CH_3-\overset{\overset{CH_3}{|}}{\underset{\underset{CH_3}{|}}{C}}-O-CH_3 + HI \longrightarrow$

$$CH_3-\overset{\overset{CH_3}{|}}{\underset{\underset{CH_3}{|}}{C}}-I + CH_3-OH$$

(1 Mark)

(b) $CH_3-CH_2-\underset{\underset{OH}{|}}{CH}-CH_3 \xrightarrow{Cu,\ 573K}$
Butan-2-ol

$$CH_3-CH_2-\overset{\overset{}{}}{\underset{\underset{O}{||}}{C}}-CH_3 + H_2$$
Butan-2-one

(1 Mark)

(c)

Phenol $+ CHCl_3 + 3NaOH \longrightarrow$

$\xrightarrow{H^+}$

Salicylaldehyde

(1 Mark)

22. **Mechanism** $H_2SO_4 \rightleftharpoons H^+ + HSO_4^-$

Step I:

$CH_3-CH_2-\overset{..}{\underset{..}{O}}-H + H^+ \longrightarrow CH_3-CH_2-\overset{..+}{\underset{\underset{H}{|}}{O}}-H$
(Proton from H$_2$SO$_4$)
Protonised alcohol

Step II: $CH_3-CH_2-\overset{..+}{\underset{\underset{H}{|}}{O}}-H \longrightarrow CH_3-\overset{+}{CH_2} + H_2O$
Carbocation

Step III:

(i) $CH_3-\overset{+}{CH_2} + :\overset{\overset{H}{|}}{O}-CH_2-CH_3 \longrightarrow$

$$CH_3-CH_2-\overset{\overset{H}{|}+}{O}-CH_2-CH_3$$

(ii) $CH_3-CH_2-\overset{\overset{H}{|}+}{O}-CH_2-CH_3 \xrightarrow{-H^\oplus}$

$$CH_3-CH_2-O-CH_2-CH_3$$

(2 Marks)

23. (i)

$CH_3-\overset{\overset{CH_3}{|}}{\underset{\underset{CH_3}{|}}{C}}-O-CH_3 + HI \longrightarrow CH_3-\overset{\overset{CH_3}{|}}{\underset{\underset{CH_3}{|}}{C}}-I + CH_3OH$

(1 Mark)

(ii) $3CH_3-CH=CH_2 \xrightarrow[(ii)\ 3H_2O_2/OH^-]{(i)\ B_2H_6}$

$$3CH_3-CH_2-CH_2OH + B(OH)_3$$

(1 Mark)

(iii) 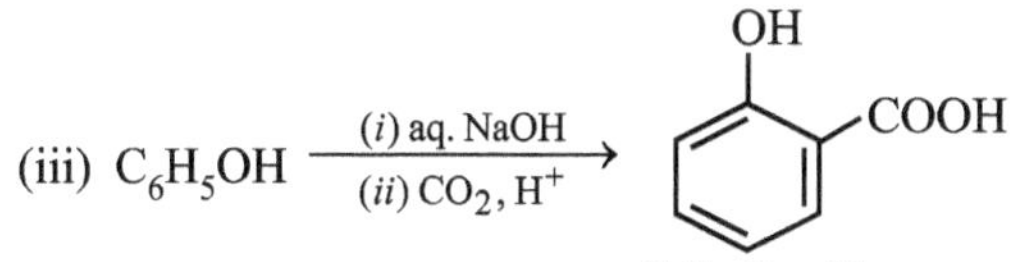 $C_6H_5OH \xrightarrow[(ii)\ CO_2,\ H^+]{(i)\ aq.\ NaOH}$ (Salicylic acid structure: benzene ring with OH and COOH)

Salicylic acid

(1 Mark)

24. (i) Since the phenoxide ion formed after the removal of a proton is stabilized by resonance whereas alkoxide ion formed after the removal of a proton from alcohol is not resonance stabilized. Thus phenol is more acidic than alcohol. **(1 Mark)**

(ii) The boiling points of ethers are lower than their isomeric alcohols, due to the absence of hydrogen bonds between ether molecules. Low polarity in ethers does not allow hydrogen bonding and hence, their boiling points are low.

On the other hand, alcohol molecules are polar and get associated through intermolecular hydrogen bonds and hence their boiling points are high.

(1 Mark)

(iii) Given reaction occurs by S_N1 mechanism and the formation of products is controlled by the stability of the carbocation resulting from the cleavage of C–O bond in protonated ether. Since tert-butyl carbocation is more stable than methyl carbocation, therefore $(CH_3)_3C - O-CH_3$ on reaction with HI gives methyl alcohol and the more stable tert-butyl iodide.

$$(CH_3)_3C-O-CH_3 \xrightarrow{H^+} \underset{\text{(more stable)}}{(CH_3)_3 \overset{+}{C}} + HOCH_3$$

(1 Mark)

25. (i) 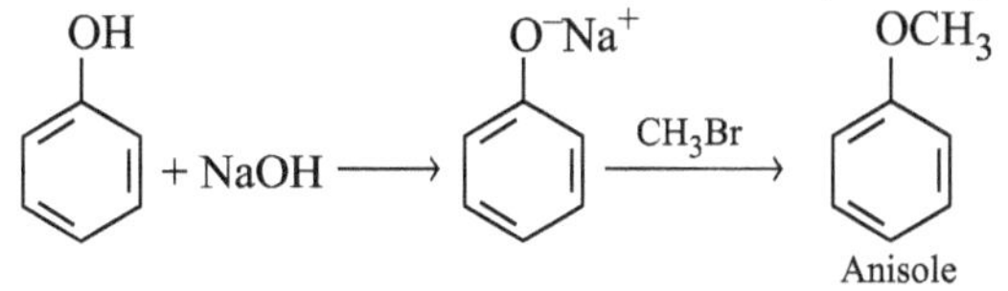 (Phenol) $+ NaOH \longrightarrow$ (Sodium phenoxide, O^-Na^+) $\xrightarrow{CH_3Br}$ (Anisole, OCH_3)

Anisole

(1 Mark)

(ii) $CH_3-\underset{\underset{OH}{|}}{\overset{\overset{H}{|}}{C}}-CH_3 \xrightarrow[\text{(oxidation)}]{Cr_2O_7^{2-}/H^+} CH_3-\underset{\underset{O}{\|}}{C}-CH_3$

Propanone

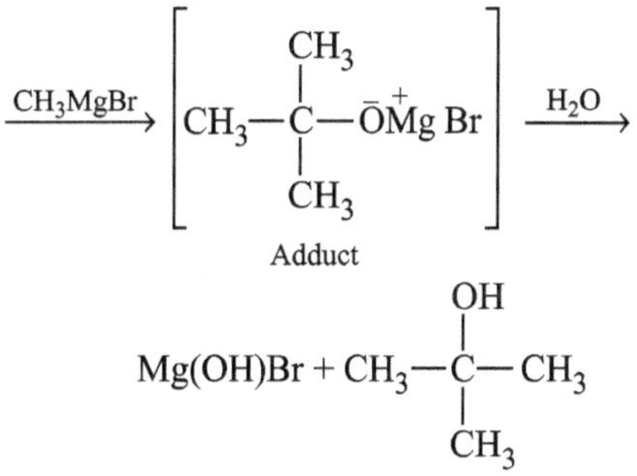

$\xrightarrow{CH_3MgBr} \left[CH_3-\underset{\underset{CH_3}{|}}{\overset{\overset{CH_3}{|}}{C}}-\bar{O}\overset{+}{Mg}\ Br \right] \xrightarrow{H_2O}$

Adduct

$$Mg(OH)Br + CH_3-\underset{\underset{CH_3}{|}}{\overset{\overset{OH}{|}}{C}}-CH_3$$

2-Methylpropan-2-ol **(1 Mark)**

(iii) 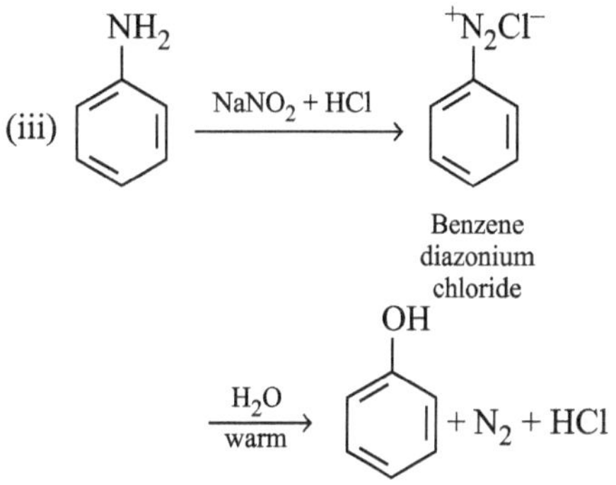 (Aniline, NH_2) $\xrightarrow{NaNO_2 + HCl}$ (Benzene diazonium chloride, $\overset{+}{N_2}Cl^-$)

Benzene diazonium chloride

$\xrightarrow[\text{warm}]{H_2O}$ (Phenol, OH) $+ N_2 + HCl$

(1 Mark)

26. (a) The given reaction follows S_N2 mechanism as shown below.

Step 1:

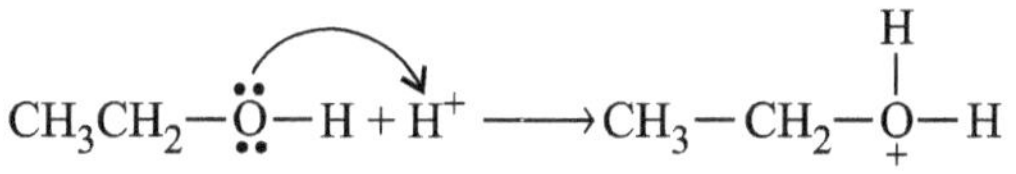

$$CH_3CH_2-\overset{..}{\underset{..}{O}}-H + H^+ \longrightarrow CH_3-CH_2-\underset{+}{\overset{\overset{H}{|}}{O}}-H$$

(½ Mark)

Step 2:

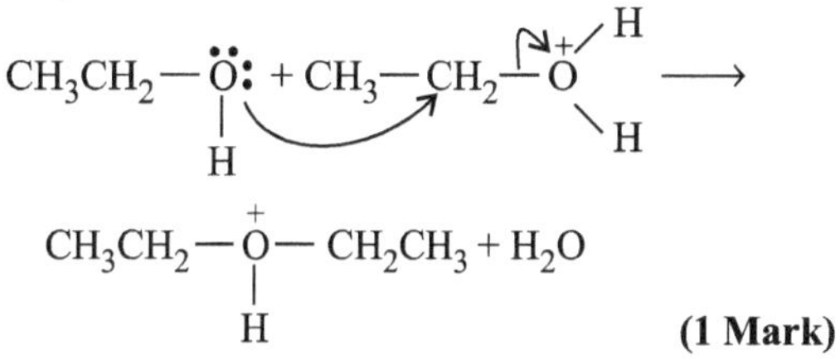

$$CH_3CH_2-\underset{\underset{H}{|}}{\overset{..}{O}}: + CH_3-CH_2-\overset{+}{\underset{\diagdown H}{\overset{\diagup H}{O}}} \longrightarrow$$

$$CH_3CH_2-\underset{\underset{H}{|}}{\overset{+}{O}}-CH_2CH_3 + H_2O$$

(1 Mark)

Step 3:

$$CH_3CH_2-\underset{\underset{H}{|}}{\overset{+}{O}}-CH_2CH_3 \longrightarrow$$

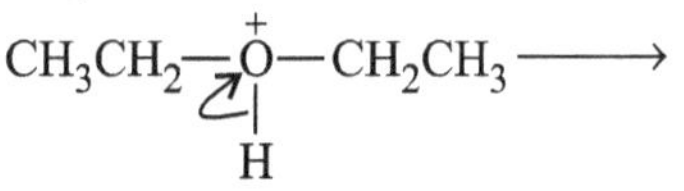

$$CH_3CH_2-O-CH_2CH_3 + H^+$$ **(½ Mark)**

(b) 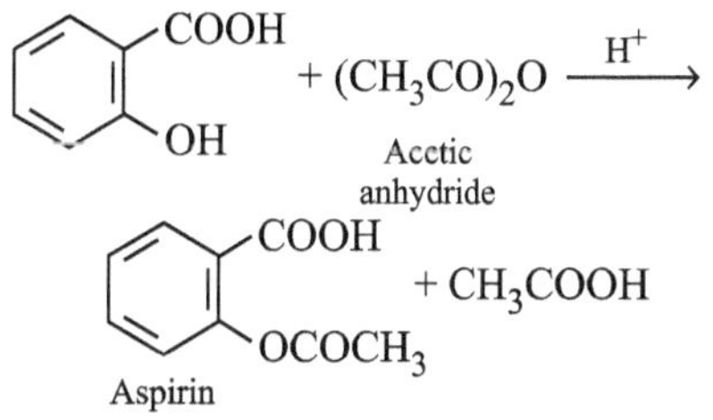 (Salicylic acid: benzene ring with COOH and OH) $+ (CH_3CO)_2O \xrightarrow{H^+}$

Acetic anhydride

(Aspirin: benzene ring with COOH and OCOCH₃) $+ CH_3COOH$

Aspirin

(1 Mark)

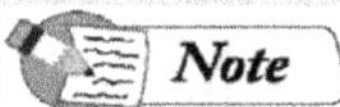

Note

Synthesis of aspirin from salicylic acid occurs by acetylation in acidic medium. Salicylic acid react with acetic anhydride in presence of few drops of concentrated sulphuric acid. Acid initiate the process of detaching the acetate ion from aceticanhydride which later get associated with H+ ion from phenolic hydroxy group in salicylic acid to be eliminated as acetic acid.

27. (i) Reimer-Tiemann reaction:

OH $\xrightarrow{\text{CHCl}_3 + \text{aq.NaOH}}$ [O⁻Na⁺ , CHCl₂] Intermediate

$\xrightarrow{\text{NaOH}}$ (O⁻Na⁺, CHO) $\xrightarrow{\text{H}^+}$ (OH, CHO)

Salicylaldehyde

Note

Heterocyclic organic compounds that are quite rich in electrons, such as pyrroles and indoles can also undergo the Reimer Tiemann reaction.

(ii) Williamson synthesis :

$$RO^-Na^+ + R'-X \xrightarrow{S_N2} R'-O-R + NaX$$

(1 + 1 = 2 Marks)

28. (i) OH + $CHCl_3$ + KOH(aq.) $\xrightarrow{-KCl, -H_2O}$

(O⁻K⁺, CHCl₂) $\xrightarrow[-2KCl]{2KOH}$ (O⁻K⁺, CH(OH)₂) unstable

$\xrightarrow{-H_2O}$ (O⁻K⁺, CHO) $\xrightarrow[\text{Dil. HCl}]{-KCl}$ (OH, CHO)

Salicylaldehyde
or
(*o*-Hydroxybenzaldehyde)

(1 Mark)

(ii) R⟨X + Na⟩ OR'⟶R – O – R' + NaX

$$CH_3- CH_2 \langle I + Na \rangle O-CH_2-CH_3$$

Ethyl Iodide   Sodium ethoxide

$$\rightarrow CH_3\text{–}CH_2\text{–}O\text{–}CH_2\text{–}CH_3 + NaI$$

(1 Mark)

29. Step-I : $C_2H_5 - \overset{..}{\underset{..}{O}} - H + H^+ \longrightarrow C_2H_5 - \overset{\overset{H}{|}}{\underset{..}{O}}{}^+ - H$

(½ Mark)

Step-II :

$$C_2H_5 - \overset{..}{\underset{..}{O}} - H + C_2H_5 - \overset{\overset{H}{|}}{O}{}^+ - H \longrightarrow C_2H_5 - \overset{\overset{H}{|}}{O}{}^+ - C_2H_5 + H_2O$$

(1 Mark)

Step-III $C_2H_5 \overset{\overset{H}{|}}{\underset{..}{O}}{}^+ - C_2H_5 \longrightarrow C_2H_5 - \overset{..}{\underset{..}{O}} - C_2H_5 + H^{\oplus}$

Diethyl ether

(½ Mark)

30. (a) In the acid catalysed dehydration of alcohols, the slowest step or the rate determining step is the formation of carbocation. Thus dehydration of tertiary alcohols will be fastest because tertiary carbocation is most stable.   **(1 + 1 = 2 Marks)**

Note

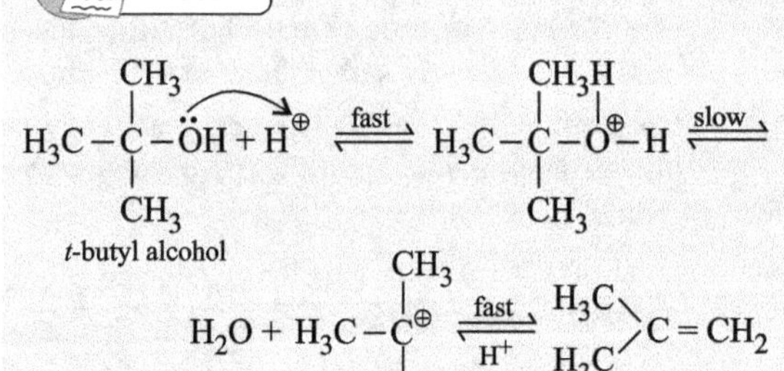

(b) (i) phenol $\xrightarrow[\text{aq.NaOH}]{\text{CHCl}_3}$ (O⁻Na⁺, CHCl₂) intermediate $\xrightarrow{\text{NaOH}}$

(O⁻Na⁺, CHO) $\xrightarrow{\text{H}^+}$ (OH, CHO)

salicylaldehyde

(1 Mark)

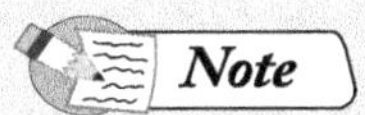

> **Note**
>
> *It is an example of Reimer-Tiemann reaction. Reimer-Tiemann reaction is an electrophillic substitution reaction in which dichlorocarbene is generated in the first step and act as strong electrophile.*

(ii) $H_3C-\overset{\overset{\displaystyle CH_3}{|}}{\underset{\underset{\displaystyle CH_3}{|}}{C}}-Cl + C_2H_5-O^-Na^+ \xrightarrow[-NaCl]{}$

t-butyl chloride

$H_3C-\overset{\overset{\displaystyle CH_3}{|}}{\underset{\underset{\displaystyle CH_3}{|}}{C}}-O-C_2H_5$

t-butyl ethyl ether

(1 Mark)

> **Note**
>
> *It is an example of Williamson Synthesis. Williamson synthesis is S_N2 reaction. Nucleophile attacks from the back side which results in inversion of configuration at the site of the leaving group.*

(iii)
$$6CH_3-CH=CH_2 + B_2H_6 \longrightarrow 2(CH_3-CH_2-CH_2)_3B$$
propene   diborane

$$(CH_3-CH_2-CH_2)_3B \xrightarrow{H_2O_2}$$

$$CH_3-CH_2-CH_2-OH + B(OH)_3$$
propanol   boric acid

(1 Mark)

31. (a) **Step1:**
$$H_2O + H_2SO_4 \longrightarrow H_3\overset{\oplus}{O} + HSO_4^{\ominus}$$

Step2:
$$CH_2=CH_2 + H_3O^+ \longrightarrow CH_3-\overset{+}{C}H_2 + H_2O$$
Ethene

Step3:
$$CH_3-\overset{+}{C}H_2 + :\overset{..}{O}H_2 \longrightarrow CH_3-CH_2-\overset{+}{O}H_2$$

Step4:
$$CH_3-CH_2-\overset{+}{O}H_2 \xrightarrow{H_2O} CH_3-CH_2+OH + H_3O^+$$
Ethanol

(2 Mark)

(b) (i)

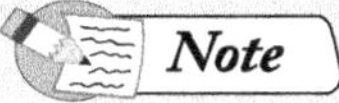

phenol   benzoquinone   **(1 Mark)**

(ii) $H_3CO-\langle\!\bigcirc\!\rangle \xrightarrow[\text{ethanoic acid}]{Br_2} H_3CO-\langle\!\bigcirc\!\rangle-Br$

anisole   *p*-bromoanisole

(1 Mark)

(iii) $\underset{\text{phenol}}{\langle\!\bigcirc\!\rangle\text{-OH}} + 3Br_2(aq.) \longrightarrow \underset{\text{2, 4, 6-tribromophenol}}{} + 3HBr$

(1 Mark)

> **Note**
>
> *Solvent has great influence in the reaction; when water act as solvent in bromination of phenol tri-subsituted product is formed, while with CS_2 as solvent, mono-subsituted products are formed with p-isomer as major product.*

32. (a) (i)

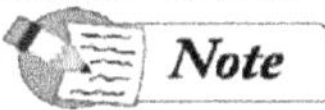

$\xrightarrow[H^+]{(CH_3CO)_2O}$

Aspirin $\quad + CH_3COOH$ Acetic acid

(1 Mark)

(ii) $CH_3-\overset{\overset{\displaystyle CH_3}{|}}{CH}-O-CH_2-CH_3 \xrightarrow{HI}$

$CH_3-\overset{\overset{\displaystyle CH_3}{|}}{\underset{\underset{\displaystyle H}{|}}{C}}-I + CH_3CH_2OH$

2-Iodopropane   ethanol

(1 Mark)

> **Note**
>
> *In acidic cleavage of ethers alkyl halide is formed from the most stable carbocation.*

(iii) $\underset{\text{But-2-en-1-ol}}{CH_3-CH=CH-CH_2-OH} \xrightarrow{PCC}$

$\underset{\text{But-2-en-1-al}}{CH_3-CH=CH-CHO}$

(1 Mark)

> **Note**
>
> *PCC→Pyridinium chlorochromate it is a reagent which is used for oxidation of alcohol to form carbonyl.*

(b) (i) Ethanol and Phenol

Iodoform test is used to distinguish between ethanol and phenol.

On heating with NaOH solution containing iodine, ethanol gives a yellow ppt of iodoform while phenol does not react.

$$C_2H_5OH + 4I_2 + 6NaOH \xrightarrow{\Delta}$$
$$CHI_3 + 5NaI + HCOONa + 5H_2O$$

Iodoform

(1 Mark)

(ii) Propanol and 2-methylpropan-2-ol

Propanol is primary alcohol while 2-methylpropan-2-ol is tertiary alcohol. Lucas test is used to distinguish bsoth of them.

Primary alcohol, i.e. propanol does not react with lucas reagent (conc.HCl + anhy. $ZnCl_2$) and no cloudiness is appeared.

Tertiary alcohol, i.e. 2-methylpropan-2-ol reacts with lucas reagent and give turbidity immediately. **(1 Mark)**

33. (a) (i) Bromination of Phenol to 2, 4, 6 tribromophenol

+ 3HBr, Reagent $\rightarrow Br_2$

(1 Mark)

(ii) Hydroboration of propene and then oxidation to propanol.

$$6(CH_3-CH=CH_2) \xrightarrow{B_2H_6}$$
$$2(CH_3CH_2CH_2)_3B \xrightarrow[H_2O/OH^-]{H_2O_2} 2H_3BO_3$$
$$+ 6CH_3CH_2CH_2OH, \text{ reagent } B_2H_6, H_2O_2$$

(1 Mark)

(b) (i) ethanol < phenol < p-nitrophenol **(1 Mark)**

> **Note**
>
> *Nitrogroup is electron withdrawing group and it decreases the electron density in $O-H$ bond therefore it easily loses a proton. Phenols and alcohols are weak acids but alcohols are less acidic than phenols.*

(ii) propane < propanal < propanol **(1 Mark)**

(c) $CH_3CH_2-\overset{+}{O} \left\langle \begin{array}{c} H \\ H \end{array} \right. + H-\overset{\bullet\bullet}{\underset{\bullet\bullet}{O}}-CH_2CH_3$

$$\longrightarrow CH_3CH_2-\overset{+}{\underset{H}{O}}-CH_2-CH_3 + H_2O$$

(1 Mark)

4   *Very Short Answer Questions (1 Mark)*

1. Write the structure of *p*-methylbenzaldehyde.   **[All India 2014, K]**
2. Write the structure of 3-methyl butanal.   **[Delhi 2023, Set-I, K]**

1   *Multiple Choice Questions*

1. Which of the following reactions is used to prepare salicylaldehyde?   **[CBSE Sample 2021-22, K]**
   (a) Kolbe's reaction
   (b) Etard reaction
   (c) Reimer-Tiemann reaction
   (d) Stephen's reduction.

1   *Multiple Choice Questions*

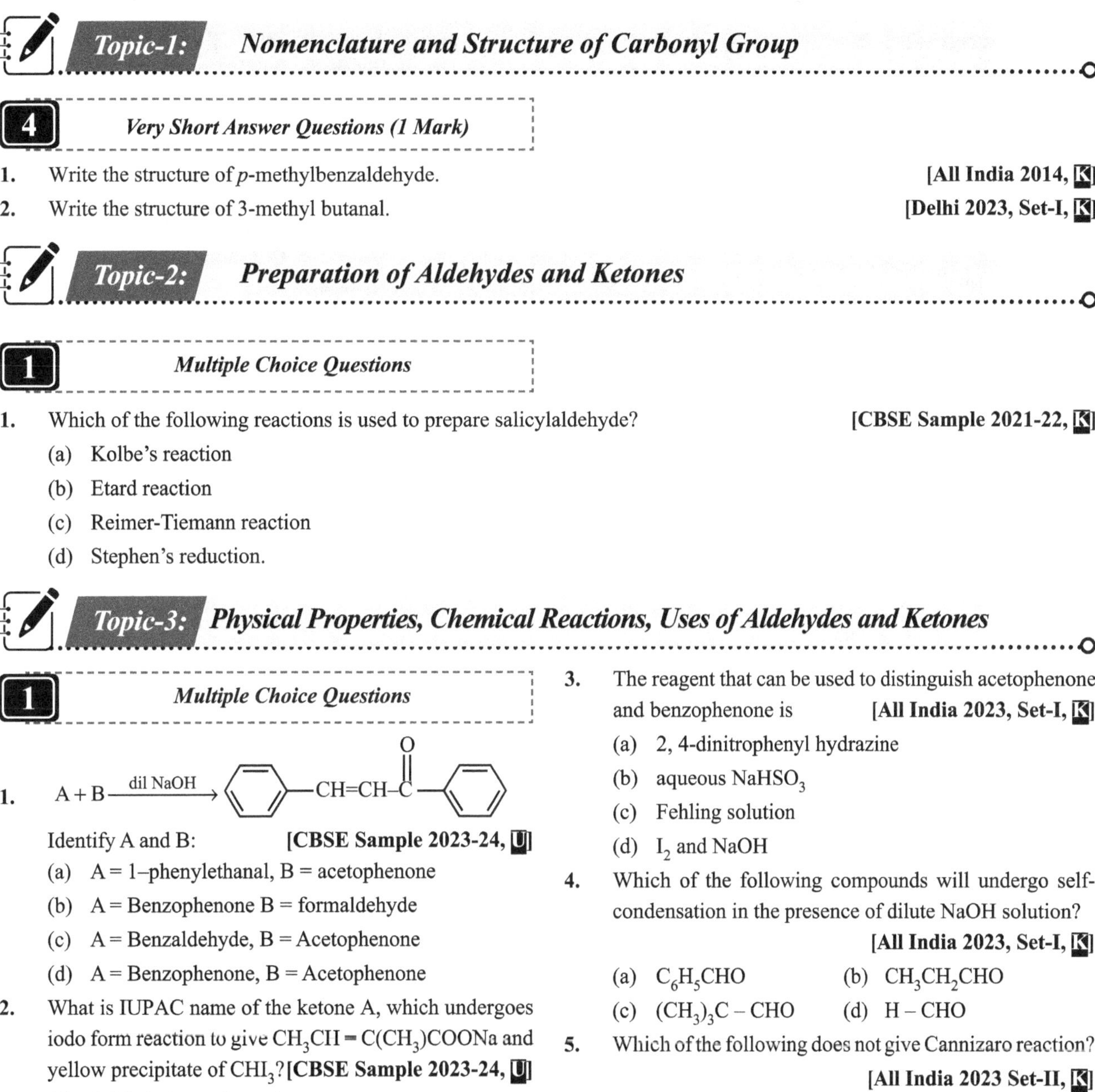

1. $A + B \xrightarrow{\text{dil NaOH}}$ (structure) $-CH=CH-C(=O)-$ (structure)

   Identify A and B: **[CBSE Sample 2023-24, U]**
   (a) A = 1–phenylethanal, B = acetophenone
   (b) A = Benzophenone B = formaldehyde
   (c) A = Benzaldehyde, B = Acetophenone
   (d) A = Benzophenone, B = Acetophenone

2. What is IUPAC name of the ketone A, which undergoes iodo form reaction to give $CH_3CH = C(CH_3)COONa$ and yellow precipitate of CHI_3? **[CBSE Sample 2023-24, U]**
   (a) 3–Methylpent–3–en–2one
   (b) 3–Methylbut–2–en–one
   (c) 2, 3–Dimethylethanone
   (d) 3–Methylpent–4–one

3. The reagent that can be used to distinguish acetophenone and benzophenone is   **[All India 2023, Set-I, K]**
   (a) 2, 4-dinitrophenyl hydrazine
   (b) aqueous $NaHSO_3$
   (c) Fehling solution
   (d) I_2 and NaOH

4. Which of the following compounds will undergo self-condensation in the presence of dilute NaOH solution?   **[All India 2023, Set-I, K]**
   (a) C_6H_5CHO (b) CH_3CH_2CHO
   (c) $(CH_3)_3C – CHO$ (d) $H – CHO$

5. Which of the following does not give Cannizaro reaction?   **[All India 2023 Set-II, K]**
   (a) $(CH_3)_3 C – CHO$ (b) $(CH_3)_2 CH – CHO$
   (c) (structure) $– CHO$ (d) HCHO

6. Aldehydes and ketones react with hydroxylamine to form   **[All India 2023 Set-II, K]**

   (a) hydrzones   (b) cyanohydrins

   (c) semicarbanzones   (d) Oxime

7. Which of the following tests/reactions is given by aldehydes as well as ketones?

                          [CBSE Sample 2022-23, K]

   (a) Fehling's test   (b) Tollen's test

   (c) 2,4 DNP test   (d) Cannizzaro reaction

8. Which of the following acids reacts with acetic anhydride to form a compound Aspirin ?

                      [All India 2022, Term-I, K]

   (a) Benzoic acid   (b) Salicylic acid

   (c) Phthalic acid   (d) Acetic acid

9. Iodoform test is not given by   **[All India 2020, K]**

   (a) Ethanol   (b) Ethanal

   (c) Pentan-2-one   (d) Pentan-3-one

2   *Assertion Reason/Two Statement Type Questions*

Given below are two statements labelled as Assertion (A) and Reason (R). Select the most appropriate answer from the options given below:

(a) Both (A) and (R) are true and (R) is the correct explanation of (A).

(b) Both (A) and (R) are true, but (R) is not the correct explanation of (A).

(c) (A) is true, but (R) is false.

(d) (A) is false, but (R) is true.

10. **Assertion (A):** The final product in Aldol condensation is always α, β- unsaturated carbonyl compound.

                     [Delhi 2023 Set-3, U]

   Reason (R): α, β- unsaturated carbonyl compound are stabilised due to conjugation.

5   *Short Answer Questions (2 or 3 Marks)*

11. (a) Out of p–toluentldehyde and p–nitrobenzaldehyde, which one is more reactive towards nucleophilic addition reactions, why?

   (b) Write the structure of the product formed when acetone reacts with 2, 4 DNP reagent.

                     [CBSE Sample 2023-24, U]

12. Write the products formed when benzaldehyde reacts with the following reagents (Any two) :

                     [All India 2022, Term-II, U]

   (i) CH_3CHO in presence of dilute NaOH

   (ii) $H_2N – OH$ in presence of weak acid

   (iii) Tollen's reagent

13. Give reasons to support the answer:

   a. Presence of Alpha hydrogen in aldehydes and ketones is essential for aldol condensation.

   b. 3 –Hydroxy pentan-2-one shows positive Tollen's test.   **[All India 2021-22, Term-II, U]**

14. An alkene 'A' (Mol. formula C_5H_{10}) on ozonolysis gives a mixture of two compounds 'B' and 'C'. Compound 'B' gives positive Fehling's test and also forms iodoform on treatment with I_2 and NaOH. Compound 'C' does not give Fehling's test but forms iodoform. Identify the compounds A, B and C. Write the reaction for ozonolysis and formation of iodoform from B and C.

                     [All India 2021-22, Term-II, A]

15. What happens when   **[All India 2020, U]**

   (a) Propanone is treated with methylmagnesium iodide and then hydrolysed, and

   (b) Benzene is treated with CH_3COCl in presence of anhydrous $AlCl_3$?

16. How will you carry out the following conversions : (Any two)   **[All India 2022, Term-II]**

   (i) Propanal to Propane

   (ii) Ethanal to But-2-enal

   (iii) Ethanoic acid to ethanamide

17. (a) Write the major products in the following :

                     [All India 2022, Term-II]

   (i) Benzaldehyde $\xrightarrow[273–283 \text{ K}]{HNO_3+H_2SO_4}$

   (ii) Cyclohexane-COONa $+NaOH \xrightarrow[\Delta]{CaO}$

   (iii) $CH_3 - \underset{\underset{H}{|}}{C} = O \xrightarrow{NH_2OH}$

18. (a) Write the equation involved in the following reactions: **[All India 2022, Term-II]**

   (i) Rosenmund reduction

   (ii) Etard reaction

   (iii) Stephen reaction

19. (A), (B) and (C) are three non-cyclic functional isomers of a carbonyl compound with molecular formula C_4H_8O. Isomers (A) and (C) give positive Tollens' test whereas isomer (B) does not give Tollens' test but give positive Iodoform test. Isomers (A) and (B) on reduction with Zn(Hg)/conc. HCl give the same product (D).

[All India 2018, ]

(a) Write the structures of (A), (B), (C) and (D).

(b) Out of (A), (B) and (C) isomers , which one is least reactive towards addition of HCN?

20. Write the equations involved in the following reactions :

(i) Wolff-Kishner reduction **[Delhi 2017, ]**

(ii) Etard reaction

 *Long Answer Questions*

21. (a) A compound 'A' of molecular formula C_2H_3OCl undergoes a series of reactions as shown below. Write the structures of A, B, C and D in the following reactions. $(C_2H_3OCl)A \xrightarrow{H_2/Pd-BaSO_4}$

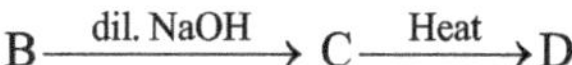

$$B \xrightarrow{\text{dil. NaOH}} C \xrightarrow{\text{Heat}} D$$

[All India 2015, ]

(b) Distinguish between the following.

(i) $C_6H_5 - COCH_3$ and $C_6H_5 - CHO$

(ii) Benzoic acid and methyl benzoate

(c) Write the structure of 2-methylbutanal.

22. (a) Write the structures of the main products when acetone $(CH_3 - CO - CH_3)$ reacts with the following reagents.

(i) $Zn - Hg$/conc. HCl

(ii) $H_2NNHCONH_2/H^+$

(iii) CH_3MgBr and then H_3O^+

(b) Arrange the following in the increasing order of their boiling points.

C_2H_5OH, $CH_3 - CHO$, $CH_3 - COOH$

(c) Give a simple chemical test to distinguish between the following pair of compounds:

CH_3CH_2CHO and $CH_3CH_2COCH_3$

 **Topic-4:** *Nomenclature and Structure of Carbonyl Group, Methods of Preparation of Carboxylic Acids*

1 *Multiple Choice Questions*

1. What is the correct IUPAC name of the given compound?

[All India 2020, ]

$$CH_3 - \underset{\underset{COOH}{|}}{\overset{\overset{CH_3}{|}}{C}} - CH_2 - CH_3$$

(a) 2, 2-Dimethylbutanoic acid

(b) 2-Carboxyl-2-methylbutane

(c) 2-Ethyl-2-methylpropanoic acid

(d) 3-Methylbutane carboxylic acid

2 *Assertion Reason/Two Statement Type Questions*

Given below are two statements labelled as Assertion (A) and Reason (R). Select the most appropriate answer from the options given below:

(a) Both (A) and (R) are true and (R) is the correct explanation of (A).

(b) Both (A) and (R) are true, but (R) is not the correct explanation of (A).

(c) (A) is true, but (R) is false.

(d) (A) is false, but (R) is true.

2. **Assertion (A):** Strong oxidising agents oxidise toluene and its derivatives to benzoic acids.

Reason (R): It is possible to stop the oxidation of toluene at the aldehyde stage with suitable reagents.

[CBSE Sample 2023-24, U]

4 *Very Short Answer Questions (1 Mark)*

3. Write the IUPAC name of the compound.

$$CH_3 - \underset{\underset{OH}{|}}{CH} - CH_2 - COOH$$

[Delhi 2014, K]

5 *Short Answer Questions (2 or 3 Marks)*

4. Convert the following: **[CBSE Sample 2023-24, U]**

(a) Benzene to m–nitrobenzaldehyde

(b) Bromobenzene to benzoic acid

5. Arrange the following in the increasing order of their property indicated (any 2):

    a. Benzoic acid, Phenol, Picric acid, Salicylic acid (pK_a values).

    b. Acetaldehyde, Acetone, Methyl-tert-butyl ketone (reactivity towards NH_2OH).

    c. ethanol, ethanoic acid, benzoic acid (boiling point)

                   [All India 2021-22, Term-II, U]

6. Write structures of compounds A and B in each of the following reactions: **[Delhi 2019, K]**

(i) 

$$\xrightarrow{KMnO_4 + KOH} A \xrightarrow{H_3O^+} B$$

(ii) 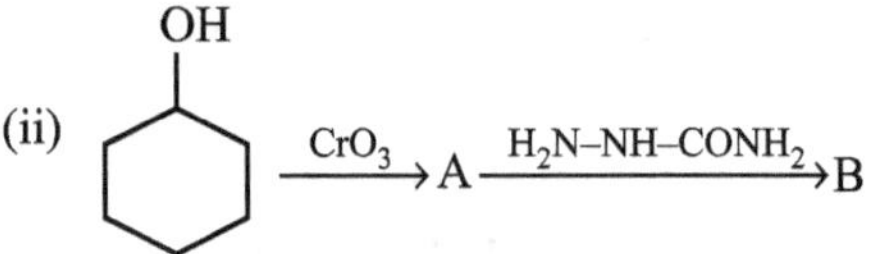

$$\xrightarrow{CrO_3} A \xrightarrow{H_2N-NH-CONH_2} B$$

7. Name the reagents used in the following reactions :

                             [Delhi 2015, K]

(i) $CH_3 - CO - CH_3 \xrightarrow{?} CH_3 - \underset{\underset{OH}{|}}{CH} - CH_3$

(ii) $C_6H_5 - CH_2 - CH_3 \xrightarrow{?} C_6H_5 - COO^-K^+$

 **Topic-5:**   *Physical Properties, Chemical Reactions, Uses of Carboxylic Acids*

---

1   *Multiple Choice Questions*

1. Which one of the following has lowest pK_a value?

                             [Delhi 2023, K]

    (a) $CH_3 - COOH$ (b) $O_2N - CH_2 - COOH$

    (c) $Cl - CH_2 - COOH$ (d) $HCOOH$

2   *Assertion Reason/Two Statement Type Questions*

Given below are two statements labelled as Assertion (A) and Reason (R). Select the most appropriate answer from the options given below:

(a) Both (A) and (R) are true and (R) is the correct explanation of (A).

(b) Both (A) and (R) are true, but (R) is not the correct explanation of (A).

(c) (A) is true, but (R) is false.

(d) (A) is false, but (R) is true.

2. **Assertion (A) :** Bromination of benzoic acid gives m-bromobenzoic acid.

    Reason (R) : Carboxyl group increases the electron density at the meta position.   **[Delhi 2023, K]**

3. **Assertion (A):** Acetic acid but not formic acid can be halogenated in presence of red P and Cl_2.

    Reason (R): Acetic acid is a weaker acid than formic acid.   **[Delhi 2023 Set-1, U]**

4. **Assertion:** Carboxylic acids are more acidic than phenols.   **[CBSE Sample 2020-21, U]**

    Reason: Phenols are ortho and para directing.

5   *Short Answer Questions (2 or 3 Marks)*

5. You are given four organic compounds "A", "B", "C" and "D". The compounds "A", "B" and "C" form an orange–red precipitate with 2, 4 DNP reagent. Compounds "A" and "B" reduce Tollen's reagent while compounds "C" and "D" do not. Both "B" and "C" give a yellow precipitate when heated with iodine in the presence of NaOH. Compound "D" gives brisk effervescence with sodium bicarbonate solution. Identify "A", "B", "C" and "D" given the number of carbon atoms in three of these carbon compounds is three while one has two carbon atoms. Give an explanation for your answer.

                  [CBSE Sample 2023-24, A]

6. Do the following conversions in not more than two steps:

                  [All India 2023 Set-2, U]

    (a) CH_3CN to $CH_3 - \underset{\underset{O}{\|}}{C} - CH_3$

    (b)  — $COOH$ to (benzene ring)

7. Do the following conversions in not more than two steps:

                  [All India 2023, Set-I, U]

    (a) CH_3COOH to CH_3COCH_3

    (b)  — CH_2CH_3 to (benzene ring) — $COOH$

8. (i) Which acid of the following pair would you expect to be stronger? **[All India 2022, Term-II, U]**

$$F - CH_2 - COOH \text{ or } CH_3 - COOH$$

(ii) Arrange the following compounds in increasing order of their boiling points :

$$CH_3CH_2OH, CH_3 - CHO, CH_3 - COOH$$

(iii) Give simple chemical test to distinguish between Benzaldehyde and Acetophanone.

9. (i) Which will undergo faster nucleophilic addition reaction? **[All India 2022, Term-II, U]**

Acetaldehyde or Propanone

(ii) What is the composition of Fehling's reagent?

(iii) Draw structure of the semicarbazone of Ethanal.

10. What happens when **[All India 2022, Term-II, U]**

(i) Propanone is treated with CH_3MgBr and then hydrolysed?

(ii) Ethanal is treated with excess ethanol and acid?

(iii) Methanal undergoes Cannizzaro reaction?

11. Write the main product in the following reactions:

[All India 2022, Term-II, U]

(i) $2CH_3COCl + (CH_3)_2Cd \rightarrow$

(ii) $CH_3CH_2CHO \xrightarrow{Zn(Hg)/conc.\ HCl}$

(iii) ⬡ $- COONa + NaOH \xrightarrow{CaO}{\Delta}$

12. Complete the following reactions: **[Delhi 2019, U]**

(i) ⬡$-CHO \xrightarrow{NaCN/HCl}$

(ii) $(C_6H_5CH_2)_2Cd + 2CH_3COCl \longrightarrow$

(iii) $CH_3 - \overset{\overset{\displaystyle CH_3}{|}}{CH} - COOH \xrightarrow[(ii)\ H_2O]{(i)\ Br_2/Red\ P_4}$

13. Write chemical equations for the following reactions:

[Delhi 2019, U]

(i) Propanone is treated with dilute $Ba(OH)_2$.

(ii) Acetophenone is treated with Zn(Hg)/Conc. HCl

(iii) Benzoyl chloride is hydrogenated in presence of Pd/$BaSO_4$.

14. How do you convert the following? **[All India 2018, U]**

(a) Ethanal to Propanone

(b) Toluene to Benzoic acid

15. Account for the following : **[All India 2018, U]**

(a) Aromatic carboxylic acids do not undergo Friedel Crafts reaction.

(b) pK_a value of 4-nitrobenzoic acid is lower than that of benzoic acid.

16. Write structures of compounds A, B and C in each of the following reactions : **[Delhi 2017, K]**

(i) $C_6H_5Br \xrightarrow{Mg/dry\ ether} A \xrightarrow[(b)\ H_3O^+]{(a)\ CO_2} B \xrightarrow{PCl_5} C$

(ii) $CH_3CN \xrightarrow[(b)H_3O^+]{(a)SnCl_2/HCl} A \xrightarrow{dil.NaOH} B \xrightarrow{\Delta} C$

17. Do the following conversions in not more than two steps :

(i) Benzoic acid to Benzaldehyde **[Delhi 2017, U]**

(ii) Ethyl benzene to Benzoic acid

(iii) Prapanone to Propene

18. Predict the products of the following reactions :

[Delhi 2015, K]

(i) $CH_3 - \overset{\overset{\displaystyle CH_3}{|}}{C} = O \xrightarrow[(ii)\ KOH/Glycol,\ \Delta]{(i)\ H_2N-NH_2} ?$

(ii) $C_6H_5 - CO - CH_3 \xrightarrow{NaOH/I_2} ? + ?$

(iii) $CH_3 COONa \xrightarrow[\Delta]{NaOH/CaO} ?$

6 — *Long Answer Questions*

19. (i) Write the reaction involved in Cannizaro's reaction **[Delhi 2023, Set-I, A]**

(ii) Why are the boiling point of aldehydes and ketones lower than that of corresponding carboxylic acids?

(iii) An organic compound 'A' with molecular formula $C_5H_8O_2$ is reduced to n-pentane with hydrazine followed by heating with NaOH and Glycol. 'A' forms a dioxime with hydroxylamine and gives a positive Iodoform and Tollen's test. Identify 'A' and give its reaction for Iodoform and Tollen's test.

20. (i) Give a chemical test to distinguish between ethanal and ethanoic acid. **[Delhi 2023, Set-I, K]**

(ii) Why is the α-hydrogens of aldehydes and ketones are acidic in nature? **[Delhi 2023, Set-I, U]**

(iii) An organic compound 'A' with molecular formula $C_4H_8O_2$ undergoes acid hydrolysis to form two compounds 'B' and 'C'. Oxidation of 'C' with acidified potassium permanganate also produces 'B'. Sodium salt of 'B' on heating with soda lime gives methane. **[Delhi 2023, Set-I, A]**

(1) Identify 'A', 'B' and 'C'.

(2) Out of 'B' and 'C', which will have higher boiling point?

Give reason.

21. A hydrocarbon (A) with molecular formula C_5H_{10} on ozonolysis gives two products (B) and (C). Both (B) and (C) give a yellow precipitate when heated with iodine in presence of NaOH while only (B) give a silver mirror on reaction with Tollen's reagent.

[CBSE Sample 2022-23, A]

(a) Identify (A), (B) and (C).

(b) Write the reaction of B with Tollen's reagent

(c) Write the equation for iodoform test for C

(d) Write down the equation for aldol condensation reaction of B and C.

22. An organic compound (A) with molecular formula $C_2Cl_3O_2H$ is obtained when (B) reacts with Red P and Cl_2. The organic compound (B) can be obtained on the reaction of methyl magnesium chloride with dry ice followed by acid hydrolysis. **[CBSE Sample 2022-23, A]**

(a) Identify A and B

(b) Write down the reaction for the formation of A from B. What is this reaction called?

(c) Give any one method by which organic compound B can be prepared from its corresponding acid chloride.

(d) Which will be the more acidic compound (A) or (B)? Why?

(e) Write down the reaction to prepare methane from the compound (B).

23. (a) Write the products formed when benzaldehyde reacts with the following reagents: **[Delhi 2020, U]**

(i) CH_3CHO in presence of dilute NaOH

(ii) H_2N-NH-⟨⟩

(iii) Conc. NaOH

(b) Distinguish between the following:

(i) $CH_3-CH=CH-CO-CH_3$ and $CH_3-CH_2-CO-CH=CH_2$

(ii) Benzaldehyde and benzoic acid.

24. (a) Write the final products in the following:

[Delhi 2020, U]

(i) $\dfrac{CH_3}{CH_3}{>}C=O \xrightarrow[\text{Conc. HCl}]{\text{Zn/Hg}}$

(ii) ⟨⟩$-COONa \xrightarrow[\Delta]{\text{NaOH/CaO}}$

(iii) $CH_2=CH-CH_2-CN \xrightarrow[\text{(b)}H_3O^+]{\text{(a)DIBAL-H}}$

(b) Arrange the following in the increasing order of their reactivity towards nucleophilic addition reaction:

CH_3COCH_3, $HCHO$, CH_3CHO, ⟨⟩$-COCH_3$

(c) Draw the structure of 2, 4-DNP derivative of acetaldehyde.

25. (a) Carry out the following conversions:

(i) *p*-nitrotoluene to 2-bromobenzoic acid

(ii) Propanoic acid to acetic acid

(b) An alkene with molecular formula C_5H_{10} on ozonolysis gives a mixture of two compounds, B and C. Compound B gives positive Fehling test and also reacts with iodine and NaOH solution. Compound C does not give Fehling solution test but forms iodoform. Identify the compounds A, B and C. **[All India2019, U]**

26. (a) Carry out the following conversions:

[All India2019, U]

(i) Benzoic acid to aniline

(ii) Bromomethane to ethanol

(b) Write the structure of major product(s) in the following:

(i) $CH_3-CH_2-\underset{\underset{O}{\|}}{C}-H \xrightarrow[\text{(b) KOH, Glycol/heat}]{\text{(a) }H_2N-NH_2}$

(ii) $CH_3-\underset{\underset{CH_3}{|}}{\overset{\overset{CH_3}{|}}{C}}-CHO \xrightarrow{\text{conc. NaOH}}$

(iii) ⟨COOH⟩ $\xrightarrow{\text{NaOH}}$

27. (a) Write the products(s) in the following reactions:

[All India 2017, K]

(i) ⟨cyclohexanone⟩O $+HCN \longrightarrow ?$

(ii) ⟨$-COONa$⟩ $+NaOH \xrightarrow[\Delta]{\text{CaO}} ?$

(iii) $CH_3-CH=CH-CN \xrightarrow[\text{(b) }H_2O/HCl]{\text{(a) DIBAL-H}} ?$

(b) Give simple chemical tests to distinguish between the following pairs of compounds

[All India 2017, K]

(i) Butanal and butan-2-one

(ii) Benzoic acid and phenol

28. (a) Write the reaction involved in the following:

 [All India 2017, U]

   (i) Etard reaction

   (ii) Stephen reduction

   (b) How will you convert the following in not more than two steps:

   (i) Benzoic acid to benzaldehyde

   (ii) Acetophenone to benzoic acid

   (iii) Ethanoic acid to 2-Hydroxyethanoic acid

29. (a) Write the structures of A and B in the following reactions: **[All India 2016, U]**

   (i) $CH_3COCl \xrightarrow{H_2,Pd—BaSO_4} A \xrightarrow{H_2N–OH} B$

   (ii) $CH_3MgBr \xrightarrow[2.\ H_3O^+]{1.\ CO_2} A \xrightarrow{PCl_5} B$

   (b) Distinguish between : **[All India 2016, K]**

   (i) $C_6H_5 – COCH_3$ and $C_6H_5 – CHO$

   (ii) CH_3COOH and $HCOOH$

   (c) Arrange the following in the increasing order of their boiling points : **[All India 2016, U]**

   $CH_3CHO, CH_3COOH, CH_3CH_2OH$

30. (a) Write the chemical reaction involved in Wolff-Kishner reduction. **[All India 2016, K]**

   (b) Arrange the following in the increasing order of their reactivity towards nucleophilic addition reaction. **[All India 2016, U]**

   $C_6H_5COCH_3, CH_3 – CHO, CH_3COCH_3$

   (c) Why a carboxylic acid does not give reactions of carbonyl group ? **[All India 2016, U]**

   (d) Write the product in the following reaction

   $CH_3CH_2CH = CH – CH_2CN \xrightarrow[2.\ H_2O]{1.\ (i–Bu)_2\ AlH}$

 [All India 2016, K]

   (e) A and B are two functional isomers of the compound C_3H_6O. On heating with NaOH and I_2, isomer B forms yellow precipitate of iodoform, whereas isomer A does not form any precipitate. Write the formulae of A and B. **[All India 2016, U]**

31. (a) Write the structures of A, B, C, D and E in the following reactions : **[Delhi 2016, U]**

   $C_6H_6 \xrightarrow[\text{Anhyd. AlCl}]{CH_3COCl} A \xrightarrow[\text{conc.HCl}]{\text{Zn–Hg/}} B \xrightarrow[(ii)\ H_3O^+]{(i)\ KMnO_4 – KOH, \Delta} C$

   $A \xrightarrow{NaOI} D + E$

32. (a) Write the chemical equation for the reaction involved in Cannizzaro reaction. **[Delhi 2016, K]**

   (b) Draw the structure of the semi-carbazone of ethanal.

 [Delhi 2016, K]

   (c) Why pK_a of $F – CH_2 – COOH$ is lower than that of $Cl – CH_2 – COOH$? **[Delhi 2016, U]**

   (d) Write the product in the following reaction:

   $CH_3 – CH = CH – CH_2CN \xrightarrow[(ii)\ H_2O]{(i)\ DIBAL-H}$

 [Delhi 2016, K]

   (e) How can you distinguish between propanal and propanone ? **[Delhi 2016, K]**

33. (a) Write the products formed when CH_3CHO reacts with the following reagents: **[All India 2014, K]**

   (i) HCN

   (ii) $H_2N–OH$

   (iii) CH_3CHO in the presence of dilute NaOH

   (b) Give simple chemical tests to distinguish between the following pairs of compounds:

 [All India 2014, K]

   (i) Benzoic acid and Phenol

   (ii) Propanal and Propanone

 [All India 2014, U]

34. (a) Account for the following: **[All India 2014, U]**

   (i) $Cl–CH_2COOH$ is a stronger acid than CH_3COOH.

   (ii) Carboxylic acids do not give reactions of carbonyl group.

   (b) Write the chemical equations to illustrate the following name reactions: **[All India 2014, K]**

   (i) Rosenmund reduction

   (ii) Cannizzaro's reaction

   (c) Out of $CH_3CH_2–CO–CH_2–CH_3$ and $CH_3CH_2–CH_2–CO–CH_3$, which gives iodoform test?

 [All India 2014, U]

35. (a) Write the products of the following reactions :

   (i) (cyclohexanone) $+ H_2N – OH \xrightarrow{H^+}$ **[Delhi 2014, U]**

   (ii) $2C_6H_5CHO + conc.\ NaOH \longrightarrow$

   (iii) $CH_3COOH \xrightarrow{Cl_2/P}$

   (b) Give simple chemical tests to distinguish between the following pairs of compounds: **[Delhi 2014, K]**

   (i) Benzaldehyde and Benzoic acid

   (ii) Propanal and Propanone

36. (a) Account for the following :   **[Delhi 2014, U]**

    (i) CH_3CHO is more reactive than CH_3COCH_3 towards reaction with HCN.

    (ii) Carboxylic acid is a stronger acid then phenol.

(b) Write the chemical equations to illustrate the following name reactions :   **[Delhi 2014, U]**

    (i) Wolff-Kishner reduction

    (ii) Aldol condensation

    (iii) Cannizzaro reaction

37. (a) How will you convert the following :   **[All India 2013, U]**

    (i) Propanone to propan-2-ol

    (ii) Ethanal to 2-hydroxy propanoic acid

    (iii) Toluene to benzoic acid

(b) Give simple chemical test to distinguish between :   **[All India 2013, U]**

    (i) Pentan-2-one and pentan-3-one

    (ii) Ethanal and propanal

38. (a) Write the products of the following reactions :   **[All India 2013, U]**

    (i) $CH_3 - \underset{\underset{O}{\|}}{C} - CH_3 \xrightarrow[\text{conc. HCl}]{\text{Zn-Hg}} ?$

    (ii) $CH_3 - \underset{\underset{O}{\|}}{C} - Cl + H_2 \xrightarrow{\text{Pd-BaSO}_4} ?$

    (iii) $\underset{\text{COOH}}{\bigcirc} \xrightarrow{Br_2 / FeBr_3} ?$

(b) Which acid of each pair shown here would you expect to be stronger?   **[All India 2013, U]**

    (i) $F - CH_2 - COOH$ or $Cl - CH_2 - COOH$

    (ii) $\underset{\text{COOH}}{\bigcirc}$ or CH_3COOH

39. (a) Although phenoxide ion has more number of resonating structures than carboxylate ion. Carboxylic acid is a stronger acid than phenol. Give two reasons.   **[Delhi 2013, U]**

(b) How will you bring about the following conversion?

    (i) Propanone to propane

    (ii) Benzoyl chloride to benzaldehyde

    (iii) ethanal to but-2-enal.   **[Delhi 2013, K]**

40. (a) Complete the following reactions : **[Delhi 2013, U]**

    (i) $2H - \underset{\underset{O}{\|}}{C} - H \xrightarrow{\text{Conc. KOH}}$

    (ii) $CH_3COOH \xrightarrow{Br_2/P}$

    (iii) $\underset{\text{CHO}}{\bigcirc} \xrightarrow[273-278\,K]{HNO_3 / H_2SO_4}$

(b) Give simple chemical tests to distinguish between the following pairs of compounds: **[Delhi 2013, K]**

    (i) Ethanal and Propanal

    (ii) Benzoic acid and Phenol.

7   *Case Based Questions*

The following questions are case based questions Read the passage carefully and answer the questions that follow:

41. The carbon - oxygen double bond is polarised in aldehydes and ketones due to higher electronegativity of oxygen relative to carbon. Therefore they undergo nucleophilic addition reactions with a number of nucleophiles such as HCN, $NaHSO_3$, alcohols, ammonia derivatives and Grignard reagents. Aldehydes are easily oxidised by mild oxidising agents as compared to ketones. The carbonyl group of carboxylic acid does not give reactions of aldehydes and ketones. Carboxylic acids are considerably more acidic than alcohols and most of simple phenols.

Answer the following: **[All India 2023, Set-I, A]**

(a) Write the name of the product when an aldehyde reacts with excess alcohol in presence of dry HCl.

(b) Why carboxylic acid is a stronger acid than phenol?

(c) (i) Arrange the following compounds in increasing order of their reactivity towards CH_3MgBr:

    CH_3CHO, $(CH_3)_3C - \underset{\underset{O}{\|}}{C} - CH_3$, $CH_3 - \underset{\underset{O}{\|}}{C} - CH_3$

    (ii) Write a chemical test to distinguish between propanal and propanone.

OR

(c) Write the main product in the following:

    (i) $\xrightarrow{[Ag(NH_3)_2]^+}$

    (ii) $\underset{\text{CHO}}{\bigcirc} \xrightarrow{H_2NCONHNH_2}$

Solutions

Topic-1: *Nomenclature and Structure of Carbonyl Group*

1. The structure of *p*-methylbenzaldehyde is:

$$CHO \text{—(benzene ring)—} CH_3$$

(1 Mark)

2. $CH_3 - \overset{\overset{\displaystyle CH_3}{|}}{CH} - CH_2 - CHO$ **(1 Mark)**
   3 –Methyl butanal

Topic-2: *Preparation of Aldehydes and Ketones*

1. **(c)** Kolbe's reaction is used to prepare salicylic acid, Etard reaction for benzaldehyde, Reimer- Tiemann reaction for salicylaldehyde and Stephen's reduction for aldehyde. **(1 Mark)**

Topic-3: *Physical Properties, Chemical Reactions, Uses of Aldehydes and Ketones*

1. **(c)** A = Benzaldehyde, B = Acetophenone. This is an example of crossed Aldol condensation. **(1 Mark)**

2. **(a)** 3–Methylpent–3–en–2–one **(1 Mark)**

3. **(d)** I_2 and NaOH;

This is the reagent of iodoform reaction. At least one methyl group to attached to $>C=O$ group is required to occur this reaction.

Acetophenone $(C_6H_5\overset{\overset{\displaystyle O}{||}}{C} CH_3)$ has $-CH_3$ group but

benzophenone $(C_6H_5\overset{\overset{\displaystyle O}{||}}{C} CH_3)$ has no $-CH_3$ group.

$$C_6H_5\overset{\overset{\displaystyle O}{||}}{C} - CH_3 \xrightarrow{I_2/NaOH} C_6H_5\overset{\overset{\displaystyle O}{||}}{C} - O\,Na + CHI_3$$

(1 Mark)

4. **(b)** CH_3CH_2CHO

It undergoes aldol condensation in presence of dil. NaOH and in order to occur this reaction at least one $\alpha - H$ has to be present.

$$2\,CH_3CH_2CHO \xrightarrow[\text{(ii) } \Delta]{\text{(i) dil. NaOH}}$$

$$CH_3 - CH = CH - CHO$$
But–2–enal   **(1 Mark)**

5. **(b)** In cannizzaro reaction, aldehydes which do not have an $\alpha -$ hydrogen atom, undergo self oxidation and reduction on heating with concentrated alkali.

Thus, $(CH_3)_2CH - CHO$ will not give cannizzaro reaction as it contains $\alpha -$ hydrogen atom.

$$(CH_3)_2 - C\overset{\displaystyle \uparrow}{H} - CHO$$
α-hydrogen   **(1 Mark)**

6. **(d)** Aldehydes and ketones react with hydroxylamine to form oxime.

$$>C = O + H_2N - OH \rightleftharpoons \left[>C<\overset{\displaystyle OH}{_{NHO_2}}\right] \longrightarrow$$

$$>C = N - OH + H_2O$$
(1 Mark)

7. **(c)** 2,4 DNP test

Fehling's, Tollen's and Cannizzaro reaction is shown by alcohols only. **(1 Mark)**

8. **(b)**

Salicylic acid (with COOH and OH) + Acetic anhydride $\xrightarrow{H^+}$

Aspirin (with COOH and $O-\overset{\overset{\displaystyle O}{||}}{C}-CH_3$) + Acetic acid (HO–)

When salicylic acid reacts with acetic anhydride then aspirin will form as a final product. **(1 Mark)**

9. **(d)** The iodoform test is a test for the presence of carbonyl compounds with the structure $RCOCH_3$ and CH_3CHO; and alcohols with the structure $R - CH(OH)CH_3$. **(1 Mark)**

10. (a) Aldol condensation is given by carbonyl compounds having at least one α – hydrogen. In this reaction, α, β – unsaturated carbonyl compounds are formed by heating the intermediate.

This reaction proceeds due to the acidic nature of α – hydrogen. The acidity of α – hydrogen is due to the strong electron withdrawing effect of the carbonyl group and resonance stabilisation of the conjugate base.

(1 Mark)

11. (a) p–nitrobenzaldehyde is more reactive towards the nucleophilic addition reaction than p–tolualdehyde as Nitro group is electron withdrawing in nature. Presence of nitro group decrease electron density, hence facilitates the attack of nucleophile. Presence of $-CH_3$ leads to +I effect as $-CH_3$ is electron releasing group. **(1 Mark)**

(b)

$CH_3COCH_3 +$

(1 Mark)

12. (i) Reaction of benzaldehyde with CH_3CHO in presence of NaOH (Aldol condensation)

3-Hydroxy-3-phenyl propanal
(Aldol) **(1 Mark)**

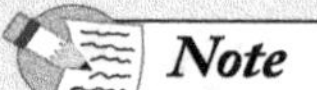

Aldols readily lose water on heating and give α, β unsaturated carbonyl compounds.

(ii) Reaction of benzaldehyde with H_2N—OH in presence of weak acid

(1 Mark)

(iii) Reaction of benzaldehyde with Tollen's reagent

$$\text{—CHO} + 2[Ag(NH_3)_2]^+ + 3OH^- \longrightarrow$$

$$\text{—COO}^- + 2Ag + 2H_2O + 4NH_3$$ **(1 Mark)**

13. (a) The alpha hydrogen atoms are acidic in nature due to presence of electron withdrawing carbonyl group. These can be easily removed by a base and the carbanion formed is resonance stabilized.

(1 Mark)

(b) Tollen's reagent is a weak oxidizing agent not capable of breaking the C-C bond in ketones . Thus ketones cannot be oxidized using Tollen's reagent itself gets reduced to Ag. But, 3-Hydroxypentan-2-one shows positive Tollen's test because it is an α-hydroxyketone that tautomerizes to an α-hydroxyenal that has an α-hydrogen atom. **(1 Mark)**

14. Compound A is an alkene, on ozonolysis it will give carbonyl compounds. As both B and C have >C=O group,

B gives positive Fehling's test so it is an aldehyde and it gives iodoform test so it is so it has $CH_3C=O$ group. This means the aldehyde is acetaldehyde

C does not give Fehling's test, so it is a ketone. It gives positive iodoform test so it is a methyl ketone means it has $CH_3C=O$ group

Compound A (C_5H_{10}) on ozonlysis gives B (CH_3CHO) + C (CH_3COR)

So "C" is CH_3COCH_3

$$CH_3CH=C(CH_3)_2 \xrightarrow{\text{(i) } O_3 \text{ (ii) } Zn/H_3O^+}$$

$$CH_3CHO + CH_3COCH_3$$

$CH_3CHO + 2Cu^{2+} + 5OH^- \longrightarrow CH_3COO^-$
$\qquad + Cu_2O \text{ (red ppt)} + 3H_2O$

$CH_3COCH_3 + 2Cu^{2+} + 5OH^- \longrightarrow$ No reaction

$CH_3CHO + 3I_2 + 3\,NaOH \longrightarrow CHI_3 \text{ (yellow ppt)}$
$\qquad + 3HI + HCOONa$

$CH_3COCH_3 + 3I_2 + 3\,NaOH \longrightarrow$
$\qquad CHI_3 \text{ (yellow ppt)} + 3HI + CH_3COONa$

$A = CH_3CH{=}C(CH_3)_2$

$B = CH_3CHO$

$C = CH_3COCH_3$ **(3 Marks)**

15. (a)

$$CH_3 - \underset{\underset{O}{\|}}{C} - CH_3 + CH_3 - MgI \longrightarrow CH_3 - \underset{\underset{O\text{-}MgI}{|}}{\overset{\overset{CH_3}{|}}{C}} - CH_3$$

$$\xrightarrow[\text{(hydolysis)}]{H_2O} CH_3 - \underset{\underset{OH}{|}}{\overset{\overset{CH_3}{|}}{C}} - CH_3 + Mg(OH)I$$

(1 Mark)

(b)

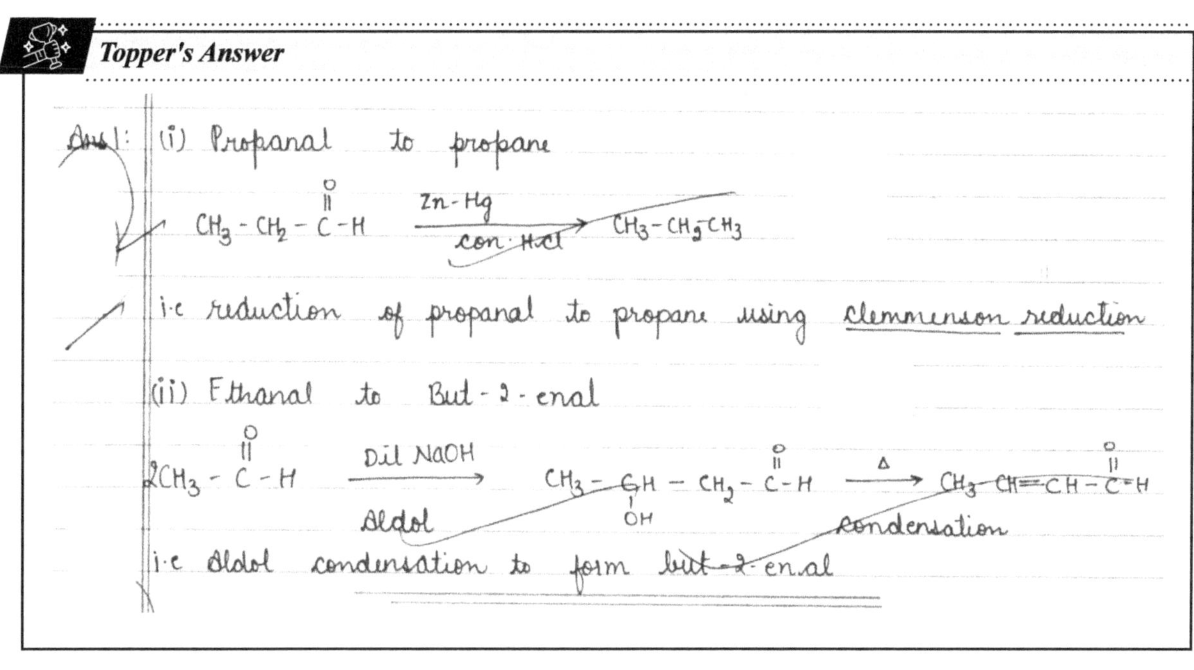

(1 Mark)

16.

17.

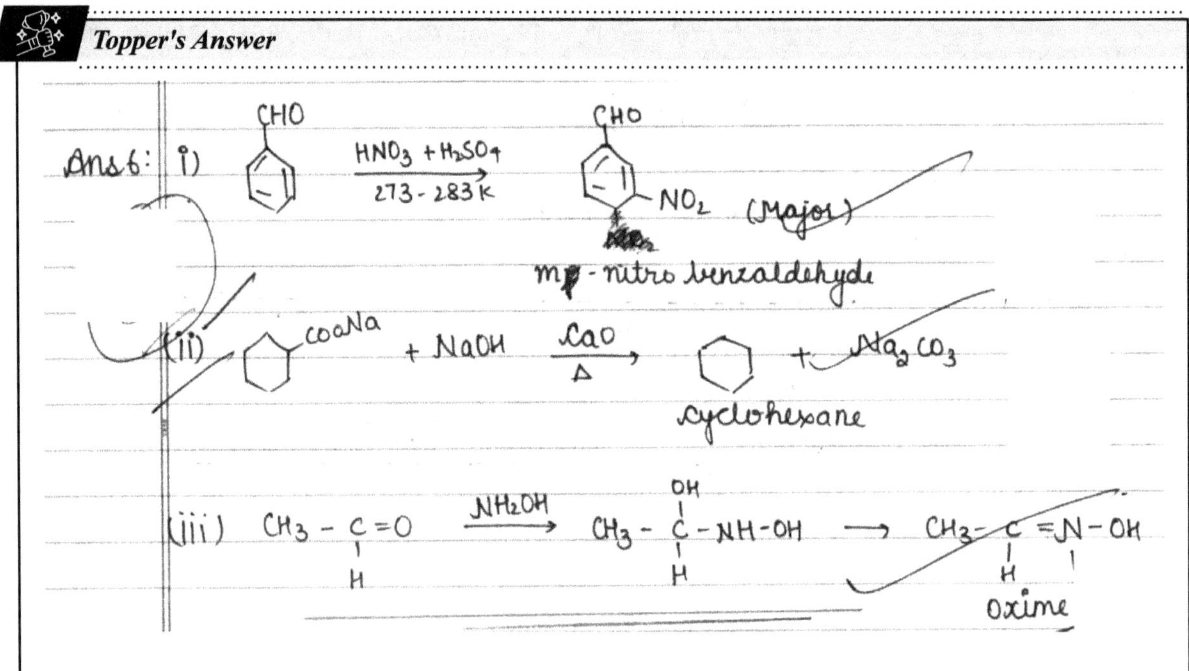

18.

Ans 10: (a) i) Rosenmund reaction
Method for preparation of aldehydes by reducing acyl halides

$$R - \overset{O}{\underset{}{C}} - Cl \xrightarrow[Pd/BaSO_4]{H_2} R - CHO$$

Acyl halide → Aldehyde

Rosenmund catalyst
(Poisoned)

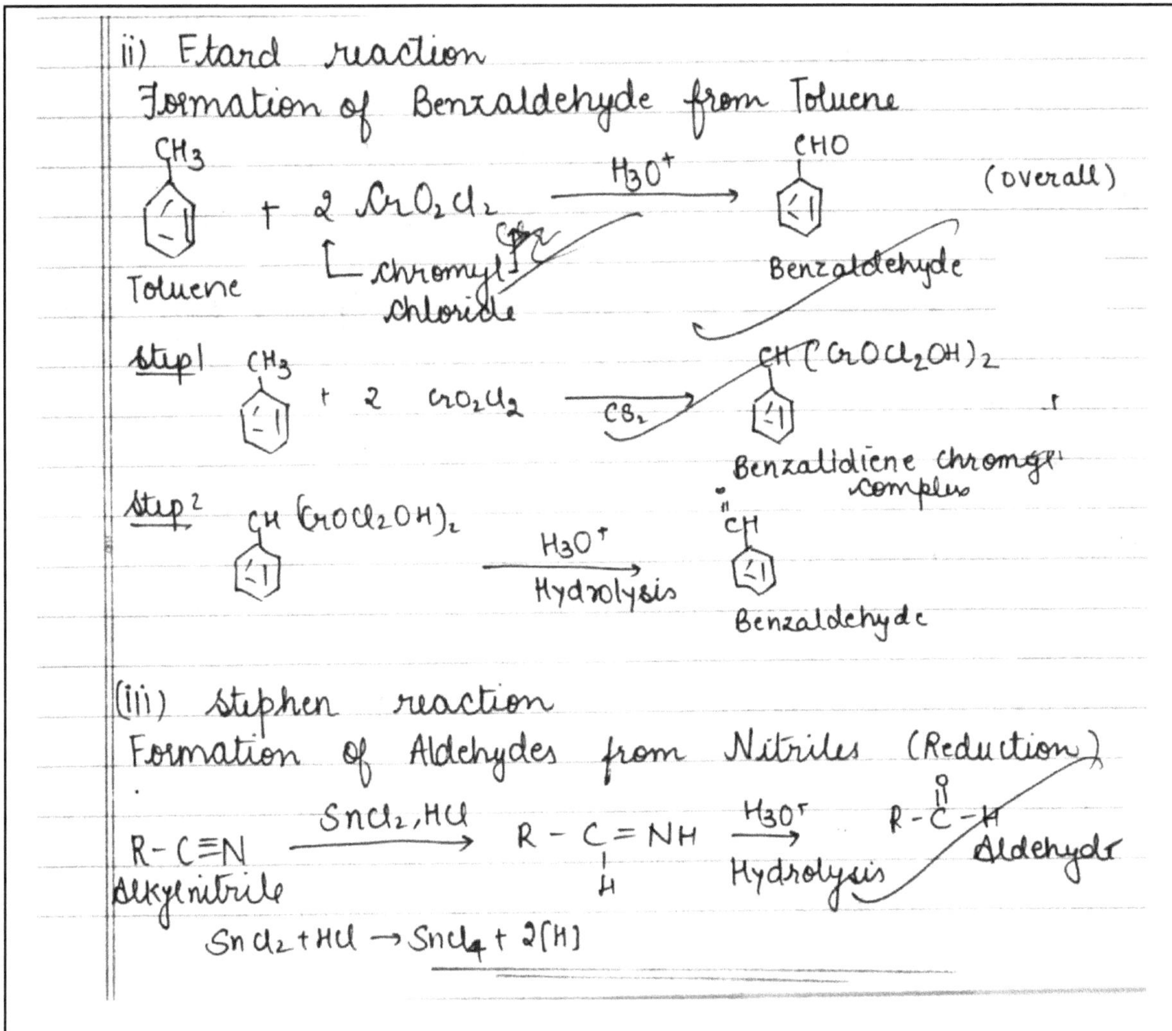

19. Given : A, B, C → molecular formula C_4H_8O

(A) and (C) → positive Tollen's test

(B) → does not give tollen's test but gives iodoform test

(A) and (B) $\xrightarrow[\substack{\text{Zn–Hg} \\ \text{conc HCl}}]{\text{reduction}}$ (D)

(a) According to the given information, as A and C give positive Tollen's test, they have an aldehydic group. Moreover, as they have 4 carbon atoms, one of them is butanal and other must be 2–methylpropanal.

Further, as B does not give positive test but gives iodoform test, so B is a ketone. It should be Butanone.

Aldehydes and ketones on reduction with Zn(Hg) in presence of conc. HCl give alkanes (Clemmensen reduction). So, D is butane.

Thus, the structures of A, B, C and D are:

(A) : $CH_3\,CH_2\,CH_2\,CHO$

Butanal

(B) : $CH_3\overset{\overset{\displaystyle O}{\|}}{C}CH_2CH_3$

Butanone

(C) : $CH_3\underset{\underset{\displaystyle CH_3}{|}}{CH}CHO$

2-Methylpropanal

(D) : $CH_3CH_2CH_2CH_3$

Butane   **(½ + ½ + ½ + ½ = 2 Marks)**

(b) Ketones are less reactive towards HCN than aldehydes due to steric and electronic factors. Thus, 'B' is least reactive towards HCN.   **(1 Mark)**

20. (i) Wolff-kishner reduction

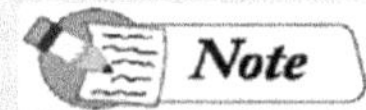

$$R_1-\overset{\overset{O}{\|}}{C}-R_2 \xrightarrow{NH_2NH_2} \left[\underset{R_1 \quad R_2}{C} = N-NH_2 \right] \xrightarrow[\Delta]{KOH} R_1-CH_2-R_2$$

(1 Mark)

(ii) *Etard reaction:*

$$CH_3 \text{-ring} \xrightarrow[+ H_2O]{CrO_2Cl_2,\ CCl_4 \atop Oxidation} CHO\text{-ring}$$

(1 Mark)

> **Note**
>
> *Chromyl chloride is a weak oxidising agent, it carry out partial oxidation of aromatic or heterocyclic bound methyl group to an aldehyde.*

21. (a)

$$\underset{(A)}{C_2H_3OCl} \xrightarrow{H_2/Pd-BaSO_4} \underset{\underset{(B)}{Acetaldehyde}}{CH_3CHO}$$

$\downarrow$ dil NaOH / Aldol reaction

$$CH_3-\underset{\underset{\underset{(C)}{\beta\text{-hydroxy butyraldehyde}}}{|}}{\underset{OH}{CH}}-CH_2-CHO$$

$\downarrow$ Heat

$$\underset{\underset{(D)}{Crotonaldehyde}}{CH_3CH = CHCHO}$$

(½ + ½ + ½ + ½ = 2 Marks)

$\therefore$ A = CH_3COCl

B = CH_3CHO

$$C = CH_3\underset{\underset{OH}{|}}{CH}-CH_2CHO$$

D = $CH_3CH = CH-CHO$

(b) (i) Benzaldehyde and acetophenone can be distinguished by iodoform test.

$$C_6H_5COCH_3 + 3NaOI \longrightarrow$$

$$C_6H_5COONa + \underset{(Yellow\ ppt.)}{CHI_3} \downarrow + 2NaOH$$

$$C_6H_5CHO + NaOI \longrightarrow \text{No yellow ppt.}$$

(1 Mark)

(ii) Benzoic acid and methyl benzoate can be distinguished by $NaHCO_3$ test.

$$\underset{Benzoic\ acid}{C_6H_5COOH} + NaHCO_3 \longrightarrow$$

$$\underset{Sodiumbenzoate}{C_6H_5COO^-Na^+ H_2O} + CO_2 \uparrow$$

$$C_6H_5COOCH_3 + NaHCO_3 \longrightarrow \text{No } CO_2$$

is formed **(1 Mark)**

(c)

$$\overset{4}{C}H_3 - \overset{3}{C}H_2 - \overset{\overset{CH_3}{|}}{\overset{2}{C}H} - \overset{1}{C}HO \qquad \textbf{(1 Mark)}$$
$$\text{2-Methylbutanal}$$

22. (a) (i)

$$\underset{Propanone}{CH_3COCH_3} \xrightarrow{Zn-Hg/conc.HCl}$$

$$\underset{Propane}{CH_3CH_2CH_3}$$

(1 Mark)

(ii)

$$\underset{Propanone}{CH_3COCH_3} \xrightarrow[H^+]{H_2N-NHCONH_2}$$

$$\underset{\underset{Propanone\ semicarbazone}{CH_3}}{CH_3-\overset{|}{C}} = NNHCONH_2 + H_2O \quad \underset{x \to \infty}{lim}$$

(1 Mark)

> **Note**
>
> $H_2N, NH, CONH_2$ *contains three nucleophilc centre i.e.,* $-NH_2, -NH-, -CONH_2, -NH_2$ *is more pronounce to attack on a electrophilic centre because its lone pair is more located at nitrogen atom compared to other which has its lone pair in conjugation with* $-CO$ *group.*

(iii)

$$\underset{Propanone}{CH_3COCH_3} \xrightarrow[(ii)H_3O^+]{(i)CH_3MgBr} CH_3-\underset{\underset{\underset{tert\text{-butyl alcohol}}{CH_3}}{|}}{\overset{\overset{OH}{|}}{C}}-CH_3$$

(1 Mark)

(b) The increasing order of boiling points is :

$$CH_3CHO < C_2H_5OH < CH_3COOH \qquad \textbf{(1 Mark)}$$

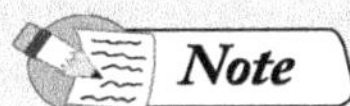

Note

The lowest boiling point of acetaldehyde is due to absence of H–bonding whereas both ethanol and acetic acid have H–bonding present in them. Now, the boiling point of acetic acid is higher due to stronger intermolecular H–bonding in it, which is due to the fact that the O–H bond in carboxylic acid is more polarized due to the presence of electron withdrawing carbonyl $\diagdown$C=O group. Moreover, the negatively polarized oxygen atom of one molecule of acetic acid can form H–bond with H-atom of the other molecule. Due to this acetic acid has higher boiling point than ethanol.

(c) $CH_3CH_2COCH_3$ gives iodoform test while CH_3CH_2CHO does not give this test.

$$CH_3CH_2COCH_3 + 3NaOI \longrightarrow$$
$$CHI_3\downarrow + CH_3CH_2COONa + 2NaOH$$

Iodoform **(1 Mark)**

Topic-4: *Nomenclature and Structure of Carbonyl Group, Methods of Preparation of Carboxylic Acids*

1. (a) 2, 2-Dimethylbutanoic acid

$$\overset{CH_3}{\underset{\underset{COOH}{|}}{\overset{|}{H_3C - \overset{2}{C} - \overset{3}{CH_2} - \overset{4}{CH_3}}}}$$

(1 Mark)

2. **(b)** Both A and R are true but R is not the correct explanation of A **(1 Mark)**

3. The IUPAC name of $CH_3 - \underset{\underset{OH}{|}}{CH} - CH_2 - COOH$ is 3- Hydroxybutanoic acid **(1 Mark)**

4. (a)

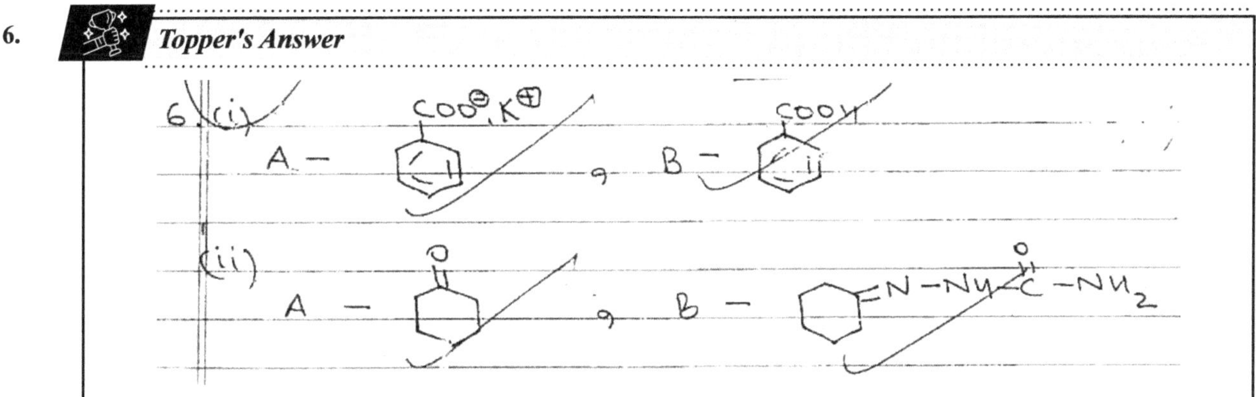

(1 Mark)

(b)

(1 Mark)

5. (a) Picric acid < salicylic acid < benzoic acid < phenol **(1 Mark)**

(b) Methyl tert – butyl ketone < acetone < Acetaldehyde **(1 Mark)**

(c) ethanol < ethanoic acid < benzoic acid (boiling point of carboxylic acids is higher than alcohols due to extensive hydrogen bonding, boiling point increases with increase in molar mass) **(1 Mark)**

6. **Topper's Answer**

(i) [structure: CH$_2$CH$_3$ on benzene] $\xrightarrow{\text{KMnO}_4-\text{KOH}}$ [structure: COOK on benzene, A] $\xrightarrow{\text{H}_3\text{O}^+}$ [structure: COOH on benzene, B]

A   B

(½ + ½ = **1 Mark**)

(ii) [cyclohexanol, OH] $\xrightarrow{\text{CrO}_3}$ [cyclohexanone, O, A] $\xrightarrow{\text{H}_2\text{N—NH—CONH}_2}$ [semicarbazone, NNHCONH$_2$, B]

A   B

(½ + ½ = **1 Mark**)

7. (i) $CH_3-CO-CH_3 \xrightarrow{\text{NaBH}_4} CH_3-\underset{\underset{OH}{|}}{CH}-CH_3$

(**1 Mark**)

(ii) $C_6H_5-CH_2-CH_3 \xrightarrow[\text{Heat}]{\text{KMnO}_4-\text{KOH}} C_6H_5-COO^-K^+$

(**1 Mark**)

Topic-5: **Physical Properties, Chemical Reactions, Uses of Carboxylic Acids**

1. **(b)** $pK_a = -\log K_a$ so the species with the highest K_a value will have the lowest pK_a value.

Highest K_a value indicates the **strongest** acid among the given options.

The presence of an electron - with drawing group increases the acidic strength of the species as it stabilizes its conjugate base. The order of acidic strength effect is $I < Br < Cl < F < NO_2$.

Thus, $NO_2 - CH_2 - COOH$ is the strongest acid and therefore its K_a value is highest or pK_a is lowest.

(**1 Mark**)

Thus, option **(b)** is correct.

2. **(a)** Benzoic acid has a $-COOH$ group on the benzene ring. Now, the $-COOH$ is a **meta-directing** and **ring-deactivating** group due to its electron-withdrawing nature.

Thus, bromination of benzoic acid gives m-bromobenzoic acid and the ring is deactivated for electrophilic substitution due to decreased charge density.

The charge density is increased at the meta-position due to which meta-bromination happens.

Therefore, both, Assertion (A) and Reason (R) are **true** and Reason (R) correctly explains Assertion (A).

Therefore, option **(a)** is correct. (**1 Mark**)

3. **(b)** Carboxylic acid having an α–hydrogen are halogenated in presence of red P and Cl_2 to give α–halocarboxylic acids. Since, acetic acid (CH_3COOH) contains α–hydrogen, so it can be halogenated using the above process. But formic acid does not have any α–hydrogen, so it cannot be halogenated using the above process.

Also, acetic acid is a weaker acid than formic acid.

(**1 Mark**)

4. **(b)** (**1 Mark**)

5. A, B and C contain carbonyl group as they give positive 2, 4 DNP test

A and B are aldehydes as aldehydes reduce Tollen's reagent

C is a ketone, as it contains carbonyl group but does not give positive Tollen's test (**½ Mark**)

C is a methyl ketone as it gives positive iodoform test

B is an aldehyde that gives positive iodoform test

(**½ Mark**)

D is a carboxylic acid

Since the number of carbons in the compounds A, B, C and D is three or two

B is CH_3CHO as this is only aldehyde which gives a positive iodoform test (**½ Mark**)

The remaining compounds A, C and D have three carbons A is CH_3CH_2CHO, C is CH_3COCH_3 and D is CH_3CH_2COOH (**½ each**)

6. **(a)** Treating a nitrile with Grignard reagent followed by hydrolysis yields a ketone.

$$CH_3C \equiv N + CH_3Mg\,Br \xrightarrow{\text{ether}} CH_3-C\overset{\overset{NMgBr}{\|}}{\diagdown}{}_{CH_3}$$

$$\xrightarrow{\text{H}_3\text{O}^+} CH_3-C\overset{\overset{O}{\|}}{\diagdown}{}_{CH_3}$$

(½ + ½ = **1 Mark**)

(b) When benzoic acid is treated with soda lime (NaOH and CaO) followed by hydrolysis, it produces benzene.

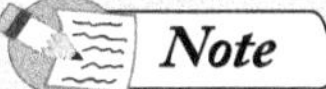

Benzoic acid → (NaOH/CaO, soda lime) → Sodium benzoate → (H_3O^+) → Benzene

(½ + ½ = 1 Mark)

7. **(a)** $CH_3COOH \xrightarrow{Ca(OH)_2} (CH_3COO)_2Ca$

$\xrightarrow[\text{distillation}]{\text{Dry}} CH_3 - \overset{\overset{\displaystyle O}{\|}}{C} - CH_3$ **(1 Mark)**

(b) Ph—$CH_2CH_3 \xrightarrow[\Delta]{KMnO_4 - KOH}$

(benzene ring with COOK) $\xrightarrow{H_3O^+}$ (benzene ring with COOH) **(1 Mark)**

8. **(i)** Acidity is directly proportional to the –I effect which means electron withdrawing group increases the acidic character. **(1 Mark)**

In case of $F–CH_2–COOH$, flourine shows–I effect due to which acidic character of this compound increases.

(ii) The compounds which have strongest hydrogen bonding between the molecules will show higher boiling point. **(1 Mark)**

CH_3COOH will have highest boiling point due to strong hydrogen bonding while CH_3CHO have lowest boiling point due to absence of hydrogen bonding.

Therefore; increasing order of boiling point is:

$CH_3CHO < CH_3CH_2OH < CH_3COOH$

(iii) Benzaldehyde contains aldehydic functional group while Acetophenone contains ketonic functional group. Tollen's test is used to distinguish between benzaldehyde and acetophenone as it only respond in case of Aldehydes.

Benzaldehyde reduces Tollen's reagent to give a silver mirror of Ag. **(1 Mark)**

9. **(i)**

$CH_3—\overset{\overset{\displaystyle O}{\|}}{C}—H$ $CH_3—\overset{\overset{\displaystyle O}{\|}}{C}—CH_3$
$+I$ $+I$ $+I$
Acetaldehyde   Propanone

propanone contains two CH_3 groups (i.e. +I effect) which makes carbonyl group less electron deficient due to which acetaldehyde show faster nucleophilic addition reaction. **(1 Mark)**

(ii) Fehling's reagent is composed of Fehling A and Fehling B. Fehling A is a blue-coloured aqueous solution of $CuSO_4$. Fehling B is colorless aqueous solution of potassium sodium tartrate $(KNaC_4H_4O_6.4H_2O)$. **(1 Mark)**

> **Note**
>
> *Fehling reagent is used to test aldehydes. Ketones and aromatic aldehyde do not respond to Fehling's test.*

(iii) Structure of semicarbazone of ethanal

$\underset{H}{\overset{CH_3}{>}}C = O + H_2N - NH - \overset{\overset{\displaystyle O}{\|}}{C} - NH_2 \longrightarrow NH - \overset{\overset{\displaystyle O}{\|}}{C} - NH_2$

$H_3C —\overset{\overset{\displaystyle H}{|}}{C} = N —NH —\overset{\overset{\displaystyle O}{\|}}{C}—NH_2$ **(1 Mark)**
Semicarbazone

10. **(i)** The reaction of propanone with Grignard reagent

$CH_3 — \overset{\overset{\displaystyle O}{\|}}{C} — CH_3 + CH_3MgBr \xrightarrow{H_2O}$
propanone

$CH_3 — \overset{\overset{\displaystyle OH}{|}}{\underset{\underset{\displaystyle CH_3}{|}}{C}} — CH_3$ **(1 Mark)**
2-methylpropan-2-ol

(ii) When ethanal is reacted with excess ethanol and acid then acetal will form as a product.

$\underset{H}{\overset{CH_3}{>}}C = O + C_2H_5OH \xrightarrow[-H_2O]{HCl} \underset{H}{\overset{CH_3}{>}}C\overset{OH}{\underset{OC_2H_5}{<}}$
Ethanal   Hemiacetal

$\xrightarrow[-H_2O]{HCl, C_2H_5OH}$

$\underset{H}{\overset{H_3C}{>}}C\overset{OC_2H_5}{\underset{OC_2H_5}{<}}$
Acetal

(1 Mark)

(iii) Methanal undergoes cannizzaro reaction

$2 \underset{H}{\overset{H}{>}}C = O + \text{conc.KOH} \longrightarrow$
Methanal

$H—\overset{\overset{\displaystyle H}{|}}{\underset{\underset{\displaystyle H}{|}}{C}}—OH + H—\overset{\overset{\displaystyle O}{\|}}{C}—OK$
   Methanol   Potassium
                    methanoate

(1 Mark)

Note

Cannizzaro reaction involves disproportionation i.e., self oxidation and self reduction of aldehydes which do not have alpha hydrogen. One molecule of aldehyde is reduced to alcohol and another is oxidised to carboxylic acid.

11. (i) $2CH_3COCl + (CH_3)_2Cd \longrightarrow CH_3 - \overset{\displaystyle O}{\underset{\displaystyle \|}{C}} - CH_3$

(1 Mark)

(ii) $CH_3CH_2CHO \xrightarrow[\text{Clemmensen Reduction}]{\text{Zn(Hg)/Conc.HCl}} CH_3CH_2CH_3$

(1 Mark)

(iii) [cyclohexyl]$- COONa + NaOH \xrightarrow[\Delta]{CaO}$ [cyclohexyl]$- H + Na_2CO_3$

(1 Mark)

12.

Topper's Answer

(i) [benzene ring] $- CHO \xrightarrow{NaCN/HCl}$ [benzene ring] $- \overset{C\equiv N}{\underset{H}{\overset{|}{C}}} - OH + NaCl$ (cyanohydrin)

(ii) $(C_6H_5CH_2)_2 Cd + 2CH_3COCl \longrightarrow CdCl_2 + 2CH_3\overset{O}{\overset{\|}{C}} - CH_2C_6H_5$

(iii) $CH_3 - \overset{CH_3}{\overset{|}{C}H} - COOH \xrightarrow[\text{(ii) H}_2O]{\text{(i) Br}_2/\text{red P}_4} CH_3 - \overset{CH_3}{\underset{Br}{\overset{|}{C}}} - \overset{O}{\overset{\|}{C}} - OH$

(i) [benzaldehyde] $\overset{O}{\overset{\|}{C}} - H \xrightarrow{NaCN}$ [phenyl]$\overset{-ONa^+}{\underset{CN}{\overset{|}{C}}} - H \xrightarrow{HCl}$ [phenyl]$\overset{OH}{\underset{CN}{\overset{|}{C}}} - H$

(1 Mark)

(ii) $(C_6H_5CH_2)_2Cd + 2CH_3COCl \longrightarrow$

$2C_6H_5CH_2COCH_3 + CdCl_2$

(1 Mark)

(iii) $CH_3 - \overset{CH_3}{\overset{|}{C}H} - COOH \xrightarrow{\text{(i) Br}_2/\text{RedP}_4}$

$\left[CH_3 - \overset{CH_3}{\underset{Br}{\overset{|}{C}}} - \overset{O}{\overset{\|}{C}} - Br \right] \xrightarrow{\text{(ii) H}_2O} CH_3 - \overset{CH_3}{\underset{Br}{\overset{|}{C}}} - \overset{O}{\overset{\|}{C}} - OH$

(1 Mark)

13. (i) $CH_3 - \overset{O}{\overset{\|}{C}} - CH_3 \underset{}{\overset{\bar{O}H}{\rightleftharpoons}} CH_3 - \overset{O}{\overset{\|}{C}} - CH_2 - \overset{OH}{\underset{CH_3}{\overset{|}{C}}} - CH_3$

(1 Mark)

Note

Mechanism:

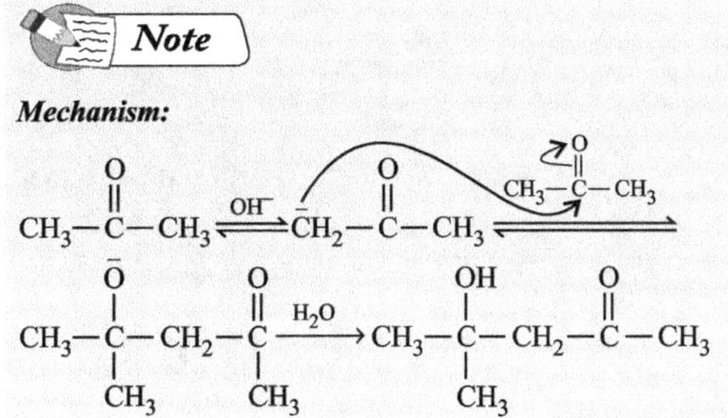

(ii)

$$C_6H_5\text{—}\overset{\displaystyle O}{\overset{\|}{C}}\text{—}CH_3 + 4[H] \xrightarrow[\Delta]{Zn-Hg + Conc.\ HCl}$$
Acetophenone

$$C_6H_5CH_2CH_3 + H_2O$$
Ethyl benzene

(1 Mark)

(iii)

$$C_6H_5\text{—}\overset{\displaystyle O}{\overset{\|}{C}}\text{—}Cl + H_2 \xrightarrow{Pd/BaSO_4}$$
Benzoyl chloride

$$C_6H_5\text{—}\overset{\displaystyle O}{\overset{\|}{C}}\text{—}H + HCl$$
Benzaldehyde

(1 Mark)

14. **(a)** **Ethanal to propanone:** CH_3CHO to CH_3COCH_3

$$CH_3CHO \xrightarrow{CH_3MgBr} CH_3\underset{\underset{OH}{|}}{C}HCH_3 \xrightarrow{CrO_3} CH_3COCH_3$$
Ethanal   Propanone

(1 Mark)

(b) **Toluene to Benzoic acid:**

Toluene $\xrightarrow[\Delta]{alk.\ KMnO_4}$ (benzene ring with COO^-K^+) $\xrightarrow{H^+}$ Benzoic acid (benzene ring with $COOH$)

(1 Mark)

15. **(a)** Aromatic carboxylic acids do not undergo Friedel crafts reaction. This is because the carboxyl group is an electron withdrawing group and hence deactivates the benzene ring towards Friedel crafts reaction. The catalyst (anhydrous $AlCl_3$) gets bonded to the carboxyl group thus preventing the desired reaction. **(1 Mark)**

Note

The Friedel-crafts alkylation may give polyalkylated products, so the Friedel-crafts acylation is a valuable alternative. The acylated products may easily be converted to the corresponding alkanes via clemmensen reduction or wolff-kishner reduction.

(b) pK_a value of 4–nitrobenzoic acid is lower than that of benzoic acid. This is because in 4-nitrobenzoic acid, nitro group being electron withdrawing in nature, makes the O–H bond in –COOH more polar, thus facilitating the release of H^+. Thus, 4-nitrobenzoic acid is more acidic. more is the acidity, lesser is the pK_a value. **(1 Mark)**

Note

Acid strength increases as we move to the right along a row of the periodic table, and as we move down a column.

16. **(i)** $C_6H_5Br \xrightarrow{Mg/dry\ ether} \underset{(A)}{C_6H_5MgBr} \xrightarrow[(b)H_3O^+]{(a)CO_2}$

$$\underset{(B)}{C_6H_5COOH} \xrightarrow{PCl_5} \underset{(C)}{C_6H_5COCl}$$

(½ + ½ + ½ = 1½ Marks)

(ii) $CH_3CN \xrightarrow[(b)H_3O^+]{(a)SnCl_2/HCl} \underset{(A)}{CH_3CHO} \xrightarrow{dil.NaOH}$

$$\underset{\underset{OH}{|}}{CH_3CH}\text{—}CH_2CHO \xrightarrow{\Delta} \underset{(C)}{CH_3CH = CHCHO}$$
(B)

(½ + ½ + ½ = 1½ Marks)

17. **(i)** Benzoic acid to Benzaldehyde

$$C_6H_5COOH \xrightarrow{SOCl_2} C_6H_5COCl$$
$$\xrightarrow{H_2,Pd-BaSO_4} C_6H_5CHO$$

(1 Mark)

(ii) Ethyl Benzene to Benzoic acid

(benzene ring with CH_2CH_3) $\xrightarrow{K_2Cr_2O_7/H^+} C_6H_5COOH$

(1 Mark)

(iii) Propanone to propene

$$CH_3COCH_3 \xrightarrow{NaBH_4} CH_3\underset{\underset{OH}{|}}{C}HCH_3$$
$$\xrightarrow{Conc.H_2SO_4} CH_3CH = CH_2$$

(1 Mark)

18. **(i)**

$$CH_3\text{—}\underset{\underset{CH_3}{|}}{C}=O \xrightarrow{H_2N-NH_2} \underset{H_3C}{\overset{H_3C}{>}}C=N-NH_2$$
Acetone phenyl hydrazine

$$\xrightarrow{KOH} \underset{H_3C}{\overset{H_3C}{>}}CH_2 + N_2$$
Propane

(1 Mark)

(ii)

$$C_6H_5\!-\!CO\!-\!CH_3 \xrightarrow{\ NaOH/I_2\ } CHI_3\!\downarrow + C_6H_5COONa$$

Iodoform
(yellow)

(1 Mark)

Note

The haloform reaction is the reaction of a methyl ketone with chlorine, bromine or iodine in the presence of hydroxide ions to give a carboxylate ion and a haloform. Only acetaldehyde is one among aldehydes which give haloform reaction. When the halogen used is iodine, the haloform reaction can be used to identify methyl ketones because iodoform is a yellow solid with a characteristic smell.

(iii) $CH_3COONa \xrightarrow{\ NaOH/CaO\ } CH_4 + Na_2CO_3$ **(1 Mark)**

Methane

19. (i) Cannizaro's reaction:

$$2R-CHO \xrightarrow[\text{conc.}]{\ OH^-\ } R-COO^- + R-CH_2-OH$$

(1 Mark)

where, R = H or ph.

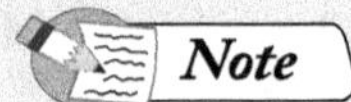

Note

Cannizaro reaction is an organic redox reaction that involves disproportionation of a carbonyl compound to a corresponding alcohol and carboxylic acid.
It takes place in carbonyl compounds that do not have α-hydrogens.

(ii) Boiling points of aldehydes and ketones are lower than that of corresponding carboxylic acids due to the absence of hydrogen bonding in aldehydes and ketones. Weaker dipole-dipole forces are present in the carbonyl compounds. **(1 Mark)**

(iii) The given compound is an oxygen containing compound and since it gives a positive Iodoform and Tollen's test, it must have an α-methyl group attached to the carbonyl group, and an aldehydic group.

Since these are five carbon atoms in the compound the structure of the compound 'A' will be:

$$\underset{\text{(A)}}{CH_3-\overset{\overset{\displaystyle O}{\|}}{C}-CH_2-CH_2-\overset{\overset{\displaystyle O}{\|}}{C}-H}$$

(1 Mark)

'A' reacts in the iodoform and Tollen's reaction as follows:

$$CH_3-\overset{\overset{\displaystyle O}{\|}}{C}-CH_2-CH_2-\overset{\overset{\displaystyle O}{\|}}{C}-H \xrightarrow{\ NaOH/I_2\ }$$

(A)

$$NaOOC-CH_2-CH_2-\overset{\overset{\displaystyle O}{\|}}{C}-H$$
$$+ CHI_3 \text{ (yellow)}$$

$$\xrightarrow[\text{Tollen's reagent}]{(Ag_2O)} CH_3-\overset{\overset{\displaystyle O}{\|}}{C}-CH_2-CH_2-\overset{\overset{\displaystyle O}{\|}}{C}-OH +$$
$$2Ag\!\downarrow$$

(2 Marks)

20. (i) Ethanal is an aldehyde that can be detected by **Tollen's test** that will give a silver mirror.

$$CH_3-CHO \xrightarrow{\ Ag_2O\ } CH_3-COOH \qquad \text{(½ Mark)}$$
$$+ 2Ag\downarrow \text{(silver)}$$

Ethanoic acid is a carboxylic acid that can be identified by **ester test** that will give a fruity smell.

$$CH_3-COOH + CH_3CH_2OH \xrightarrow{\ H^+\ }$$
$$CH_3-COOCH_2CH_3 + H_2O$$

Fruity smell

(½ Mark)

(ii) The α-hydrogens of aldehydes and ketones are bonded to the carbon atom that is bonded to the carbonyl group.

The conjugate base is called enolate ion which is stabilized by resonance and the strong electron-withdrawing nature of the carbonyl group makes the α-hydrogens acidic. **(1 Mark)**

(iii) The given compound contains oxygen so it can be an alcohol ether, aldehyde or ketone or a carboxylic acid/derivative. Since it is hydrolysed, it can be an ether or an ester. Since one of the products of hydrolysis can be oxidized to give the other product, the compound 'A' has to be an **ester**.

(1) So, A = $CH_3 - \overset{\overset{O}{\|}}{C} - OCH_2CH_3$ **(1 Mark)**

$CH_3 - \overset{\overset{O}{\|}}{C} - OCH_2CH_3 \xrightarrow{H_2O/H^+}$

$CH_3 - \overset{\overset{O}{\|}}{C} - OH + CH_3CH_2OH$
    (B)   (C)

$CH_3CH_2OH \xrightarrow[\text{[O]}]{KMnO_4/H+} CH_3COOH$
  (C)   (B)

$CH_3COONa \xrightarrow[\Delta]{CaO/NaOH} CH_4 + CO_2 \uparrow$

(1 Mark)

(2) Compound (B) CH_3COOH will have a higher boiling point as the extent of hydrogen bonding is greater in (B) than in (C). **(1 Mark)**

21. A is an alkene

B is an aldehyde with $-CH_3$ group

C is a methyl ketone

$CH_3CHO + [Ag(NH_3)_2]^+ + OH^- \longrightarrow$

$\qquad CH_3COO^- + Ag + NH_3 + H_2O$ **(1/2 mark)**

$CH_3COCH_3 + NaOH + I_2 \longrightarrow$

$\qquad\qquad CHI_3 + CH_3COONa$ **(1/2 mark)**

A : $CH(CH_3)=C(CH_3)_2$, B: CH_3CHO, C: $O=C(CH_3)_2$

(1.5 = 1/2 mark each)

$CH_3COCH_3 + CH_3CHO$

$\downarrow Ba(OH)_2$

$(CH_3)_2C(OH)CH_2COCH_3 + CH_3CH(OH)CH_2CHO +$
$(CH_3)_2C(OH)CH_2CHO + CH_3CH(OH)CH_2COCH_3$

$\downarrow$ heat

$(CH_3)_2C=CHCOCH_3 + CH_3CH=CHCHO$
$+ (CH_3)_2C=CHCHO + CH_3CH=CHCOCH_3$

(2.5 = 1/2 mark for each product, ½ for the reaction)

22. (a) (A): CCl_3COOH, (B): CH_3COOH **(1 mark)**

(b) $CH_3COOH \xrightarrow[\text{(ii) } H_2O]{\text{(i) Red P/Cl}_2} CCl_3COOH$,

Hell Volhard Zelinsky reaction **(1/2 +1/2 = 1 mark)**

(c) $CH_3COCl \xrightarrow{H_2O} CH_3COOH$ **(1 mark)**

(d) A will be more acidic due to presence of 3 Cl groups (electron withdrawing groups) which increase acidity of carboxylic acid. **(1 mark)**

(e) $CH_3COOH \xrightarrow{\text{(i) NaOH, CaO (ii) heat}} CH_4 + Na_2CO_3$ **(1 mark)**

23.

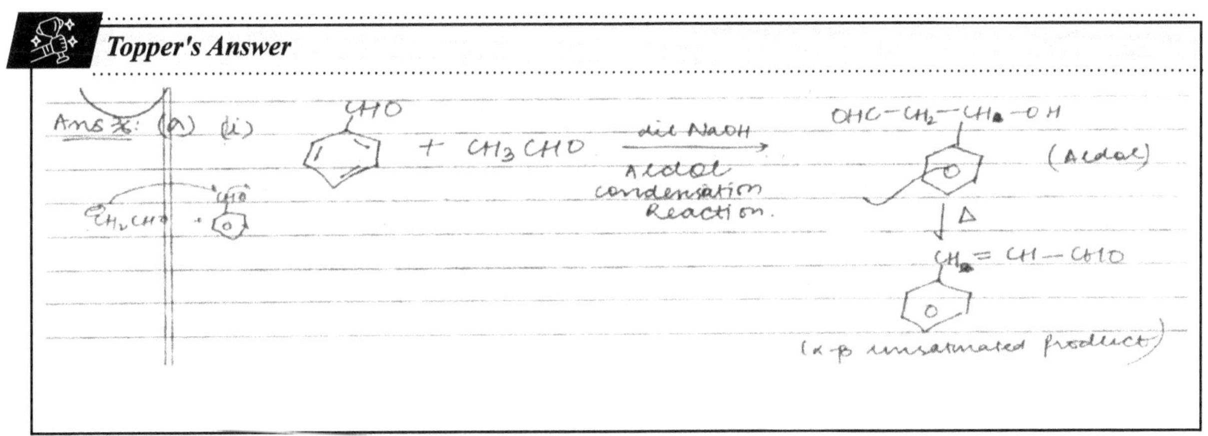

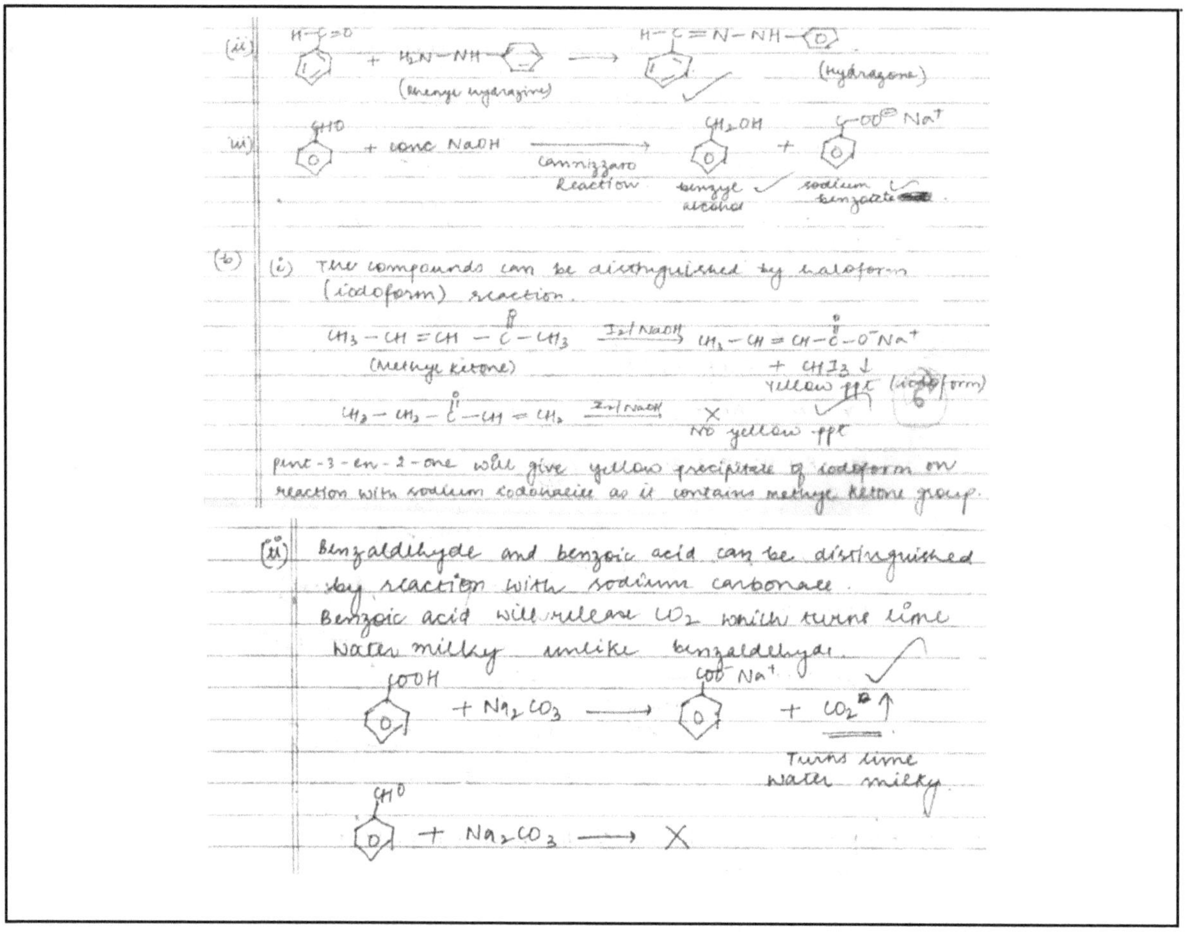

(ii) [handwritten reaction] Ph–CHO + $H_2N–NH–$Ph (phenyl hydrazine) $\longrightarrow$ Ph–CH=N–NH–Ph (hydrazone)

(iii) [handwritten reaction] Ph–CHO + conc. NaOH $\xrightarrow{\text{Cannizzaro Reaction}}$ Ph–CH_2OH (benzyl alcohol) + Ph–$COO^- Na^+$ (sodium benzoate)

(b) (i) The compounds can be distinguished by haloform (iodoform) reaction.

$CH_3–CH=CH–\overset{O}{\overset{\|}{C}}–CH_3$ (methyl ketone) $\xrightarrow{I_2/NaOH}$ $CH_3–CH=CH–\overset{O}{\overset{\|}{C}}–O^- Na^+$ + $CHI_3 \downarrow$ Yellow ppt (iodoform)

$CH_3–CH_2–\overset{O}{\overset{\|}{C}}–CH=CH_2$ $\xrightarrow{I_2/NaOH}$ ✗ No yellow ppt

pent-3-en-2-one will give yellow precipitate of iodoform on reaction with sodium iodoxide as it contains methyl ketone group.

(ii) Benzaldehyde and benzoic acid can be distinguished by reaction with sodium carbonate. Benzoic acid will release CO_2 which turns lime water milky unlike benzaldehyde.

Ph–COOH + $Na_2CO_3 \longrightarrow$ Ph–$COO^- Na^+$ + $CO_2 \uparrow$ Turns lime water milky

Ph–CHO + $Na_2CO_3 \longrightarrow$ ✗

(a) (i) $H–\overset{}{C}=O$ (Ph) + $CH_3–\underset{H}{C}=O$ $\xrightarrow{\text{dil. NaOH}}_{\text{aldol condensation}}$ $H–C=CH–\overset{O}{\overset{\|}{C}}–H$ (Ph)

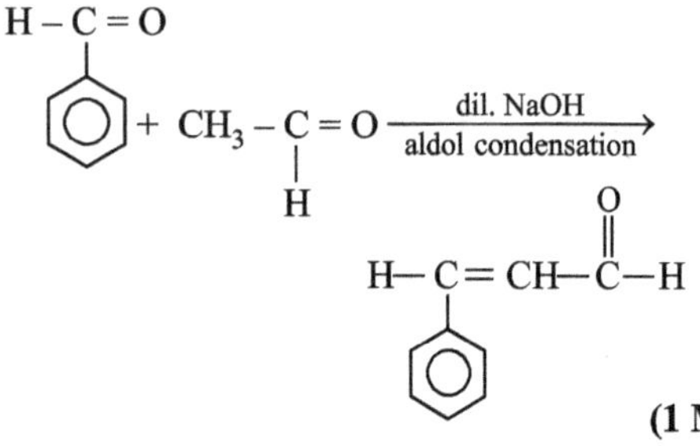

(1 Mark)

(ii) Ph$–\underset{H}{C}=O + H_2N–\underset{H}{N}–$Ph $\xrightarrow{-H_2O}$ Ph$–\underset{H}{C}=N–\underset{H}{N}–$Ph

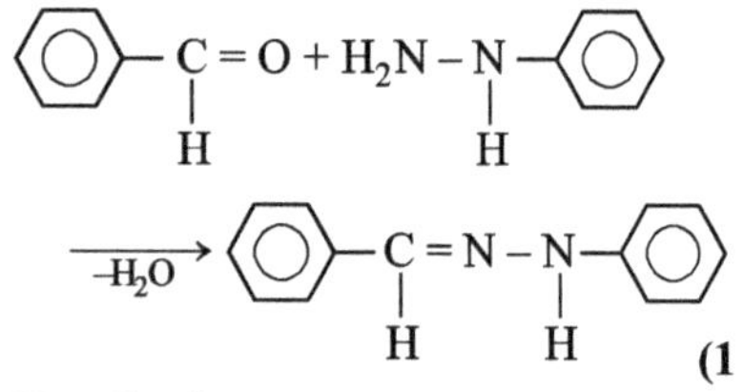

(1 Mark)

(iii) $2\ $ Ph$–\overset{H}{\underset{}{C}}=O$ + conc. NaOH $\xrightarrow[\text{Cannizzaro reaction}]{\Delta}$ Ph$–CH_2–OH$ + Ph$–COO^- Na^+$

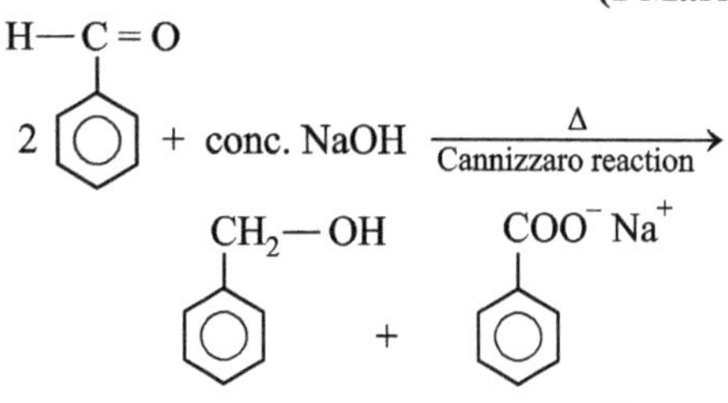

(1 Mark)

(b) (i) $CH_3CH=CH–COCH_3$ and $CH_3CH_2–CO–CH=CH_2$ can be distinguished by the iodoform test as the first compound contains a methyl ketonic group $\left(-\overset{}{\underset{O}{\overset{\|}{C}}}–CH_3\right)$ and undergoes iodoform test, whereas the other compound does not.

(1 Mark)

(ii) Benzaldehyde does not react with sodium bicarbonate ($NaHCO_3$) whereas benzoic acid evolves carbon dioxide upon reaction with $NaHCO_3$ because of its acidic character.

(1 Mark)

24. **(a)** (i) $\underset{CH_3}{\overset{CH_3}{>}}C=O$ $\xrightarrow[\text{Conc.HCl}]{\text{Zn/Hg}}$ $\underset{CH_3}{\overset{CH_3}{>}}CH_2$

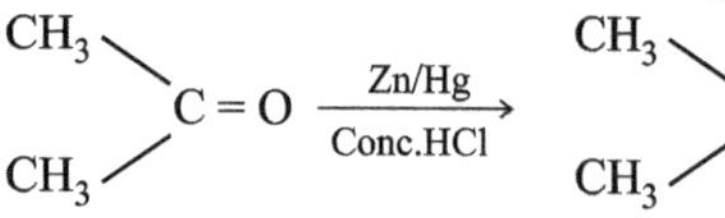

(1 Mark)

(ii) Ph$–COONa + NaOH \xrightarrow[\Delta]{CaO}$ Ph $+ Na_2CO_3$

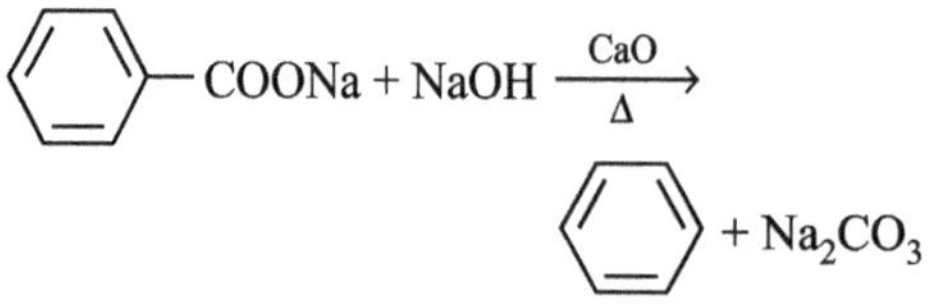

(1 Mark)

(iii) $CH_2 = CH - CH_2 - CN \xrightarrow[\text{(b) } H_3O^+]{\text{(a) DIBAL–H}}$

$$CH_2 = CH—CH_2—\underset{\underset{O}{\|}}{C}—H$$

(1 Mark)

(b)

$$\underset{\underset{O}{\|}}{C}—CH_3 < CH_3—\underset{\underset{O}{\|}}{C}—CH_3$$

$$< CH_3—\underset{\underset{O}{\|}}{C}—H < H—\underset{\underset{O}{\|}}{C}—H$$

(1 Mark)

(c) $CH_3—\underset{\underset{H}{|}}{C} = O + H_2N—\underset{\underset{H}{|}}{N}$—[ring: O_2N, NO_2] $\xrightarrow{-H_2O}$

Acetaldehyde   2, 4 – DNP

$$CH_3—\underset{\underset{H}{|}}{C} = N—\underset{\underset{H}{|}}{N}—[\text{ring: } O_2N, NO_2]$$

2, 4 – DNP derivative of acetaldehyde

(1 Mark)

25. (a) (i)

[p-Nitrotoluene: ring with CH_3, NO_2] $\longrightarrow$ [2-Bromobenzoic acid: ring with $COOH$, Br]

p-Nitrotoluene   2-Bromobenzoic acid

[ring: CH_3, NO_2] $\xrightarrow{Br_2}$ [ring: CH_3, Br, NO_2] $\xrightarrow{Sn/HCl}$

[ring: CH_3, Br, NH_2] $\xrightarrow[0-5\,°C]{NaNO_2/HCl}$ [ring: CH_3, Br, $N_2^+Cl^-$] $\xrightarrow[H_3PO_2]{H_2O}$

[ring: CH_3, Br] $\xrightarrow[KOH, \Delta]{KMnO_4}$ [ring: $COOH$, Br]

(1 Mark)

In step (I), the trisubstitution is controlled by - o, - p directing group i.e., CH_3 group. Because -p position with respect to CH_3 is blocked then Br will substitute - o position with respect to CH_3.

(ii) $CH_3CH_2COOH \xrightarrow[\Delta]{NH_3} CH_3CH_2CONH_2$

$\xrightarrow[\substack{\text{(Hofmann} \\ \text{bromamide} \\ \text{reaction)}}]{Br_2/KOH} CH_3CH_2NH_2 \xrightarrow{HONO} CH_3CH_2OH$

$CH_3COOH \xleftarrow[\text{(Oxidation)}]{(O)}$
Acetic acid

(1 Mark)

(b) $C_5H_{10} \xrightarrow{\text{ozonolysis}} B + C$

Compound B gives +ve Fehling test and reacts with I_2, NaOH. This implies that compound B is an aliphatic aldehyde, it should be CH_3CHO.

Compound C does not give Fehling test, but forms iodoform. This implies compound C is a ketone and contains a methyl ketone group. Therefore, compound A is

$$CH_3 – CH = \underset{\underset{CH_3}{|}}{C} — CH_3$$

$$CH_3 – CH = \underset{\underset{CH_3}{|}}{C} — CH_3 \xrightarrow[\text{(ii) } Zn/H_2O]{\text{(i) } O_3}$$

(A) C_5H^{10}

$$CH_3 – \underset{\underset{}{\overset{O}{\|}}}{C} – H + CH_3 – \underset{\underset{}{\overset{O}{\|}}}{C} – CH_3$$
(B)   (C)

(1 + 1 + 1 = 3 Marks)

Fehling test : In this test the presence of aldehyde but not ketones is detected by reduction of the deep blue solution of copper (II) to a red ppt. of insoluble copper oxide. It is commonly used for reducing sugars. Iodoform test is used to check the presence of carbonyl compounds with the structure $R – CO – CH_3$ or alcohols with the structure $RCH(OH) – CH_3$ in a given unknown substance.

26. (a) (i)

$$\underset{\text{Benzoic acid}}{C_6H_5COOH} \longrightarrow \underset{\text{Aniline}}{C_6H_5NH_2}$$

$$\underset{COOH}{} \xrightarrow[\Delta]{NH_3} \underset{CONH_2}{} \xrightarrow{Br_2/KOH} \underset{NH_2}{}$$

(1 Mark)

(ii) $\underset{\text{Bromomethane}}{CH_3Br} \longrightarrow \underset{\text{Ethanol}}{CH_3CH_2OH}$

$$CH_3Br \xrightarrow{KCN(alc.)} CH_3 - CN \xrightarrow{H_3O^+}$$

$$CH_3COOH \xrightarrow{LiAlH_4} CH_3CH_2OH$$

(1 Mark)

(b) (i) $CH_3CH_2 - CH_3$ **(1 Mark)**

(ii) $(CH_3)_3CCH_2OH + (CH_3)C_3COONa$ **(1 Mark)**

(iii)

$$\underset{COONa}{}$$

(1 Mark)

Reaction (i) is an example of wolf-Kishner reduction. In this reaction carbonyl compounds are reduced to alkane. Reaction (ii) is on example of cannizzaro reaction in which one molecule of an alkehyde is reduced to produce a primary alcohol and another oxidised to carboxylic acid using a hydroxide base Reaction (iii) is an example of acid base reaction.

27. (a) (i)

$$\underset{}{C_6H_{10}O} + HCN \longrightarrow \underset{OH}{\overset{CN}{C_6H_{10}}}$$

(1 Mark)

(ii)

$$\underset{\substack{\text{Sodium} \\ \text{benzoate}}}{C_6H_5-COONa} \xrightarrow[-Na_2CO_3]{NaOH/CaO, \Delta} \underset{\text{Benzene}}{C_6H_6}$$

(1 Mark)

(iii) $CH_3 - CH = CH - CN \xrightarrow[\text{(b) } H_2O/HCl]{\text{(a) DIBAL-H}}$

$$CH_3 - CH = CH - CHO$$ **(1 Mark)**

Equation (i) is an example of nucleophilic substitution reaction. Equation (ii) is an example of decarboxylation reaction. In this reaction the COOH or COONa group is removed and replaced with a hydrogen atom. In equation (iii) DIBAL being a reducing agents, reduces partially nitriles to imines then imines are hydrolysed to aldehyde.

(b) (i) **Tollen's test :** Butanal gives positive test with Tollen's reagent whereas butan-2-one gives negative test.

$$CH_3CH_2CH_2CHO + 2\,[Ag(NH_3)_2]^+ + 3OH^-$$

$$\downarrow$$

$$CH_3CH_2CH_2CO\bar{O} + 2Ag + 2H_2O + 4NH_3$$

(1 Mark)

(ii) **FeCl_3 test :** Benzoic Acid gives a buff coloured ppt with neutral $FeCl_3$ solution whereas phenol gives a violet colour with neutral $FeCl_3$ solution. **(1 Mark)**

28. (a) (i) **Etard reaction.**

$$\underset{CH_3}{C_6H_5} + CrO_2Cl_2 \xrightarrow{CS_2} \underset{CH(OCrOHCl_2)_2}{C_6H_5} \xrightarrow{H_3O^+} \underset{CHO}{C_6H_5}$$

(1 Mark)

Etard Reaction: *Chromyl chloride (CrO_2Cl_2) oxidises methyl group of toluene to a chromium complex, which on hydrolysis gives corresponding benzaldehyde.*

(ii) **Stephen reaction.**

$$RCN + SnCl_2 + HCl \longrightarrow RCH = NH \xrightarrow{H_3O^+} RCHO$$

(1 Mark)

Stephen Reaction: *Nitriles are reduced to corresponding imine with stannous chloride in the presence of hydrochloric acid, which on hydrolysis give corresponding aldehyde.*

(b) (*i*) Benzoic acid to benzaldehyde :

$$COOH \xrightarrow[-SO_2, -HCl]{SOCl_2} COCl \xrightarrow[\text{S or quinoline}]{H_2/Pd + BaSO_4} CHO$$

(1 Mark)

(ii) Acetophenone to benzoic acid :

$$\underset{\text{Acetophenone}}{COCH_3} \xrightarrow[\Delta]{KMnO_4/KOH} COO^-K^+ \xrightarrow{H_3O^+} \underset{\text{Benzoic acid}}{COOH}$$

(1 Mark)

(iii) Ethanoic acid to 2-hydroxyethanoic acid :

$$\underset{\text{Ethanoic acid}}{CH_3-COOH} \xrightarrow[\text{(ii)}\,H_2O]{\text{(i)}\,Cl_2/Red\,P} CH_2(Cl)-COOH$$

$$\xrightarrow{aq\cdot KOH} \underset{\text{2-Hydroxyethanoic acid}}{CH_2(OH)-COOH}$$

(1 Mark)

29. (a) (i) $CH_3COCl \xrightarrow{H_2,\ Pd-BaSO_4} \underset{(A)}{CH_3CHO}$

$\xrightarrow{H_2N-OH} \underset{(B)}{CH_3CH=N-OH}$

(½ + ½ = 1 Mark)

(ii) $CH_3MgBr \xrightarrow[2.\ H_3O^+]{1.\ CO_2} \underset{(A)}{CH_3COOH}$

$\xrightarrow{PCl_5} \underset{(B)}{CH_3COCl}$ **(½ + ½ = 1 Mark)**

(b) (i) $C_6H_5-COCH_3$ is a methyl ketone and therefore, gives a yellow precipitate of iodoform when reacted with NaOH and I_2 (haloform test).

$$C_6H_5-COCH_3 \xrightarrow[I_2]{NaOH} C_6H_5COONa + CHI_3$$

C_6H_5-CHO does not give this reaction.

(1 Mark)

(ii) As shown below, methanoic acid gives silver mirror test, while ethanoic acid will not give this test.

$$HCOOH + 2[Ag(NH_3)_2]NO_3$$
$$\longrightarrow 2Ag + CO_2 + 2NH_4NO_3 + 2NH_3$$

(1 Mark)

(c) The increasing order of boiling points of the given compounds is as follows :

$CH_3CHO < CH_3CH_2OH < CH_3COOH$ **(1 Mark)**

The boiling point of the given compounds can be compared on the basis of the extent of intermolecular hydrogen bond formation.

30. (a)
$$\underset{\text{Acetaldehyde}}{CH_3-\overset{\displaystyle |}{\underset{\displaystyle H}{C}}=O} + NH_2NH_2 \xrightarrow{-H_2O}$$

$$\underset{\text{Hydrazone}}{CH_3-\overset{\displaystyle |}{\underset{\displaystyle H}{C}}=NNH_2} \xrightarrow[\text{Glycol}]{KOH,\ 453-473\ K} CH_3-CH_3 + N_2$$

(1 Mark)

(b) The increasing order of reactivity towards nucleophilic addition reaction for the given compounds is as follows:

$$CH_3COCH_3 < C_6H_5COCH_3 < CH_3-CHO$$

(1 Mark)

Aldehydes are more reactive than ketones towards the nucleophillic addition reaction. Among the ketones, aromatic ketones are more susceptible to nucleophilic attack than an aliphatic one.

(c) The carbon of carboxylic acid is much less electrophilic as compared to aldehydes and ketones because the lone pair of oxygen attached to hydrogen is involved in resonance, as shown below:

$$R-\overset{\displaystyle O}{\overset{\displaystyle \|}{C}}-\ddot{O}H \longleftrightarrow R-\overset{\displaystyle O^-}{\overset{\displaystyle |}{C}}=\overset{+}{O}H$$

(1 Mark)

(d) $CH_3CH_2CH=CHCH_2CN \xrightarrow[\text{(ii)}\ H_2O]{\text{(i)}\ (i-Bu)_2\ AlH}$

$CH_3CH_2CH=CH-CH_2-CHO$

(1 Mark)

(e) The possible functional isomers of C_3H_6O are CH_3-CH_2-CHO and CH_3COCH_3

Out of these, methyl ketone can give iodoform test as shown :

$$CH_3COCH_3 \xrightarrow[\Lambda]{NaOH+I_2} \underset{\text{yellow ppt.}}{CH_3COONa + CHI_3}$$

Hence, isomer A is CH_3CH_2CHO and B is CH_3COCH_3 **(1 Mark)**

31.

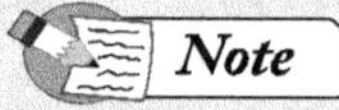

$$C_6H_6 \xrightarrow[\text{Anhyd. AlCl}_3]{\text{CH}_3\text{COCl}} \text{(A)}$$

(A) — $COCH_3$ attached to benzene ring

(A) → NaOI → COONa (benzene ring) (D) + CHI$_3$ (E)

(A) → Zn–Hg/ Conc. HCl → CH_2CH_3 (benzene ring) (B)

(B) → (i) KMnO$_4$ – KOHΔ (ii) H$_3$O$^+$ → COOH (benzene ring) (C)

(1 + 1 + 1 + 1 + 1 = 5 Marks)

32. (a) $HCHO + HCHO \xrightarrow[\Delta]{\text{Conc. NaOH}} CH_3OH + HCOONa$

formaldehyde   methyl   sodium formate
              alcohol

(1 Mark)

> **Note**
>
> *For aldehydes which do not have a-hydrogen atom undergoes self oxidation and reduction in the presence of concentrated alkali. This produces one mole of alcohol and one mole of salt of carboxylic acid. This is called cannizzaro's reaction.*

(b) $\underset{\text{ethanal}}{\overset{H_3C}{\underset{H}{>}}C=O} + \underset{\text{semicarbazide}}{H_2N-NH-\overset{\overset{O}{\|}}{C}-NH_2} \longrightarrow$

$$\underset{\substack{\text{semicarbazone} \\ \text{of} \\ \text{ethanal}}}{CH_3-\overset{\overset{H}{|}}{C}=N-NH-\overset{\overset{O}{\|}}{C}-NH_2}$$

(1 Mark)

(c) Fluorine is more electronegative than chlorine. The presence of fluorine in a molecule will make it more acidic. Thus, the pKa of $F-CH_2COOH$ is lower than that of $Cl-CH_2COOH$. **(1 Mark)**

(d) $CH_3-CH=CH-CH_2CN \xrightarrow[\text{(ii) H}_2\text{O}]{\text{(i) DIBAL-H}}$

$$CH_3CH=CHCH_2CHO$$

(1 Mark)

(e) Tollen's reagent will give a positive test of silver mirror formation with propanal, while propanone does not give this test.

$$R-CHO + 2[Ag(NH_3)_2]^+ + 3OH^- \longrightarrow$$
$$2Ag\downarrow + R-COO^- + H_2O + NH_3$$

Tollen's Reagent

(1 Mark)

> **Note**
>
> *Ammonical silver nitrate solution act as mild oxidising agent and oxidises aldehyde to acetate ion and itself reduced to metallic silver.*

33. (a) (i) $CH_3CHO \longrightarrow \underset{\text{Cyanohydrin}}{CH_3CH(OH)CN}$ **(1 Mark)**

(ii) $CH_3-\overset{\overset{H}{|}}{C}=\boxed{O+H_2}-NOH \longrightarrow$
$\underset{\text{Oxime}}{CH_3-CH=NOH}$ **(1 Mark)**

(iii) $CH_3CHO + CH_3CHO \xrightarrow[\text{NaOH}]{\text{dil.}}$
$CH_3-CH(OH)-CH_2-CHO$ **(1 Mark)**

(b) (i) **Ferric chloride test :** Phenol reacts with neutral FeCl$_3$ to form an iron phenol complex giving violet colouration.

$$6C_6H_5OH + FeCl_3 \longrightarrow$$
$$\underset{\text{Violet colour}}{[Fe(OC_6H_5)_6]^{3-} + 3H^+ + 3Cl^-}$$

But benzoic acid reacts with neutral FeCl$_3$ to give a buff coloured ppt. of ferric benzoate.

$$3C_6H_5COOH + FeCl_3 \longrightarrow$$
$$\underset{\text{Buff colour}}{(C_6H_5COO)_3 Fe + 3HCl}$$

(1 Mark)

(ii) Proponal is an aldehyde, thus, it reduces Tollen's reagent. But propanone being a ketone does not reduce Tollen's reagent. **(1 Mark)**

34. (a) (i) $ClCH_2COOH$ is a stronger acid than CH_3COOH. This is because Cl atom exhibits – I effect, withdraw electron denstity from O–H bond. As a result, polarity of O–H bond increases and hence release of H$^+$ becomes easier. **(1 Mark)**

(ii) Carboxylic acids do not give reactions of carbonyl group because carbonyl carbon in carboxyl group is less electropositive than carbonyl carbon in aldehydes and ketones due to resonance. **(1 Mark)**

(b) (i) **Rosenmund Reduction** is used to prepare aldehydes from acid chloride by passing H_2 gas through xylene in presence of Pd catalyst and partially poisoned by addition of S or quinoline.

$$CH_3 - \overset{\overset{O}{\|}}{C} - Cl + H_2 \xrightarrow[\text{boiling xylene}]{Pd, BaSO_4, S}$$

$$CH_3 - \overset{\overset{O}{\|}}{C} - H + HCl \qquad \textbf{(1 Mark)}$$

(ii) **Cannizzaro reaction:** Aldehydes which do not contain α-hydrogen atom, when treated with conc. alkali solution undergo self oxidation and reduction to form alcohol and carboxylate ion.

$$\underset{\text{Formal dihyde}}{HCHO} + \underset{\text{(conc)}}{NaOH} \longrightarrow \underset{\text{Methanol}}{CH_3OH} + \underset{\text{Sodium formate}}{HCOO^- Na^+}$$

(1 Mark)

(c) $CH_3CH_2CH_2COCH_3$ will give iodoform test due to presence of $CH_3 - CO -$ group. **(1 Mark)**

35. (a) (i) $\bigcirc = O + H_2N - OH \xrightarrow{H^+}$

$\bigcirc = N - OH$

(1 Mark)

(ii) $2C_6H_5CHO + \text{conc.NaOH} \longrightarrow$
$$C_6H_5CH_2OH + C_6H_5COOH$$

(1 Mark)

(iii) $CH_3COOH \xrightarrow{Cl_2 + P \text{ (red)}} \underset{\underset{Cl}{|}}{CH_2COOH}$

(1 Mark)

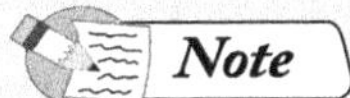
Note

Cannizzaro Reactions are the base induced disproportionation of two molecules of a non-enolizable aldehyde to yield a carboxylic acid and a primary alcohol. The reaction is also said to be redox process because one aldehyde oxidised to give carboxylic acid while other aldehyde undergoes reduction to yield the alcohol.

(b) (i) $NaHCO_3$ is used distinguish benzaldehyde and benzoic acid,

CHO

$\bigcirc + NaHCO_3 \longrightarrow$ No reaction

COOH

$\bigcirc + NaHCO_3 \longrightarrow$

$$C_6H_5COONa + CO_2\uparrow + H_2O \quad \textbf{(1 Mark)}$$

(ii) Fehling's test is used to distinguish propanal and propanone

$$\underset{\text{propanal}}{CH_3CH_2CHO} + 2Cu^{2+} + 5OH^- \longrightarrow$$

$$\underset{\text{(Red Colour)}}{Cu_2O + CH_3CH_2COO^- + 3H_2O}$$

$$\underset{\text{propanal}}{CH_3COCH_3} + Cu^{2+} + OH^- \longrightarrow \text{No reaction}$$
(1 Mark)

36. (a) (i) CH_3CHO is more reactive than CH_3COCH_3 towards reaction with HCN. This is because there is more steric hindrance in case of CH_3COCH_3, so the attack by the nucleophile (CN^-) becomes difficult. This is not the case in CH_3CHO.

$\boxed{CN^-}$ $\qquad$ $\boxed{CN^-}$

$$\underset{H}{\overset{H_3C}{\diagdown}} C = O \qquad \underset{H_3C}{\overset{H_3C}{\diagdown}} C = O$$

less steric hindrance $\qquad$ more steric hindrance **(1 Mark)**

(ii) Carboxylic acid is a stronger acid than phenol. This is because in the resonating structures of carboxy anion, the $-$ve charge is on the more electro $-$ve O-atom whereas in phenoxide ion, $-$ve charge is on less electronegative carbon atom. Moreover, the $-$ve charge is delocalised over two oxygen atoms in carboxylate anion whereas is phenoxide ion, it is delocalised over one oxygen atom and less electro negative carbon-atoms. **(1 Mark)**

(b) (i) **Wolff-Kishner reduction**

$$\underset{\text{ald/ketone}}{\overset{\diagdown}{\diagup}} C = O \xrightarrow[-H_2O]{NH_2NH_2} \overset{\diagdown}{\diagup} C = NNH_2$$

$$\xrightarrow[\Delta]{KOH/glycol} \underset{\text{alkane}}{\overset{\diagdown}{\diagup} CH_2} + N_2$$

(1 Mark)

(ii) **Aldol condensation**

$$\underset{R}{\overset{O}{\|}}\diagup_{R^I} \xrightarrow{NaOH} \underset{R}{\overset{O}{\|}}\diagup^{R^I}\diagdown_{R}^{OH}$$

β-Hydroxy Ketone

$$\xrightarrow{-H_2O} \underset{R}{\overset{O}{\|}}\diagup C \diagdown_{R^I}^{R}$$

Aldol Condensation Product

(1 Mark)

(iii) Cannizaro Reaction

$$2HCHO \xrightarrow[NaOH]{conc} CH_3OH + HCOONa$$

(1 Mark)

37. (a)

(i)

$$CH_3 - \overset{\overset{\displaystyle O}{\|}}{C} - CH_3 + H_2 \xrightarrow{Ni, Pt \ or \ Pd}$$

Propanone

$$\underset{\text{Propan-2-ol}}{CH_3 - \overset{\overset{\displaystyle OH}{|}}{CH} - CH_3}$$

(1 Mark)

(ii)

$$\underset{\text{Ethanal}}{CH_3 - CHO} \xrightarrow{HCN} CH_3 - \overset{\overset{\displaystyle H}{|}}{\underset{\underset{\displaystyle OH}{|}}{C}} - CN$$

$$\xrightarrow{H^+/H_2O} \underset{\text{2 - Hydroxy propanoic acid}}{CH_3 - \overset{\overset{\displaystyle OH}{|}}{CH} - COOH}$$

(1 Mark)

(iii)

Toluene $\xrightarrow[\text{(ii)} H^+/H_2O]{\text{(i)} KMnO_4/OH^-, \Delta}$ Benzoic acid

(1 Mark)

(b) Chemical tests to distinguish between :

(i) Pentan-2-one and pentan-3-one : On treating with NaOI (I_2/NaOH) pentan-2-one gives yellow ppt. of iodoform but pentan-3-one does not. (only methyl ketones give iodoform test)

$$CH_3 - CH_2 - CH_2 - \overset{\overset{\displaystyle O}{\|}}{C} - CH_3 + 3NaOI \rightarrow$$

Pentan-2-one

$$\underset{\underset{\text{(Yellow ppt.)}}{\text{Iodoform}}}{CH_3CH_2CH_2COONa + CHI_3 \downarrow + 2NaOH}$$

$$\underset{\text{Pentan-3-one}}{CH_3 - CH_2 - \overset{\overset{\displaystyle O}{\|}}{C} - CH_2 - CH_3} \xrightarrow{NaOI} \text{No yellow ppt. of iodoform}$$

(1 Mark)

(ii) Ethanal and propanal : Ethanal when treated with I_2/NaOH (or NaOI) gives yellow ppt. of iodoform but propanal does not.

$$\underset{\text{Ethanal}}{CH_3CHO} + 3NaOI \longrightarrow \underset{\underset{\text{ppt.}}{\text{Yellow}}}{CHI_3} \downarrow + HCOONa + 2NaOH$$

$$\underset{\text{Propanal}}{CH_3CH_2CHO} \ \Big\downarrow {\scriptstyle I_2/NaOH}$$

No yellow ppt. of iodoform

(1 Mark)

38. (a) (i)

$$\underset{\text{Acetone}}{CH_3 - \overset{\overset{\displaystyle O}{\|}}{C} - CH_3} + 4[H] \xrightarrow[\text{conc.HCl}]{Zn-Hg} \underset{\text{Propane}}{CH_3CH_2CH_3} + H_2O$$

(1 Mark)

(ii)

$$\underset{\text{Ethanoyl chloride}}{CH_3 - \overset{\overset{\displaystyle O}{\|}}{C} - Cl} + H_2 \xrightarrow{Pd - BaSO_4}$$

$$\underset{\text{Ethanal}}{CH_3CHO} + HCl$$

(1 Mark)

> **Note**
>
> *The rosenmund reaction is catalysed by palladium on barium sulphate. Barium sulphate reduces the activity of palladium due to its low surface area hence decreases the reducing power of palladium in order to prevent over-reduction of the acid.*

(iii)

Benzoic acid $\xrightarrow{Br_2/FeBr_3}$ m-Bromo benzoic acid $+ HBr$

(1 Mark)

(b) (i) F – CH_2COOH is stronger acid than Cl – CH_2COOH because F is more electronegative than Cl. F withdraws electrons from O – H bond more strongly than Cl and helps in easier release of H^+ ions by making O – H bond weaker relative to Cl. The stronger - I effect of F also disperses the –ve charge on carboxylate anion and stabilises it to a greater extent than Cl. **(1 Mark)**

(ii) In benzoic acid, benzene ring is present which is an electron withdrawing group and hence it makes the O – H bond more polar and easier to break. This means benzoic acid is more acidic, while, there is no electron withdrawing group in ethanoic acid. Therefore, benzoic acid is more acidic than ethanoic acid. **(1 Mark)**

39. (a) Reasons for carboxylic acid being stronger acid than phenols are as follows.

(i) Carboxylate ion, the conjugate base of carboxylic acid is stablised by two equivalent resonance structures in which the negative charge is effectively delocalised between two more electronegative oxygen atoms.

(ii) The conjugate base of phenol, a phenoxide ion has non equivalent resonance structures in which the negative charge is at the less electronegative carbon atom. **(2 Marks)**

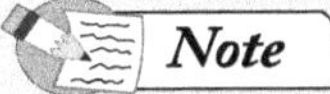 *Note*

Consider the resonating structures of carboxylate and phenoxide ion

$$RCOOH \rightleftharpoons RCOO^- + H^+$$

Carboxylate ion

Resonance hybrid

In case of phenoxide ion, structures (II – IV) carry a negative charge on the less electronegative carbon atom. Therefore, their contribution towards the resonance stabilization of phenoxide ion is very small.

(b) (i) $CH_3COCH_3 + 4[H] \xrightarrow{Zn-Hg,HCl}$
Propanone

$$CH_3CH_2CH_3 + H_2O$$
Propane **(1 Mark)**

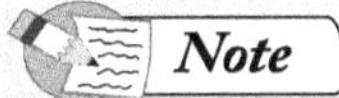 *Note*

Clemmensen reduction is complementary to wolf-kishner reduction, which also convert aldehyde and ketones to hydrocarbons. Clemmensen reduction carried out in strongly acidic conditions and wolf kishner reduction carried out in strongly basic conditions.

(ii) Benzoyl chloride $\xrightarrow[H_2]{Pd-BaSO_4}$ Benzaldehyde **(1 Mark)**

(iii) $2CH_3CHO \xrightarrow[\text{Aldol condensation}]{Dil.NaOH}$
Ethanal

$$CH_3 - \overset{OH}{\underset{|}{CH}} - CH_2 - CHO$$

$$\xrightarrow[\Delta, -H_2O]{H^+/H_2O} CH_3 - CH = CH - CHO$$
But–2–enal **(1 Mark)**

40. (a) (i) $2H - \overset{O}{\overset{||}{C}} - H \xrightarrow[\text{cannizzaro reaction}]{Conc. KOH}$
Formaldehyde

$$CH_3OH \quad + \quad HCOOK$$
Methyl alcohol Potassium formate **(1 Mark)**

(ii) $CH_3COOH \xrightarrow{Br_2/P} Br - CH_2 - COOH$
Acetic acid Bromoacetic acid

(1 Mark)

Note

Hell-volhard-zelinsky reaction:
Carboxylic acids having an α-hydrogen are halogenated at the α-position on treatment with chlorine or bromine in the presence of small amount of red phosphoms to give α-halocarboxylic acids. The reaction fails to accomplish the fluorination and iodination of carboxylic acids.

(iii) Benzaldehyde $\xrightarrow[273-283 K]{HNO_3 / H_2SO_4}$ *m*-Nitrobenzaldehyde $+ H_2O$

(1 Mark)

(b) (i) **Ethanal and propanal :** On reacting with I_2/NaOH (or NaOI) ethanal gives yellow precipitate of iodoform but propanal does not.

$$CH_3CHO + 3I_2 + 4NaOH \xrightarrow{heat}$$

$$CHI_3 + HCOONa + 3NaI + 3H_2O$$
Iodoform
(Yellow ppt.

$$CH_3CH_2CHO + I_2 + NaOH \longrightarrow$$

No yellow ppt.   **(1 Mark)**

(ii) **Benzoic acid and phenol :** On reacting with $NaHCO_3$ solution, benzoic acid evolves CO_2 but phenol does not.

$$C_6H_5COOH + NaHCO_3 \longrightarrow$$
Benzoic acid

$$C_6H_5COONa + CO_2 \uparrow + H_2O$$
Sodium benzoate

$$C_6H_5OH \xrightarrow{NaHCO_3} No\ evolution\ of\ CO_2$$
Phenol

(1 Mark)

41. (a) Aldehyde + Alcohol $\xrightarrow[\text{(excess)}]{\text{Dry} \atop \text{HCl}}$ Acetal

$$R-CHO \underset{}{\overset{R'OH_2HCl\ gas}{\rightleftharpoons}} \left[R-C {\overset{\displaystyle OR'}{\underset{\displaystyle OH}{}}} \right]$$

Hemiacetal

$$\xrightarrow[H^+]{R'OH} R-C {\overset{\displaystyle OR'}{\underset{\displaystyle OR'}{}}}$$

Acetal   **(1 Mark)**

(b) Acidity of a substance is judged by the stability of its conjugate base.

$$R-COOH \longrightarrow R-C{\overset{\displaystyle O}{\underset{\displaystyle O^-}{}}} + H^+ ;$$

Conjugate base

$$R-C{\overset{\displaystyle O}{\underset{\displaystyle O^-}{}}} \longleftrightarrow R-C{\overset{\displaystyle O^-}{\underset{\displaystyle O}{}}}$$

Two equivalent cannonical structures
of conjugate base

Further, in these two cannonical structures, the negative charge is symmetrically distributed over the more electronegative atom 'O'.

Therefore, carboxylic acids are the most acidic organic compound among the other organic substances.

(1 Mark)

(c) (i)

$$CH_3CHO,\ (CH_3)_3C-\underset{\underset{O}{\|}}{C}-CH_3,\ CH_3-\underset{\underset{O}{\|}}{C}-CH_3$$
(I)   (II)   (III)

Increasing order of reactivity toward CH_3MgBr

(II) < (III) < (I)

+I effect of alkyl group(s) reduces the electrophilicity of carbonyl carbon.   **(1 Mark)**

(ii) The mild oxidizing agents, e.g. Tollen's reagent, Fehling's reagent can easily oxidize aldehydes but not ketones.

$$R-CHO + 2\left[Ag(NH_3)_2\right]^+ + 3OH^- \longrightarrow$$
(Freshly prepared
ammoniacal silver
nitrate solution)

$$RCOO^- + 2Ag + 4NH_3 + 2H_2O$$

$$R-\underset{\underset{}{\overset{\displaystyle O}{\|}}}{C}-R + \left[Ag(NH\ )\ \right] \xrightarrow{OH^-}$$

no reaction **(1 Mark)**

OR

(c) (i)

$$\xrightarrow{[Ag(NH_3)_2]^+}$$

(cyclohexane ring with CHO) → (cyclohexane ring with COO^-)

(keto group remains
unaffected with mild
oxidizing agent)

(1 Mark)

(ii)

(benzaldehyde, CHO) $\xrightarrow[\text{(semicarbazide)}]{H_2N\ CO\ NH\ NH_2}$

(benzene ring with $CH=N-NH\ CONH_2$)

semicarbazone.   **(1 Mark)**

9 Amines

Topic-1: *Structure of Amines, Classification, Nomenclature*

---

4   *Very Short Answer Questions (1 Mark)*

1. Write the IUPAC name of $CH_3-N-C_6H_5$ with CH_3 on nitrogen

   [Delhi 2020, K]

2. Write the IUPAC name of the given compound:

   [Delhi 2016, K]

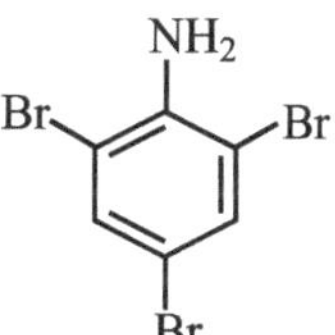

3. Write the structure of N-methylethanamine.

   [All India 2013, K]

Topic-2: *Preparation of Amines*

---

1   *Multiple Choice Questions*

1. Amides can be converted into amines by the reaction named   **[Delhi 2023, Set-I, K]**

   (a) Hoffmann degradation

   (b) Ammonolysis

   (c) Carbylamine

   (d) Diazotisation

2. Which of the following would not be a good choice for reducing nitrobenzene to aniline? **[Delhi 2023, Set-I, K]**

   (a) $LiAlH_4$ (b) H_2/Ni

   (c) Fe and HCl   (d) Sn and HCl

3. CH_3CONH_2 on reaction with NaOH and Br_2 in alcoholic medium gives   **[Delhi 2020, Set-I]**

   (a) $CH_3CH_2NH_2$ (b) CH_3CH_2Br

   (c) CH_3NH_2 (d) CH_3COONa

4   *Very Short Answer Questions (1 Mark)*

4. What happens when $CH_3 - Br$ is treated with KCN?

   [Delhi 2013, K]

Topic-3: *Physical Properties, Chemical Reactions*

---

1   *Multiple Choice Questions*

1. In which of the following solvents, the $C_4H_8NH_3{}^+X^-$ is soluble;   **[CBSE Sample 2023-24, K]**

   (a) ether   (b) acetone

   (c) water   (d) bromine water

2. Among the following which has the highest value of p^Kb?   **[All India 2023, Set-I, U]**

   (a) $C_6H_5-NH_2$

   (b) $C_6H_5-CH_2-NH_2$

   (c) $H_3C-C_6H_4-NH_2$

   (d) $O_2N-C_6H_4-NH_2$

3. In the reaction [Delhi 2023 Set-III $\boxed{K}$]

$C_6H_5NH_2 + CHCl_3 + 3\ KOH \rightarrow A + 3B + 3C$ the product A is

(a) C_6H_5NC (b) C_6H_5CN

(c) C_6H_5Cl (c) $C_6H_5NHCH_3$

4. Arrange the following in the increasing order of their boiling points: [CBSE Sample 2022-23, $\boxed{U}$]

A : Butanamine, B: N,N-Dimethylethanamine, C: N-Etthylethanaminamine

(a) C<B<A   (b) A<B<C

(c) A<C<B   (d) B<C<A

5. Which of the following statements is not correct for amines? [CBSE Sample 2022-23, $\boxed{U}$]

(a) Most alkyl amines are more basic than ammonia solution.

(b) pK_b value of ethylamine is lower than benzylamine.

(c) CH_3NH_2 on reaction with nitrous acid releases NO_2 gas.

(d) Hinsberg's reagent reacts with secondary amines to form sulphonamides.

6. Propanamide on reaction with bromine in aqueous NaOH gives: [CBSE Sample 2020-21, $\boxed{U}$]

(a) Propanamine

(b) Ethanamine

(c) N-Methyl ethanamine

(d) Propanenitrile

7. IUPAC name of product formed by reaction of methyl amine with two moles of ethyl chloride

[CBSE Sample 2020-21, $\boxed{U}$]

(a) N,N-Dimethylethanamine

(b) N,N-Diethylmethanamine

(c) N-Methyl ethanamine

(d) N-Ethyl - N-methylethanamine

8. Out of the following, the strongest base in aqueous solution is [All India 2020, $\boxed{K}$]

(a) Methylamine

(b) Dimethylamine

(c) Trimethylamine

(d) Aniline

2   *Assertion Reason/Two Statement Type Questions*

Given below are two statements labelled as Assertion (A) and Reason (R). Select the most appropriate answer from the options given below:

(a) Both (A) and (R) are true and (R) is the correct explanation of (A).

(b) Both (A) and (R) are true, but (R) is not the correct explanation of (A).

(c) (A) is true, but (R) is false.

(d) (A) is false, but (R) is true.

9. **Assertion (A):** Tertiary amines are more basic than corresponding secondary and primary amines in gaseous state.

Reason (R): Tertiary amines have three alkyl groups which cause +I effect.

4   *Very Short Answer Questions (1 Mark)*

10. Write the reaction involved in the Hoffmann bromamide degradation reaction. [All India 2019, $\boxed{U}$]

11. Propanamine and N, N-dimethylmethanamine contain the same number of carbon atoms, even though propanamine has higher boiling point than N, N-dimethylmethanamine. Why?

12. Arrange the following in increasing order of boiling points: [Delhi 2019, $\boxed{K}$]

$(CH_3)_3N, C_2H_5OH, C_2H_5NH_2$

13. Arrange the following compounds in increasing order of solubility in water : [Delhi 2014, $\boxed{K}$]

$C_6H_5NH_2, (C_2H_5)_2NH, C_2H_5NH_2$

14. Arrange the following in increasing order of their basic strength in aqueous solution :

$CH_3NH_2, (CH_3)_3N, (CH_3)_2NH$ [Delhi 2013, $\boxed{K}$]

5   *Short Answer Questions (2 or 3 Marks)*

15. An organic compound (A) with molecular formula C_3H_7NO on heating with Br_2 and KOH forms a compound (B). compound (B) on heating with $CHCl_3$ and alcoholic KOH produces a foul smelling compound (C) and on reacting with $C_6H_5SO_2Cl$ forms a compound (D) which is soluble in alkali. Write the structures of (A), (B), (C) and (D). [All India 2022, Term-II, A]

16. Give reasons : [All India 2022, Term-II, $\boxed{U}$]

(i) Ammonolysis of alkyl halides is not a good method to prepare pure primary amines.

(ii) Aniline does not give Friedel-crafts reaction.

(iii) Although $-NH_2$ group is o/p directing in electrophilic substitution reactions, yet aniline on nitration gives good yield of *m*-nitroaniline.

17. Give reasons for **any 3** of the following observations:
    [CBSE Sample 2022-23, U]
    (a) Aniline is acetylated before nitration reaction.
    (b) pK_b of aniline is lower than the m-nitroaniline.
    (c) Primary amine on treatment with benzenesulphonyl chloride forms a product which is soluble in NaOH however secondary amine gives product which is insoluble in NaOH.
    (d) Aniline does not react with methyl chloride in the presence of anhydrous $AlCl_3$ catalyst.

18. Account for the following:
    [CBSE 2021-22, Term-II, U]
    a. Aniline cannot be prepared by the ammonolysis of chlorobenzene under normal conditions.
    b. N-ethylethanamine boils at 329.3K and butanamine boils at 350.8K, although both are isomeric in nature.
    c. Acylation of aniline is carried out in the presence of pyridine.

19. Convert the following: **[CBSE 2021-22, Term-II, U]**
    a. Phenol to N-phenylethanamide.
    b. Chloroethane to methanamine.
    c. Propanenitrile to ethanal.

20. What happens when reactions:
    [CBSE 2021-22, Term-II, U]
    a. N-ethylethanamine reacts with benzenesulphonyl chloride.
    b. Benzylchloride is treated with ammonia followed by the reaction with Chloromethane.
    c. Aniline reacts with chloroform in the presence of alcoholic potassium hydroxide.

21. a. Write the IUPAC name for the following organic compound: **[CBSE 2021-22, Term-II, U]**

    $CH_3 - N - CH_2CH_3$

    b. Complete the following:
    [CBSE 2021-22, Term-II, U]

    $C_6H_5NO_2 \xrightarrow{Sn/HCl} A \xrightarrow{Br_2/H_2O}$

    $B \xrightarrow[273-278K]{NaNO_2/HCl} C \xrightarrow[\Delta]{HBF_4} D$

22. Give reasons: **[Delhi 2020, U]**
    (a) Aniline does not undergo Friedal-Craft's reaction.

    (b) Aromatic primary amines cannot be prepared by Gabriel phthalimide synthesis.
    (c) Aliphatic amines are stronger bases than ammonia.

23. (a) How will you distinguish between the following pairs of compounds: **[All India 2020, U]**
    (i) Aniline and Ethanamine
    (ii) Aniline and N-Methylaniline
    (b) Arrange the following compounds in decreasing order of their boiling points:
    Butanol, Butanamine, Butane

24. (a) Give one chemical test to distinguish between the compounds of the following pairs :
    (i) CH_3NH_2 and $(CH_3)_2NH$ **[All India2019, K]**
    (ii) Aniline and Ethanamine
    (b) Why aniline does not undergo Friedel-Crafts reaction? **[All India2019, U]**

25. An aromatic compound 'A' on heating with Br_2 and KOH forms a compound 'B' of molecular formula C_6H_7N which on reacting with $CHCl_3$ and alcoholic KOH produces a foul smelling compound 'C'. Write the structures and IUPAC names of compounds A, B and C.
    [Delhi 2019, U]

26. Write the structures of compounds A, B and C in the following reactions. **[All India 2017, U]**
    (a) $CH_3 - COOH \xrightarrow{NH_3/\Delta} A \xrightarrow{Br_2/KOH(aq)} B$
    $\xrightarrow{CHCl_3 + alc.KOH} C$
    (b) $C_6H_5N_2^+BF_4^- \xrightarrow[\Delta]{NaNO_2/Cu} A \xrightarrow{Fe/HCl} B$
    $\xrightarrow{CH_3COCl/pyridine} C$

27. Give reasons for the following : **[All India 2017, U]**
    (a) Acetylation of aniline reduces its activation effect.
    (b) CH_3NH_2 is more basic than $C_6H_5NH_2$.
    (c) Although $- NH_2$ is *o/p* directing group, yet aniline on nitration gives a significant amount of *m*-nitroaniline.

28. Give reasons : **[Delhi 2017, U]**
    (i) Acetylation of aniline reduces its activation effect.
    (ii) CH_3NH_2 is more basic than $C_6H_5NH_2$.
    (iii) Although $-NH_2$ is o/p directing group, yet aniline on nitration gives a significant amount of m-nitroaniline.

29. Write the chemical equations involved in the following reactions : **[All India 2016, K]**
    (i) Hoffmann-bromamide degradation reaction
    (ii) Carbylamine reaction

30. Give reasons for the following :   [**All India 2016, U**]

   (i) Aniline does not undergo Friedel-Craft's reaction.

   (ii) $(CH_3)_2NH$ is more basic than $(CH_3)_3N$ in an aqueous solution.

   (iii) Primary amines have higher boiling point than tertiary amines.

31. Arrange the following in increasing order of their basic strength.   [**All India 2015, K**]

   (i) $C_6H_5 - NH_2$, $C_6H_5 - CH_2 - NH_2$, $C_6H_5 - NH - CH_3$

   (ii) 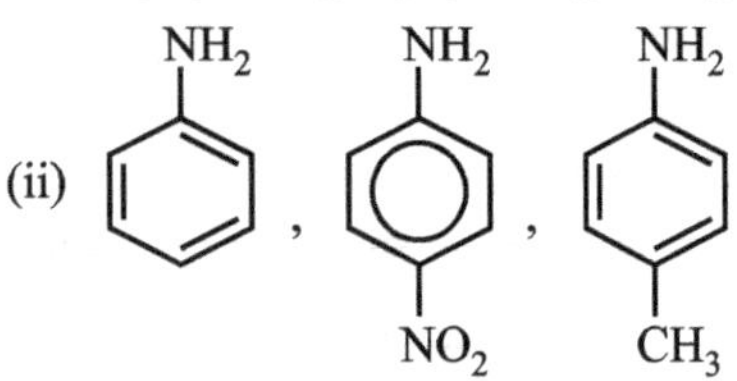

32. How do you convert the following.   [**All India 2015, K**]

   (i) $C_6H_5CONH_2$ to $C_6H_5NH_2$

   (ii) Aniline to phenol

   (iii) Ethanenitrile to ethanamine

33. Write the chemical equations involved when aniline is treated with the following reagents.   [**All India 2015, K**]

   (i) Br_2 water

   (ii) $CHCl_3 + KOH$

   (iii) HCl

34. Account for the following:

   (i) Primary amines $(R-NH_2)$ have higher boiling point than tertiary amines (R_3N).

   (ii) Aniline does not undergo Friedel - Crafts reactions:

   (iii) $(CH_3)_2NH$ is more basic than $(CH_3)_3N$ in an aqueous solution.   [**All India 2014, U**]

35. Give the structures of A, B and C in the following reactions: [**All India 2014, U**]

   (i) $C_6H_5NO_2 \xrightarrow{Sn+HCl} A \xrightarrow[273K]{NaNO_2+HCl} B \xrightarrow{H_2O} C$

   (ii) $CH_3CN \xrightarrow[A]{H_2O/H^+} A \xrightarrow[\Delta]{NH_3} B \xrightarrow{Br_2+KOH} C$

36. Give the structures of A, B and C in the following reactions :   [**Delhi 2014, U**]

   (i) $CH_3Br \xrightarrow{KCN} A \xrightarrow{LiAlH_4} B \xrightarrow[273K]{HNO_2} C$

   (ii) $CH_3COOH \xrightarrow[\Delta]{NH_3} A \xrightarrow{Br_2+KOH}$

      $B \xrightarrow{CHCl_3+NaOH} C$

37. How will you convert the following :   [**Delhi 2014, U**]

   (i) Nitrobenzene into aniline

   (ii) Ethanoic acid into methanamine

   (iii) Aniline into N-phenylethanamide

   (Write the chemical equations involved.)

6   *Long Answer Questions*

38. An organic compound with molecular formula $C_7H_7NO_2$ exists in three isomeric forms, the isomer 'A' has the highest melting point of the three. 'A' on reduction gives compound 'B' with molecular formula C_7H_9N. 'B' on treatment with $NaNO_2/HCl$ at 0–5°C to form compound 'C'. On treating C with H_3PO_2, it gets converted to D with formula C_7H_8, which on further reaction with CrO_2Cl_2 followed by hydrolysis forms 'E' C_7H_6O. Write the structure of compounds A to E. Write the chemical equations involved.   [**CBSE Sample 2023-24, A**]

39. (a) Account for the following:

      [**CBSE Sample 2023-24, K**]

   (i) N–ethylbenzenesulphonyl amide is soluble in alkali.

   (ii) Reduction of nitrobenzene using Fe and HCl is preferred over Sn and HCl.

  (b) Arrange the following in:

      [**CBSE Sample 2023-24, K**]

   (i) decreasing order of pK_b values

     $C_6H_5NH_2$, $C_6H_5NHCH_3$, $C_6H_5CH_2NH_2$, CH_3NH_2, NH_3

   (ii) increasing order of solubility in water

     C_2H_5Cl, $C_2H_5NH_2$, C_2H_5OH

   (iii) decreasing boiling point

     CH_3COOH, C_2H_5OH, CH_3NH_2, CH_3OCH_3

40. (I) Give reasons: [**All India 2023, Set-I, K**]

   (i) Aniline on nitration gives good amount of m-nitroaniline, though $-NH_2$ group is o/p directing in electrophilic substitution reactions.

   (ii) $(CH_3)_2NH$ is more basic than $(CH_3)_3N$ in an aqueous solution.

   (iii) Ammonolysis of alkyl halides is not a good method to prepare pure primary amines.

  (II) Write the reaction involved in the following:

      [**All India 2023, Set-I, K**]

   (i) Carbyl amine test

   (ii) Gabriel phthalimide synthesis

41. (a) Write the structures of the main products of the following reactions : **[All India 2023, U]**

(i)

(ii)

(iii)

(b) Give a simple chemical test to distinguish between aniline and N, N- dimethylaniline.

[All India 2023, K]

(c) Arrange the following in the increasing order of their pK_b values : **[All India 2023, K]**

$C_6H_5NH_2$, $C_2H_5NH_2$, $C_6H_5NHCH_3$

42. (a) Write the structures of main products when aniline reacts with the following reagents :

[Delhi 2015, K]

(i) Br_2 water

(ii) HCl

(iii) $(CH_3CO)_2O$ / pyridine

(b) Arrange the following in the increasing order of their boiling point : **[Delhi 2015, U]**

$C_2H_5NH_2, C_2H_5OH, (CH_3)_3N$

(c) Give a simple chemical test to distinguish between the following pair of compounds : **[Delhi 2015, K]**

$(CH_3)_2NH$ and $(CH_3)_3N$

7   *Case Based Questions*

43. Read the following passage and answer the questions that follow : **[All India 2022, Term-II A]**

Amines constitute an important class of organic compounds derived by replacing one or more hydrogen atoms of ammonia molecule by alkyl/aryl groups. Amines are usually formed from nitro compounds, halides, amides, etc. They exhibit hydrogen bonding which influences their physical properties. Alkyl amines are found to be stronger bases than ammonia. In aromatic amines, electron releasing and withdrawing groups, respectively increase and decrease their basic character.

Reactions of amines are governed by availability of the unshared pair of electrons on nitrogen. Influence of the number of hydrogen atoms at nitrogen atom on the type of reactions and nature of products is responsible for identification and distinction between primary, secondary and tertiary amines. Reactivity of aromatic amines can be controlled by acylation process.

(i) Why does aniline not give Friedel-Crafts reaction ?

(ii) Arrange the following in the increasing order of their pK_b values :

$C_6H_5NH_2$, NH_3, $C_2H_5NH_2$, $(CH_3)_3N$

(iii) How can you distinguish between $CH_3CH_2NH_2$ and $(CH_3CH_2)_2NH$ by Hinsberg test ?

(iv) Write the structures of A and B in the following reactions :

(I)

$$CH_3CH_2CONH_2 \xrightarrow[]{Br_2 / alc. KOH} A \xrightarrow[Pyridine]{CH_3COCl} B$$

(II)

Topic-4: *Method of Preparation of Diazonium Salts, Physical Properties, Chemical Reactions, Importance of Diazonium Salts in Synthesis of Aromatic Compounds*

1   *Multiple Choice Questions*

1. When Benzene diazonium choride reacts with phenol, it forms a dye. This reaction is called

[All India 2023 Set-II, K]

(a) Diazotisation reaction

(b) Condensation reaction

(c) Coupling reaction

(d) Acetylation reaction

4   *Very Short Answer Questions (1 Mark)*

2. The conversion of primary aromatic amines into diazonium salts is known as _______ . **[All India 2014, K]**

5   Short Answer Questions (2 or 3 Marks)

3. (i) Draw the zwitter ion structure for sulphanilic acid

   (ii) How can the activating effect of $-NH_2$ group in aniline be controlled? **[Delhi 2023, Set-I, U]**

4. (i) Complete the reaction with the main product formed: **[2 × 1 = 2 Marks]**

$$N_2^+Cl^-$$ on benzene ring $\xrightarrow{CH_3CH_2OH}$

   (ii) Convert Bromoethane to Propanamine.

5. (a) Illustrate Sandmeyer's reaction with an equation.

   (b) Explain, why $(CH_3)_2NH$ is more basic than $(CH_3)_3N$ in aqueous solution. **[Delhi 2023, Set-I, U]**

6. Give the structures of A and B in the following sequence of reactions: **[All India 2020, U]**

   (a) $CH_3COOH \xrightarrow[\Delta]{NH_3} A \xrightarrow{NaOBr} B$

   (b) $C_6H_5NO_2 \xrightarrow{Fe/HCl} A \xrightarrow[0°-5°C]{NaNO_2 + HCl} B$

   (c) $C_6H_5N_2^+Cl^- \xrightarrow[\Delta]{CuCN} A \xrightarrow{H_2O/H^+} B$

7. Write the structures of main products when benzene diazonium chloride reacts with the following reagents : **[All India 2019, Set-II]**

   (i) CuCN

   (ii) CH_3CH_2OH

   (iii) KI

8. Write the structures of A, B and C in the following : **[Delhi 2016, K]**

   (i) $C_6H_5-CONH_2 \xrightarrow{Br_2/aq.KOH} A \xrightarrow[0-5\,°C]{NaNO_2+HCl}$ $B \xrightarrow{KI} C$

   (ii) $CH_3-Cl \xrightarrow{KCN} A \xrightarrow{LiAlH_4} B \xrightarrow[\Delta]{CHCl_3+alc.KOH} C$

9. Complete the following reactions : **[All India 2013, K]**

   (i) $CH_3CH_2NH_2 + CHCl_3 + KOH\,(alc.) \longrightarrow$

   (ii) $C_6H_5N_2^+\,Cl^- \xrightarrow[(Room\,temp.)]{H_2O}$

   (iii) NH_2 on benzene ring $+\,HCl\,(aq.) \longrightarrow$

10. Give the structures of A, B and C in the following reaction : **[Delhi 2013, U]**

   (i) $C_6H_5N_2^+Cl^- \xrightarrow{CuCN} A$ $\xrightarrow{H_2O/H^+} B \xrightarrow[\Delta]{NH_3} C$

   (ii) $C_6H_5NO_2 \xrightarrow{Sn+HCl} A$ $\xrightarrow[273\,K]{NaNO_2+HCl} B \xrightarrow[\Delta]{H_2O/H^+} C$

6   Long Answer Questions

11. (I) Write the structure of A, B and C in the following reactions: **[All India 2023, Set-I, U]**

   (i) Benzene ring $-N_2^+Cl \xrightarrow{CuCN} A$ $\xrightarrow{H_2O/H^+} B \xrightarrow[\Delta]{NH_3} C$

   (ii) Nitrobenzene (NO_2) $\xrightarrow{Fe/HCl} A \xrightarrow[273\,K]{NaNO_2+HCl} B$ $\xrightarrow{C_2H_5OH} C$

   (II) Why aniline does not undergo Friedal-Crafts reaction? **[All India 2023, Set-I, K]**

   (III) Arrange the following in increasing order of their boiling point: **[All India 2023, Set-I, U]**

$$C_2H_5OH, C_2H_5NH_2, (C_2H_5)_3N$$

12. (a) Write the reactions involved in the following : **[All India 2018, K]**

   (i) Hoffmann bromamide degradation reaction

   (ii) Diazotisation

   (iii) Gabriel phthalimide synthesis

   (b) Give reasons : **[All India 2018, U]**

   (i) $(CH_3)_2NH$ is more basic than $(CH_3)_3N$ in an aqueous solution.

   (ii) Aromatic diazonium salts are more stable than aliphatic diazonium salts.

13. An aromatic compound 'A' of molecular formula C_7H_7ON undergoes a series of reactions as shown below. Write the structures of A, B, C, D and E in the following reactions : **[Delhi 2015, U]**

$$(C_7H_7ON) \xrightarrow{Br_2+KOH} C_6H_5NH_2 \xrightarrow[273\,K]{NaNO_2+HCl} B \xrightarrow{CH_3CH_2OH} C$$

A $\xrightarrow{CHCl_3+NaOH} D$ B $\xrightarrow{KI} E$

Solutions

Topic-1: *Structure of Amines, Classification, Nomenclature*

1. N, N – Dimethylaniline **(1 Mark)**
2. 2, 4, 6-Tribromoaniline **(1 Mark)**
3. $CH_3 – CH_2 – NH – CH_3$. **(1 Mark)**

Topic-2: *Preparation of Amines*

1. **(a)** Amides are converted into primary amines by the reaction called Hoffmann bromamide degradation reaction.

$$R \overset{\overset{O}{\|}}{-C} - NH_2 + Br_2 + 4NaOH \longrightarrow \underset{1°\,amine}{R - NH_2} +$$

$$Na_2CO_3 + 2NaBr + 2H_2O$$

Therefore, option (a) is correct. **(1 Mark)**

Ammonolysis, carbylamine reaction and Diazotization are all reactions of amines and for their preparation from amides.

2. **(a)** Using $LiAlH_4$ for reduction of nitrobenzene to aniline is not a good choice because it converts nitrobenzene to diazobenzene. $(Ph – N = N – Ph)$.

Therefore, option **(a)** is correct. **(1 Mark)**

3.

Topper's Answer

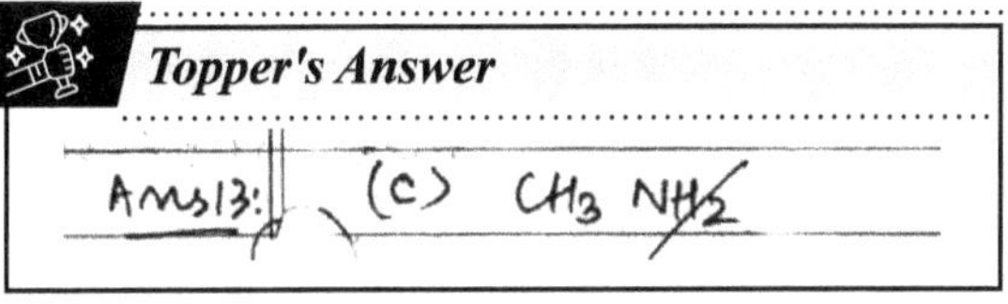

(1 Mark)

4. $CH_3Br + KCN \longrightarrow \underset{Acetonitrile}{CH_3CN} + KBr$ **(1 Mark)**

Topic-3: *Physical Properties, Chemical Reactions*

1. **(c)** water **(1 Mark)**

2. **(d)** 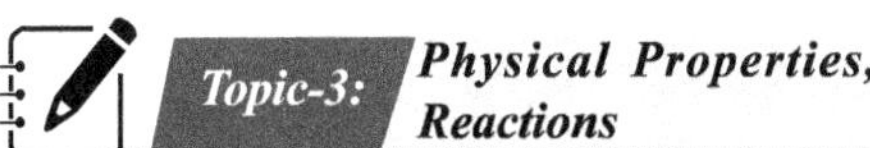

$O_2N-\langle\text{ }\rangle-NH_2$; $K_b = \dfrac{[\overset{+}{RNH_3}][OH^-]}{[RNH_2]}$

Larger K_b value → smaller pK_b value → higher basicity.

– NO_2 group exerts – I effect on the lone pair of – NH_2 group.

This results into the difficulty of lone pair towards acid. Therefore, K_b value becomes smaller, pK_b value larger. **(1 Mark)**

3. **(a)** Aliphatic and aromatic primary amines on heating with chloroform and ethanolic KOH form isocyanides or carbylamines which are foul smelling substances.

$$C_6H_5NH_2 + CHCl_3 + 3\,KOH \rightarrow$$
$$\underset{(A)}{C_6H_5 – NC} + \underset{(B)}{3\,KCl} + \underset{(C)}{3H_2O}$$

(1 Mark)

4. **(d)** B<C<A

In primary amine intermolecular association due to H-bonding is maximum while in tertiary it is minimum. **(1 Mark)**

5. **(c)** CH_3NH_2 on reaction with nitrous acid releases NO_2 gas

Wrong statement. The evolution of nitrogen gas takes place. **(1 Mark)**

6. **(b)** **(1 Mark)**

7. **(d)** **(1 Mark)**

8. **(b)** Order of basicity in aqueous solution for amines :

$2° > 1° > 3° > NH_3$ **(1 Mark)**

9. **(a)** Both A and R are true and R is the correct explanation of A. **(1 Mark)**

10. $\underset{\substack{Ethanamide\,(2C)\\(Acetamide)}}{CH_3-\overset{\overset{O}{\|}}{C}-NH_2} + Br_2 + 4NaOH \longrightarrow$

$$\underset{Methylamine\,(1C)}{CH_3NH_2} + Na_2CO_3 + 2NaBr + 2H_2O$$

(1 Mark)

 **Note**

Hoffmann bromamide reaction: *Reaction of an acid amide with bromine in an aqueous or ethanolic solution of sodium hydroxide to form a primary amine, with one carbon atom less, is known as Hoffmann bromamide reaction.*

11. $CH_3CH_2CH_2NH_2$ (1° amine)

propanamine

and $CH_3 - \overset{\overset{\displaystyle CH_3}{|}}{N} - CH_3$ (3° amine)

N,N-Dimethylmethanamine

Due to the presence of two H-atoms on N-atom of primary amines, they undergo extensive intermolecular H-bonding while tertiary amines due to the absence of H-atom on the N-atom do not undergo H-bonding. As a result, primary amines (*e.g.* propanamine) have higher boiling points than tertiary amines (*e.g.* N, N-dimethyl methanamine) of comparable molecular mass. **(1 Mark)**

12. $(CH_3)_3 N < C_2H_5NH_2 < C_2H_5OH$ **(1 Mark)**

> ***Note***
>
> *Alcohols have a higher boiling point as compared to that of amines because of strong hydrogen bonding. Oxygen being more electronegative forms strong hydrogen bond as compared to nitrogen. In tertiary amine, there is no hydrogen to form hydrogen bond. Hence it has lowest boiling point.*

13.   The order of solubility in water is :

$C_6H_5NH_2 < (C_2H_5)_2NH < C_2H_5NH_2$ **(1 Mark)**

> ***Note***
>
> *Solubility of amines in water depends upon the extent of H-bonding between amine and water molecules. Extent of intermolecular H-bonding is highest for primary amine followed by secondary amine. Aniline does not form intermolecular H-bond with water to very large extent due to bulky hydrophobic phenyl group.*

14. $(CH_3)_2NH > CH_3NH_2 > (CH_3)_3NH$ **(1 Mark)**

> ***Note***
>
> *Basic strength of alkyl amines in the aqueous state is determined by inductive effect, solvation effect and stearic hinderance of the alkyl group. As –CH$_3$ group is smaller than –C$_2$H$_5$, it offers less stearic hinderance to hydrogen bonding. Therefore order of basic strength will be different for ethyl substituted amines.*
>
> $(C_2H_5)_2NH > (C_2H_5)_3N > C_2H_5NH_3 > NH_3$
>
> $(CH_3)_2NH > CH_3NH_2 > (CH_3)_3N > NH_3$

15.

(A)   (D)   (B)   (C)

(B) $\xrightarrow[\substack{KOH \\ \text{Carbylamine reaction}}]{CHCl_3/\Delta}$ (C)

(2 Marks)

16. (i)   Ammonolysis yields a mixture of primary, secondary, tertiary and quaternary salts. The separation of pure primary amines from ammonolysis of alkyl halide is a difficult process. **(1 Mark)**

(ii) Aniline does not give friedel-crafts reaction as it forms anilinium chloride salt which deactivates the ring for further acylation and alkylation reaction. **(1 Mark)**

(iii) –NH$_2$ group is electron donating group which activates the ring and gives ortho, para product but in case of nitration it will form anilinium ion in presence of acid and gives meta directing product. **(1 Mark)**

17. (a) Aniline is acetylated, before nitration reaction in order to avoid formation of tarry oxidation products and protecting the amino group, so that p-nitro derivative can be obtained as major product. **(1 mark)**

(b) pK$_b$ of aniline is lower than the m-nitro aniline. The basic strength of aniline is more that m-nitroaniline. pk$_b$ value is inversely proportional to basic strength. Presence of Electron withdrawing group decrease basic strength. **(1 mark)**

(c) Due to the presence of acidic hydrogen in the N-alkylbenzenesulphonamide formed by the treatment of primary amines. **(1 mark)**

(d) Aniline does not react with methylchloride in the presence of AlCl$_3$ catalyst, because aniline is a base and AlCl$_3$ is Lewis acid which lead to formation of salt. **(1 mark)**

18. (a) In case of chlorobenzene, the C—Cl bond is quite difficult to break as it acquires a partial double bond character due to conjugation.

So Under the normal conditions, ammonolysis of chlorobenzene does not yield aniline. **(1 Mark)**

(b) Primary and secondary amines are engaged in intermolecular association due to hydrogen bonding between nitrogen of one and hydrogen of another molecule. Due to the presence of three hydrogen atoms, the intermolecular association is more in primary amines than in secondary amines as there are two hydrogen atoms available for hydrogen bond formation in it. **(1 Mark)**

(c) During the acylation of aniline, stronger base pyridine is added. This done in order to remove the HCl so formed during the reaction and to shift the equilibrium to the right hand side. **(1 Mark)**

19. (a) Phenol into N-phenylethanamide **(1 Mark)**

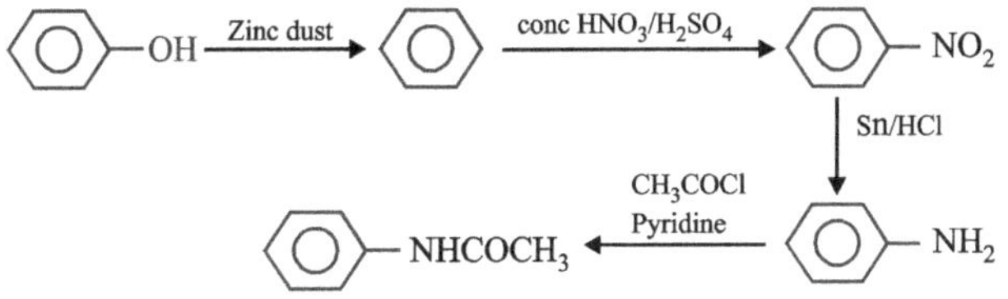

$$CH_3CH_2CN \xrightarrow{H_3O^+} CH_3CH_2CONH_2 \xrightarrow{Br_2/NaOH} CH_3CH_2NH_2 \xrightarrow{HNO_2} CH_3CH_2OH \xrightarrow{PCC} CH_3CHO$$

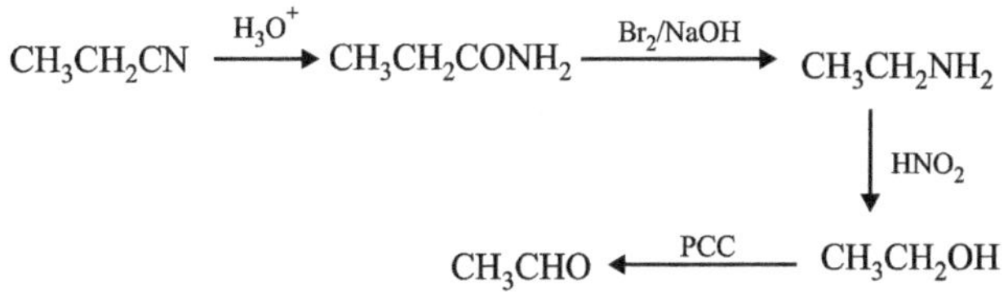

20. (a) When N-ethylethanamine reacts with benzenesulphonyl chloride, N, N-diethylbenzenesulphonamide is formed. Which is insoluble in alkali. **(1 Mark)**

(b) When benzylchloride is treated with ammonia, Benzylamine is formed which on reaction with chloromethane yields a secondary amine, N-methylbenzylamine. **(1 Mark)**

(c) When aniline reacts with chloroform in the presence of alcoholic potassium hydroxide, phenyl isocyanides or phenyl isonitrile is formed that has foul small. **(1 Mark)**

21. (a) N-Ethyl-N-methylbenzenamine or N-Ethyl-N-ethylaniline **(1 Mark)**

(b)

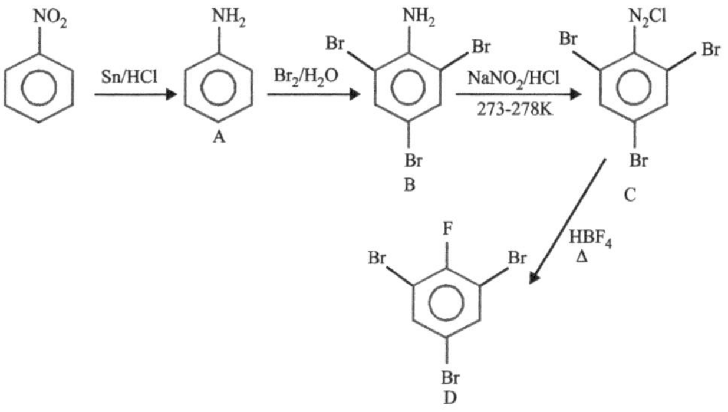

(b) Chloroethane to methanamine **(1 Mark)**

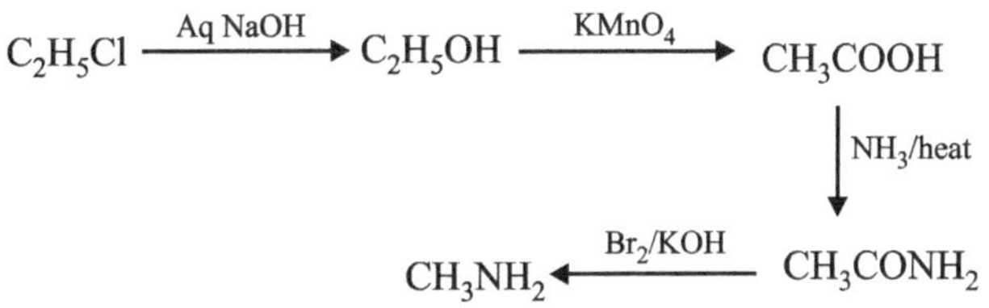

$$C_2H_5Cl \xrightarrow{Aq\ NaOH} C_2H_5OH \xrightarrow{KMnO_4} CH_3COOH \xrightarrow{NH_3/heat} CH_3CONH_2 \xrightarrow{Br_2/KOH} CH_3NH_2$$

(c) Propanenitrile to ethanal **(1 Mark)**

(2 Marks)

22.

Ans 33: (i) Aniline consists of amine attached to benzene ring. Amine Nitrogen in amine consists lone pair which it delocalises in the ring by resonance. Due to this resonance, through which it can act as a strong lewis base.

In friedal craft, $AlCl_3$ is used as a catalyst which is a strong lewis acid. The lone pair of nitrogen easily attacks vacant orbital of $AlCl_3$ and forms salt and doesn't undergo friedal crafts reaction.

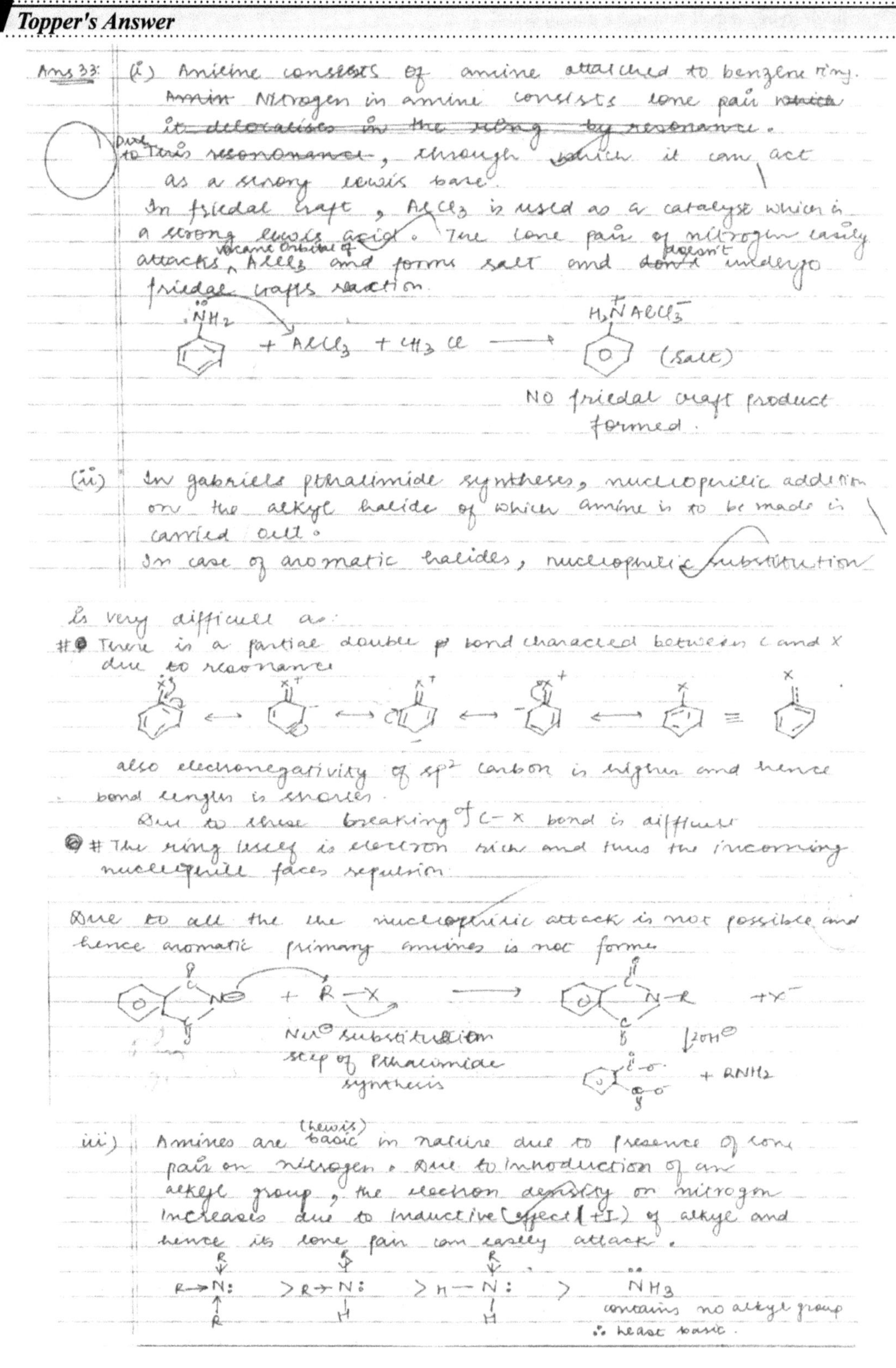

+ $AlCl_3$ + CH_3Cl ⟶ (salt)

NO friedal craft product formed.

(ii) In gabriels pthalimide syntheses, nucleophilic addition on the alkyl halide of which amine is to be made is carried out.

In case of aromatic halides, nucleophilic substitution is very difficult as:

\# ● There is a partial double p bond character between C and X due to resonance

also electronegativity of sp^2 carbon is higher and hence bond length is shorter.

Due to these breaking of C–X bond is difficult

● \# The ring itself is electron rich and thus the incoming nucleophile faces repulsion

Due to all the the nucleophilic attack is not possible and hence aromatic primary amines is not formed

Nu⁻ substitution step of Pthalimide synthesis

+ RNH₂

iii) Amines are basic (lewis) in nature due to presence of lone pair on nitrogen. Due to introduction of an alkyl group, the electron density on nitrogen increases due to inductive effect (+I) of alkyl and hence its lone pair can easily attack.

$$R \rightarrow \overset{R}{\underset{R}{N:}} \;>\; R \rightarrow \overset{R}{\underset{H}{N:}} \;>\; H - \overset{R}{\underset{H}{N:}} \;>\; NH_3$$

contains no alkyl group ∴ least basic.

(a) Aniline is basic in nature. It does not undergo Friedal-Crafts reaction due to salt formation with aluminium chloride, the Lewis acid, which is used as a catalyst. Anilinium ion is formed in which nitrogen of aniline acquires positive charge and hence acts as a strong deactivating group for further reaction. **(1 Mark)**

(b) Aromatic primary amines cannot be prepared by Gabriel phthalimide synthesis because aryl halides do not undergo nucleophilic substitution with the anion formed by phthalimide. **(1 Mark)**

(c) Aliphatic amines are stronger bases than ammonia due to + I effect of alkyl groups leading to high electron density on the nitrogen atom. **(1 Mark)**

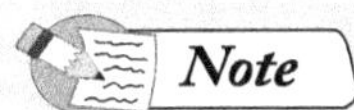

Note

Aromatic primary amines cannot be prepared by this method.

23. (a) (i) Aniline and ethanamine can be distinguished by the azo-dye test.

An orange dye is obtained when aniline reacts with ($NaNO_2$ + dil. HCl) at 0°–5°C followed by a reaction with alkaline solution of 2-naphthol.

Ethanamine gives a brisk effervescences with the same solution due to evolution of N_2 gas.

(ii) 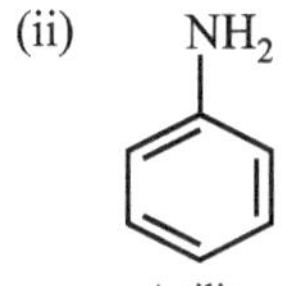

Only primary amines react with ($CHCl_3$ + KOH) to give a foul odour of isocyanide (carbylamine reaction). Hence, aniline will give this test but N-methylaniline will not. Also, aniline will form azo dye as in (i), but N-methylaniline will not form dye. **(1 + 1 = 2 Marks)**

(b) $CH_3 - CH_2 - CH_2 - CH_2 - OH$ (butanol)
$CH_3 - CH_2 - CH_2 - CH_2 - NH_2$ (butanamine)
$CH_3 - CH_2 - CH_2 - CH_3$ (butane)

Due to hydrogen bonding, the decreasing order of boiling point is:

Butanol > Butanamine > Butane **(1 Mark)**

24. (a)

(i) CH_3NH_2 and $(CH_3)_2NH$
Methyl amine   Dimethyl amine

Methyl amine, being a primary amine, undergoes carbylamine reaction (carbylamines have foul smell).

$$CH_3NH_2 + CHCl_3 + 3KOH \longrightarrow$$
$$CH_3NC + 3KCl + 3H_2O$$
Methylisocyanide
(carbylamine)

Dimethyl amine, a secondary amine, does not respond carbylamine reaction. **(1 Mark)**

(ii) $C_2H_5NH_2$ and $C_6H_5NH_2$
Ethanamine   Aniline

Aniline, a primary aromatic amine, when treated with a solution of sodium nitrite in dil. HCl at 273–278 K followed by treatment with an alkaline solution of β-naphthol gives an orange coloured dye (**azo dye test**).

$$\text{Ph}-NH_2 + HONO + HCl \xrightarrow[\text{(diazotisation)}]{273\text{-}278K}$$

$$\text{Ph}-\overset{+}{N} \equiv NCl^-$$
Benzene diazonium chloride

$$\text{Ph}-N^+ \equiv NCl^- + \text{β-Naphthol} \xrightarrow[\text{(Coupling)}]{\text{dil. NaOH}}$$
β-Naphthol

1-Phenylazo-2-naphthol
(**orange dye**)

Ethyl amine, a primary aliphatic amine, when treated with a solution of $NaNO_2$ in dil. HCl gives a primary alcohol along with a brisk evolution of N_2 gas.

$$C_2H_5NH_2 + HONO \xrightarrow{273-278K}$$
$$C_2H_5OH + N_2\uparrow + H_2O$$

(1 Mark)

(b)   Aniline, being a Lewis base, reacts with the Lewis acid ($AlCl_3$, catalyst for Friedel-Craft reaction) to form a salt. Thus the catalyst $AlCl_3$ is consumed. Moreover, the product has positive charge on N, which is deactivating for electrophilic substitution.

$$\underset{\substack{\text{Aniline (Lewis base)}\\\text{(having activating}\\\ddot{N}H_2\text{ group)}}}{\ddot{N}H_2} + \underset{\text{Lewis acid}}{AlCl_3} \longrightarrow \underset{\substack{\text{Salt}\\\text{(having deactivting}\\\overset{+}{N}H_2A\bar{l}Cl_3\text{ group)}}}{\overset{+}{N}H_2A\bar{l}Cl_3}$$

(1 Mark)

25.   Benzamide (A) $\xrightarrow[\substack{\text{Hoffman}\\\text{bromamide}\\\text{degradation}}]{\dfrac{Br_2}{KOH}}$ Aniline or Phenylamine (B) $\xrightarrow[\substack{\text{Carbylamine}\\\text{reaction}}]{\dfrac{CHCl_3}{KOH}}$ Phenylisocyanide (C)

(1 + 1 + 1 = 3 Marks)

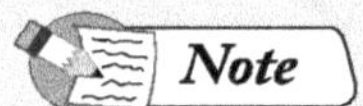

> ### Note
>
> *Carbylamine reaction is given by aliphatic and aromatic primary amine only.*

26.   (a) $CH_3COOH \xrightarrow{NH_3/\Delta} \underset{(A)}{CH_3CONH_2} \xrightarrow{Br_2/KOH(eq)}$

$\underset{(B)}{CH_3NH_2} \xrightarrow{CHCl_3 + \text{alc. KOH}} \underset{(C)}{CH_3NC}$

(½ + ½ + ½ = 1½ Marks)

(b) $\underset{}{C_6H_5N_2BF_4^+} \xrightarrow[\Delta]{NaNO_2/Cu} \underset{(A)}{C_6H_5NO_2}$

$\xrightarrow{Fe/HCl} \underset{(B)}{C_6H_5NH_2} \xrightarrow[\text{pyridine}]{CH_3COCl} \underset{(C)}{C_6H_5-NH-\overset{\overset{O}{\|}}{C}-CH_3}$

(½ + ½ + ½ = 1½ Marks)

27.   (a)   The lone pair present on nitrogen will get involved in resonance with the carbonyl group. Thus it will reduce the activation effect in aniline. The resonance is shown below.   **(1 Mark)**

$$\underset{H}{\overset{H}{>}}\ddot{N}-\overset{\overset{O}{\|}}{C}-CH_3 \longleftrightarrow \overset{+}{>}N=\overset{\overset{O^-}{|}}{C}-CH_3$$

(b)   Aniline may be regarded as a resonance hybrid of the following structures:

As a result of resonance, the lone pair of electrons on the nitrogen atom gets delocalized over the benzene ring and thus is less easily available for protonation. Therefore, aromatic amines are weaker bases than primary amine.   **(1 Mark)**

(c)   Nitration is carried out with a mixture of concentrated HNO_3 and concentrated H_2SO_4. Aniline gets protonated to form anilinium ion. Therefore, in presence of acids, the reaction mixture consists of aniline and anilinium ion. Nitration of aniline due to steric hindrance at ortho position mainly gives para nitroaniline and the nitration of anilinium ion gives m-nitroaniline as it is meta directing.

$$\text{Aniline} \xrightarrow{NO_2^+} \underset{\substack{p\text{-Nitroaniline}\\(51\%)}}{NO_2} + \underset{\substack{o\text{-Nitroaniline}\\(2\%)}}{NO_2}$$

$$\underset{\substack{\text{Anilinium}\\\text{ion}}}{\overset{+}{N}H_3} \xrightarrow{NO_2} \underset{\substack{m\text{-Nitroaniline}\\(47\%)}}{\xrightarrow{NH_4OH}}$$

Thus due to protonation of the amino group nitration of aniline gives a substantial amount of m-nitroaniline.   **(1 Mark)**

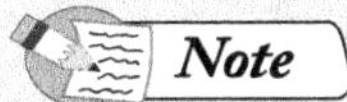

m-directing groups deactivate the -o and -p position but not affected the -m position. So electron density is enhanced at m-position, hence preferably electrophilic substitution reaction occurs at m-position, results substantial amount of m-derivative.

28. (i) Acetyl group is an electron withdrawing group which attracts the lone pair of electrons on the N-atom towards itself as a result, the activation effect of amino group is reduced.

Due to the resonance, the electron pair of nitrogen atom gets delocalised towards carbonyl group so activation effect is reduced.

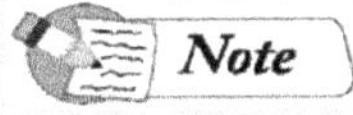

(1 Mark)

(ii) Due to resonance the lone pair of electron on the nitrogen in aniline get delocalised over benzene ring and electron density over nitrogen decreases thus making it less easily available for protonation. Hence aniline is weaker base than methyl amine.

(1 Mark)

> **Note**
>
> *The order of basic strength of amines in aqueous solution is as follows:*
> $(CH_3)_2NH > CH_3NH_2 > (CH_3)_3N > NH_3 > C_6H_5NH_2$

(iii) Nitration is carried out with a mixture of conc. HNO_3 and conc H_2SO_4, (acidic medium). So in the presence of these acids aniline protonated to form anilinium ion. Anilinium ion is m-directing and deactivating. Therefore the nitration of anilinium ion gives m-nitroaniline as major product.

(1 Mark)

> **Note**
>
> *Due to inductive effect anilinium nitrogen strongly withdraw electron density from the ortho position consequently deactivate the ortho position followed by meta and para position.*

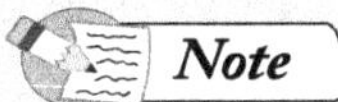

29. (i) Hoffmann bromamide degradation reaction

$$R-\overset{O}{\overset{\|}{C}}-NH_2 + Br_2 + 4NaOH \longrightarrow$$

$$R-NH_2 + Na_2CO_3 + 2NaBr + 2H_2O$$

(1 Mark)

> **Note**
>
> *The reaction is an example of molecular rearrangement and involves migration of an alkyl or aryl group from the carbon group to the adjacent nitrogen atom.*

(ii) Carbylamine reaction

$$R-NH_2 + CHCl_3 + 3KOH(alc.) \overset{\Delta}{\longrightarrow}$$
$$R-NC + 3KCl + 3H_2O \quad \textbf{(1 Mark)}$$

> **Note**
>
> *The carbylamine reaction, also known as Hoffmann's cyanide test, is a chemical test for the detection of primary amine.*

30. (i) Aniline forms salt with aluminium chloride, the catalyst of the Friedel-Crafts reaction. As a result, the nitrogen atom in aniline acquires a positive charge, which deactivates the benzene ring towards the electrophillic reaction. Thus, aniline does not undergo the Friedel-Crafts reaction. **(1 Mark)**

(ii) There are two factors that affect the basicity of the amines in an aqueous solution : solvation of ammonium ions and inductive effect. Inductive effect of the alkyl group is greater in $(CH_3)_3N$ than in $(CH_3)_2NH$. However, due to greater stabilisation by increased hydrogen bonding in $(CH_3)_2NH$ on solvation with water molecules, $(CH_3)_2NH$ is more basic than $(CH_3)_3N$. **(1 Mark)**

(iii) Primary amines are engaged in intermolecular association because of hydrogen bonding between nitrogen of one molecule and hydrogen of another molecule, as shown below.

On the other hand, no such interaction is possible in tertiary amines because of absence of the hydrogen atom directly attached to nitrogen. Therefore, due to stronger intermolecular forces, the boiling point of primary amines is higher than that of secondary amines. **(1 Mark)**

31. (i) The order of increasing basic strength is

$$C_6H_5NH_2 < C_6H_5NHCH_3 < C_6H_5CH_2NH_2$$

least basic   most basic   **(1 Mark)**

> **Note**
>
> e^- pair of N delocalised e^- pair on N, not delocalised e^- pair on N delocalised; $-CH_3$ group increases, e^- density on N due to $+I$ effect
>
> *A pair of electron of nitrogen in $C_6H_5CH_2.NH_2$ is available for donation.*

(ii) 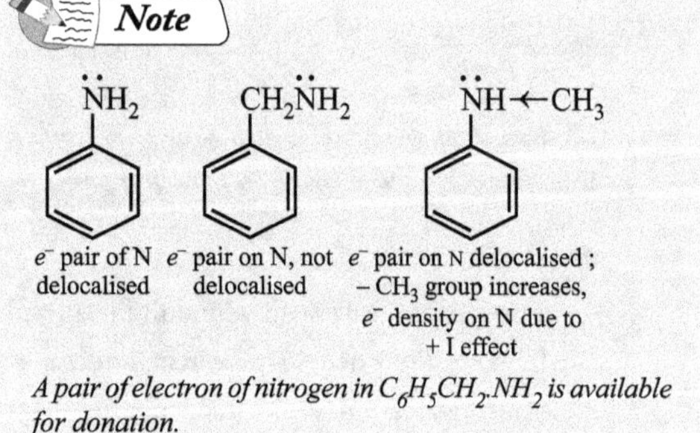

least basic (*p*-nitroaniline)   (aniline)   most basic (*p*-toluidine)

(1 Mark)

> **Note**
>
> *Nitro group is electron withdrawing hence reduces basic character, while methyl group is electron repelling hence increases basic character of aniline.*

32. (i) Benzamide $\xrightarrow[\text{(Hoffmann's bromamide reaction)}]{Br_2/NaOH}$ Aniline **(1 Mark)**

(ii) Aniline $\xrightarrow{NaNO_2/HCl}$ Benzenediazonium chloride $\xrightarrow{H_2O}$ Phenol **(1 Mark)**

(iii) $CH_3CH_2CN \xrightarrow{H_2O/H^+} CH_3CH_2COOH \xrightarrow[\Delta]{NH_3}$

Ethanenitrile   Propanoic acid

$CH_3CH_2CONH_2 \xrightarrow{Br_2/KOH} CH_3CH_2NH_2$

Propanamide   Ethylamine **(1 Mark)**

33. (i) Aniline $\xrightarrow{Br_2/H_2O}$ 2,4,6-Tribromoaniline **(1 Mark)**

(ii) Aniline $\xrightarrow{CHCl_3/KOH}$ Benzene isocyanide **(1 Mark)**

(iii) Aniline $\xrightarrow{HCl}$ Anilinium chloride **(1 Mark)**

34. (i) RNH_2 have higher boiling point than 3° amines (R_3N). This is because of intermolecular H-bonding in RNH_2 which is absent in 3° amines. **(1 Mark)**

(ii) Aniline being a Lewis base reacts with Lewis acid $(AlCl_3)$ to form a salt.

$$C_6H_5NH_2 + AlCl_3 \longrightarrow C_6H_5NH_2{}^+AlCl_3{}^-$$

As a result, N of aniline acquires positive charge and hence it acts as a strong deactivating group for electrophilic substitution reactions. Consequently, aniline does not undergo Fridel Crafts reaction.

(1 Mark)

(iii) $(CH_3)_2NH$ is a stronger base than $(CH_3)_3N$ in aqueous solution because in aqueous solution, basicity is controlled by three factors: +I-effect of alkyl group, H-bonding and steric factors. All these factors are favourable for 2° amines and hence 2°amines are strongest bases in solution. **(1 Mark)**

35. (i) $C_6H_5NO_2 \xrightarrow[HCl]{Sn} C_6H_5NH_2 \xrightarrow[273\ K]{NaNO_2 + HCl}$
$\qquad\qquad\qquad\qquad$ (A)

$C_6H_5N_2^+Cl^- \xrightarrow{H_2O} C_6H_5OH + N_2 + HCl$
$\quad$ (B) $\qquad\qquad$ (C)

(1½ Marks)

(ii) $CH_3CN \xrightarrow{H_2O/H^+} CH_3COOH \xrightarrow[\Delta]{NH_3}$
$\qquad\qquad\qquad\qquad$ (A)

$CH_3CONH_2 \xrightarrow{Br_2 + KOH} CH_3NH_2$
$\quad$ (B) $\qquad\qquad\qquad$ (C)

(½ + ½ + ½ = 1½ Marks)

36. (i) $CH_3Br \xrightarrow{KCN} CH_3CN \xrightarrow{LiAlH_4}$
$\qquad\qquad\qquad\qquad$ (A)

$CH_3CH_2NH_2 \xrightarrow{HNO_2}{273K} CH_3CH_2OH + N_2 + H^+$
$\quad$ (B) $\qquad\qquad\qquad\qquad$ (C)

(½ + ½ + ½ = 1½ Marks)

(ii) $CH_3COOH \xrightarrow[\Delta]{NH_3} CH_3CONH_2$
$\qquad\qquad\qquad\qquad$ (A)

$\xrightarrow[KOH]{Br_2} CH_3NH_2 \xrightarrow[NaOH]{CHCl_3} CH_3NC$
$\qquad\qquad$ (B) $\qquad\qquad$ (C)

(½ + ½ + ½ = 1½ Marks)

37. (i) Nitrobenzene into aniline

$$NO_2 \xrightarrow[HCl]{Fe} NH_2 + 2H_2O$$

(1 Mark)

(ii) Ethanoic acid to methanamine

$CH_3COOH \xrightarrow{SOCl_2} CH_3COCl$

$\xrightarrow{NH_3} CH_3CONH_2 \xrightarrow{Br_2/KOH} CH_3NH_2$

(1 Mark)

(iii) Aniline into N-phenylethanamide

$$NH_2 \xrightarrow[Pyridine]{(CH_3CO)_2O} HNCOCH_3$$

(1 Mark)

38. Compound "A" is p–methylnitrobenzene Compound 'B' is p– methylbenzenamine

Compound C is p–methylbenzenediazoiumchloride

Compound D – Toluene

Compound E – Benzaldehyde

The chemical reactions involved are

A (p-nitrotoluene, CH_3 / NO_2) $\xrightarrow{Sn/HCl}$ B (p-toluidine, CH_3 / NH_2) $\xrightarrow[0°C-5°C]{NaNO_2/HCl}$ C (diazonium salt, CH_3 / N_2Cl) $\xrightarrow{H_3PO_2}$ D (toluene, CH_3) $\xrightarrow[H_3O^+]{CrO_2Cl_2}$ E (benzaldehyde, $C-H$ with $=O$)

(1 mark for correct identification of A, 1 each for identification and reaction of formation of B, C, D and E from A)

39. **(a) (i)** The hydrogen attached to N–Ethylbenzene sulphonamide is acidic in nature. This is due to the presence of strong electron withdrawing sulphonyl group. Hence, it is soluble in alkali.

(1 Mark)

(ii) Reduction with iron scrap and hydrochloric acid is preferred because $FeCl_2$ formed gets hydrolysed to release hydrochloric acid during the reaction. Thus, only a small amount of hydrochloric acid is required to initiate the reaction. **(1 Mark)**

(b) (i) $C_6H_5NH_2 > C_6H_5NHCH_3 > NH_3 > C_6H_5CH_2NH_2 > CH_3NH_2$ **(1 Mark)**

(ii) $C_2H_5Cl < C_2H_5NH_2 < C_2H_5OH$ **(1 Mark)**

(iii) $CH_3COOH > C_2H_5OH > CH_3NH_2 > CH_3OCH_3$

(1 Mark)

40. (I) (i)

Aniline $\xrightarrow[H_2SO_4, 288k]{HNO_3,}$ p-nitroaniline (NH_2 / NO_2, 51%) + m-nitroaniline (NH_2 / NO_2, 47%) + o-nitroaniline (NH_2 / NO_2, 2%)

In a strong acidic medium, aniline gets protonated to form anilinium ion ($C_6H_5\overset{+}{N}H_3$) which is meta directing.

(1 Mark)

(ii) In aqueous solution $(CH_3)_3N$ is less basic than $(CH_3)_2NH$ due to the difficulty in solvation of tertiary amine group than secondary amine after protonation. Therefore, the instability of conjugate acids of t-amines leads to the less basicity.

$(CH_3)_3N \xrightarrow{H^+}$ Conjugate acid (less soluble in water)

$(CH_3)_2NH \xrightarrow{H^+}$ Conjugate acid (comparatively better solubility)

So, $(CH_3)_2NH$ is more basic than $(CH_3)_3N$.

(1 Mark)

(iii) $R-X + \overset{..}{N}H_3 \longrightarrow R\overset{+}{N}H_3X^- \longrightarrow RNH_2$ (1° amine)

Primary amine or 1° amine obtained by ammonolysis of alkyl halide further reacts as nucleophile to react with alkyl halide and leads to the formation of secondary and tertiary amines and finally, quaternary amines.

$R-NH_2 \xrightarrow{RX} R_2NH \xrightarrow{RX} R_3N \xrightarrow{RX} R_4\overset{+}{N}X^-$

(1 Mark)

(II) (i) Carbylamine Test or Isocyanide Test: This reaction is used for primary amine test.

$R-NH_2 + CHCl_3 + 3KOH \xrightarrow{\Delta} RNC + 3KCl + 3H_2O$ **(1 Mark)**

(ii) Gabriel Phthalimide Synthesis:

N-alkylphthalimide → $R — NH_2$ (1°-amine)

(1 Mark)

41. (a) (i) Aniline $\xrightarrow[\text{pyridine}]{(CH_3CO)_2O}$ NHCOCH₃ product

(1 Mark)

(ii) $\bigcirc—SO_2Cl \xrightarrow{(CH_3)_2NH}$

(1 Mark)

product with $S—N(CH_3)_2$

(iii) $N_2^+Cl^-$ compound $\xrightarrow{CH_3CH_2OH}$ benzene

(1 mark)

(b) Aniline and N, N-dimethylaniline can be distinguished using the **carbylamine** test :

Aniline being primary aromatic amine give a positive carbylamine test whereas N, N-dimethylaniline does not.

$C_6H_5NH_2 + CHCl_3 \xrightarrow{KOH}$ NC (Phenyl isocyanide) (foul smell)

$C_6H_5N(CH_3)_2 + CHCl_3 \xrightarrow{KOH}$ No reaction

(1 mark)

(c) $C_2H_5NH_2 < C_6H_5NH\,CH_3 < C_6H_5NH_2$ **(1 mark)**

Increasing order of pK_b : pK_b tells the strength of a base. Lower is pK_b value, stronger is the base. Now $C_6H_5NH_2$ is a weak base because the lone pair is involved in resonance with the benzene and is thus not available for donation while in $C_2H_5NH_2, C_2H_5$ is an electron donating group, which increases the e– density on N thus facilitating the release of lone pair. Hence, $C_2H_5NH_2$ is a strong base.

42. (a) (i) Aniline $\xrightarrow{Br_2\ water}$ 2,4,6-tribromoaniline

(1 Mark)

(ii) Aniline $\xrightarrow{HCl}$ $\overset{+}{N}H_3Cl^-$ compound

(1 Mark)

(iii) Aniline $\xrightarrow{(CH_3CO)_2O/Pyridine}$ NHCOCH₃ compound

(1 Mark)

(b) Increasing order of boiling point

$(CH_3)_2N < C_2H_5NH_2 < C_2H_5OH$ **(1 Mark)**

Alcohols have higher boiling point as compared to that of amines because of strong intermolecular hydrogen bond. Oxygen is more electronegative than nitrogen, so, it forms strong hydrogen bond as compared to nitrogen. In tertiary amine, there is no hydrogen atom to form hydrogen bond and hence, it has the lowest boiling point.

(c) $(CH_3)_2$ NH reacts with benzenesulphonyl chloride to give sulfonamides.

N, N-Dimethyl benzen sulphonamide

$(CH_3)_3$ N does not reacts with benzenesulphonyl chloride. **(1 Mark)**

43.

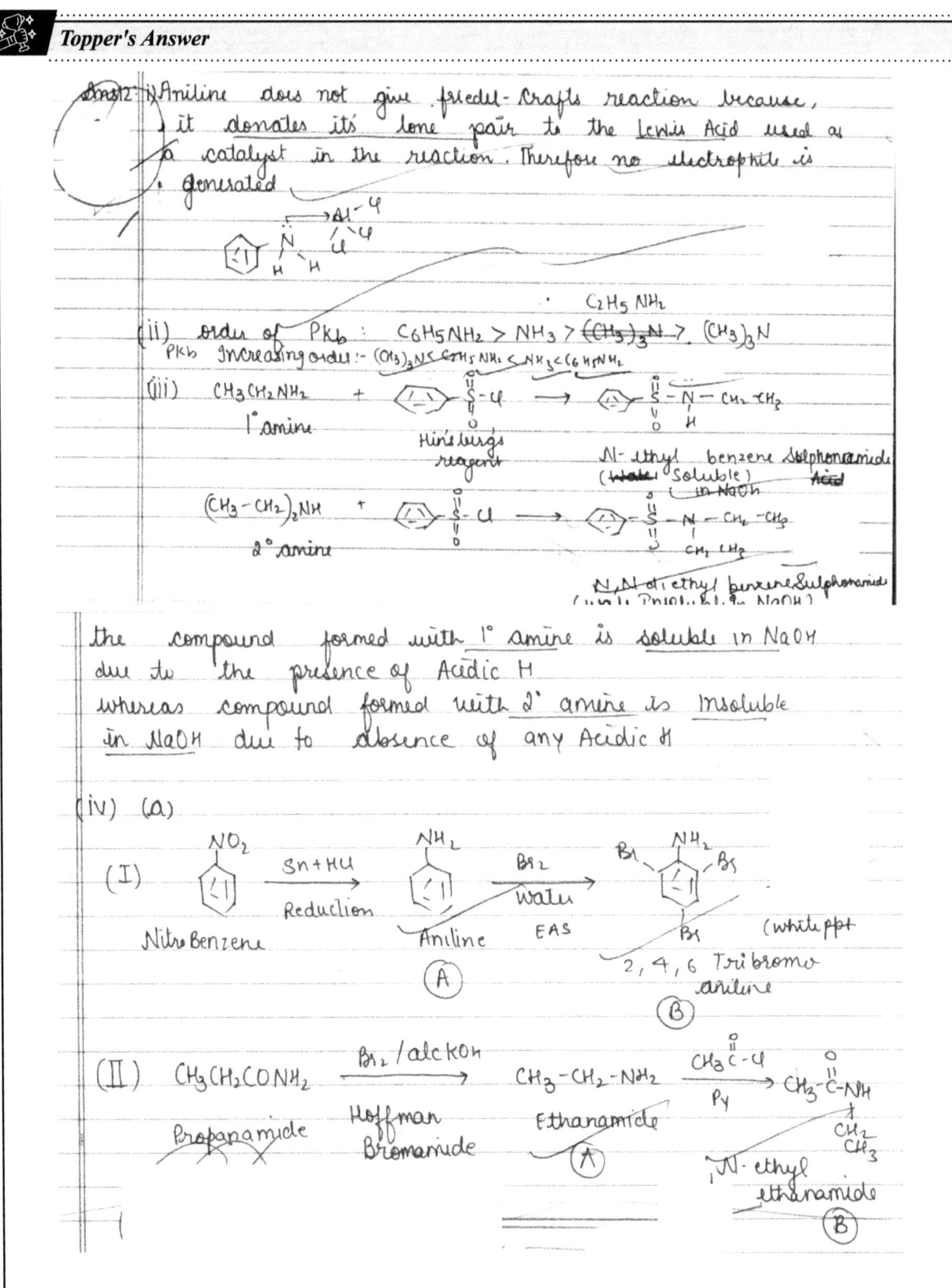

Topic-4: *Method of Preparation of Diazonium Salts, Physical Properties, Chemical Reactions, Importance of Diazonium Salts in Synthesis of Aromatic Compounds*

1. **(c)** When Benzene diazonium chloride reacts with phenol, it forms *p*-Hydroxyazobenzene (orange dye). This type of reaction is known as coupling reaction.

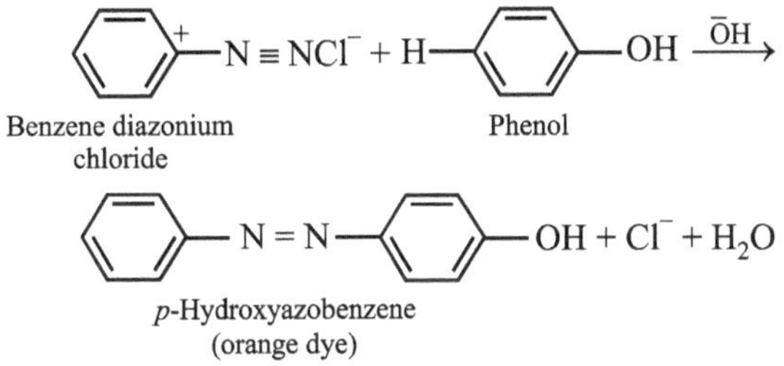

$$\underset{\substack{\text{Benzene diazonium}\\\text{chloride}}}{C_6H_5\overset{+}{-}N\equiv NCl^-} + H\underset{\text{Phenol}}{-C_6H_4-OH} \xrightarrow{\bar{O}H}$$

$$\underset{\substack{p\text{-Hydroxyazobenzene}\\\text{(orange dye)}}}{C_6H_5-N=N-C_6H_4-OH} + Cl^- + H_2O$$

(1 Mark)

2. The conversion of primary aromatic amines into diazonium salts is known as **diazotization.** **(1 Mark)**

3. **(i)** The zwitter ion structure of an amino acid is a dipolar ion and has both, amino and carboxylic groups (acidic) ionized.

The ionized form of sulphanilic acid has the following structure:

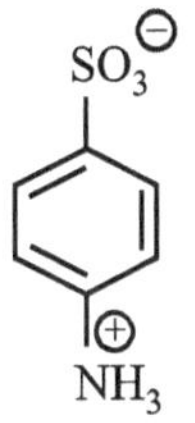

$$\overset{SO_3^{\ominus}}{\underset{\overset{\oplus}{NH_3}}{C_6H_4}}$$

(1 Mark)

(ii) The activating effect of $-NH_2$ group in aniline can be controlled by protecting it by acetylation.

(1 Mark)

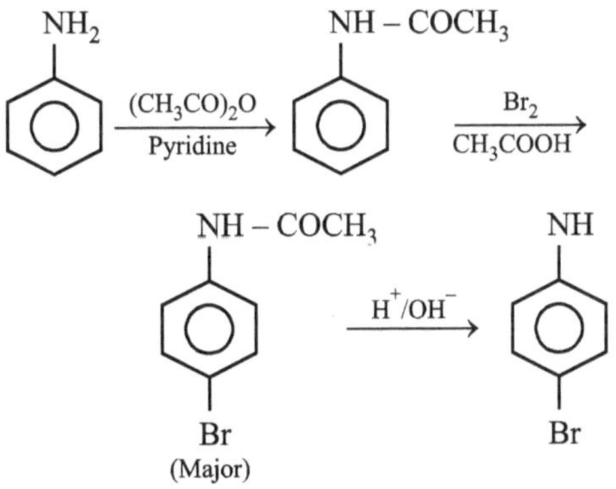

$$\underset{NH_2}{C_6H_5} \xrightarrow[\text{Pyridine}]{(CH_3CO)_2O} \underset{NH-COCH_3}{C_6H_5} \xrightarrow[CH_3COOH]{Br_2}$$

$$\underset{\substack{NH-COCH_3\\\\Br\\(Major)}}{C_6H_4} \xrightarrow{H^+/OH^-} \underset{\substack{NH\\\\Br}}{C_6H_4}$$

4. **(i)** The given reaction is an electrophilic substitution reaction that involves replacement of N_2^+ by H^+.

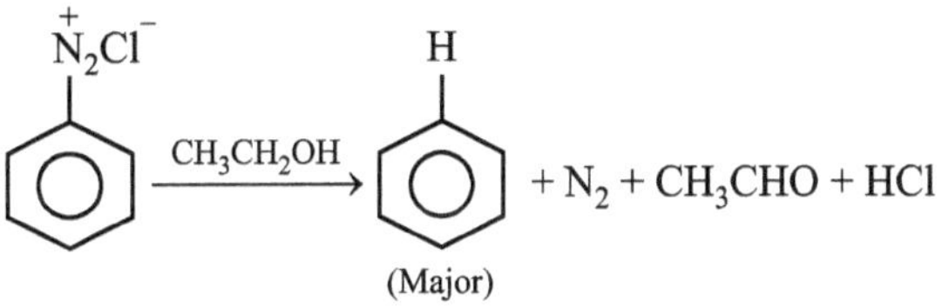

$$\underset{\overset{+}{N_2Cl^-}}{C_6H_5} \xrightarrow{CH_3CH_2OH} \underset{\substack{H\\(Major)}}{C_6H_5} + N_2 + CH_3CHO + HCl$$

(1 Mark)

(ii) The conversion requires one extra carbon atom and the replacement of bromo group by amino group.

$$\underset{\text{Bromo ethane}}{CH_3CH_2-Br} \xrightarrow[\text{(aq.)}]{KCN} CH_3CH_2-CN \xrightarrow{LiAlH_4}$$

$$\underset{\text{Propanamine}}{CH_3CH_2-CH_2-NH_2}$$

(1 Mark)

5. **(a)** **Sandmeyer's reaction:**

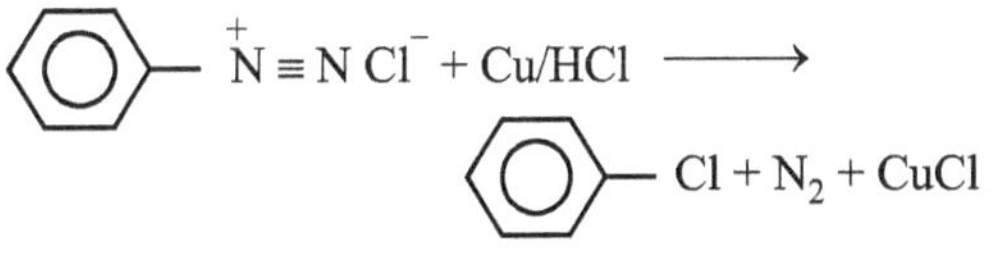

$$C_6H_5-\overset{+}{N}\equiv N\ Cl^- + Cu/HCl \longrightarrow$$

$$C_6H_5-Cl + N_2 + CuCl$$

(1 Mark)

(b) In aqueous solutions, factors like hydrogen bonding and stabilization of the conjugate acid determine the strength of the amine. **(1 Mark)**

$(CH_3)_2\,NH$ is a secondary amine while $(CH_3)_3N$ is a tertiary amine.

Due to the absence of a hydrogen atom on nitrogen for hydrogen bonding in $(CH_3)_3N$, which is available in $(CH_3)_2\,NH$, and steric factors along with the effect of Inductive effect, the secondary amine $(CH_3)_2\,NH$ is more basic than primary and tertiary amine $(CH_3)_3N$. **(1 Mark)**

6. **(a)** $CH_3-COOH + NH_3 \longrightarrow$

$$CH_3COO^-NH_4^+ \xrightarrow[-H_2O]{\Delta}$$

$$\underset{(A)}{CH_3-CO-NH_2} \xrightarrow{NaOBr} \underset{(B)}{CH_3-NH_2}$$

(½ + ½ = 1 Mark)

Note

Conversion of A to B is Hofmann Degradation reaction.

Step 1:

$$R-\overset{\overset{O}{\|}}{C}-\underset{\underset{H}{|}}{N}-H \overset{OH^-}{\rightleftharpoons} R-\overset{\overset{O}{\|}}{C}-\underset{\underset{H}{|}}{N^-} \overset{Br-Br}{\longrightarrow} R-\overset{\overset{O}{\|}}{C}-\underset{\underset{H}{|}}{N}-Br + Br^-$$

Step 2:

$$R-\overset{\overset{O}{\|}}{C}-\underset{\underset{H}{|}}{N}-Br \overset{OH^-}{\rightleftharpoons} R-\overset{\overset{O}{\|}}{C}-\overset{\cdot\cdot}{N}-Br \overset{-Br^-}{\longrightarrow}$$

$$R-N=C=O$$
Isocyanate

Step 3:

$$R-N=C=O \overset{OH^-}{\longrightarrow} R-\overset{\cdot\cdot}{N}-\overset{\overset{OH}{|}}{C}-O \rightleftharpoons$$

$$R-\underset{\underset{H}{|}}{N}-\overset{\overset{O^-}{|}}{C}-O \overset{H^+}{\longrightarrow} R-NH_2 + CO_2$$

(b)

$$\underset{(A)}{\overset{NO_2}{\bigcirc}} \overset{Fe/HCl}{\longrightarrow} \underset{}{\overset{NH_2}{\bigcirc}} \overset{NaNO_2\ +HCl}{\underset{0°-5°C}{\longrightarrow}} \underset{(B)}{\overset{\overset{+}{N}\equiv NCl^-}{\bigcirc}}$$

(½ + ½ = 1 Mark)

(c)

$$\underset{(A)}{\overset{N_2^+Cl^-}{\bigcirc}} \overset{CuCN}{\underset{\Delta}{\longrightarrow}} \underset{(A)}{\overset{CN}{\bigcirc}} \overset{H_2O/H^+}{\longrightarrow} \underset{(B)}{\overset{COOH}{\bigcirc}}$$

(½ + ½ = 1 Mark)

7.

Topper's Answer

21.(i)
⊕N≡N Cl⊖
CuCN / KCN
CN
main product
(ii)
⊕N≡N Cl⊖
CH₃CH₂OH
main product
(iii)
⊕N≡N Cl⊖
KI
I
main product

8. (i) $C_6H_5CO\,NH_2 \xrightarrow{Br_2/aq.\ KOH} C_6H_5NH_2$
(A)
Aniline

$\xrightarrow{NaNO_2 + HCl} C_6H_5N_2^+Cl^- \xrightarrow{KI} C_6H_5I$
(B) (C)
Benzene Iodobenzene
diazonium
chloride

$$(\tfrac{1}{2} + \tfrac{1}{2} + \tfrac{1}{2} = 1\tfrac{1}{2}\ \textbf{Mark})$$

(ii) $CH_3Cl \xrightarrow{KCN} CH_3CN \xrightarrow{LiAlH_2} CH_3CH_2NH_2$
(A) (B)
Ethanenitrile Ethanamine

$\xrightarrow{CHCl_3 + alc.\ KOH} CH_3CH_2NC$
(C)
Ethyl
isocynide

$$(\tfrac{1}{2} + \tfrac{1}{2} + \tfrac{1}{2} = 1\tfrac{1}{2}\ \textbf{Mark})$$

9. (i) $CH_3CH_2NH_2 + CHCl_3 + 3\ KOH\ (alc.) \longrightarrow$

$CH_3CH_2N{\equiv}C + 3KCl + 3H_2O$
Ethylisocyanide

$$(\textbf{1 Mark})$$

(ii) $C_6H_5N_2^+Cl^- \xrightarrow[\text{Room temp.}]{H_2O} C_6H_5OH + N_2 + HCl$
Phenol

$$(\textbf{1 Mark})$$

(iii) 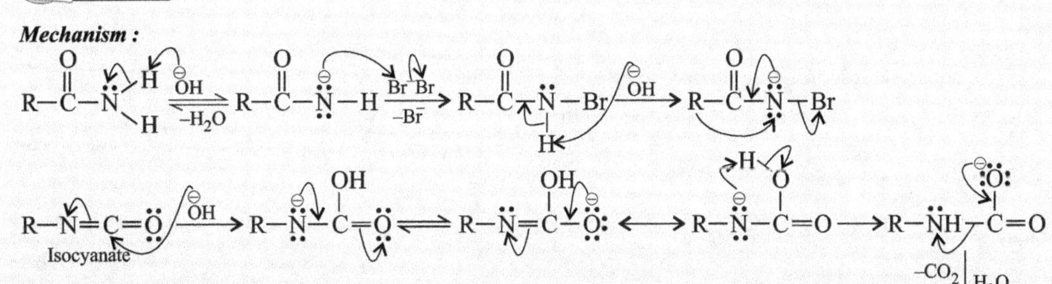

$$(\textbf{1 Mark})$$

10. (i) $C_6H_5N_2^+Cl^- \xrightarrow{CuCN} C_6H_5CN \xrightarrow{H_2O/H^+}$
(A)

$C_6H_5COOH \xrightarrow[\Delta]{NH_3} C_6H_5CONH_2$
(B) (C)

$$(\tfrac{1}{2} + \tfrac{1}{2} + \tfrac{1}{2} = 1\tfrac{1}{2}\ \textbf{Marks})$$

(ii) $C_6H_5NO_2 \xrightarrow{Sn+HCl} C_6H_5NH_2 \xrightarrow[273K]{NaNO_2+HCl}$
(A)

$C_6H_5N_2^+Cl^- \xrightarrow[\Delta]{H_2O/H^+} C_6H_5OH$
(B) (C)

$$(\tfrac{1}{2} + \tfrac{1}{2} + \tfrac{1}{2} = 1\tfrac{1}{2}\ \textbf{Marks})$$

11. (I) (i)

$$(\textbf{1½ Marks})$$

(ii)

$$(\textbf{1½ Marks})$$

(II) Aniline acts as Lewis base and forms salt with Lewis acid ($AlCl_3$) used in Friedel Craft reaction.

$$(\textbf{1 Mark})$$

(III) C_2H_5OH, $C_2H_5NH_2$, $(C_2H_5)_3N$
(I) (II) (III)
78.37°C 16 – 20°C 88.6 – 89.8°C

Boiling pt. $\propto$ molecular wt.; $\propto$ H-bonded substance

$\therefore$ order = (II) < (I) < (III) $\qquad$ $(\textbf{1 Mark})$

12. (a) The reaction involed in :

(i) **Hoffmann bromamide degradation reaction:**

$R - \overset{\overset{\displaystyle O}{||}}{C} - NH_2 + Br_2 + 4NaOH \longrightarrow$
$R - NH_2 + Na_2CO_3 + 2NaBr + 2H_2O$

$$(\textbf{1 Mark})$$

Note

Mechanism :

(ii) Diazotisation :

$$\underset{\text{(Aniline)}}{C_6H_5NH_2} + NaNO_2 + 2HCl \xrightarrow{273\text{-}278K}$$

$$C_6H_5\overset{+}{N_2}Cl^- + NaCl + 2H_2O$$

(1 Mark)

(iii) Gabriel phthalimide synthesis :

Phthalimide $\xrightarrow{\text{KOH (alc)}}$

$$\text{Phthalimide} \xrightarrow{\text{KOH (alc)}}$$

$$\xrightarrow[S_N2]{R-X}$$

Phthalimide + R—NH₂ (1° amine)

(1 Mark)

(b) (i) In aqueous solution, the factors controlling basicity of amines are inductive effect, solvation effect and steric hindrance of the alkyl group. Based on these, $(CH_3)_2NH$ is found to be more basic than $(CH_3)_3N$. **(1 Mark)**

$$C_6H_5NH_2 \xrightarrow[\text{pyridine}]{(CH_3CO)_2O} C_6H_5NHCOCH_3$$

(ii) Aromatic diazonium salts are more stable than aliphatic diazonium salts. The stability of aromatic diazonium salts is due to resonance which is absent in aliphatic diazonium salts. **(1 Mark)**

13. (a)

$$\underset{(A)}{C_6H_5CONH_2} \xrightarrow{Br_2/KOH} \underset{(A)}{C_6H_5NH_2} \xrightarrow[273\ K]{NaNO_2/HCl} \underset{(B)}{C_6H_5\overset{+}{N_2}Cl^-}$$

$$C_6H_5NH_2 \xrightarrow{CHCl_3 + NaOH} \underset{(D)}{C_6H_5NC}$$

$$\underset{(B)}{C_6H_5\overset{+}{N_2}Cl^-} \xrightarrow{CH_3CH_2OH} \underset{(C)}{C_6H_6}$$

$$\underset{(B)}{C_6H_5\overset{+}{N_2}Cl^-} \xrightarrow{KI} \underset{(E)}{C_6H_5I}$$

(1 + 1 + 1 + 1 + 1 = 5 Marks)

Chapter 10 — Biomolecules

1   *Multiple Choice Questions*

1. When D-glucose reacts with HI, it forms

[All India 2023, Set-I, K]

  (a) Gluconic acid   (b) n-hexane

  (c) Saccharic acid   (d) Iodohexane

2. Which of the following statements is not true about glucose?   **[Delhi 2023, Set-I, K]**

  (a) It is an aldohexose

  (b) On heating with HI it forms n-hexane

  (c) It is present in pyranose form

  (d) It gives 2, 4 DNP test

3. Hydrolysis of sucrose is called   **[Delhi 2023 Set-I, K]**

  (a) inversion   (b) hydration

  (c) esterification   (d) saponification

4. Which of the following sugar is known as dextrose ?

[All India 2022, Term-I, K]

  (a) Glucose   (b) Fructose

  (c) Ribose   (d) Sucrose

5. Glucose on reaction with Br_2 water gives :

[All India 2022, Term-I, K]

  (a) Saccharic acid   (b) Hexanoic acid

  (c) Gluconic acid   (d) Salicyclic acid

6. Which one of the following reactions is not explained by the open chain structure of glucose:

[CBSE Sample 2021-22, Term-I, K]

  (a) Formation of pentaacetate of glucose with acetic anhydride.

  (b) formation of addition product with 2,4 DNP reagent.

  (c) Silver mirror formation with Tollen's reagent.

  (d) existence of alpha and beta forms of glucose.

7. Which one of the following statement is correct about sucrose: **[CBSE Sample 2021-22, Term-I, K]**

  (a) It can reduce tollen's reagent however cannot reduce fehling's reagent

  (b) It undergoes mutarotation like glucose and fructose

  (c) It undergoes inversion in the configuration on hydrolysis

  (d) It is laevorotatory in nature .

8. In the following reaction, identify A and B:

[All India 2021-22, Term-I, U]

$$C_6H_{12}O_6 \xrightarrow{\text{Acetic anhydride}} A$$

$$\Big| \text{Conc.nitric acid}$$

$$B$$

  (a) $A = COOH - (CH_2)_4 - COOH,\ B = OHC - (CHOCOCH_3)_4 - CH_2OCOCH_3$

  (b) $A = COOH - (CH_2)_4 - CHO,\ B = OHC - (CHOCOCH_3)_4 - CH_2OCOCH_3$

  (c) $A = OHC - (CHOCOCH_3)_3 - CH_2OCOCH_3,\ B = COOH - (CH_2)_4 - CHO$

  (d) $A = OHC - (CHOCOCH_3)_4 - CH_2OCOCH_3,\ B = COOH - (CH_2)_4 - COOH$

9. Which one of the following reactions is not explained by the open chain Structure of glucose:

[CBSE Sample 2021-22, U]

(a) Formation of pentaacetate of glucose with acetic anhydride.

(b) formation of addition product with 2,4 DNP reagent.

(c) Silver mirror formation with Tollen's reagent.

(d) existence of alpha and beta forms of glucose.

10. Which of the following is a polysaccharide?

[CBSE Sample 2021-22, K]

(a) glucose   (b) maltose

(c) glycogen   (d) lactose

11. Which one of the following statement is correct about sucrose: **[CBSE Sample 2021-22, U]**

(a) It can reduce tollen's reagent however cannot reduce fehling's reagent

(b) It undergoes mutarotation like glucose and fructose

(c) It undergoes inversion in the configuration on hydrolysis

(d) It is laevorotatory in nature .

12. In the following reaction, identify A and B:

[CBSE Sample 2021-22, U]

$$C_6H_{12}O_6 \xrightarrow{\text{Acetic anhydride}} A$$

Conc.nitric acid

B

(a) $A = COOH-(CH_2)_4-COOH, B = OHC-(CHOCOCH_3)_4-CH_2OCOCH_3$

(b) $A = COOH - (CH_2)_4 - CHO, B = OHC - (CHOCOCH_3)_4 - CH_2OCOCH_3$

(c) $A = OHC - (CHOCOCH_3)_3 - CH_2OCOCH_3, B = COOH - (CH_2)_4 - CHO$

(d) $A = OHC - (CHOCOCH_3)_4 - CH_2OCOCH_3, B = COOH - (CH_2)_4 - COOH$

13. Dissachrides that are reducing in nature are:

[CBSE Sample 2020-21, K]

(a) sucrose and lactose

(b) sucrose and maltose

(c) lactose and maltose

(d) sucrose, lactose and maltose

2   *Assertion Reason/Two Statement Type Questions*

Given below are two statements labelled as Assertion (A) and Reason (R). Select the most appropriate answer from the options given below:

(a) Both (A) and (R) are true and (R) is the correct explanation of (A).

(b) Both (A) and (R) are true, but (R) is not the correct explanation of (A).

(c) (A) is true, but (R) is false.

(d) (A) is false, but (R) is true.

14. **Assertion (A) :** Sucrose is a non-reducing sugar.

[All India 2020, K]

Reason (R) : Sucrose has glycosidic linkage.

4   *Very Short Answer Questions (1 Mark)*

15. What type of linkage is present in polysaccharides?

[Delhi 2020, K]

16. What is the basic structural difference between glucose and fructose?   **[Delhi 2019, K]**

17. Write the products obtained after hydrolysis of lactose.

[Delhi 2019, K]

18. What are the products of hydrolysis of sucrose?

[All India 2014, K]

19. Which of the two components of starch is water soluble ?

[Delhi 2014, K]

20. What are the products of hydrolysis of sucrose?

[All India 2013, K]

 **Short Answer Questions (2 or 3 Marks)**

21. When sucrose is hydrolysed the optical rotation values are measured using a polarimeter and are given in the following table: **[CBSE Sample 2023-24, Ap]**

S.No.	Time (hours)	Specific Rotation
1	0	$+66.5°$
2	∞	$-39.9°$

(a) Account for the two specific rotation values.

(b) What is the specific name given to sucrose based on the above observation.

(c) One of the products formed during the hydrolysis of sucrose is a glucose, that reacts with hydroxylamine to give compound A. Identify compound A.

22. Give the reaction of heating glucose with hydroxylamine. Presence of which group is confirmed by this reaction?

[Delhi 2023 Set-III, K]

23. Give the reaction of glucose with hydrogen cyanide. Presence of which group is confirmed by this reaction?

[Delhi 2023 Set-II, K]

24. Give the reaction of glucose with acetic anhydride. Presence of which group is confirmed by this reaction?

[Delhi 2023, Set-I, K]

25. Account for the following: **[CBSE Sample 2022-23, U]**

(a) There are 5 OH groups in glucose

(b) Glucose is a reducing sugar

26. What happens when D-glucose is treated with the following reagents **[CBSE Sample 2022-23, U]**

(a) Bromine water

(b) HNO_3

27. Give the plausible explanation for the following:

[All India 2020, U]

(a) Glucose doesn't give 2,4-DNP test.

(b) The two strands in DNA are not identical but are complementary.

(c) Starch and cellulose both contain glucose unit as monomer, yet they are structurally different.

 **Topic-2:** **Proteins, Enzymes**

 **Multiple Choice Questions**

1. Protein are polymers of **[All India 2023 Set-II, K]**

(a) Nucleic acids

(b) Amino acids

(c) Monosaccharides

(d) Amines

2. β-pleated sheet structue in proteins refers to

[Delhi 2023 Set-III, K]

(a) primary structure

(b) secondary structure

(c) tertiary structure

(d) quaternary structure

3. Amino acids which cannot be synthesized in the body and must be obtained through diet are known as

[All India 2022, Term-I, K]

(a) Acidic amino acids

(b) Essential amino acids

(c) Basic amino acids

(d) Non-essential amino acids

4. Complete the following analogy :

[All India 2022, Term-I, K]

Curdling of milk : A :: α-helix : B

(a) A : Primary structure   B : Secondary structure

(b) A : Denatured protein   B : Primary structure

(c) A : Secondary structure   B : Denatured protein

(d) A : Denatured protein   B : Secondary structure

5. Which of the following statement is correct:

[CBSE Sample 2021-22, Term-I, U]

(a) Fibrous proteins are generally soluble in water

(b) Albumin is an example of fibrous proteins

(c) In fibrous proteins, the structure is stabilised by hydrogen bonds and disulphide bonds

(d) pH does not affect the primary structure of protein.

6. Which of the following statement is correct:

[CBSE Sample 2021-22, U]

(a) Fibrous proteins are generally soluble in water

(b) Albumin is an example of fibrous proteins

(c) In fibrous proteins, the structure is stabilised by hydrogen bonds and disulphide bonds

(d) pH does not affect the primary structure of protein.

7. Curdling of milk is an example of:

[CBSE Sample 2020-21, K]

(a) breaking of peptide linkage

(b) hydrolysis of lactose

(c) breaking of protein into amino acids

(d) denauration of proetin

8. Amino acids are   **[Delhi 2020, Set-I]**

(a) acidic   (b) basic

(c) amphoteric   (d) neutral

2   *Assertion Reason/Two Statement Type Questions*

Given below are two statements labelled as Assertion (A) and Reason (R). Select the most appropriate answer from the options given below:

(a) Both (A) and (R) are true and (R) is the correct explanation of (A).

(b) Both (A) and (R) are true, but (R) is not the correct explanation of (A).

(c) (A) is true, but (R) is false.

(d) (A) is false, but (R) is true.

9. **Assertion (A):** Enzymes are very specific for a particular reaction and for a particular substrate.

Reason (R): Enzymes are biocatalysts.

[CBSE Sample 2023-24, U]

10. **Assertion (A):** Proteins are polymers of α-amino acids connected by a peptide bond.   **[Delhi 2023 Set-I, K]**

Reason (R): A tetrapeptide contains 4 amino acids linked by 4 peptide bonds.

11. **Assertion (A):** Proteins are found to have two different types of secondary structures viz alpha-helix and beta-pleated sheet structure.

Reason (R): The secondary structure of proteins is stabilized by hydrogen bonding.

[CBSE Sample 2022-23, U]

5   *Short Answer Questions (2 or 3 Marks)*

12. Define the following terms with a suitable example in each: **[Delhi 2020, K]**

(a) Polysaccharides

(b) Denatured protein

(c) Fibrous protein

13. Differentiate between following :   **[Delhi 2020, Set-I]**

(i) Amylose and Amylopectin

(ii) Globular protein and Fibrous protein

(iii) Nucleotide and Nucleoside

14. Differentiate between the following: **[Delhi 2019, K]**

(i) Amylose and Amylopectin

(ii) Peptide linkage and Glycosidic linkage

(iii) Fibrous proteins and Globular proteins

15. Write chemical reactions to show that open structure of D-glucose contains the following: **[Delhi 2019, K]**

(i) Straight chain

(ii) Five alcohol groups

(iii) Aldehyde as carbonyl group

16. Define the following with an example of each :

[All India 2018, K]

(a) Polysaccharides

(b) Denatured protein

(c) Essential amino acids

17. (a) Write the product when D-glucose react with conc. HNO$_3$. **[Delhi 2019, K]**

(b) Amino acids show amphoteric behaviour. Why?

(c) Write one difference between α-helix and β-pleated structures of proteins.

18. Define the following terms as related to proteins:

(i) Peptide linkage

(ii) Primary structure

(iii) Denaturation

[All India 2014, K]

  **Topic-3: *Vitamins, Nucleic Acids, Hormones***

1 *Multiple Choice Questions*

1. The vitamins which can be stored in our body are:

[CBSE Sample 2023-24, K]

(a) Vitamin A, B, D and E

(b) Vitamin A, C, D and K

(c) Vitamin A, B, C and D

(d) Vitamin A, D, E and K

2. Nucleosides are composed of

[All India 2022, Term-I, K]

(a) a pentose sugar and phosphoric acid

(b) a nitrogenous base and phosphoric acid

(c) a nitrogenous base and a pentose sugar

(d) a nitrogenous base, a pentose sugar and phosphoric acid

3. The base which is present in DNA but not in RNA, is

[All India 2022, Term-I, K]

(a) Cytosine

(b) Guanine

(c) Adenine

(d) Thymine

4. Nucleic acids are polymer of

[All India 2022, Term-I, K]

(a) amino acids

(b) nucleosides

(c) nucleotides

(d) glucose

2 *Assertion Reason/Two Statement Type Questions*

Given below are two statements labelled as Assertion (A) and Reason (R). Select the most appropriate answer from the options given below:

(a) Both (A) and (R) are true and (R) is the correct explanation of (A).

(b) Both (A) and (R) are true, but (R) is not the correct explanation of (A).

(c) (A) is true, but (R) is false.

(d) (A) is false, but (R) is true.

5. **Assertion (A) :** Vitamin C cannot be stored in our body.

Reason (R) : Vitamin C is fat soluble and is excreted from the body in urine. **[Delhi 2023, K]**

6. **Assertion (A):** The backbone of DNA and RNA molecules is a chain consisting of heterocyclic base, pentose sugar nd phosphate group. **[Delhi 2023 Set-3, U]**

Reason (R): Nucleotides and nucleosides mainly differ from each other in presence of phosphate group.

7. **Assertion:** The two strands of DNA are complementary to each other **[CBSE Sample 2020-21, U]**

Reason: The hydrogen bonds are formed between specific pairs of bases.

3 — Matching Based Questions

8. Match the following: [CBSE Sample 2021-22, **K**]

	I		II
(i)	Amino acids	(A)	Protein
(ii)	Thymine	(B)	Nucleic acid
(iii)	Insulin	(C)	DNA
(iv)	Phosphodiester linkage	(D)	Zwitter ion
(v)	Uracil		

Which of the following is the best matched options?

(a) (i) – A; (v) – D; (iii) – C; (iv) – B

(b) (i) – D; (ii) – C; (iii) – A; (iv) – B

(c) (i) – D; (v) – D; (iii) – A; (iv) – B

(d) (i) – A; (ii) – C; (iii) – D; (iv) – B

4 — Very Short Answer Questions (1 Mark)

9. What are three types of RNA molecules which perform different functions? [Delhi 2013, **K**]

5 — Short Answer Questions (2 or 3 Marks)

10. (a) DNA fingerprinting is used to determine paternity of an individual. Which property of DNA helps in the procedure? [CBSE Sample 2023-24, **U**]

(b) What structural change will occur when a native protein is subjected to change in pH?

11. What are nucleic acids? Why two strands in DNA are not identical but are complementary?

[All India 2023, Set-I, **K**]

12. (a) What is the difference between a nucleoside and nucelotide? [All India 2023 Set-II, **K**]

(b) What products would be formed when a nucleotide from DNA containing thymine is hydrolysed?

13. Give reasons for any 3 of the following observations:

[Delhi 2023, Set-I, **U**]

(a) Penta-acetate of glucose does not react with hydroxylamine.

(b) Amino acids behave like salts.

(c) Water soluble vitamins must be taken regularly in diet.

(d) The two strands in DNA are complimentary to each other.

14. (a) What is the difference between native protein and denatured protein? [All India2019, **K**]

(b) Which one of the following is a disaccharide : Glucose, Lactose, Amylose, Fructose

(c) Write the name of the vitamin responsible for the coagulation of blood.

15. (i) Write the structural difference between starch and cellulose.

(ii) What type of linkage is present in nucleic acids ?

(iii) Give one example each for fibrous protein and globular protein. [All India 2016, **K**]

16. (i) Write the name of two monosaccharides obtained on hydrolysis of lactose sugar. [Delhi 2016, **K**]

(ii) Why Vitamin C cannot be stored in our body ?

[Delhi 2015, **K**]

(iii) What is the difference between a nucleoside and nucleotide ? [Delhi 2015, **K**]

17. (i) Write the product obtained when D-glucose reacts with H_2N –OH. [All India 2015, **K**]

(ii) Amino acids show amphoteric behaviour. Why?

[Delhi 2015, **K**]

(iii) Why cannot vitamin C be stored in our body?

[Delhi 2015, **K**]

18. (i) Which one of the following is a disaccharide : Starch, Maltose, Fructose, Glucose ? [Delhi 2015, **K**]

(ii) What is the difference between fibrous protein and globular protein ? [Delhi 2015, **K**]

(iii) Write the name of vitamin whose deficiency causes bone deformities in children. [Delhi 2015, **K**]

19. (i) Deficiency of which vitamin causes night blindless?

[Delhi 2014, ]

(ii) Name the base that is found in nucleotide of RNA only. [Delhi 2014, K]

(iii) Glucose on reaction with HI gives n-hexane. What does it suggest about the structure of glucose ?

[Delhi 2014, K]

7 *Case Based Questions*

20. Carbohydrates are optically active polyhydroxy aldehyde and ketones. They are also called saccharides. All these carbohydrates which reduce. Fehling's solution and Tollen's reagent are referred to as reducing sugar. Glucose, the most important source of energy for mammals is obtained by the hydrolysis of starch. Vitamins are necessary food factors required in the diet. Proteins are the polymers of amino acids and perform various structural and dynamic functions in the organisms. Deficiency of vitamins leads to many diseases.

Answer the following: [All India 2023, Set-I, K]

(a) The penta-acetate of glucose does not react with Hydroxylamine. What does it indicate?

(b) Why cannot vitamin C be stored in our body?

(c) Define the following as related to proteins.

(i) Peptide linkage [All India 2023, Set-I, K]

(ii) Denaturation

OR

(c) Define the following as related to carbohydrates:

(i) Anomers [All India 2023, Set-I, K]

(ii) Glycoside linkage

21. Strengthening the Foundation: Chargaff Formulates His "Rules"

Many people believe that James Watson and Francis Crick discovered DNA in the 1950s. In reality, this is not the case. Rather, DNA was first identified in the late 1860s by Swiss chemist Friedrich Miescher. Then, in the decades following Miescher's discovery, other scientists–notably, Phoebus Levene and Erwin Chargaff- -carried out a series of research efforts that revealed additional details about the DNA molecule, including its primary chemical components and the ways in which they joined with one another. Without the scientific foundation provided by these pioneers, Watson and Crick may never have reached their groundbreaking conclusion of 1953: that the DNA molecule exists in the form of a three-dimensional double helix.

Chargaff, an Austrian biochemist, as his first step in this DNA research, set out to see whether there were any differences in DNA among different species. After developing a new paper chromatography method for separating and identifying small amounts of organic material, Chargaff reached two major conclusions:

[CBSE Sample 2022-23, A]

(i) the nucleotide composition of DNA varies among species.

(ii) Almost all DNA, no matter what organism or tissue type it comes from maintains certain properties, even as its composition varies. In particular, the amount of adenine (A) is similar to the amount of thymine (T), and the amount of guanine (G) approximates the amount of cytosine (C). In other words, the total amount of purines $(A + G)$ and the total amount of pyrimidines $(C + T)$ are usually nearly equal. This conclusion is now known as "Chargaff's rule."

Chargaff's rule is not obeyed in some viruses. These either have single- stranded DNA or RNA as their genetic material. **Answer the following questions:**

(a) A segment of DNA has 100 adenine and 150 cytosine bases. What is the total number of nucleotides present in this segment of DNA?

(b) A sample of hair and blood was found at two sites. Scientists claim that the samples belong to same species. How did the scientists arrive at this conclusion?

(c) The sample of a virus was tested and it was found to contain 20% adenine, 20% thymine, 20 % guanine and the rest cytosine. Is the genetic material of this virus (a) DNA- double helix (b) DNA-single helix (c) RNA? What do you infer from this data?

OR

How can Chargaff's rule be used to infer that the genetic material of an organism is double- helix or single- helix?

22. After watching a programme on TV about the presence of carcinogens (cancer causing agents) potassium bromate and potassium iodate in bread and other bakery products, Rupali a class XII student decided to make others aware about the adverse effects of these carcinogens in foods. She consulted the school principal and requested him to instruct the canteen contractor to stop selling sandwiches pizzas, burgers and other bakery products to the students. The principal took an immediate action and instructed the canteen contractor to replace the bakery products with some protein and vitamin rich food like fruits, salads, sprouts, etc. The decision was welcomed by the parents and the students. **[All India 2017, A]**

After reading the above passage, answer the following question:

(a) What are the values (atleast two) dispalyed by Rupali?

(b) Which polysaccharide component of carbohydrates is commonly present in bread?

(c) Write the two type of secondary structures of proteins.

(d) Give two examples of water soluble vitamins.

23. After watching a programme on TV about the presence of carcinogens(cancer causing agents) Potassium bromate and Potassium iodate in bread and other bakery products, Ritu a class XII student decided to aware others about the adverse effects of these carcinogens in foods. She consulted the school principal and requested him to instruct canteen contractor to stop selling sandwiches, pizza, burgers and other bakery products to the students. Principal took an immediate action and instructed the canteen contractor to replace the bakery products with some proteins and vitamins rich food like fruits, salads, sprouts etc. The decision was welcomed by the parents and students. **[Delhi 2017, A]**

After reading the above passage, answer the following questions :

(i) What are the values (at least two) displayed by Ritu ?

(ii) Which polysaccharide component of carbohydrates is commonly present in bread ?

(iii) Write the two types of secondary structure of proteins.

(iv) Give two examples of water soluble vitamins.

24. Shanti, a domestic helper of Mrs. Anuradha, fainted while mopping the floor. Mrs. Anuradha immediately took her to the nearby hospital where she was diagnosed to be severely 'anaemic'. The doctor prescribed an iron rich diet and multivitamins supplement to her. Mrs. Anuradha supported her financially to get the medicines. After a month, Shanti was diagnosed to be normal.

[All India 2013, K]

After reading the above passage, answer the following questions :

(i) What values are displayed by Mrs. Anuradha?

(ii) Name the vitamin whose deficiency causes 'pernicious anaemia'.

(iii) Give an example of a water soluble vitamin.

25. After watching a programme on TV about the adverse effects of junk food and soft drinks on the health of school children, Sonali, a student of Class XII, discussed the issue with the school principal. Principal immediately instructed the canteen contractor to replace the fast food with the fibre and vitamins rich food like sprouts, salad, fruits etc. This decision was welcomed by the parents and the students. After reading the above passage, answer the following questions : **[Delhi 2013, K]**

(a) What values are expressed by Sonali and the Principal of the school?

(b) Give two examples of water-soluble vitamins.

Solutions

Topic-1: *Carbohydrates*

1. (b) n-hexane;

$$CHO - (CHOH)_4 - CH_2OH \xrightarrow{HI, \Delta} CH_3 - (CH_2)_4 - CH_3$$

D-Glucose → n-Hexane **(1 Mark)**

2. (d) The molecular formula of glucose is $C_6H_{12}O_6$ and it contains an aldehydic (–CHO) functional group.

Thus, it is an aldohexose.

On prolonged heating with HI, it forms n-Hexane suggesting a straight chain form.

It exists in a six-membered pyranose ring form.

Due to the cyclic structure, it does not give 2, 4–DNP test.

Therefore, option **(d)** is correct. **(1 Mark)**

3. (a) Hydrolysis of sucrose to give equimolar mixture of D – (+) – glucose and D – (–) – fructose is called inversion. It is because it brings about a change in the sign of rotation, from dextro (+) to laevo (–) and the product is named as invert sugar.

$$\underset{\text{Sucrose}}{C_{12}H_{22}O_{11}} + H_2O \rightarrow \underset{D-(+)-Glucose}{C_6H_{12}O_6} + \underset{D-(-)-Fructose}{C_6H_{12}O_6}$$

(1 Mark)

4. (a) Glucose is a carbohydrate and act as a reducing sugar. It is also known as dextrose as it rotates the plane polarised light to the right. **(1 Mark)**

5. (c)

$$\underset{\text{Glucose}}{CHO - (CHOH)_4 - CH_2OH} + [O] \xrightarrow{Br_2/water} \underset{\substack{\text{Gluconic} \\ \text{acid}}}{COOH - (CHOH)_4 - CH_2OH}$$

(1 Mark)

6. (d) Glucose is found to exist in two different crystalline forms which are named as α and β which can not be explained by open chain structure of glucose. **(1 Mark)**

7. (c) It undergoes inversion in the configuration on hydrolysis. **(1 Mark)**

8. (d) A = OHC – (CHOCOCH₃)₄ – CH₂OCOCH₃

B = COOH – (CH₂)₄ – COOH

$$\underset{\text{Glucose}}{CHO - (CHOH)_4 - CH_2OH} \xrightarrow{HNO_3} \underset{\text{Saccharic acid}}{COOH - (CHOH)_4 - COOH}$$

$$\underset{\text{Glucose}}{CHO - (CHOH)_4 - CH_2OH} + 5\underset{\text{Acetic anhydride}}{(CH_3CH_2)_2O} \longrightarrow$$

$$\underset{\substack{\text{Glucose penta acetate}}}{CHO - (CHOCOCH_3)_4 - CH_2O - \overset{O}{\overset{\|}{C}} - CH_3} + 5CH_3COOH$$

(1 Mark)

9. (d) Glucose is found to exist in two different crystalline forms which are named as α and β which can not be explained by open chain structure of glucose.

(1 Mark)

10. (c) Glycogen (It is a polymer of glucose) **(1 Mark)**

11. (c) It undergoes inversion in the configuration on hydrolysis. **(1 Mark)**

12. (d) A = OHC – (CHOCOCH₃)₄ – CH₂OCOCH₃

B = COOH – (CH₂)₄ – COOH

$$\underset{\text{Glucose}}{CHO - (CHOH)_4 - CH_2OH} \xrightarrow{HNO_3} \underset{\text{Saccharic acid}}{COOH - (CHOH)_4 - COOH}$$

$$\underset{\text{Glucose}}{CHO - (CHOH)_4 - CH_2OH} + 5\underset{\text{Acetic anhydride}}{(CH_3CH_2)_2O} \longrightarrow$$

$$\underset{\substack{\text{Glucose penta acetate}}}{CHO - (CHOCOCH_3)_4 - CH_2O - \overset{O}{\overset{\|}{C}} - CH_3} + 5CH_3COOH$$

(1 Mark)

13. (c)   **(1 Mark)**

14. (b) Sucrose is a non-reducing sugar because the two monosaccharide units are held together by a glycosidic linkage between C_1 of α-glucose and C_2 of β-fructose. The reducing groups are involved in glycosidic bond formation. **(1 Mark)**

15. Glycosidic linkage is present in polysaccharides. **(1 Mark)**

16. *Glucose:*
- It is a aldohexose and contains aldehyde functional group. **(½ Mark)**

Fructose:
- It is a ketohexose contains ketone functional group. **(½ Mark)**

17.

> **Topper's Answer**
>
> 4. Products of hydrolysis of lactose :— β-D-galactose, β-D-glucose
>
> β-D-galactopyranose   β-D-glucopyranose.

The products of hydrolysis of lactose are β-D-glucose and β-D-galactose. **(1 Mark)**

18. The products of hydrolysis of sucrose are: D-glucose and D-fructose **(½ + ½ = 1 Mark)**

19. Amylose is water soluble component of starch which constitute about 15-20%. **(1 Mark)**

20. Glucose and fructose.

$$C_{12}H_{22}O_{11} + H_2O \xrightarrow{\text{HCl}} \underset{\text{Glucose}}{C_6H_{12}O_6} + \underset{\text{Fructose}}{C_6H_{12}O_6}$$

(1 Mark)

21. (a) The reactant Sucrose is dextrorotatory. On hydrolysis it give glucose dextrorotatory and fructose which is leavoroatatory. The specific rotation of fructose is higher than glucose

Sucrose is dextrorotatory but after hydrolysis gives dextrorotatory glucose and laevorotatory fructose. Since the laevorotation of fructose ($-92.4°$) is more than dextrorotation of glucose ($+52.5°$), the mixture is laevorotatory. **(1 Mark)**

(b) Invert sugar, The hydrolysis of sucrose brings about a change in the sign of rotation, from dextro (+) to laevo (–) and the product is named as invert sugar. **(1 Mark)**

(c) Glucose **(1 Mark)**

$$\begin{array}{c} CH{=}N{-}OH \\ | \\ (CHOH)_4 \\ | \\ CH_2OH \end{array}$$

22. Glucose reacts with hydroxylamine to form an oxime. This reaction confirms the presence of a carbonyl group $\left(\!\!>\!\!C{=}O\right)$ in glucose. **(1 Mark)**

$$\begin{array}{c} CHO \\ | \\ (CHOH)_4 \\ | \\ CH_2OH \end{array} \xrightarrow{\text{NH}_2\text{OH}} \begin{array}{c} CH{=}N{-}OH \\ | \\ (CHOH)_4 \\ | \\ CH_2OH \end{array}$$

(1 Mark)

23. Glucose reacts with hydrogen cyanide to give cyanohydrin. This reaction confirms the presence of a carbonyl group ($>C{=}O$) in glucose. **(1 Mark)**

$$\begin{array}{c} CHO \\ | \\ (CHOH)_4 \\ | \\ CH_2OH \end{array} \xrightarrow{\text{HCN}} \begin{array}{c} CH{\overset{\displaystyle CN}{\underset{\displaystyle OH}{<}}} \\ | \\ (CHOH)_4 \\ | \\ CH_2OH \end{array}$$

(1 Mark)

24. Glucose reacts with acetic anhydride and undergoes acetylation and gives pentaacetate.

$$\underset{\substack{|\\CH_2OH}}{\overset{\substack{CHO\\|}}{(CHOH)_4}} \xrightarrow{\text{Acetic anhydride}} \underset{\substack{|\\CH_2-O-\overset{O}{\overset{||}{C}}-CH_3}}{\overset{\substack{CHO\\|}}{(CH-O-\overset{O}{\overset{||}{C}}-CH_3)_4}}$$

(1 Mark)

The formation of pentaacetate confirms the presence of five –OH groups. **(1 Mark)**

25. **(a)** Acetylation of glucose with acetic anhydride gives glucose pentaacetate which confirms the presence of five –OH groups. Since it exists as a stable compound, five –OH groups should be attached to different carbon atoms. **(1 Mark)**

$$\underset{\substack{|\\CH_2OH}}{\overset{\substack{CHO\\|}}{[CHOH]_4}} \xrightarrow{\text{Acetic anhydride}} \underset{\substack{|\\CH_2-O-\overset{O}{\overset{||}{C}}-CH_3}}{\overset{\substack{CHO\\|}}{[CH-O-\overset{O}{\overset{||}{C}}-CH_3]_4}}$$

(b) Glucose reduces Fehlings reagent

$$\underset{\substack{|\\CH_2OH}}{\overset{\substack{H\\\diagdown\,C\diagup O}}{\underset{\substack{H-C-OH\\HO-C-H\\H-C-OH\\H-C-OH}}{}}} + 2Cu^{2+} + 2H_2O \longrightarrow$$

$$\underset{\substack{|\\CH_2OH}}{\overset{\substack{HO\\\diagdown\,C\diagup O}}{\underset{\substack{H-C-OH\\HO-C-H\\H-C-OH\\H-C-OH}}{}}} + Cu_2O + 4H^+$$

(1 mark)

26. **(a)**
$$\underset{\substack{|\\CH_2OH}}{\overset{\substack{CHO\\|}}{[CHOH]_4}} \xrightarrow{Br_2\ \text{water}} \underset{\substack{|\\CH_2OH}}{\overset{\substack{COOH\\|}}{[CHOH]_4}}$$
Gluconic acid **(1 mark)**

(b)
$$\underset{\substack{|\\CH_2OH}}{\overset{\substack{CHO\\|}}{[CHOH]_4}} \xrightarrow{\text{Oxidation}} \underset{\substack{|\\COOH}}{\overset{\substack{COOH\\|}}{[CHOH]_4}} \xleftarrow{\text{Oxidation}} \underset{\substack{|\\CH_2OH}}{\overset{\substack{COOH\\|}}{[CHOH]_4}}$$
Saccharic acid   Gluconic acid

(1 mark)

27. **(a)** Aldehyde group is not free in glucose, it is involved in the formation of cyclic structure in glucose. Thus, it does not react with 2, 4-dinitrophenylhydrazine. **(1 Mark)**

(b) The two strands in DNA are held together by hydrogen bonds between specific pair of bases (cytosine with guanine and adenine with thymine). Thus, the two strands are complementary to each other. **(1 Mark)**

(c) Starch contains α-D-glucose, while cellulose contains β-D-glucose as their monomers. **(1 Mark)**

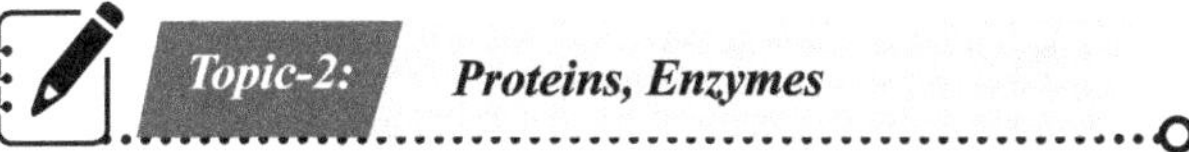

Topic-2:   *Proteins, Enzymes*

1. **(b)** All proteins are polymers of α–amino acids. **(1 Mark)**

2. **(b)** β – pleated sheet structure and α – Helix in proteins refers to secondary structure. These structures arise due to the regular folding of the backbone of the polypeptide chain due to hydrogen bonding between $-\overset{O}{\overset{||}{C}}-$ and – NH – groups of the peptide bond. **(1 Mark)**

3. **(b)** The amino acids which are not synthesized in our body and obtained through diet are essential amino acids. For example: histidine, lysine, leucine etc. **(1 Mark)**

4. **(d)** A : Denatured protein

B : Secondary protein

- Curdling of milk is due to denaturation of proteins.
- α-helix is an element of secondary structure in which the amino acid chain is arranged in a spiral.

(1 Mark)

5. **(d)** pH does not affect the primary structure of protein while pH affects the tertiary structure. **(1 Mark)**

6. **(d)** pH does not affect the primary structure of protein while pH affects the tertiary structure. **(1 Mark)**

7. **(d)** **(1 Mark)**

8. **Topper's Answer**

Ans 15 (c) Amphoteric

(1 Mark)

9. **(b)** Both A and R are true and R is not the correct explanation of A. **(1 Mark)**

10. **(c)** All proteins are polymers of α–amino acids. A tetrapeptide contains four amino acids linked by three peptide bonds. **(1 Mark)**

11. **(b)** Both A and R are true but R is not the correct explanation of A. **(1 Mark)**

12. (a) **Polysaccharides:** Carbohydrates which yield a large number of monosaccharide units on hydrolysis are called polysaccharides. *Example:* Starch **(1 Mark)**

    (b) **Denatured protein:** When a protein is subjected to physical change like change in pH, the hydrogen bonds are disturbed. Due to this, globules unfold and helix get uncoiled and protein loses its biological activity. This form is called 'denatured protein'. *Example:* Coagulation of egg white on boiling **(1 Mark)**

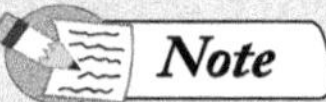

Denaturation destroys secondary and tertiary structures of protein, but primary structure remains intact.

    (c) **Fibrous protein:** When the polypeptide chains run parallel and are held together by hydrogen and disulphide bonds, then fibre like structure is formed. Such type of proteins are called 'fibrous proteins' *Example:* Keratin **(1 Mark)**

13.

Topper's Answer

Ans 30. (a) (i)

Amylose	Amylopectin
1) It comprises 15–20% of starch	1) It comprises 80–85% of starch
2) It is water soluble	2) It is water insoluble
3) It consists of linear chain polymers of α-D glucose with C1-C4 linkage	3) It consists of branched chain polymers of α-D glucose with C1-C4 linkage and C1-C6 linkage between the 2 linear chains

(b)(ii)

Globular Protein	Fibrous protein
1) In this the polypeptide chains are coiled together in a spherical shape	1) In this, 2 polypeptide chains run parallel to each other and are bonded to each other by disulphide bonds
2) They are water soluble	2) They are water insoluble
3) Eg: Insulin, albumin	3) Eg: Keratin, myosin
4) It is 3° structure of protein	4) It is 3° structure of protein

(iii) (A)

Nucleotide (Phosphorus - sugar - base)	Nucleoside (sugar - Base)
1) When the phosphorous compound are attached to 5' position of the sugar moiety which already has a base attached to its 1' position	1) When the nitrogen base pairs are attached with the 1' position of sugar (Ribose sugar or β-D-2-deoxyribose sugar)
2) It polymerises to form poly-nucleotides through phospho-dester linkages	2) It first attaches itself to phosphorus compound at 5' and then form polynucleotides.

14. **(i)** Amylose and Amylopectin

Amylose: It is a linear polymer of α-D glucose having approximately 200 –1000 α-D-glucose units. C-1 of one α-D glucose is attached to C-4 of another α-D glucose with glycosidic bond. It is water soluble and it forms 15-20% part of starch and give blue colour with I_2.

Amylopectin: It is a branched chain polymer of α-D glucose which is constituted by hundreds of small chain having 20-30 α-D glucose unit. In it small chain are formed by glycosidic bonds between C-1 and C-4. These chain are joined by C_1— C_6 bonds. This fraction does not give blue colour with I_2

(1 Mark)

(ii) Peptide linkage and Glycosidic linkange

The bond conecting two or more similar or different amino acid in protein is commonly called *peptide bond* or *peptide linkage.* In the formation of peptide bond —NH_2 group of one amino acid is condensed with —COOH of adjacent amino acid to form —CONH linkage.

When —OH group of hemiacetal carbon of one monosaccharide is condensed with — OH group of another, glycosidic bond is formed, which links two monosacharide together. **(1 Mark)**

(iii)

Fibrous Proteins		Globular Proteins	
(i)	Proteins which are made up of linear, thread like molecules are called fibrous protein. In these molecules, poly-peptide chains are held together with H bonds.	(i)	In these proteins poly-peptides attain spherical shape and poly-peptides are held together with relatively weaker-H-bonds.
(ii)	They are insoluble in water but soluble in strong acid and bases. **Example:** Keratin, Myosin	(ii)	They are soluble in water, alkalies, salt solutions and acid solutions. **Example:** Globulin, Pepsin

(1 Mark)

15.

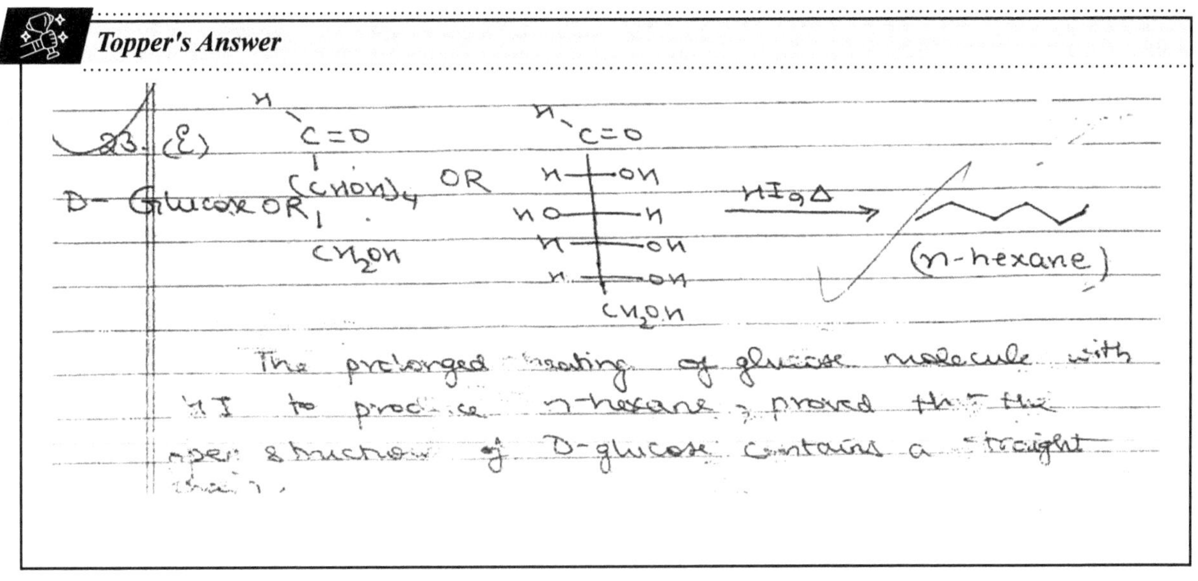

The prolonged heating of glucose molecule with HI to produce n-hexane, proved that the open structure of D-glucose contains a straight chain.

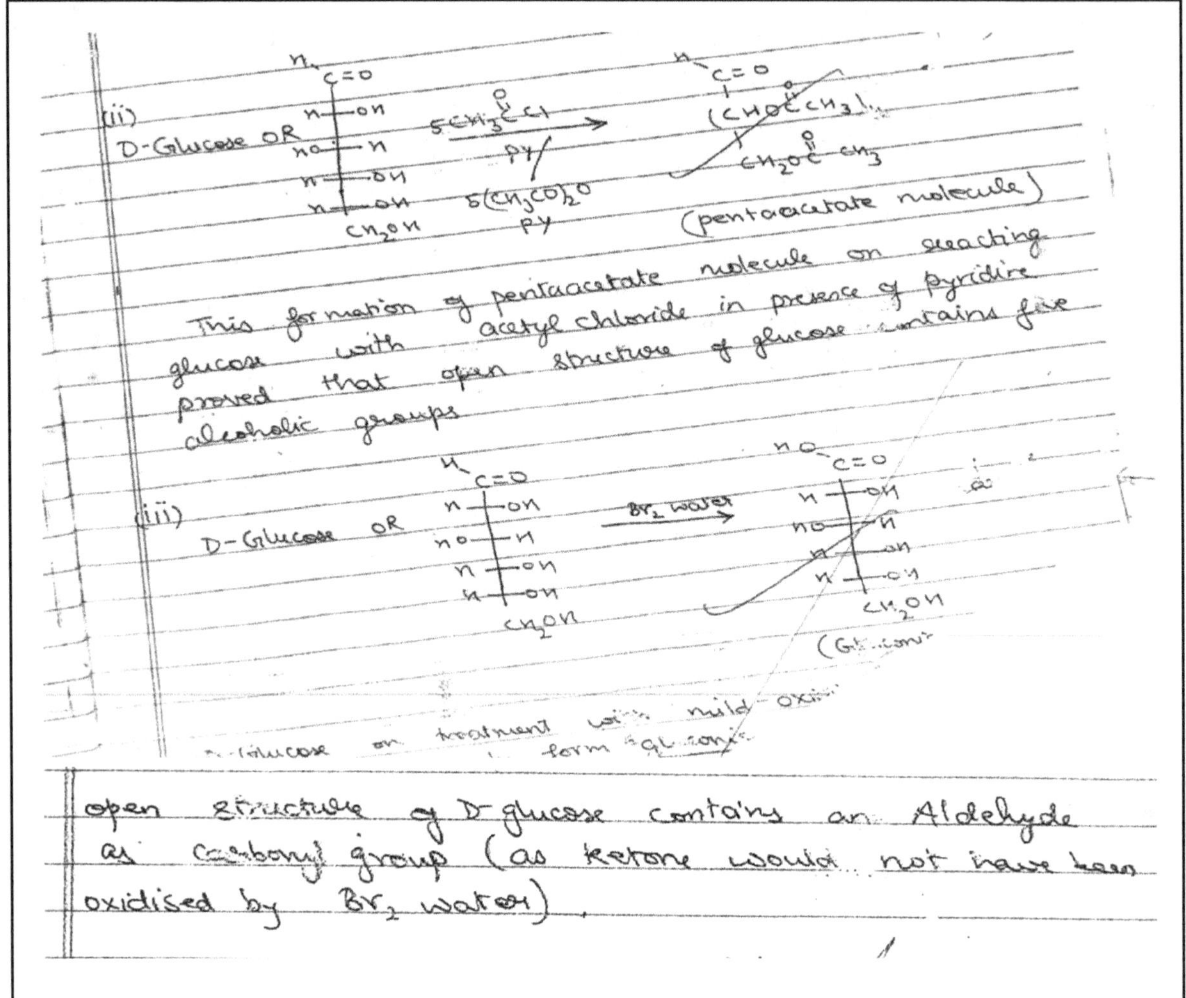

(i) Glucose on heating with HI and red phosphorous at 100°C, it forms *n*-hexane. This proves the presence of straight chain of six carbon atom in glucose.

$$\begin{array}{c} CHO \\ | \\ (CHOH)_4 \\ | \\ CH_2OH \end{array} \xrightarrow[\Delta]{HI,\ Red\ P}$$

$$CH_3—CH_2—CH_2—CH_2—CH_2—CH_3$$
n-hexane

(1 Mark)

(ii) Glucose forms pentaacetyl derivatives with acid chloride and acid anhydride in the presence of anhydrous zinc chloride. It proves that one molecule of glucose contains five —OH groups.

$$\begin{array}{c} CHO \\ | \\ (CHOH)_4 \\ | \\ CH_2OH \end{array} + 5\ CH_3COCl \xrightarrow[\Delta]{ZnCl_2}$$
acetylchloride

$$\begin{array}{c} CHO \\ | \\ (CHOCOCH_3)_4 \\ | \\ CH_2OCOCH_3 \end{array} + 5\ HCl$$
Glucose pentaacetate

(1 Mark)

(iii) Glucose reacts with hydrogen cyanide to form, cyanohydrin. This reaction proves the presence of carbonyl group.

$$
\begin{array}{c}
\text{CHO} \\
| \\
\text{(CHOH)}_4 \\
| \\
\text{CH}_2\text{OH}
\end{array}
\xrightarrow{\text{HCN}}
\begin{array}{c}
\text{CH}\diagup^{\text{CN}}_{\diagdown\text{OH}} \\
| \\
\text{(CHOH)}_4 \\
| \\
\text{CH}_2\text{OH}
\end{array}
$$

Glucose cyanohydrin

(1 Mark)

16. (a) **Polysaccharides :** These carbohydrates yield a large number of monosaccharide units on hydrolysis. For ex : starch, cellulose, gums (any one)

(1 Mark)

   (b) **Denatured protein :** When a protein in its native form is subjected to a physical change like change in temperature or chemical change like change in pH, the H-bonds break, globules unfold, the helix gets uncoiled and the protein loses its biological activity. This is denatured protein.

   For ex : coagulation of egg white on boiling, curdling of milk (any one) **(1 Mark)**

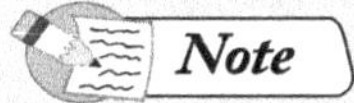

Food, especially meat is cooked in order to denature the proteins within and make them easier to digest.

   (c) **Essential amino acids :** These amino acids cannot be synthesised in the body and must be obtained through diet.

   For ex : Valine, leucine, lysine **(1 Mark)**

The nine essential amino acids are histidine, isoleucine, leucine, lysin, methionine, phenylalanine, threonine, tryptophan and valine.

17. (a) When glucose reacts with conc HNO_3, saccharic acid is formed.

$$
\begin{array}{c}
\text{CHO} \\
| \\
\text{(CHOH)}_4 \\
| \\
\text{CH}_2\text{OH} \\
\text{glucose}
\end{array}
\xrightarrow[\text{HNO}_3]{\text{Conc.}}
\begin{array}{c}
\text{COOH} \\
| \\
\text{(CHOH)}_4 \\
| \\
\text{COOH} \\
\text{saccharic acid}
\end{array}
$$

(1 Mark)

   (b) Amino acids show amphoteric behaviour in zwitter ionic form as they react both with acids and bases.

   Due to presence of both acidic (carboxyl group) and basic (amino group) in same molecule, amino acids exist as zwitter ion form and can react with acids as well bases. **(1 Mark)**

   (c) **α-Helix:** The polypeptide chains twist into a right handed screw with –NH group of amino acid hydrogen bonded with $>C = O$ group of an adjacent turn of the helix.

   β-pleated: The polypeptide chains stretch to maximum extension and lay side by side in a zig-zag manner to form a flat sheet. Each chain is held to two neighbouring chains by hydrogen bond. **(1 Mark)**

18. (a) **Peptide linkage:** A peptide bond is an amide linkage formed between – COOH group of one α-amino acid and NH_2 group of other α-amino acid by loss of a water molecule. For example:

$$
\text{H}_2\text{N} - \text{CH}_2 - \overset{\overset{\textstyle O}{\|}}{\text{C}} - \text{OH} + \text{H} - \underset{\underset{\textstyle H}{|}}{\text{N}} - \underset{\underset{\textstyle CH_3}{|}}{\text{CH}} - \text{COOH}
$$

$$
\longrightarrow \text{H}_2\text{N-CH}_2 \overset{\overset{\textstyle O}{\|}}{\text{C}} \text{-NH} \overset{\overset{\textstyle CH_3}{}}{\text{CH}}\text{-COOH}
$$

Peptide bond

(1 Mark)

   (b) **Primary structure:** Each polypeptide chain of proteins has a large number of α-amino acids which are linked to one another in a specific manner. The specific sequence in which various α-amino acids present in a protein are linked to one another is called its primary structure. Any change in sequence of α-amino acids creates a different protein.

(1 Mark)

   (c) **Denaturation:** When a protein in its native form is subjected to physical changes such as change in temperature, pH, etc., H-bonds are broken. Due to cleavage of H-bonds, unfolding of protein molecule occurs and the protein loses its biological activity. This loss of biological activity is called denaturation.

(1 Mark)

Note

Denaturation of proteins involves the disruption of both secondary and tertiary structures. Denaturation reactions are not enough strong to break the peptide bonds therefore primary structure of proteins remain intact. Denaturation process disrupt the normal alpha-helix and beta sheets in protein and uncoils them into random shape.

Topic-3: *Vitamins, Nucleic Acids, Hormones*

1. **(d)** Vitamin A, D, E and K. These are fat soluble vitamins **(1 Mark)**

2. **(c)** Nucleosides are composed of a nitrogenous base, and a pentose sugar. **(1 Mark)**

3. **(d)** The bases which are present in RNA are adenine, uracil, guanine and cytosine. **(1 Mark)**

4. **(c)** Nucleic acids are biological macromolecules which are polymers of repeating monomeric units called nucleotides. **(1 Mark)**

5. **(c)** Vitamin C is a **water - soluble** vitamin that is released from our body through urine and therefore cannot be stored in our body.

   Therefore, Assertion (A) is **true** but Reason (R) is **false.**

   Therefore, option **(c)** is correct. **(1 Mark)**

6. **(a)** The backbone of both DNA and RNA molecules consists of a chain of nucleotides which consists of a heterocyclic nitrogeneous base (either adenine, guanine, cytosine or thymine in DNA or uracil in RNA), pentose sugar molecule (deoxyribose in DNA and ribose in RNA) and a phosphate group.

   Nucleosides contains only sugar and a base while & nucleotides contain sugar, base and a phosphate group.

   (1 Mark)

7. **(a)** **(1 Mark)**

8. **(b)** (i) – (D); (ii) – (C); (iii) – (A); (iv) – (B)

   Amino acids form proteins and exist as zwitter ion, Thymine is a nitrogenous base in DNA, Insulin is a protein, phosphodiester linkage is found in nucleic acids so also in DNA and Uracil is nitrogenous base found in RNA which is a nucleic acid. **(1 Mark)**

9. The three types of RNA which perform different functions are :
   (i) Transfer RNA or tRNA.
   (ii) Ribosomal RNA or rRNA.
   (iii) Messenger RNA or mRNA. **(1 Mark)**

10. **(a)** Replication
    A sequence of bases on DNA is unique for a person and is the genetic material transferred to the individual from the parent which helps in the determination of paternity. **(1 Mark)**
    (b) During denaturation secondary and tertiary structures are destroyed but the primary structure remains intact. **(1 Mark)**

11. Nucleic Acids, the long chain polymeric biomolecules, are one of the components of chromosome present in the nucleus of the cell. These are responsible for transmitting the genetic information. The monomer of the biopolymer is known as nucleotide. **(1 Mark)**
    The two strands in DNA are complementary to each other because the H-bonds form between specific pairs of bases belong to different chains. **(1 Mark)**

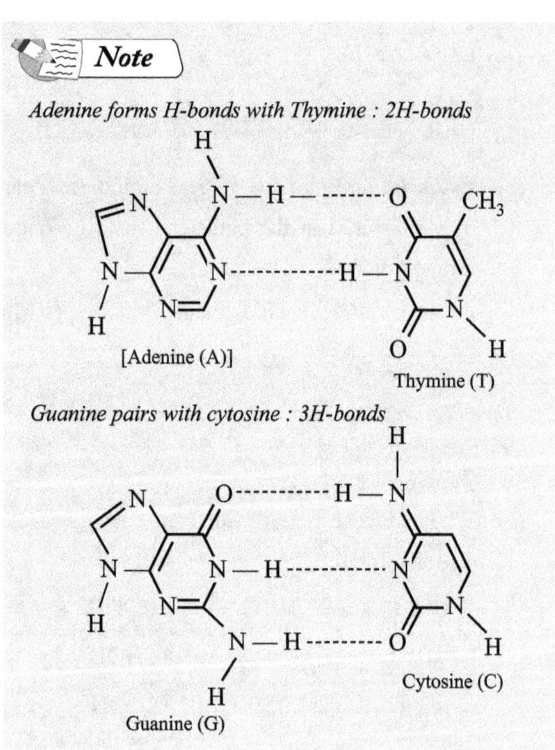

Note

Adenine forms H-bonds with Thymine : 2H-bonds

Guanine pairs with cytosine : 3H-bonds

12. **(a)** Nucleoside is formed by the attachment of a base to 1'-position of sugar while a nucleotide is formed when a nucleoside is linked to phosphoric acid at 5'-position of sugar moiety.

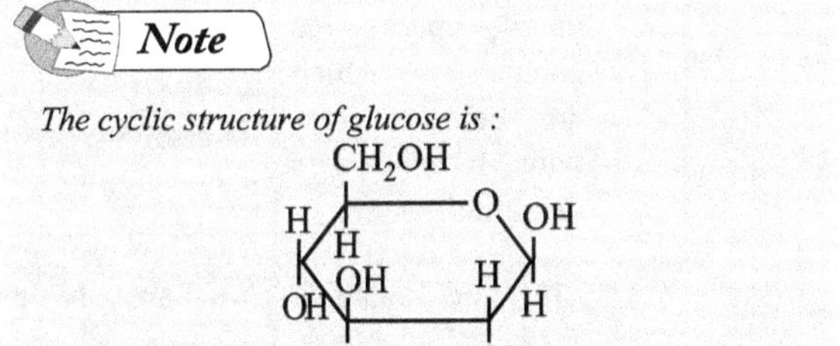

(a) Nucleoside

(b) Nucleotide **(1 Mark)**

(b) When a nucleotide from DNA containing thymine is hydrolysed, thymine $\beta - D - 2 -$ deoxyribose and phosphoric acid are obtained as products. **(1 Mark)**

13. (a) Pentaacetate of glucose does not react with hydroxylamine because of the absence of a free – CHO group in the cyclic structure of glucose.

(1 Mark)

> **Note**
>
> *The cyclic structure of glucose is :*

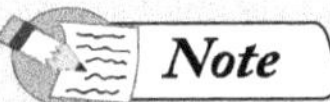

(b) Amino acids behave like salts because they have both, an acidic – COOH group and basic – NH_2 group due to which it forms a dipolar zwitter ion.

(1 Mark)

$$H_3N - \overset{\overset{\displaystyle R}{|}}{\underset{\underset{\displaystyle H}{|}}{C}} - COOH \rightleftharpoons H_4N^+ - \overset{\overset{\displaystyle R}{|}}{\underset{\underset{\displaystyle H}{|}}{C}} - COO^-$$

Zwitter-ion

(c) Water - soluble vitamins must be taken regularly in diet because they are excreted out of our body through urine.

These vitamins include vitamin B and C.

(1 Mark)

(d) The two strands in DNA are complimentary to each other because the purines and pyrimidines of one strand bond to their counterparts in the second strand according to the rule A $\rightarrow$ T and G $\rightarrow$ C through Hydrogen bonds. **(1 Mark)**

14. (a) Proteins which are found in a biological system with unique 3D-structure and biological activity are called native proteins. When a native protein is subjected to physical and chemical change, it loses its biological activity and are called as denatured protein. **(1 Mark)**

(b) Lactose is a disaccharide. **(1 Mark)**

(c) Vitamin K is responsible for the coagulation of blood. **(1 Mark)**

> **Note**
>
> *Deficiency of vitamin K is rare, but, in severe cases, it can increase clotting time, leading to the hemorrhage and excessive bleeding.*

15. (i) Cellulose is a linear polymer made up of β-glucose having the C1-C4 glycosidic linkage, whereas starch is a polymer of α-glucose having two components: amylose and amylopectin. Amylose is a long, unbranched chain with 200-1,000 α-D-(+) glucose units held by the C1-C4 glycosidic linkage.

Amylopectin is a branched-chain polymer of α-D-glucose unit in which the chain is formed by the C1-C4 glycosidic linkage and branching occurs at the C1-C6 glycosidic linkage. **(1 Mark)**

(ii) Three types of linkage are found in nucleic acids.

(1) Hydrogen bonds

(2) Glycosidic linkage

(3) Phosphodiester linkage **(1 Mark)**

(iii) Fibrous protein: Keratin

Globular protein: Egg albumin **(1 Mark)**

16. **(i)** Two monosaccharides obtained on hydrolysis of lactose sugar are β-D-glucose and β-D-galactose.

(1 Mark)

(ii) Vitamin C cannot be stored in our body because it is water soluble in nature so it repeatedly gets eliminated through urine. **(1 Mark)**

(iii) When a base (purine or pyrimidine) get attached to 1′ position of a pentose sugar a nucleoside is formed.

When a nucleoside is further linked to phosphoric acid at 5′ position of the sugar moiety, we get a nucleotide.

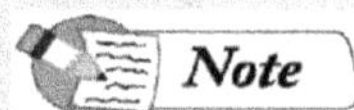

(1 Mark)

17. **(i)**

$$HOH_2C-(CHOH)_4-CHO+NH_2OH \xrightarrow{-H_2O}$$
D-Glucose

$$HOH_2C-(CHOH)_4-CH=NOH$$
Glucose oxime

(1 Mark)

> **Note**
>
> *The structure of glucose can be confirmed by various evidences which are as follows.*

	Reagent	*Product*	*Conformation*
(i)	*HI/Δ*	*n-hexane*	*Confirms the presence of six carbon atoms which are linked in a straight chain.*
(ii)	*NH$_2$OH/HCN*	*Oxime/cyano hydrin*	*Confirms the presence of carbonyl group.*
(iii)	*Br$_2$ water*	*Gluconic acid*	*Confirms the presence of aldehyde group.*
(iv)	*Acetic anhydride*	*Glucose pentaacetate*	*Confirms the presence of 5 –OH group.*
(v)	*HNO$_3$*	*Saccharic acid*	*Confirms the presence of primary alcoholic group.*

(ii) Amino acids are amphoteric in nature because they exist as zwitterion and react with both acids as well as bases.

- **Reaction with acids**

$$R-CH-COO^- \xrightarrow{H^+} R-CH-COOH$$
$$\quad\;\; |\qquad\qquad\qquad\;\; |$$
$$\quad\; {}^+NH_3 \qquad\qquad\quad {}^+NH_3$$

- **Reaction with bases**

$$R-CH-COO^- \xrightarrow{OH^-} R-CH-COO^-$$
$$\quad\;\; |\qquad\qquad\qquad\;\; |$$
$$\quad\; {}^+NH_3 \qquad\qquad\quad {}^+NH_2$$

(1 Mark)

(iii) Vitamin C cannot be stored in the body because it is water soluble, so easily excreted through urine.

(1 Mark)

18. **(i)** Maltose is a disaccharide, as it consist of two α-D glucose units. **(1 Mark)**

> **Note**
>
> *Starch is a polysaccharide, whereas fructose and glucose are monosaccharides.*

(ii)

	Fibrous Protein	**Globular Protein**
(a)	They are made up of parallel polypeptide chains which are held together with H-bond and disulphide bond.	The polypeptide chains in these protein are folded around themselves, giving these proteins a spherical structure.
(b)	They are insoluble in water but soluble in strong acid and base	They are soluble in water, alkalies, salt solution and acid solution.

(1 Mark)

(iii) Deficiency of vitamin D causes bone deformities in children. **(1 Mark)**

19. **(i)** The deficiency of vitamin A causes night blindness.

(1 Mark)

(ii) Uracil (U) is the base that is found in nucleotide of RNA only. **(1 Mark)**

(iii) On prolonged heating with HI, glucose forms n-hexane. This shows that all the six carbon atoms in glucose are linked in a straight chain. **(1 Mark)**

20. (a) Pentacetate of glucose does not react with hydroxylamine (NH_2OH). This indicates the absence of aldehyde (–CHO) group.   **(1 Mark)**

(b) Vitamin C is a water soluble vitamin. That is why it cannot be stored in body but excreted in urine.

(1 Mark)

(c) (i) Peptide linkage is nothing but the amide linkage which is formed between – COOH group and – NH_2 group of two same or different amino acid molecules. This results to the elimination of a water molecule and formation of a peptide bond – CO – NH – .

$$H_2N - CH_2 - \overset{\overset{O}{\|}}{C} - \boxed{OH + H}\ N - CH\overset{R}{\underset{COOH}{\diagdown}} \xrightarrow{-H_2O}$$

$$H_2N - CH_2 - \overset{\overset{O}{\|}}{C} - NH\ CH\overset{R}{\underset{COOH}{\diagdown}}$$

Peptide linkage

(1 Mark)

(ii) Denaturation: When a protein, in its native form, is subjected to a physical or chemical change like change in temperature, or pH, the native conformation of the molecule is disrupted as the secondary and tertiary linkages get destroyed but primary linkage remains intact. This phenomenon is known as denaturation of protein.   **(1 Mark)**

OR

(c) (i) Anomers: Carbohydrates which differ in configuration at the glycosidic carbon (i.e., C_1 in aldoses and C_2 in ketoses) are called anomers.

e.g. α-D-Glucose and β-D-Glucose are anomers.

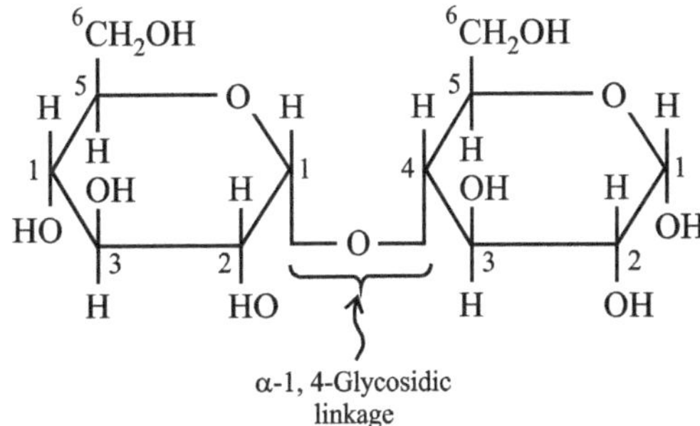

(1 Mark)

(ii) Glycosidic Linkage:

The two monosaccharides are joined together by an oxide linkage formed by the loss of a water molecule. Such a linkage between two monosaccharide units through oxygen atom is called glycosidic linkage.   **(1 Mark)**

21. (a) A = 100 so T = 100

C = 150 so G = 150

Total nucleotides = 100+100+150+150 = 500

(1 mark)

(b) They studied the nucleotide composition of DNA. It was the same so they concluded that the samples belong to same species.   **(1 mark)**

(c) A = T = 20%

But G is not equal to C so double helix is ruled out.

(1/2 mark)

The bases pairs are ATGC and not AUGC so it is not RNA   **(1/2 mark)**

The virus is a single helix DNA virus   **(1 mark)**

OR

According to Charagaff rule, all double helix DNA will have the same amount of A and T as well as C will be same amount as G. If this is not the case then the helix is single stranded. **(2 marks)**

22. (a) The values displayed by Rupali are self awareness, confidence, decision-making and concern towards adverse effect of harmful ingredients used in school canteen. **(2 Marks)**

(b) Polysaccharide component commonly present in bread is starch. **(1 Mark)**

(c) α-helix and β-pleated sheet are the two types of secondary structure of proteins. **(1 Mark)**

(d) Water soluble vitamins are B and C. **(1 Mark)**

23. (i) Caring, concerned, socially alert and leadership values displaced by Ritu. **(1 Mark)**

(ii) Starch is commonly present in bread. **(1 Mark)**

(iii) (a) α-Helix structure

(b) β-Pleated sheet structure **(1 Mark)**

(iv) water soluble vitamins: vitamin B, vitamin C **(1 Mark)**

24. (i) The incident displayed that Mrs. Anuradha is a nice human being associated with some values like presence of mind, kind hearted, helping nature, concern for others etc. **(1 Mark)**

(ii) Vitamin B_{12} deficiency causes pernicious anaemia. **(1 Mark)**

(iii) Vitamin C is a types of water soluble vitamin. **(1 Mark)**

25. (a) The values expressed by Sonali are concern for health of her school mates, observation and analysis of a problem.

Taking initiative for a good cause agreeing to valuable ideas of others, taking prompt action for the valuable ideas given by Sonali are some values expressed by Principal of the school. **(2 Marks)**

(b) Two water soluble vitamins are Vitamin B_{12} and Vitamin C. **(1 Mark)**